GLOBAL ILLICIT DRUG TRENDS 2001

New York, 2001

UNITED NATIONS PUBLICATION
Sales No. E.01.XI.11
ISBN 92-1-148140-6

This publication has not been
formally edited.

PREFACE

At the twentieth special session of the General Assembly in 1998, States Members agreed to make significant progress towards the control of supply and demand for illicit drugs by the year 2008. They noted that this objective could only be achieved by means of the 'balanced approach' (giving demand as much attention as supply), and on the basis of regular assessments of the drug problem. (General Assembly Resolution S-20/2 and S-20/3). The aim of the present report is to contribute to such assessments by presenting supply and demand statistics and analysis on the evolution of the global illicit drug problem.

However, reliable and systematic data to assess the drug problem, and to monitor progress in achieving the goals set by the General Assembly, is not readily available. The present report is based on data obtained primarily from the annual reports questionnaire (ARQ) sent by Governments to UNDCP in 2000, supplemented by other sources when necessary and where available. Two of the main limitations encountered by UNDCP in using ARQ and other sources are: (a) that ARQ reporting is not systematic enough, both in terms of number of countries responding and of content, and (b) that most countries lack the adequate monitoring systems required to produce reliable, comprehensive and internationally comparable data.

The report tries to overcome these limitations by presenting, annually, **Estimates** of illicit drug **Production**, **Trafficking** and **Consumption**. These statistics form the main body of the report. They are supplemented by a section on **Analysis**, which focuses on different themes each year. Last year, a chapter in the Analysis section dealt with amphetamine-type stimulants (ATS),summarizing the evolution of relevant international drug control activities in that area, and updating trends in their illicit manufacture, trafficking and abuse. This year, the broader issue of **Clandestine Synthetic Drugs** is addressed as a special theme. It provides an overview of the synthetic drug phenomenon, its intrinsic characteristics, and some of its likely future developments. It complements trend data which can be found in the statistical sections on Estimates. The second special theme which is addressed in the report concentrates on the **Main Centres of Illicit Opium Production**, and tries to explain why production has reached such high levels in two countries, **Afghanistan** and **Myanmar**.

United Nations International Drug Control Programme (UNDCP)
Vienna

EXPLANATORY NOTE

This report was prepared by the Research Section of UNDCP and has been reproduced without formal editing. The chapter "Understanding Clandestine Synthetic Drugs"was prepared by the Scientific Section of UNDCP.

The designations employed and the presentation of the material in this publication do not imply the expression of any opinion whatsoever on the part of the Secretariat of the United Nations concerning the legal status of any country, territory, city or area or of its authorities, or concerning the delimitation of its frontiers or boundaries. The names of territories and administrative areas are in italics.

The following abbreviations have been used in this report:

ARQ	annual reports questionnaire
ATS	amphetamine-type stimulants
CICAD	Inter-American Drug Abuse Control Commission
CIS	Commonwealth of Independent States
DEA	Drug Enforcement Administration (United States of America)
DMT	N,N - dimethyltryptamine
DOB	brolamfetamine
EMCDDA	European Monitoring Centre for Drugs and Drug Addiction
ESPAD	European School Survey Project on Alcohol and other Drugs
F.O.	UNDCP Field Office
HNLP	Meeting of Heads of National Law Enforcement Agencies - Asia and the Pacific
IDU	injecting drug use
INCB	International Narcotics Control Board
INCSR	International Narcotics Control Strategy Report (United States of America)
Interpol/ICPO	International Criminal Police Organization
LSD	lysergic acid diethylamide
NAPOL	National Police
ODCCP	United Nations Office for Drug Control and Crime Prevention
PCP	phencyclidine
UNDCP	United Nations International Drug Control Programme
UNAIDS	Joint and Co-sponsored United Nations Programme on Human Immunodeficiency Virus/Acquired Immunodeficiency Syndrome
WCO	World Customs Organization
WHO	World Health Organization
Govt.	Government
u.	Unit
lt.	Litre
kg	Kilogram
ha	Hectare
mt	Metric ton

TABLE OF CONTENTS

HIGHLIGHTS

UNDERSTANDING CLANDESTINE SYNTHETIC DRUGS

- Introduced as licit medicines at the end of the 19th century, synthetic drugs as a clandestine phenomenon, related mainly to the so-called 'designer drugs', only became an issue of global concern over the past decade.

- Compared to the plant-based drugs cocaine and heroin, clandestine synthetic drugs are spreading rapidly as part of mass youth culture, attractive to consumers because of their benign and modern image as well as their performance-enhancing and communication-facilitating effects.

- On the supply side, the wide availability of their starting materials, the simplicity of their manufacturing process, the flexibility of their evolving chemical composition and the difficulty of controlling perpetually changing starting materials and end-products have also contributed to their spread.

- The dynamics resulting from those demand and supply characteristics in the current socioeconomic context, make clandestine synthetic drugs very strong candidates for assuming an increasing share of world-wide drug markets.

- Further research appears crucial to deepening our understanding of the phenomenon in order to develop policy options and provide practical responses.

MAIN CENTRES OF ILLICIT OPIUM PRODUCTION

- At the end of the twentieth century, illicit opium poppy cultivation became concentrated in just two countries, Afghanistan and Myanmar, which accounted for more than 90% of global production.

- The consequences of over twenty years of protracted war have contributed to Afghanistan becoming the largest producer of opium in the 1990s.

- A full fledged "opium economy" entrenched itself in the country from the 1980s, filling the voids left by the lack of any effective central government capable of controlling the entire country and the destruction of the most income generating opportunities in the countryside.

- Following large increases in the production of opium in the late 1990s there was a downward turn in 2000, and this appears to have become more pronounced in 2001. Given the enormous economic and political uncertainty currently prevailing in the country, it is too early to assess the effect on the global illicit opiate market.

- A century and a half of troubled history brought Myanmar to the second rank among the world suppliers of illicit opiates during the last decade.

- The 1990's may also have constituted a turning point in that history, with the beginning of the pacification of the remote and rugged opium producing areas controlled by ethnic minorities and of reductions in opium poppy cultivation.

- However, remaining obstacles on the road to the total elimination of opium production in Myanmar are still considerable and recent progress on the opium control front are offset by increasing levels of illicit methamphetamine manufacture.

PRODUCTION

- The total area cultivated in **opium** poppy increased slightly (3%), to reach 222,000 ha in 2000, but global opium production decreased by 19%, to about 4700 tonnes. The divergence between the two trends was caused by a 9% decrease in the area cultivated in Afghanistan and a 21% increase in Myanmar (where yields per hectare are four times lower than in Afghanistan).

- 70% of global opium production still came from Afghanistan in 2000 (3276 mt), against 23% from Myanmar (1087 mt), 5% from other Asian countries (primarily Lao PDR, Thailand and Pakistan) and 2% from Latin America (Colombia and Mexico). The current ban on opium poppy cultivation in Afghanistan is likely to dramatically reduce opium production in 2001.

- Global cultivation of **coca** bush, production of coca leaf and potential production of cocaine remained more or less stable in 2000.

- However, the overall stabilization masks diverging trends in the three main producing areas: (i) eradication in Bolivia brought the cultivation area down to 14,600 ha (including 12,000 ha authorized under national law 1008 for traditional use); (ii) cultivation continued to decline in Peru; (iii) some increase in Colombia, however at a slower pace than during previous years.

- In the absence of reliable information on global **cannabis** cultivation, seizure data (with a 35% increase for herbal cannabis in 1999) suggest continued wide-spread production and trafficking.

TRAFFICKING

- 1999 seizures show that about a third of all drugs were seized in North America, a quarter in West Europe, a fifth in Asia and a tenth in South America.

- 1999 interception rates (quantities seized / quantities produced) were 39% for cocaine and 15% for opiates.

- ATS seizures more than doubled in 1999 on a year earlier; cannabis herb rose by a third and opiates by 14%; cocaine seizures fell by 6%.

- The ten-year trend (1990-1999) shows ATS growing at an annual average rate of 30%, compared to 6% for cannabis herb, 5% for heroin, 4% for cannabis resin and 3% for cocaine.

CONSUMPTION

- UNDCP estimates 180 million people consume illicit drugs (annual prevalence in the late 1990s). This includes 144 million for cannabis, 29 million for ATS, 14 million for cocaine and 13.5 million for opiates (of which 9 million for heroin). These numbers are not cumulative because of poly-drug use.

- The strongest increases recorded in 1999 were for cannabis and ATS consumption.

- At the regional level, cocaine consumption remained stable in North America (though significantly down compared to the mid-1980s), but increased in West Europe, as well as in a number of countries in South America in 1999.

- Heroin abuse remained generally stable in West Europe, but increased in East Europe, Central Asia, South-West Asia and, to a lesser degree, in some countries of East and South-East Asia.

- ATS abuse increased strongly in East and South-East Asia and appeared to be stabilizing, after years of increase, in West Europe, as well as in North America (except for ecstasy).

- Cannabis abuse is generally increasing in Europe, the Americas, Africa and Oceania (though there are signs of stabilization in some major markets in West Europe and North America), and decreasing in South and South-West Asia.

ANALYSIS

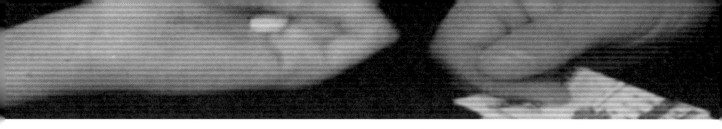

UNDERSTANDING CLANDESTINE SYNTHETIC DRUGS

INTRODUCTION

Trends in drug abuse frequently follow a cycle whereby individual drugs or consumption patterns re-emerge at different times and/or in different regions. Understanding those trends and their underlying dynamics can therefore contribute to improving policy responses and early reactions to the repetition of previously known problems.

In contrast to the long history of abuse of plant-based drugs such as heroin and cocaine, it is only over the past decade that the 'synthetic drug phenomenon', i.e., the widespread recreational use of certain psychoactive drugs by a mostly young consumer population, frequently as part of a certain life-style or sub-cultural group identity, has become an issue of global concern. While it is now clear that certain clandestine synthetic drugs are rapidly spreading around the globe, there are still considerable differences in the magnitude of the problem, both in geographical terms, as well as with regard to consumer populations.

This paper is intended to provide an overview of and background information on clandestine synthetic drugs. The emphasis is on the intrinsic characteristics of their illicit manufacture, trafficking and abuse, compared to heroin and cocaine. The role and complex interplay of those characteristics in the evolution and geographical spread of the current synthetic drug phenomenon are described, and past and current trends are examined in order to identify possible future developments.

CLANDESTINE SYNTHETIC DRUGS: EVOLUTION OF A PROBLEM

From 'plant-based' to 'synthetic' drugs

The modern drug problem evolved gradually from the use of crude plant products/preparations of relatively low psychoactive potency for ritual, spiritual or healing purposes. With the advancement of natural science and pharmaceutical technology, it became possible to refine the (psycho)active compounds (e.g., morphine, cocaine) of the crude plant products (opium and coca leaf respectively). With the availability of the pure active principle, more reliable and specific medical applications became possible, although therapeutic use of those substances was still dependent on the availability of the plant raw material. It was only in the late 19th and early 20th centuries, when pharmaceutical research and industry reached a reasonable size and level of sophistication, that the synthetic manufacture of therapeutic drugs began to compete, in terms of cost-effectiveness, with the isolation of active principles from natural raw materials. As a result, it became possible to manufacture the pure active principles of several traditionally-used plant-based products in laboratories around the world[a], for the most part using easily available and cheap chemical starting materials, and to make many of those medications available at low cost to large sections of society (The main developments in the evolution of the modern drug problem are shown in Figure 2 below).

The search for drugs with identical or similar therapeutic effects, yet with higher potency or improved specificity, i.e., with fewer undesirable side-effects, marked the next stage in the evolutionary process. The principle of modifying the chemical structure of a given, well-studied parent molecule, known as drug design or drug modeling, is a basic concept in modern pharmaceutical research and industrial manufacture. An example of modern synthetic drugs modeled on the structural features of morphine is a group of synthetic opioids, the fentanyls, which are used as analgesics (painkillers) and in anaesthesia.

The early days of synthetic pharmaceutical drugs were characterized by a general enthusiasm for virtually all new products. This, together with the easy availability of some medicines, lax prescribing practices and/or over-prescription, caused a somewhat careless use of these drugs. Gradually, awareness of and concern for the potential dangers associated with the widespread use of some psychoactive medicines began to grow. Regulatory restrictions were introduced, medical use was gradually discouraged, and subsequently started to decline. Diversions from licit into illicit trade then became the major source of supply for non-medical use.

---

a) In some cases, it can still be more cost-effective to isolate the active principle (e.g., morphine) from the plant material, even though the required synthesis technology is available.

Box A Classes of drugs ('plant-based' versus 'synthetic')

Broadly speaking, there are two major classes of drugs, 'synthetic' drugs, and 'plant-based' (or 'botanical' or 'natural') drugs. Although the term 'synthetic drug', is nowadays frequently equated with 'ecstasy'[b] or 'amphetamine-type stimulants', it covers, in fact, a much broader spectrum of man-made substances. The distinctive feature of synthetic drugs, as opposed to plant-based drugs is that they are synthesized in a chemical laboratory, usually from 'off-the-shelf' chemicals (so-called precursors or starting materials). Plant-based drugs, by contrast, are obtained by refining or processing the plant material.

Synthetic drugs can be copies of substances occurring in nature, they can be modifications of such naturally occurring substances, or they can be entirely new creations with no natural counterparts. This implies that almost every substance can also be synthesized in a chemical laboratory (see Figure 1), i.e., it is the _process_ of obtaining a given drug, which differs between natural and synthetic drugs, namely extraction/isolation from the plant material, or multi-step chemical synthesis from various simpler chemicals (precursors). When natural precursors are used in the manufacturing process, the resulting products are called 'semi-synthetic' drugs.

Examples of plant-based drugs are cocaine and morphine, the active principles in coca leaf and opium poppy respectively[c]. Heroin is sometimes also considered 'plant-based', although it is produced by minor chemical modification of morphine, and should therefore be more accurately classified a 'semi-synthetic' drug. The group of synthetic drugs comprises, for example, the stimulants amphetamine and methamphetamine, ecstasy, the depressant drugs methaqualone (known as Mandrax), various benzodiazepines (commonly known under such trade names as Valium or Librium), and synthetic painkillers related to fentanyl, to name but a few.

The further tightening and extension of control measures prompted the establishment of clandestine laboratories in which, in order to meet illicit demand, illicit manufacturers synthesized copies of the desired products from the very same chemicals used in the pharmaceutical industry[d].

The last phase in the evolution of the modern drug problem was the 'design' of new drugs based on the chemical structure of a parent substance, which produced the desired effects. This principle is very similar to that of pharmaceutical research. However, while the aims of the pharmaceutical industry are to develop safer medications or to increase specificity for a given type of desired therapeutic effect, the goal of clandestine manufacturers is to create substances with pharmacological profiles that are sought after by the user population. Clandestine manufacturers are also driven by the desire to create substances that fall outside national and/or international control regimes in order to circumvent existing laws and to avoid prosecution. These clandestinely manufactured, so-called 'designer drugs' are sometimes also referred to as 'synthetic drugs of the second generation' since they are not simply illicitly manufactured copies of existing substances, but entirely new creations in the clandestine sector[e].

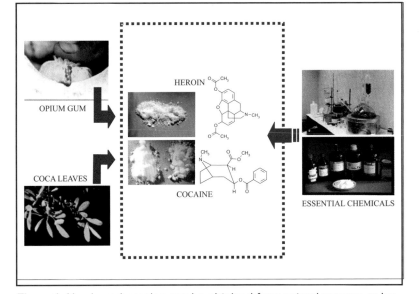

Figure 1: Heroin and cocaine can be obtained from natural sources or by chemical synthesis.

---

b) Throughout this chapter, the term 'ecstasy' is used to describe any of a group of related substances which are sold on the streets as 'ecstasy'; ecstasy refers to the chemical substance MDMA.

c) In the context of this paper, 'plant based drugs' means cocaine and morphine/heroin. It does not refer to the plant materials themselves (coca leaf and opium), and therefore, does not include cannabis either.

d) This description of 'evolutionary states' reflects the development in many developed countries starting in the first half of the 20th century. While the sequence applies to the global level as well, exact dates vary from one geographical region to another.

e) While the consumption of illicitly manufactured drugs always carries the risk of adverse reactions to by-products generated during the synthesis process, designer drugs carry the added resik of side effects of unknown severity in response to the new drugs themselves. Users are thus offering themselves as experimental subjects for drugs which have not undergone any quality control during their manufacturing process, and which have never been tested adequately in humans.

There are five major classes of designer drugs:
- (i) synthetic opioids,
- (ii) phencyclidine (PCP) derivatives,
- (iii) tryptamines,
- (iv) methaqualone derivatives, and
- (v) phenylalkylamines (PAAs).

Most synthetic opioids are close chemical relatives of fentanyl or pethidine (meperidine). Fentanyls appeared on the street in response to the diminished availability of heroin in the late 1970s / early 1980s. They were consequently marketed as 'synthetic heroin', yet were several hundred times more potent than heroin itself. As a result of their great potency there were many cases of overdose and death, and fentanyls soon lost popularity. The second group of synthetic opioid derivatives subject to clandestine modification are pethidines. Abuse of pethidines is associated with the most serious designer drug catastrophe so far, when a neurotoxic reaction to a pethidine by-product led to irreversible Parkinsonism among young intravenous drug abusers in the early 1980s. PCP derivatives, which are based on the molecule of the general anaesthetic phencyclidine, came to the attention of drug control agencies in the latter part of the 1960s. As a consequence of their strong hallucinogenic and frequently bizarre effects, their use never became particularly widespread. Tryptamines are another group of hallucinogenic compounds that lend themselves to structural modification. They are related to LSD in chemical structure and, like LSD, were fairly popular during the 'psychedelic' years of the 1960s. Clandestine modifications of the central nervous system depressant methaqualone, despite relative ease of synthesis, have made only a limited appearance on the streets. By contrast, various substances related to amphetamine in their chemical structure, the phenylalkylamines, have been seen on the streets in several waves since the mid-1960s. The latest wave started in the mid-1980s / early 1990s when various amphetamine-type stimulants (ATS) made their appearance on the dance drug scene. For a number of reasons, the ATS phenomenon in all its dimensions exemplifies the peculiarities, on both the demand and supply side, of clandestine synthetic drugs in general.

Amphetamine-type stimulants: a case scenario[1]

Social and geographical spread of ATS abuse

Immediately after their introduction into medical practice in the 1930s, amphetamine and methamphetamine - considered to be the parent drugs of the ATS group -

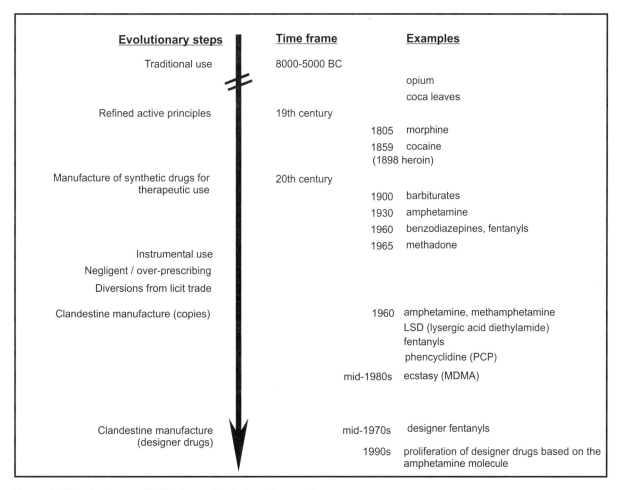

Evolutionary steps	Time frame		Examples
Traditional use	8000-5000 BC		
			opium
			coca leaves
Refined active principles	19th century		
		1805	morphine
		1859	cocaine
		(1898	heroin)
Manufacture of synthetic drugs for therapeutic use	20th century		
		1900	barbiturates
		1930	amphetamine
		1960	benzodiazepines, fentanyls
		1965	methadone
Instrumental use			
Negligent / over-prescribing			
Diversions from licit trade			
Clandestine manufacture (copies)		1960	amphetamine, methamphetamine
			LSD (lysergic acid diethylamide)
			fentanyls
			phencyclidine (PCP)
		mid-1980s	ecstasy (MDMA)
Clandestine manufacture (designer drugs)		mid-1970s	designer fentanyls
		1990s	proliferation of designer drugs based on the amphetamine molecule

Figure 2. Clandestine synthetic drugs: Evolution of a problem.

began to be used for non-medical purposes. Lax prescribing, together with instrumental use among soldiers during the Second World War contributed to the subsequent spread of abuse among the general public. Abuse started among occupational groups, moved on to students and athletes and then to recreational users. Chronic abuse in a core group of heavy abusers became a problem in a few countries, notably in northern Europe and Japan. Epidemics of non-instrumental use of ATS usually started among *avant garde* sections of society, spread through the middle classes and finally reached the marginal sections of society.

In geographical terms, ATS abuse gradually spread from a few countries, including Sweden, Japan, and the United States, to neighbouring countries within the same regions, and then to other regions as well. Since the mid-1990s, and subsequent to the start of the 'ecstasy' epidemic in Europe, abuse of ATS has been perceived as a global phenomenon, although with different substances predominating in different parts of the world (see Figure 3). Today, recreational use of ATS is most prevalent in several developed countries, particularly in Europe, but is also increasing rapidly in other regions, in particular in South-East Asia, where instrumental use, for example by long-distance truck drivers, used to be the prevailing pattern of use.

Sources of supply

In the early days, when amphetamines were considered a panacea for many ailments, non-medical use of ATS was facilitated by over-prescribing and negligent prescribing practices. With potential dangers associated with the widespread use of ATS becoming a matter of concern, and with regulatory restrictions being introduced, large-scale diversions from licit trade soon became the principal source of supply to meet non-medical demand. From the early 1970s, the application of more stringent controls on several traditional ATS led to what is often called the 'balloon' effect, i.e., the displacement of supply from one source to another. In this case, the 'balloon effect' refers to the displacement from the licit to the illicit sector, leading to the emergence of clandestine manufacture, initially of amphetamine and methamphetamine, and later of structurally modified designer ATS.

With the extension of control measures to cover the manufacture of starting materials, another facet of the 'balloon' effect became apparent, i.e., the shift from one well established precursor to another, followed by the displacement of clandestine manufacture to a neighbouring country where control measures were less stringent. The shift in the United States in the 1980s from

1-phenyl-2-propanone (P2P; also known as benzyl methyl ketone, or BMK) to ephedrine as key precursors for methamphetamine synthesis, and the subsequent displacement of clandestine methamphetamine manufacture to Mexico, illustrate such 'ballooning'. Another example of 'ballooning', linked to the introduction of stricter controls, is the historical displacement, from the 1950s onwards, of clandestine manufacture of methamphetamine from Japan to Korea, the Philippines, and later to China.

Today, in most regions where consumption figures are high, clandestine synthesis is the main source of supply of ATS for the illicit market. Advanced stages of 'innovative' clandestine drug design are currently underway in Europe and, to a lesser extent, in North America and Australia. In several Asian countries, clandestine synthetic drug manufacture has entered the first stage in the illicit copying of existing drugs such as methamphetamine and, more recently, ecstasy. By contrast, the situation in many developing countries - in particular African and Latin American countries - is still characterized by oversupply, including lax prescribing practices and the availability of pharmaceutical drugs through unregulated channels. In those regions there is a risk that the history of Europe, the United States and Japan in the 1960s and 1970s may be repeating itself: oversupply may be followed by clandestine synthesis, initially by the copying of existing pharmaceutical drugs, and eventually by the manufacture of structurally-related 'designer ATS'.

CLANDESTINE SYNTHETIC DRUGS VIS-À-VIS PLANT-BASED DRUGS

Against the background of the ATS case scenario described above, the following section looks at the complex interrelationship between incentives and disincentives on both the demand and the supply side for different types of drugs. It also analyses some of the underlying characteristics that drive drug supply and demand, highlighting major differences between plant-based drugs (as illustrated by the cases of heroin and cocaine) and synthetic drugs (see also Boxes B and C).

On the supply side, one crucial factor for a clandestine operator is the availability of, and access to, the required starting materials. While the production of the classical plant-based drugs, heroin and cocaine, is dependent on natural raw materials only produced in certain geographical locations, manufacture of synthetic drugs typically requires starting materials that are most often readily available worldwide[f]. The chemicals concerned are usually cheap and the desired end-product can be produced in a few simple reaction steps. Lengthy and

---

f) It should be noted that for some groups of synthetic drugs natural raw materials are also available, for instance, ephedrine for the manufacture of methamphetamine or methcathinone, or certain safrole-containing essential oils for some ecstasy-type substances.

Figure 3. Historical spread of abuse of amphetamine-type stimulants*

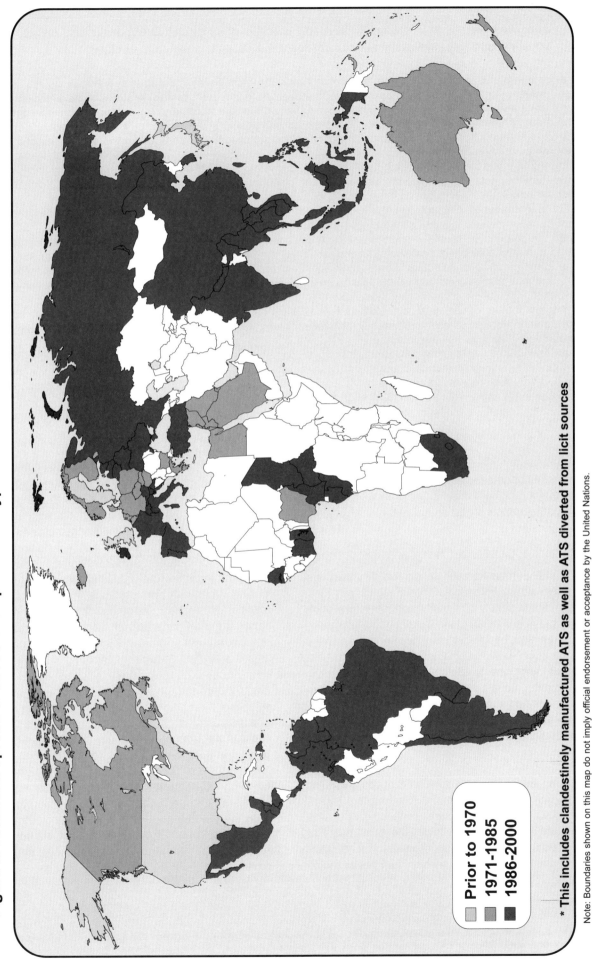

Prior to 1970
1971-1985
1986-2000

* This includes clandestinely manufactured ATS as well as ATS diverted from licit sources

Note: Boundaries shown on this map do not imply official endorsement or acceptance by the United Nations.

BOX B: Specific differences in the manufacturing process of synthetic and plant-based drugs, which contribute to the attractiveness of clandestine synthetic drug manufacture:

(i)   the relative volume of starting materials required is considerably smaller in the case of synthetic drugs;

(ii)   the immediate precursors of synthetic drugs are comparable, in terms of processing stage, to the intermediate products coca paste and morphine. Clandestine synthetic drug laboratories are therefore comparable to laboratories processing the final stage of the conversion of morphine into heroin, or coca paste into cocaine (see Figure 4 below);

(iii)   the scale of production of synthetic drugs is very flexible: depending on the drug to be synthesized, clandestine laboratories can be 'kitchen'-type for personal supply using primitive technology and often literally set up in domestic kitchens; or they can be elaborate, purpose-built constructions with the latest technical equipment. Clandestine synthetic drug laboratories can thus easily be set up in the form of makeshift laboratories supplying a single order, and then dismantled to prevent detection;

(iv)   while for plant-based drugs one starting material yields one end-product, clandestine synthetic drug manufacture is more flexible in terms of number of synthesis routes, alternate precursors and end-products;

(v)   while the production process of plant-based drugs is essentially an extraction / isolation process, i.e., the end-products, cocaine and morphine, are present from the very beginning, the synthetic end-products are only constructed during the final stages of the synthesis. This reduces the risk of detection, while at the same time, it makes the seizure of a clandestine synthetic drug laboratory an effort requiring precise timing (not before the end-product is finished, not after it has been distributed) in order to prove that synthesis actually did take place;

(vi)   the large number of structural modifications with similar pharmacological profiles, which can substitute for one other (designer analogues) offers the opportunity for clandestine experimentation or 'research' which frequently cannot be countered by existing laws in many countries;

(vii)   the possibility of manufacturing tailor-made synthetic drugs allows clandestine chemists to satisfy particular consumer needs and to respond quickly to changes in fashion/consumer preferences once they have recognized a market potential. By contrast, the scope for clandestine 'innovation' related to plant-based drugs is very limited and largely restricted to changes in the presentation/mode of administration of the drug.

---

labour-intensive harvesting and extraction/isolation procedures are not required, and risks associated with the protection of cultivation areas do not exist.

Another important factor is the access to information and to the required scientific and technical know-how. 'Recipes' for the manufacture of synthetic drugs are widely available through specific underground literature, or through the Internet. In fact, modern information technology plays a crucial role in the spread of clandestine drug synthesis by offering any lay person answers to questions such as: what chemical precursors to use; where to get them; how to evade detection; and how to set up a simple 'kitchen' laboratory. All of this is compounded by the fact that a typical synthesis is relatively simple in terms of number of reaction steps required and the technology involved. Synthesis yields are usually high.

The global spread of certain synthetic drugs over the past decade can also be attributed to economic incentives that affect their manufacture, trafficking and, ultimately, abuse. On the supply side, the profitability of synthetic drugs, in the consumer markets, is frequently higher than that of cocaine or heroin. Not restricted to specific geographical areas, the manufacture of synthetic drugs can easily occur close to the place of final consumption[g]. As a consequence, almost all of the total retail price of a synthetic drug remains in the region where the drug is consumed. In addition, the close vicinity of places of clandestine manufacture and consumption reduces the risk of detection, for example, at border crossings and because it enables trafficking in smaller quantities. The facts that synthetic drug laboratories are less conspicuous also contributes to reducing the overall risks for clandestine operators, when compared with illicit cocaine or heroin production.

On the demand side, several factors influence the final decision of a user to choose a particular drug. The pharmacological characteristics of the drug itself, i.e., the sought-after effects of the drug weighed against its undesirable side effects and risks, inasmuch as they are known to the user, probably play a significant role. Similarly, the suitability of a drug for administration routes other than by intravenous injection and, increasingly, methods other than smoking, also seem to be contributing factors. Other elements include cultural, social and economic considerations, the image and social representation of individual drugs, and the

---

g) This is particularly true for 'ecstasy' and amphetamine in Europe, and for methamphetamine in the United States. Exceptions are the trafficking of 'ecstasy' from Europe to Australia, South-East Asia/Far East, and the United States. Demand for methamphetamine in the Far East is met by supply from within the region.

BOX C: Intrinsic characteristics of synthetic drugs contributing to their attractiveness to consumers vis-à-vis the traditional plant-based drugs:

(i)   many synthetic drugs can be taken by mouth. In addition to being 'convenient' for the user, the use of pills also avoids injection or smoking and the dangers or social stigma associated with these administration routes;

(ii)   compared to heroin and cocaine, the use of which has been stigmatized among drug users as well as the general public, the recreational use of synthetic drugs, is generally perceived as being less harmful, and controllable. Since several synthetic drugs are used to enhance performance or cope with difficult /unpleasant situations (tension, stress, depression and so on), they are often perceived as being beneficial to the individual rather than destructive;

(iii)   with the internationalization of societies and in an increasingly technology-oriented world, synthetic drugs are frequently seen as representations of technological advances, of modernism, affluence and success.

---

availability/accessibility of alternative substances. The situation is, therefore, more complex on the demand side than the supply side, and consumer preferences may change over time.

Economic incentives on the demand side are likely to become particularly important when there is an alternative substance available that offers the consumer similar pharmacological effects at a lower cost and no higher risk. In pharmacological terms alone, the stimulant drugs cocaine and methamphetamine/amphetamine are competitors for the same user population. Similarly, heroin and fentanyls can compete and used to compete, in the late 1970s/early 1980s, for the same illicit narcotic analgesic (opioid) market. Reality however is far more complex since additional factors such as purity, the duration of the effects and the image of the drugs also play significant roles.

APPROACHES TO THE CONTROL OF CLANDESTINE SYNTHETIC DRUGS

The international drug control system is guided by the need to strike a balance between ensuring the availability of substances used for legitimate medical purposes, and preventing their diversion into illicit markets. Procedures to extend control measures to new substances have been carefully formulated, taking into account the need to maintain legitimate trade in those substances for medical purposes. They consist of a monitoring system of licit transactions of individual substances, which are related to manufacture, stocks, trade and use, and estimates for quantities needed for medical and research purposes. In such a system, any inconsistency or change would be apparent and would prompt caution and eventually corrective measures, thus preventing the leakage of a controlled substance into illicit channels.

Clandestine synthetic drugs challenge the current drug control system in several ways:

- firstly, because they are manufactured clandestinely, there is no legitimate trade, and their distribution cannot be monitored by the traditional drug control system;

- secondly, as a result of the so-called substance-by-substance scheduling approach, the appearance of new substances, which are not included in the schedules of the conventions, cannot be countered immediately with appropriate measures, given that their manufacture, trafficking and abuse are not 'illicit', i.e., they do not constitute a criminal offense at that point in time. This offers room for clandestine experimentation or 'research' into individual substances within a class of drugs with similar pharmacological profiles;

- thirdly, as a consequence of the clandestine nature of the substances concerned, there are usually not sufficient data available for the required scheduling assessments. The procedure for their inclusion into the control system is thus a lengthy one, and this allows clandestine manufacturers to continue to operate for some time and sell their products without immediately facing legal consequences.

Through the 1988 Convention, the international community has attempted to strengthen the existing drug control system which mostly focuses on end-products, with legislative tools which also address diversion and the illicit use of starting materials and other chemicals required in clandestine drug manufacture. Precursor control has now become one of the cornerstones of most drug control strategies. It is particularly important in the area of synthetic drugs, given their flexibility within the manufacturing process, and the wide range of starting materials that can substitute for one other.

In addition, before the 1988 Convention came into effect, there had been no international system for the control of precursors for synthetic drugs, not even for the most immediate starting materials. This is in contrast to the situation with plant-based drugs, where the same international control regime (1961 Convention) applies to immediate starting materials (coca leaf, opium), intermediates (coca paste, morphine) and end-products (cocaine, heroin), and only the chemicals required in the extraction and purification processes are monitored through the 1988 Convention. Figure 4 provides an overview of the different control regimes as they apply to plant-based drugs, to synthetic drugs, and to the precursors and other chemicals required for their manufacture.

The large number of legitimate uses, and the frequently large volumes of licit trade also tend to set practical limitations on a particularly strict control system for precursors. Moreover, unlike most end-products, many precursors are manufactured and traded by a large number of companies worldwide. There are, therefore, various sources of licit supply, enabling clandestine operators (i) to adapt quickly to the introduction of

stricter controls in major supplier and transit countries, and (ii) to place orders with several suppliers world-wide simultaneously. As a result, trafficking and diversion routes are highly flexible. Effective monitoring of movements of precursors is also complicated by the variety of shipping routes through a number of intermediaries in different countries, which are used to disguise the final destination of the shipments.

Another trend over the past few years has been the increasing use in illicit drug manufacture of legitimately obtained, non-controlled substances as substitutes for precursors that are already under control. From a drug control perspective, this development gives rise to two problems. First, the large number of potential substitutes makes strict control of the licit trade of such substances unrealistic, and secondly, many of those substitutes have an even broader range of legitimate uses than the 'traditional' precursor substances. The situation is more disturbing with regard to synthetic than plant-based drugs, since even the most essential precursors of certain synthetic drugs can be substituted by non-controlled precursors, or can be synthesized from a non-controlled pre-precursor 'down the chain'[h]. In the

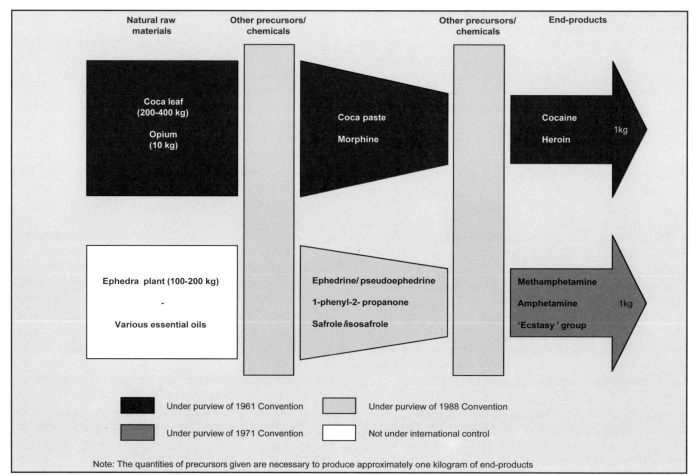

Figure 4. Comparison of processing stages and control regimes of selected plant-based narcotic drugs, synthetic drugs, and their precursors / starting materials.

h) Examples are the use of benzaldehyde and benzyl cyanide in the manufacture of P2P and amphetamine.

case of heroin and cocaine, by contrast, only the chemicals for the isolation, conversion and purification can be replaced by non-controlled substitutes, whereas sufficient supply of opium or coca leaf, respectively, is always crucial for their manufacture.

THE DEVELOPMENT OF A TREND - DEMAND PULL OR SUPPLY PUSH?

Preferences for individual substances (or substance classes) are the result of a complex interplay between cultural, social, economic and other factors. As a consequence, they vary within and between countries, as well as over time. The emergence of a new drug trend seems usually to be the result of clandestine manufacturers exploring the market potential, followed by consumer acceptance. This satisfaction of consumer preference, at a given time and in a given socio-cultural context, is a precondition for the popularity of a new drug. Subsequently, supply may be gradually replaced by demand as the major driving force in an expanding market. For synthetic drugs, on a global scale, most new trends emerged in western countries, notably the United States, and then gradually spread to less developed countries[i].

Shifts in preferences for individual drugs are correlated to some extent with a change in the social representation of a given substance, which itself may partly be the result of more and more detailed, accurate and exhaustive information on side effects and risks involved in the consumption of that particular substance. In the absence of a sub-cultural memory of the hazards of the use of a given drug, each new generation of users seems to rediscover the pleasurable effects of that drug. This, together with the subsequent rediscovery and dissemination of information on adverse health and psychological consequences is part of the cyclical pattern which characterizes most epidemics of illicit drug use.[2]

In the case of the classical plant-based drugs, a new trend is largely limited to changes in the route of administration, accompanied by the necessary change in the presentation of the drug (e.g., cocaine and crack cocaine, or heroin hydrochloride and heroin base). As a consequence, only a few products are available to consumers. Synthetic drugs, by contrast, allow for the clandestine manipulation of a 'successful' drug molecule, frequently without changing the pharmacological effects sought after by the consumers, thus opening access to an entire class of related substances. This flexibility makes synthetic drugs highly suitable for situations of changing trends and fashion and, at the same time, a nightmare for law enforcement and forensic chemists.

Globalization and the internationalization of societies appear to have contributed to creating an environment conducive to the spread of clandestine synthetic drugs, both from the supply and the demand point of view. On the demand side, there are at least three phenomena that can be observed over the last decade:

(i) changes in social structures in many societies around the world, which lead, among other things, to an emphasis on individual success and performance;
(ii) a growing global trend towards fashionable lifestyles, short-lived amusement and a 'consumption culture' which trusts in 'pills' as universal remedies (see also Box D); and
(iii) the spread of modern communication technology.

While the first two phenomena may translate into distinct consumption patterns, namely instrumental/occupational use to achieve desired goals, and recreational/social use, the last one contributes to the rapidity of the spread of synthetic drugs and to the convergence in consumption patterns in different parts of the world. The media industry and modern communication technology, in particular the Internet, enable fashions to become increasingly global and expand public access to specific information on various drugs, including their effects, where to get them, and the comparison of prices.

From the demand perspective

Today's situation with regard to the consumption of psychoactive drugs for recreational purposes can be seen in the social context of the 'mass culture' of the youth of the 1990s. Synthetic drug consumption since the beginning of the 1990s has not been associated with distinct social classes of drug users, nor does it appear to have any political dimension. Instead, pleasure-seeking, amusement and fun in a controlled way without any perceived impact on work performance, seem to be at the heart of that drug culture in many countries. As such, consumption of certain psychoactive drugs has become a mass phenomenon: school children and college and high-school students are growing up in an environment where drugs are almost constantly present and where their availability has become the norm. Certain synthetic drugs have become an integral part of mainstream youth culture in many countries where they are used as representations of a fashionable life-style. Among wide sectors of increasingly younger segments of the population of all social strata, synthetic drugs seem to be valued for facilitating communication, socializing with others and for creating a sense of belonging and integration. This is particularly true for the drugs with predominantly stimulant effects which were origi-

---

i) An exception to this trend is methcathinone (ephedrone), an ATS which was seen in 1982 in St. Petersburg about ten years before it made its first appearance in the USA. Also the current wave of 'ecstasy' consumption in the context of the club and dance culture emerged in Europe, and has only hit the United States much later.

BOX D: 'Lifestyle products'

One facet of contemporary consumption culture is the rapidly increasing demand for products which enable people to manage their lives more easily. A vast number of so-called lifestyle products is now available, usually in the form of pills, which can be easily swallowed. They are alleged to increase both the mental and physical well-being of the user, and enable him/her to cope with a variety of 'lifestyle' problems. For instance, the need to enhance mental performance, i.e., concentration, cognition or memory, is reflected in the increasing popularity of so-called 'smart drugs'. 'Smart drugs' or 'cognition enhancers' refer to a group of substances ranging from mixtures of vitamins, minerals and amino acids to pharmaceutical drugs used to treat memory loss associated with ageing. They act by increasing the blood flow to the brain, or by boosting the levels of certain neurotransmitters which play a role in learning and memory. In addition to stimulant effects (like energy drinks), 'smart products' can also have relaxing effects. Use of 'slimming pills', anabolic steroids and doping agents also reflect the need to conform with certain popularly-held views, norms and behaviours. Some authors go even so far as to include Viagra, a prescription medication used to treat certain forms of sexual impotence, in this category, since its popularity can be attributed to the same driving forces behind many of today's lifestyle drugs. Irrational (and frequently unethical) marketing of certain licit medications may thus create an environment where consumption of 'pills', licit or illicit, is perceived as a panacea to cope with any of the stressful problems of modern life.

---

nally associated with the dance culture. However, the individual drug - or its specific pharmacological effect - might often be less important to the users than the role it plays as a component of a certain lifestyle.

Drug type

In terms of pharmacological effects, the current requirements of the synthetic drug market translate into only a few drug classes. These are substances that increase performance, enhance or alter sensory perception and/or facilitate inter-personal communication, and help socializing with others. Current youth values do not seem to favour synthetic drugs with calming effects, which tend to isolate the user. For the (sub)cultural phenomena closely related to the dance drug scene, the overall pharmacology of drugs used continues to be the same, namely a combination of stimulation and enhancement of sensory perception. Apart from their pharmacological effects, the intrinsic characteristics of the substances themselves which also contribute to their suitability for a given consumer population, include the speed of onset and the duration of effects. Considering the current fashion of dance or lifestyle drugs, the duration of action of an 'ideal' future synthetic drug should not be too long, ideally a few hours; it should not produce a 'hangover' the following day, and it should meet the criterion of oral bioavailability, i.e., it must be effective when taken by mouth, perhaps by smoking, although the social acceptance of smoking is steadily declining in several societies.

While not all synthetic drugs meet those criteria, many ATS do, and in view of the reputation and social acceptance some established drugs have gained on the dance drug market, it can be expected that they will continue to

be available, and that they will spread increasingly outside the dance scene. The reputation, in particular, of ecstasy has resulted in several other substances being marketed under that name, and the term 'ecstasy' has increasingly become synonymous with a recreational drug in the dosage form of a tablet. While some of the substances offered for marketing purposes under the name 'ecstasy' are also available as separate entities under their own names like amphetamine and LSD, several others, especially chemically- and pharmacologically-related substances, lack a separate market and consumer identity. Another drug which may experience faster and widespread abuse in the future is gamma-hydroxybutyrate, or GHB[j]. Although structurally unrelated to ATS, GHB was introduced into the market by successfully using the 'ecstasy analogy' marketing concept. It is known to users at dance settings as 'liquid ecstasy', or 'the ultimate drug', which is said to produce euphoric and hallucinogenic effects, to enhance sexual pleasure and to have no 'come-down' effect.

In an environment of constant change in terms of availability of drugs, where a large number of drugs and drug combinations are available simultaneously, polydrug use is common. Such drug use involves the deliberate combination of drugs to alter, strengthen or prolong certain effects, or to alleviate the after-effects of the main drug used. Another aspect is the combination of illicit drugs with certain licit pharmaceuticals, in particular those which slow the metabolic breakdown of the illicit drug in the body, thus prolonging and/or enhancing its effects. The added risks which such consumption patterns bear are significant, and can even be fatal, as there may be unpredictable interactions with other therapeutic agents and even normal biochemical processes in the body.

---

j) Note that in March 2001, following a recomendation by WHO, GHB (as *gamma*-hydroxybutyric acid) was included in Schedule IV of the 1971 Convention.

BOX E: Other classes of synthetic drugs

Other classes of synthetic drugs which have been synthesized clandestinely in the past are phencyclidine (PCP) and its analogues, including ketamine, synthetic opioids (fentanyls and pethidines) and methaqualone derivatives. However, apart from PCP analogues, widespread consumption of these substance classes does not appear to be likely against the background of current societal norms and values and consumer preferences.

Analogues of phencyclidine are a group of hallucinogens which may become more important in the future. While some of them are still used in veterinary medicine, such as ketamine, and may find their way onto the streets by diversion from licit trade, others may be created in clandestine laboratories. Recreational use of ketamine, for instance, already appears to be increasing in several regions around the world, mainly as part of the 'ecstasy' / party drug market. When offered as a separate drug, it is favoured for its relatively short-term hallucinogenic properties. The ease with which PCP analogues can be synthesized may lead to even more analogues appearing in the future.

By contrast, and as a result of their negative image, the probability that synthetic opioids such as derivatives of pethidine (meperidine) or of fentanyl will regain popularity among consumers in the future is relatively small. For pethidines, the experience of the early 1980s is too well remembered, when several young users destroyed their lives with irreversible Parkinsonism induced by a neurotoxic by-product (MPTP) in a batch of a clandestinely manufactured pethidine derivative. As a consequence, pethidine derivatives are fraught with considerable risk from the inadvertent production of either MPTP or from an as yet unexplored congener also having neurotoxic properties. A similar negative image is associated with the abuse of fentanyl derivatives, which caused numerous overdose deaths in the 1980s as a result of their extreme potency.

Among clandestinely manufactured synthetic central nervous system (CNS) depressants, the only drug with a distinct, though restricted consumer market is methaqualone. Traditionally, supply for illicit markets in southern and eastern Africa used to be met by illicit manufacture in India, but more recently, methaqualone is predominantly being manufactured locally. While consumption of methaqualone has for a long time been chiefly confined to southern and eastern Africa, it appears to be gaining in popularity as 'poor man's ecstasy' in a particular sub-group of the nightclub and dance party scene, for instance, in Australia because of its euphoric, aphrodisiac, and disinhibiting effects in certain individuals. As such, it is particularly popular with gay men, and is usually used together with alcohol.

While PCP analogues, synthetic opioids and methaqualone are usually manufactured illicitly, clandestine manufacture is not necessarily the only source of supply for drugs encountered on the streets. CNS depressants, in particular benzodiazepines, and volatile substances (inhalants) are two major groups of synthetic drugs of abuse which are obtained from licit sources. The attractiveness of benzodiazepines, for example, can be attributed, among other things, to the pharmaceutical-grade of the drugs, i.e., their guaranteed quality and the knowledge about the dose level of the active ingredient, thus assuring the consumer that the same effect can be expected.

For benzodiazepines, two major patterns of misuse are encountered: (i) in the context of therapeutically unjustified overuse and (ii) as part of polydrug use. For instance, benzodiazepines are used in the dance scene after an event in order to recover from the effects of ATS and to avoid an unpleasant 'come-down', particularly insomnia, which may last for several days following ATS consumption. They may also be used to boost the effects of heroin. Another development, which may continue and expand in the future, is the use of some synthetic CNS depressants within the context of committing a crime which involves dazing the victim, prior to robbery or sexual assault (hence the term 'date-rape' drugs). The amnesia (limited loss of memory) following drug intake prevents the victim from recalling details of the crime and of its perpetrator.

Another aspect of the drug market which should not be overlooked is the problem of volatile substance use ('glue sniffing'). This form of drug use certainly has the potential for expansion although in a different consumer population, namely children and teenagers, and in particular from lower income families. None of the inhalant products concerned is under international control, and the majority of these chemicals are commercially available and are legal to possess. In fact, many of them are contained in common household products. Since they are cheap and widely available, volatile substances are the drugs of choice for adolescents in many countries, reflected in lifetime prevalence rates of up to 25 percent (compared to up to 9 percent for 'ecstasy')[3]. In contrast to the frequently-held belief that such products are harmless, non-addictive and undetectable, volatile substance use can cause health and social problems of considerable magnitude. Inhalation of many volatile substances produces adverse effects similar to those of central nervous system depressants such as alcohol and barbiturates. From the illicit supply point of view, retailing of such products can be a lucrative business.

The range of drugs which provide the effects favoured by current 'youth cultures', and which are frequently used simultaneously, extends from ecstasy and related substances to stimulants and hallucinogens. In terms of substance classes which may attract attention by consumers in the recreational drug scene, hallucinogens will continue to be strong candidates. The past has shown that ecstasy use may be followed by hallucinogen use as a consequence of users finding the effects of ecstasy insufficiently attractive.[4] They then turn either to mixtures containing hallucinogens or directly to hallucinogens. In this context, the resurgence of LSD in the mid-1990s should not be disregarded. LSD appeals to the younger market because it is frequently easy to obtain, often cheap to purchase, and produces a lasting high. Since LSD is now usually available at a much lower strength per dosage unit than in the 1960s, it may also trigger the spread of other mild hallucinogens among young consumers. One group of hallucinogens which may become more popular is the tryptamines. They provide brief and intense 'trips' when smoked or injected, and although some of them have been banned in most countries since the early 1970s, there are reports that some party drug users are experimenting with tryptamines as an alternative to LSD. However, there are drawbacks to tryptamines, including their mode of administration. Some of them have to be smoked, snorted, or injected in order to be pharmacologically effective. In addition, many of them, at common dose levels, are far more hallucinogenic in nature than ecstasy. They may therefore not appeal as much to the youth culture as other party drugs, unless their pharmacological drawback is balanced by a relatively low price.

Considering the overall consumer preferences characterizing the current wave of abuse of synthetic drugs, a similarly widespread consumption of substances of other chemical / pharmacological classes (Box E) in the immediate future seems unlikely.

Geographical trends

In geographical terms, the demand for performance-enhancing and dance drugs can be expected to spread along with improvements in standard of living, stronger buying power and free-market economies. The growth of a middle class, accompanied by a growing interest in imported fashions may make certain communities vulnerable to the use of synthetic drugs. Within individual regions or countries, synthetic drug use can be expected to spread both vertically and horizontally, i.e., from higher to lower social strata and from larger cities to towns and rural areas. Falling prices as a consequence of an expansion of the market may further contribute to this development.

'Ecstasy' and related ATS have already been spreading in countries of South and South-East Asia. In China, for instance, and more specifically in Hong Kong, Shanghai, Canton, and in the 'special economic zones', demand for synthetic drugs is rising in night-clubs, dance-halls or Karaoke bars. For similar reasons, i.e., because of their modern image and their generally lower prices compared to traditional drugs, synthetic drugs can also be expected to continue spreading in eastern Europe. Demand for synthetic drugs may also further increase in several countries in South America, where 'ecstasy' has recently become fashionable among youth.[5]

From the supply perspective

On the supply side, synthetic drugs enable clandestine chemists to follow developments in a consumer market which is subject to trends of fashion and in which the individual drug plays less of a role compared to the rituals/myths surrounding its use. However, a clandestine chemist would not normally want to replace a more potent drug which is well accepted in the consumer population with a less potent one unless he is forced to do so, for instance, by the unavailability of the required precursor chemicals. While staying within the confines of consumer acceptance and preferences, a clandestine chemist will tend, within a group of related substances, to synthesize the drugs which carry the highest profits and have the lowest risks of detection. The focus will therefore be on those substances which have the highest possible potency and which can be synthesized, to the extent possible, from unsuspicious starting materials.

Drug type

Several of the substances and substance classes which are attractive to consumers in the recreational drug scene are equally attractive for clandestine manufacturers in terms of level of risk and financial returns. This is particularly true for some synthetic stimulants and hallucinogens, which offer opportunities for structural modification and drug design. However, since consumer acceptance is a factor beyond the direct control of clandestine manufacturers, creating an entirely 'new' substance class involves a certain degree of risk. As a consequence, future trends are likely to evolve from what is already discernable today:

- increased availability of traditional ATS such as amphetamine and methamphetamine, to be used for their performance-enhancing effects;
- re-emergence of other ATS already banned in most countries as a consequence of previous periods of abuse[k]; and/or

---

k) The most recent example in this context is the re-emergence of PMA (*para*-methoxyamphetamine) in 2000 as part of the 'ecstasy' market. PMA has been under international control since 1986.

BOX F: AlexanderShulgin and the PIKHKAL / TIHKAL dilemma

PIHKAL and TIHKAL are two books published by Alexander and Ann Shulgin in 1991 and 1997 respectively. Detailed descriptions of the pharmacology and chemistry of phenethylamines and tryptamines are interwoven with autobiographical details about the authors. For almost 30 years, Alexander Shulgin synthesized and evaluated, mainly through self-monitoring, a broad range of psychoactive substances. The first book, PIHKAL, is based on his life's research into the effects of phenethylamines in human beings, hence the acronym in the title which stands for *P*henethylamines *I* *H*ave *K*nown *A*nd *L*oved (TIHKAL, by analogy, stands for *T*ryptamines *I* *H*ave *K*nown *A*nd *L*oved). While valued by some psychotherapists for providing first-hand accounts of the use of a number of psychoactive compounds, the level of detail - which affords the reader a realistic feeling for the effects of the compounds described - worries drug control authorities, who fear that the descriptions could encourage drug use. Of even more concern is the fact that the books offer quasi-encyclopedic compendiums of dosages, durations of action, and syntheses in recipe form for almost 200 chemical compounds of the class of phenethylamines and for more than 50 tryptamines. There is thus justifiable concern that the availability of PIHKAL and TIHKAL may bring a whole range of new substances and precursors to the attention of both consumers and illicit producers. Manufactured under clandestine laboratory conditions, the 'quality' of the substances is very likely to be dissimilar to those described by Shulgin; low purity, presence of impurities and insufficient testing of these street products are major contributors to the considerable health risks they pose for consumers.

- increase in consumption of new designer ATS, or of substances which have so far only appeared sporadically in illicit markets. The so-called phenethylamines (PEAs), which are close chemical relatives of ATS not controlled in most countries, and which can be expected to produce similar effects, can be included in this category.

The only other pharmacological drug class which, like the ATS, lends itself to structural modification (and which may also be attractive in the immediate future from the consumers' point of view), are the hallucinogenic tryptamines. Although their synthesis is usually more complex than ATS synthesis, the availability of the book TIHKAL[6], in the same way as PIHKAL (and other similar underground 'recipe' books), may contribute to new trends in the future (Box F).

Geographical trends

In geographical terms, western Europe has been the world's major illicit manufacturing region for amphetamine and ecstasy-type substances during most of the last decade. On the whole, as long as ATS consumption continues in Europe, large-scale production can be expected to continue in this region as well. At the same time, there are indications that 'marketing activities' are being expanded from regional to international consumer markets, e.g., North America, Australia / New Zealand, South Africa, Asia and South America.[7]

The extension of clandestine manufacture to eastern Europe, the Baltic States and CIS Member States is also likely to continue as the economic situation in many of those countries is still fragile, expertise and technical capabilities to synthesize drugs are readily available, labour is cheap, and precursors are mostly also easily available.

Illicit manufacture of synthetic drugs also continues to rise in South-East Asia with traditional heroin-producing organizations now increasingly diversifying into ATS, in particular methamphetamine. While many of these products are destined for consumption within the region, an increasing number of seizures of South-East Asian methamphetamine - mostly from Thailand - were made in Europe, and more recently also in the United States[8]. This indicates the reversal of a trend which has been true for some time for 'ecstasy', with the drug being exported from Europe to South-East Asia. There are now also indications that clandestine manufacturers in South-East Asia may soon be able to produce high quality 'ecstasy' comparable to that imported from Europe. As a consequence, prices can be expected to go down, thus making the drug affordable to larger segments of society. This may be a concern particularly in China, where seizure data indicate that the country has become important as a point of distribution of various synthetic drugs.

A similar trend to that seen in South-East Asia may eventually also emerge in some Latin American countries, where demand for 'ecstasy' is already evolving. Africa, by contrast, with the exception of South Africa, does not appear to face a risk of a major clandestine synthetic drug manufacture in the immediate future, as the situation in that region is still characterized by the availability of pharmaceutical drugs through unregulated channels (parallel markets).

As pointed out earlier, trends on the demand side are mainly driven by the drugs themselves, their representation, and intrinsic characteristics, such as overall pharmacology, suitability for certain mode of administration, duration of action, etc.. On the supply side, as well as the drugs themselves, there are other factors that have an impact on trends in clandestine manufacture and

BOX G: Other likely developments on the supply side of clandestine synthetic drug manufacture and trafficking

A) A diversification in the clandestine sector aimed partly at avoiding possible detection by ordering monitored chemicals, and partly at making up for the shortages in some essential precursors which have occurred as a result of increased alertness and monitoring within the industry. Activities may include:
- the search for substitutes of essential, yet controlled precursors;
- the synthesis of controlled precursors from so-called pre-precursors;
- investigations into alternative synthesis routes for a given end-product;
- an increase in the use of natural raw materials to obtain the required precursors;
- the use of non-controlled chemical modifications of precursors (so-called 'hidden precursors'), which can be easily converted, usually in one single step, into the primary, controlled chemical;
- the illicit manufacture and trafficking of drug intermediates, which are usually not included in any control regime; and
- the recycling of used chemicals.

In the longer run, stricter precursor legislation may thus force more clandestine chemists to synthesize their own starting materials or use less well described synthesis routes. An increased level of such activity may lead, subsequently, to the presence of more by-products/impurities of unknown toxicity in the end-product. However, as user acceptance will remain the ultimate yardstick for any individual product on the illicit market, a reputation for selling 'bad stuff' would not be conducive to good business on the part of the drug dealers.

B) A compartmentalization of illicit synthetic drug laboratory operations into the different stages along the manufacturing process, aimed at spreading the risk. This includes:
- the acquisition of precursor chemicals, illicit synthesis, and any further manipulation of the drug substance such as tableting being carried out separately and in different locations;
- the various stages of illicit synthesis itself being broken up into separate activities;
- an increasing number of clandestine chemists operating on a more independent, 'order and cash' basis when offering their skills.

C) An increased level of 'borrowing' concepts and adopting practices of the pharmaceutical and chemical industries, including for example:
- the maintenance of clandestine 'research' laboratories to develop new designer drugs; and
- the manufacture of so-called prodrugs, or metabolic precursors, of established (and usually regulated) drugs of abuse.

trafficking. On the manufacturing side, they may include, for example, the focus and level of law enforcement and regulatory activities, the skills of clandestine chemists and the level of sophistication of their laboratories. On the trafficking side, they include, importantly, the 'marketing' issue, i.e., the ability of clandestine operators to 'market' their products (Boxes G and H).

CLANDESTINE SYNTHETIC DRUGS AND LINKS WITH ORGANIZED CRIME

One of the worrying developments in the recent history of clandestine synthetic drugs is that their production and distribution are increasingly becoming structured, and integrated into international organized criminal activities. Driven by high profits, a clandestine synthetic drug 'industry' characterized by large-scale manufacture and international distribution networks is evolving.

'Market opportunities' are also likely to lead to a surge of polydrug trafficking and distribution, mirroring the polydrug abuse phenomenon. Intelligence information in several western European countries also suggests that criminals who have been involved in violent crime and the importation of traditional drugs are getting increasingly involved in the production and distribution of synthetic drugs. Some criminal 'investors' from western Europe exploit the economic and employment situation in eastern Europe. They invest the necessary capital, deliver the precursor chemicals for manufacturing ATS, take orders for markets abroad and launder profits through front companies. With large amounts of ready cash at their disposal, there is also a risk that criminal organizations may even purchase formerly state-owned and fully equipped premises for large-scale clandestine synthetic drug manufacture. There are also indications that criminal organizations are starting to control retail level distribution of synthetic drugs by taking over the

---

BOX H: 'Product design' and 'marketing concepts'

Since the recreational synthetic drug market is flexible and driven to a large extent by fashion, marketing concepts are of great importance. Based on the rather scattered evidence available, it can be expected that future clandestine chemists will be even more sensitive to the perceptions and needs of their clients, for example, by exploiting the closeness in appearance to legitimate products. To this end, they will continue to promote the tablet as a dosage form, and avoid the marketing of powders or liquids which need to be smoked, snorted or injected, and which lack the convenience and more benign image of 'pills'. Some law enforcement authorities also expect that in the future, in addition to the instructions on 'proper' use available on the Internet, some kind of written 'customer information' may be provided together with the drug.

Increasingly, 'new' drugs on the street are actually preexisting drugs with new names and alternative marketing. This usually involves taking an existing synthetic drug of low quality and simply modifying its appearance (colour and/or texture). A well-known example is 'ice', a particularly pure form of d-methamphetamine hydrochloride suitable for smoking. Adding food colouring is another simple marketing gimmick used in an attempt to differentiate various substances or to suggest to consumers a certain composition and quality of a given product. Moreover, combinations of drugs may be given a new name or may be marketed as a cocktail of drugs.

establishments where large dance parties are held, and where these drugs are sold.

From a historical perspective, the expansion of criminal groups engaged in the production and trafficking of plant-based drugs into synthetic drugs appears to have frequently started with trafficking in precursor chemicals, an activity which, unlike the distribution of the synthetic end-products, has always been international and multi-stage in character. Similarities to trafficking patterns of plant-based drugs have suggested for a long time that the same groups might be involved in both activities, and that the two markets are actually linked[9]. The next step, which is now underway in several parts of the world, is the move into the distribution of synthetic end-products. It is now generally acknowledged that, in some regions, the illicit activities in plant-based and synthetic drugs are already intertwined. In North America for example, criminal groups, once primarily involved in the trafficking of cannabis and cocaine from Mexico, seem to be using their existing distribution networks to supply the US market with methamphetamine, thus enabling a more rapid spread of methamphetamine throughout the country. According to some reports, Mexican drug trafficking groups are increasingly involved in illicit trafficking in 'ecstasy', exchanging cocaine from Latin America for 'ecstasy' manufactured in Europe[10]. A similar development can also be seen with heroin networks in East and South-East Asia, with the appearance of links between illicit activities in heroin and ATS, both at the manufacturing and trafficking levels: heroin and ATS may be increasingly manufactured in the same laboratories and distributed through the same distribution channels.

CONCLUSIONS AND FUTURE OPTIONS

This paper has attempted to give an overview of the synthetic drug phenomenon, its evolution, and likely future developments. While a number of conclusions emerge directly from the body of the paper itself, and are not summarized here in detail, this section highlights some major linkages between the peculiarities of clandestine manufacture, trafficking and abuse of synthetic drugs, and policy responses, other approaches and options for future consideration.

Understanding the phenomenon

While for decades the drug phenomenon was equated with the classical drugs of abuse, notably heroin and cocaine, there is now a new challenge in the form of synthetic drugs. This latest drug phenomenon is characterized by the recreational use of a number of synthetic psychoactive substances by a socially-integrated, mostly young, consumer population. Commonly held views about the harmlessness of those substances, and about their 'value' in helping to manage one's life more easily, or to experience pleasure and amusement in a controllable way without impacting on work performance, have contributed to their global spread, as has their association with technological advancements, modernism, and affluence. Economic models and societal norms and values emphasizing performance and individual success explain current pharmacological preferences and the attractiveness of substances which can be used to increase performance, to enhance or alter sensory perception and/or to facilitate inter-personal communication and social interaction.

Globalization and the emergence of performance-oriented societies in an increasing number of countries around the world seem to be drawing a growing number of people, particularly the young, to seek comfort and pleasure in synthetic drugs. This trend may be accelerated by a supply 'push' inasmuch as clandestine manufacturers may explore the area of synthetic drugs further once they have recognized the potential inherent in the market: products can be tailor-made to satisfy consumer needs, and changes in fashion and consumer preferences can be responded to quickly. Considering the specificities of demand and supply of synthetic drugs together, there is thus good reason to anticipate an expansion of the synthetic drug phenomenon beyond the confines of certain sub-cultural or social groups to wider sections of society and to geographical areas where manufacture, trafficking and/or consumption have been hitherto unknown. Modern communication technology such as the Internet plays a critical role in this development by linking the world in terms of preferences and consumption patterns, and by rapidly and globally disseminating information on synthetic drugs and recipes for their manufacture. The potential therefore exists for synthetic drugs, in particular ATS, to become one of the major global concerns for drug control in the twenty-first century. Growing pressure to eliminate or significantly reduce coca and opium poppy cultivation[11] may also contribute to this development.

Reducing demand

Largely driven by demand and subject to clandestine experimentation and 'research', the new synthetic drug market is a flexible area. Mechanisms to obtain relevant and reliable information on emerging drugs and patterns of use in a timely manner are crucial for health and regulatory authorities alike, to ensure, for example, rapid dissemination of information on potential hazards related to the use of a new drug, or to design appropriate prevention and control strategies. Success may depend upon early warning mechanisms and the rapid and global dissemination of information gathered on new drugs, drug combinations, or patterns of use. In view of the widespread availability of certain synthetic drugs and the integration of their use in mainstream youth culture and leisure-time activities, prevention programmes tailored to specificities of the phenomenon (young age of consumer population, perceived harmlessness, etc.) and integrated into the wider concept of health promotion, can be considered key elements in any approach or strategy to reduce demand for clandestine synthetic drugs over the longer term.

Reducing supply

Measures to reduce supply need to address both the emergence of new synthetic drugs and the continued widespread availability of already banned substances. They also need to build on existing successes in the area of precursor control. Consequently, effective supply reduction strategies have to combine a broadening of the scope and flexibility of control systems with the harmonization of national legislation and the strengthening of law enforcement activities in the area of illicit manufacture, trafficking and distribution of synthetic drugs.

Improving the knowledge base

In order to tackle an area as dynamic as the synthetic drug market in a comprehensive and pro-active manner on both the demand and the supply sides, a better understanding of the factors driving its evolution is required. Systematic investigations of the way that attitudes and perspectives of youth are affected by rapid social and economic changes and more detailed examinations of the complex interplay between demand and supply of individual synthetic drugs or drug classes, and how they relate to different geographical and cultural contexts are needed. Driving forces on the supply side will be better understood once the question of the impact of progress in science on the emergence of new synthetic drugs has been investigated. However, in view of the epidemic and global dimensions of synthetic drug use by young people, more systematic research into the (long-term) health consequences of synthetic drug use will be one of the most important and challenging areas of future work. This will allow for drawing together the diverging perceptions of synthetic drug use being seen as a blessing for some and a curse for others.

The findings from such investigations could contribute to improving the design of health education and prevention programmes as well as treatment services which meet the needs of (recreational) synthetic drug users. But such findings are also crucial for an assessment of the wider health and social implications of specific consumption patterns of synthetic drugs, now and particularly for the future. While research on ecstasy, for example, has for some time suggested cognitive, behavioural and emotional alterations in users, and suggestive evidence of human neurotoxicity has emerged during the past decade, it was only recently that the dose-dependent (cumulative) nature of the neuro-psychological deficits was confirmed in a larger sample of ecstasy users[12]. Since the current status of knowledge does not exclude possible long-term consequences on cognitive functioning, it is thus only further systematic and unbiased research that can help to answer one of the most worrying questions, namely whether current consumption patterns of certain synthetic drugs by young people will precipitate or exacerbate neurological problems, and whether we should expect that a whole generation of elderly, former synthetic drug users will in future suffer from a decline in mental functioning, much earlier or more pronounced than that associated with the normal ageing process.

Developing a global response

Over the past few years, growing international concern about rapidly increasing and widespread use of amphetamines has prompted the international community to call for a thorough global review of synthetic stimulants and their precursors[13]. A number of policy options for counter-measures and practical solutions have been developed. They include regional initiatives such as the 'Joint Action on New Synthetic Drugs' of the European Union[14], which provides for the establishment of an early warning system to identify new synthetic drugs as they appear on the European market, for a mechanism to assess the risks of these drugs, and for a procedure to bring specific new synthetic drugs under control in EU Member States. At the international level, an Action Plan Against Illicit Manufacture, Trafficking and Abuse of Amphetamine-type Stimulants and their Precursors, including a time-frame for the establishment of national legislation and programmes, was adopted at the Special Session of the General Assembly (UNGASS) in June 1998. The action plan covers key areas of raising awareness and providing accurate information, reducing demand, limiting supply, and strengthening control systems, and proposes countermeasures at all levels. Concrete steps are being developed for a coordinated effort to implement the action plan in the Far East, one of the regions most affected by the ATS problem.

On a global basis, a number of high level international meetings[15] have addressed the synthetic drug problem in all its dimensions, including regulatory action in precursor control, activities in the area of demand reduction and primary prevention, and improved operational capabilities of law enforcement authorities. Most recently, G8 experts have agreed on the need to tackle the synthetic drug problem at a global level, and in particular have re-emphasized the need for enhanced cooperation, at all levels, and for better and faster means for information collection and exchange.[16]

Full implementation of the UNGASS Action Plan on ATS will provide the necessary experience and an appropriate basis for tackling the problem of clandestine synthetic drugs in general.

ENDNOTES

1. Summarized from UNDCP, *Amphetamine-type Stimulants: A Global Review* (UNDCP/TS.3, Vienna, 1996). This study was the result of the first comprehensive analysis of the issue of ATS, including two expert group meetings in Vienna, Austria, in February 1996, and Shanghai, China PDR, in November 1996.

2. Hando, J. and Hall, W. (1997), Patterns of Amphetamine Use in Australia, in: *Amphetamine Misuse: International Perspectives on Current Trends* (H. Klee, ed.), Harwood Academic Publishers, The Netherlands.

3. Economic and Social Council (ECOSOC) (1998), *Youth and Drugs: A Global Overview*, United Nations (E/CN.7/1998/8).

4. Schuster. P., et al., Is the use of ecstasy and hallucinogens increasing?, *European Addiction Research*, 4, pp. 75-82, 1998.

5. International Narcotics Control Board (INCB), *Report 2000*, United Nations, New York, 2001, para321.

6. Shulgin, A. and Shulgin, A. (1991), PIHKAL, *A Chemical Love Story*, Transform Press, Berkeley; Shulgin, A. and Shulgin, A., (1997), TIHKAL, *The Continuation*, Transform Press, Berkeley.

7. ICPO Interpol, 1999 *Trends and Patterns of Illicit Drug Traffic*, prepared for 43rd Session of the Commission on Narcotic Drugs, Vienna, 6-15 March 2000.

8. ICPO Interpol, *Drug Alert*, 9/2000.

9. UNDCP, 1996, *op.cit.*.

10. INCB, 2001, *op.cit.*, para294.

11. *Political declaration and action plan on international cooperation on the eradication of illicit crops and on alternative development,* adopted at the Special Session of the General Assembly Devoted to Countering the World Drug Problem Together, 8-10 June 1998 (Resolution S-20/1).

12. Thomasius, R. (2000), *Ecstasy: eine Studie zu gesundheitlichen und psychosozialen Folgen des Missbrauchs*, Wissenschaftliche Verlagsgesellschaft mbH Stuttgart, 2000.

13. Economic and Social Council (ECOSOC) resolution 1995/20; Comprehensive reviews of the ATS phenomenon in recent years include (i) the study by UNDCP on 'Amphetamine-type Stimulants: A Global Review' (UNDCP/TS.3, 1996); (ii) a WHO Meeting and report on 'Amphetamines, MDMA and other Psychostimulants', November 1996; and (iii) a book edited by H.Klee on 'Amphetamine Misuse: International Perspectives on Current Trends', Harwood Academic Publishers, 1997.

14. 'Joint Action on New Synthetic Drugs' of the European Union (16 June 1997).

15. "Anti-Drug Conference, Tokyo, 2000", Japan, January 2000; 33rd ASEAN Ministerial Meeting, Bangkok, Thailand, July 2000; G8 Kyushu-Okinawa Summit Meeting, Japan, July 2000; International Congress "In pursuit of a drug-free ASEAN 2015, Sharing the vision, leading the change", Bangkok, Thailand, October 2000.

16. G8 Ad-hoc Meeting of Drug Experts, Miyazaki, Japan, December 2000.

MAIN CENTERS OF ILLICIT
OPIUM PRODUCTION

Addressing the subject of global opiate markets for the first time[*], the Analysis section of *Global Illicit Drug Trends* concentrates this year on the first link of the opiate supply-demand chain. The data clearly show Afghanistan and Myanmar as the previous decade's main sources of illicit opium. How did the territories of those two countries become the source of 90% of global illicit opium? What are some of the main characteristics of the problem at present? Which factors could influence its future evolution? Those questions are of direct relevance to understanding global trends in the illicit opiate market today.

Examining the roots and the dynamics of a problem whose dimensions have always extended well beyond the boundaries of Afghanistan and Myanmar, the following two profiles propose some elements of an answer.

---

*The Analysis section of the 2000 edition of the report focused on the European cocaine market and the world amphetamine-type stimulant market. The first part of the Analysis section in this year's edition covers clandestine synthetic drugs.

AFGHANISTAN

HOW DID AFGHANISTAN BECOME A MAJOR SUPPLIER OF ILLICIT OPIUM?

During the 1990's Afghanistan became the world's largest producer of illicit opium. In 1999, it produced 79% of global illicit opium. In 2000, this proportion reduced, but it was still 70%. In order to understand how a single country came to play such a dominant role in the illicit opiate market, it is necessary to review the recent historical background.

Opium poppy has been cultivated in Afghanistan throughout the last century, but never to the extent that it has been since the 1980s. The country's dominant role in global opium production is really a story of the last two decades, but the story has developed against a background of the convergence of a complex set of economic, political and geo-strategic factors which have been in place for a long time, and eventually led, at least in part, to an average annual growth rate of 23% in the cultivation of opium poppy from 1986 to 2000. Three different factors are basic to explaining the entrenchment and expansion of opium poppy cultivation in Afghanistan: the lack of effective government control over the whole country; the degradation of agriculture and most economic infrastructure due to more than twenty years of civil war; and the acceptance of opium poppy cultivation as a livelihood strategy by many rural households in the country. The first of the three factors can only be explained historically; the latter two acquire meaning within this context, as well as in the context of Afghanistan's more contemporary history.

It is no coincidence that Afghanistan began to emerge as a significant producer of illicit opium in precisely the period of protracted war, which began in 1979 and still persists. Peace has not yet been made in Afghanistan and faction-fighting, warlordism and particularistic nationalisms remain endemic. Though the recent historical record is patchy, it is clear that the country was not among the world's main opium producers until the late 1970s. Opium has been cultivated and consumed in the region for centuries and there is some evidence that opium poppy has been a traditional crop in parts of Afghanistan since the 18th century. With the emergence of the international drug control system in the early 20th century, a clearer historical picture begins to emerge because the government of the country participated in the meetings of the Permanent Central Opium Board[a] under the auspices of the League of Nations in the 1920s and 1930s. Afghanistan did report some opium production, but the amounts were small compared to other reporting countries.

At the Second Opium Conference of 1924 under the auspices of the League of Nations, Afghanistan reported cultivation in the provinces of Herat, Badakshan and Jalalabad. It was reported that "opium ceased to be a government monopoly and any person may deal in it"[1]. At this time a 5% export duty was levied upon opium under the Afghan Customs authority. In 1932, the first year for which estimates of production are reported, Afghanistan produced 75 tons of opium. China, in comparison, produced about 6,000 tons in the same year[2]. The area under cultivation in 1932 was reported to be less than 4,000 hectares. (In comparison, 82,000 ha were under cultivation in 2000). Reports on opium exports from Afghanistan in the late 1930s, though fragmentary, establish that opium production was limited, in the order of magnitude of less than 100 tons per annum.[3] Afghanistan prohibited opium production in 1945, although continued smuggling through India was reported after the ban[4]. In 1956, Afghanistan reported production of only 12 tons of opium[5].

In November 1957, another law prohibiting the production of opium was promulgated. The United Nations Commission on Narcotic Drugs considered this, and in the debate it was noted that the solution of the serious economic problems attendant on the prohibition of opium production was of cardinal importance, because the failure to address this had been a material factor in Afghanistan's abrogation of a policy of prohibition on a previous occasion[6]. This was a clear indication that the government was growing concerned about the production of opium within its borders. The concern probably led to the country removing itself from what could otherwise have been a viable export market. In the previous year, 1956, Afghanistan had requested official recogni-

---

a) The predecessor of the International Narcotics Control Board (INCB).

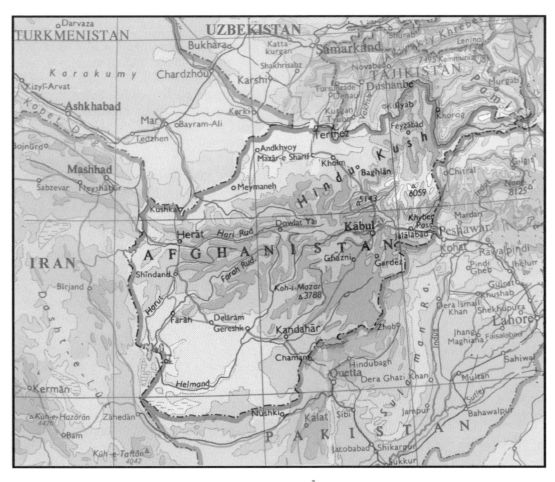

Note: Boundaries and names shown and designations used on this map do not imply official endorsement or acceptance by the United Nations.

tion as a state producing opium for export at the Commission on Narcotic Drugs[7]. This was superseded by the ban of 1957. Subsequent reports indicate that the government was not able to enforce the ban fully and sought international assistance to address the problem. During the 1961 Plenipotentiary Conference for the adoption of a Single Convention on Narcotic Drugs the country was listed among those "in which narcotics constitute a serious problem"[8]. It should be noted, in this context, that a clear distinction between licit and illicit opium production was only established after the adoption of the 1961 Convention[b].

During the 1960s and 1970s, Afghanistan's state-directed economic development was dependent on foreign aid. In the 1960's, for instance, foreign aid accounted for 40% of the budget[9]. Controlling opium production also became dependent upon securing international assistance. Though production was at relatively low lev-

els, the government's efforts to impose the ban were constrained by the availability of resources. The report of the International Narcotics Control Board in 1970 noted that while opium production was forbidden by the Afghan government, the outflow of opium into adjoining regions indicated that the ban was not being enforced[10]. In 1971, the view was expressed at the Commission on Narcotic Drugs that "the attitude of the government of Afghanistan was perhaps too passive,"[11] in response to Afghanistan's recognition that illicit opium production was increasingly taking place and its stated inability to achieve a significant suppression of production. As early as 1972 the Board listed Afghanistan among those countries which presented the strongest immediate challenge in terms of control of illicit production and traffic. Turkey abolished opium production in 1972, and it was already clear that Afghanistan could become an alternative source of supply[12]. The same year the Board sent representatives to

---

b) Though the 1953 Protocol began this process of regulating the cultivation of opium poppy, it was only with the 1961 Convention that the cultivation and production of opium were brought under comprehensive control; see I. Bayer and H. Godse, "Evolution of international drug control, 1945 - 95," *Bulletin on Narcotics*, Vol LI, 1 and 2, 1999, pp. 1-17.

Kabul to review the situation and concluded that the capacity of the country to effectively implement drug control policies was low. The most acute problem was found to be in Badakhshan. Representatives of the United Nations Food and Agriculture Organisation were also in the delegation with a view to initiating projects for crop substitution and community development[13].

After the war began in 1979, the government lost control of the countryside. The rural economy deteriorated as a result of the fighting (food production fell by half to two thirds) and this meant that growing urban populations were depending more on government assistance[14]. Both sides of the war relied on imports of arms and cash, which resulted in a rapid monetization of the economy[15]. By the 1980's there were indications that the *mujahideen* were using the production and sale of opium to finance some weapons needs. An increasingly structured and formalized economic system grew from this nascent "drugs for arms trade." Opium was one of the only commodities which could generate enough income for large scale arms purchases. Shrinking sources of illicit opium for international markets - Iran effectively prohibited poppy cultivation after the 1979 revolution[16] - again made Afghanistan an alternative source of supply.

OPIUM PRODUCTION FROM 1979 TO 1989

From 1979 opium production began to increase in Afghanistan. This is shown in Figure 1 which also shows Afghanistan's share in world production from 1980 to 2000. The marked increase from 1987 onwards probably indicates a shift in agricultural livelihood strategies as the collateral damage from years of intense fighting destroyed other income generating activities.

The growth in cultivation (see figures in the following section) though data is only available from 1986, shows the same picture. Of Afghanistan's total land area of 65 million ha, only an estimated 8m. ha are considered to be arable, and it is thought that less than one half of that is cultivated every year, some 2.6 million hectares[17]. From 1958 until 1978, 85% of the then total population of 15 million lived in the countryside, and most of the rest were involved in one way or another with rural enterprise[18]. Almost 90 percent of all food and agricultural crops were harvested on irrigated land[19]. In 1978, just prior to the outbreak of the war, three quarters of Afghanistan's farmers had access to and could afford fertilizers[20].

Between 1979 and 1989, and especially in the latter half of this period, regular agricultural production was severely disrupted. About one third of all farms were abandoned. Between one half to two-thirds of all villages were bombed; between one quarter and one third of the country's irrigation systems were destroyed [21]; and, the amount of livestock fell by 70 percent[22]. By

1988 total food production had declined to around 45% of the level prevailing before 1979, the number of livestock had fallen precipitously and the country was importing 500,000 metric tons of wheat annually from the Soviet Union[23]. The reduction in fertilizer availability and affordability would have lowered crop yield further; in some areas, fertilizer use declined by 90 percent[24].

All of this went hand in hand with a severe depopulation in the rural parts of the country. Between 1978 and 1989, some 9 percent of the Afghan population were killed; another third fled the country; 11 percent became internal refugees, many heading to the urban centers[25].

As noted above, the 1970s witnessed basic changes in the illicit opium market. Between 1972 and the early 1980s three main sources of opium production, Iran, Pakistan and Turkey, were enforcing bans or severe drug control laws, creating an opening for other sources of opium in South-West Asia[26]. In the 1980s, the trend became clear: just as internal factors were leading to an upswing in Afghan opium production, external factors were opening major markets, ensuring the economic viability of this production. Afghanistan's major role in the global production of opium thus became established during this period (see Figure 1).

THE "OPIUM ECONOMY"

By 1989, the production of opium, which had reached 1,200 tons, and was 35% of global production, had firmly established itself in the country as a major source of income generation. (see Figure 1) Over ten years, opium production had effectively been included in the livelihood strategies of individual farmers, itinerant labourers and rural communities for a variety of reasons. These changes were barely noticed, since the civil war continued to attract all the attention. The withdrawal of Soviet troops, the dissolution of the Soviet Union and the end of the Cold War changed Afghanistan's geo-strategic situation at the beginning of the 1990s. Yet peace remained elusive, the civil war continued, and the opium economy became firmly entrenched in the country through the 1990s.

The average annual growth rate for the production of opium in Afghanistan was 14% between 1979 and 1989. It accelerated to 19% between 1989 and 1994. Opium production accelerated after the Soviet withdrawal for two reasons: first, it provided a viable source of income for waring factions; and secondly, it had proven itself to be a viable crop for cultivation and rural livelihood and unlike the destroyed licit agricultural sector, had developed systems and infrastructure which actually functioned. After the Soviet withdrawal and through the mid 1990s, when the Taleban took control of most of the country, sources of external support and patronage of the various fighting factions lessened[27]. This forced

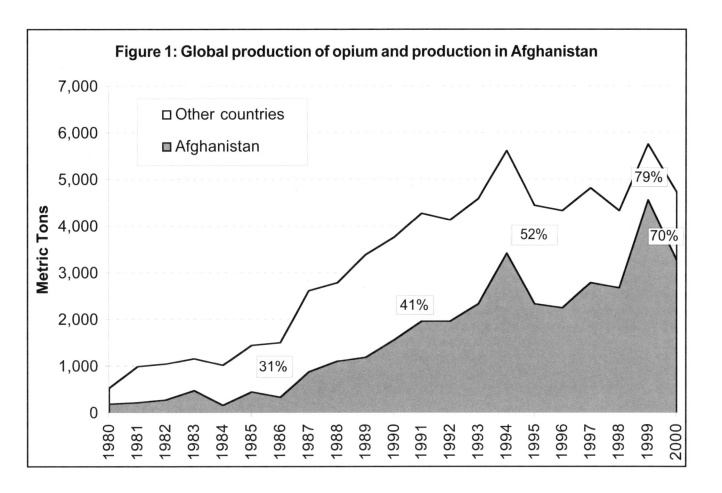

Figure 1: Global production of opium and production in Afghanistan

factions, which were still fighting to gain new spheres of influence, to devise new sources of financing. As war raged in Afghanistan, opium became an important method of generating income and thereby, almost intrinsically, developed further the systems of investment and growth which had begun in the 1980s. By 1989 the production of opium had reached a critical mass. The "opium economy" was firmly in existence, providing funding for various activities when patronage dried up. Also, by the beginning of the 1990s the increasing monetization of the economy necessitated by the war had created incentives for cash based activities. Among these, the cultivation of opium emerged as one of the most lucrative for a large sector of the population[28].

The ability of the government to continue allocating resources remained constrained for obvious reasons after 1989. Few resources were allocated to the agricultural sector; when they were, the allocation was inefficient. Though, as late as 1992, the government was still providing wheat subsidies to selected provinces, they were often badly coordinated. The lack of coordination often resulted, for example, in a disruption of the wheat supply from one province to another, giving an unintended incentive for the cultivation of opium poppy[29].

By the late 1980s, the breakdown of any form of governance in Afghanistan resulted in a weakening of social and legal constraints on the cultivation of opium poppy.

While at various points in its history the cultivation of opium poppy was actually forbidden, or *haram*, under Islam, this did not prevent people from cultivating it. Although economic considerations were often given priority over religious customs, the acceptance of the agricultural tax, now known as *ushur*, by mullahs and the local authorities, was often interpreted by farmers and itinerant workers as implicit support for the cultivation of opium poppy[30].

By 1989 those involved in the cultivation, harvesting and production of opium, including both peasants and landless labourers, had been involved in it for at least a decade. They had developed and expanded know-how and technical expertise and were using established markets, infrastructure and trading systems. Though a large amount of roads and transport infrastructure had been destroyed by the fighting, the various factions had a direct interest in maintaining those necessary for the opium trade - giving opium a market of increasingly viability while markets for other crops continued to be underdeveloped.

The harvest of opium poppy, although labour intensive, had proven to be a "sustainable alternative" in the prevailing circumstances. Opium itself is durable and commanded a higher price on average. Also, because fresh opium can be retained and stocked by farmers and sold later as dry opium, the product itself gave farmers cru-

Box 1: Opium as a livelihood strategy [36]
In and of themselves, the effects of war on the agricultural sector would argue against the selection of opium poppy as a cash crop in Afghanistan. The decrease in available farm labour would in particular make cultivating opium poppy an unattractive option. The fragility of the opium poppy, and the shortage of fertilizers during the war would militate against its large-scale cultivation in Afghanistan. Nevertheless, surveys have found that opium poppy in Afghanistan is grown on the best land, and on the best *irrigated* land, with much of the available fertilizer devoted to its cultivation.[37] This apparent paradox can be explained by the strong financial incentives for poppy cultivation. Another factor that helps explains the high profitability of opium is its physical durability. This makes it a precious commodity in situations of severely damaged transport infrastructure. It is estimated that nearly 60 per cent of Afghanistan's road network was destroyed during the conflict[38]. What distinguishes opium from perishable produce is the fact that, even when roads are destroyed to the extent that they were during the series of armed conflicts in Afghanistan, the investment made in poppy cannot be jeopardized by longer travel times to the market. Furthermore, opium's high cash value/volume ratio can in part offset its high labour requirements; the labour invested in it can, at least in part, be made up by less travel time per unit of profit. In terms of household level decision-making, opium provided a low-risk strategy in a high-risk environment.

Opium as source of credit
With no formal system of credit in place in Afghanistan, one of the reasons for the entrenchment of the opium economy is because of its value to people as a source of credit. Similar to formal systems of credit elsewhere, opium is used by the landless (about one third of the population) in Afghanistan to obtain basic human needs, such as food, clothes and medicine. Amongst the wealthier and land owning groups it is used to facilitate productive investment in agricultural production, not only of opium poppy but of other crops as well.

A typology of the different types of informal credit systems operating in opium growing regions would include: the advance sale of a fixed amount of agricultural production, the delayed payment for commodities from shopkeepers or traders, and interest free loans from immediate or extended family members. A significant number of households in Afghanistan obtain advance payments, known as *salaam*, on future agricultural production (including opium, wheat and black cumin). The findings of one UNDCP study indicate that this a widespread and accepted system[39] of informal credit. While *Salaam* provides advanced payments on wheat and black cumin, in the poppy growing districts, the majority of farmers receive advance payment on the opium crop. Much of this has to due with the nature of the crop itself. Opium poppy is a very dependable crop. In times of drought for example, it is considered to be more dependable than wheat or black cumin. Because of this and because of the complex system of credit which arose, opium is considered by many to be the optimal crop for recourse to credit. Opium is also one of the commodities which can be purchased and resold as a means of obtaining loans under the so-called *anawat* system: commodities are purchased on credit, at an agreed price which is considerably higher than the cash price.

Because opium is relatively non-perishable and maintains a relatively stable value (in terms of local currency), it is also used as a means of household saving. It is known that because of small price differentials between regions, opium can be used for short-term financial speculation by those with disposable income. Lenders can include family members, landlords and commercial traders -- this enables almost any individual involved in the trade to access the market for credit, allowing households to spread their liabilities across a range of lenders, rationally hedging all investments similar to any other system of credit.

The expansion of production in the context of the lack of other income generating activities
The expansion of opium poppy cultivation over the last two decades is related to the absence of non-farm income opportunities in the country. A large portion of the economy of Afghanistan has always been agriculturally based, with a large portion of agricultural production taking place at the subsistence level. However, even the agricultural sector is structurally weak largely due to the absence or destruction of appropriate infrastructure and the lack of any significant development. In the main, agricultural production in Afghanistan is characterised by poor marketing, small landholdings, no formal recourse to credit and an extreme shortage of irrigation.

One UNDCP study found that when the cultivation of opium poppy is first introduced to an area it tends to be grown on relatively small plots of land by a small number of households in a limited number of villages. However, the process of expansion in the second or third years can be significant, with increasing numbers of households emulating their neighbours by cultivating opium across an increasing number of villages within the district. The study further discovered that the labour intensive nature of the crop was thought by farmers to be the major cost associated with its cultivation. For this reason, many households were found to cultivate opium poppy at a level that was commensurate with the supply of household labour or reciprocal labour arrangements, particularly in its initial year of cultivation[40].

The role of opium in the labour market especially for itinerant harvesters
Opium poppy is a labour intensive crop and the majority of households require hired labour during the opium poppy harvest. Estimates suggest that approximately 350 person days are required to cultivate one hectare of opium poppy, compared to approximately 41 person days per hectare for wheat and 135 person days per hectare for black cumin. Harvesting alone is reported to require as much as 200 person days per hectare[41]. Therefore, the majority of opium producing households require hired labour during the opium planting harvest. In many cases this hired labour migrates from other districts in search of opportunities to cultivate opium poppy. A UNDCP study found that in Helmand province, the largest producer of opium in Afghanistan, only 20% of the hired labour originates in the province.[42] To spread the demand for both hired and family labour during the harvest period, households cultivate different varieties of opium poppy with differing maturation periods. Differences in climate across Afghanistan mean that the opium poppy harvest is staggered throughout the season. Opium poppy provides an important source of income for some of the population in poppy growing areas. A large number of itinerant harvesters in Afghanistan are also subsistence farmers who own land themselves. In some cases they travel to harvest opium and return home to harvest rain-fed wheat from their own land.

cial collateral to use for access to credit and invest- ment. The stocks of dry opium play an important role in the overall price structure for the crop, enabling farmers to hedge against both oversupply and under-production. The different ways in which the production of opium had become incorporated into the livelihood strategies of agricultural communities is discussed in greater depth in Box 1.

Through the early 1990s the civil war continued and all economic activity was increasingly subordinated to sup- porting the power struggles between the various fac- tions. A large industry had arisen to provide the infra- structure - transport, communications, arms, and pro- tection - which the warring factions needed to retain their zones of influence. This was one component of a new war economy which grew up in Afghanistan; the other two components were a transit trade linking the region and the opium trade[c]. Food prices rose by fac- tors of five or ten and the government financed its grow- ing budget deficits by printing money[31]. The govern- ment was increasingly isolated, the areas under its con- trol contracted and by 1994 the faction known as the Taleban[d] emerged as a major contender in the struggle. The Taleban took the city of Qandahar, concentrated in the southern provinces and had seized Kabul by 1996. Today they control most of Afghanistan with only areas in the north (the location of the opposition groups, loose- ly termed the Northern Alliance) outside their control.

OPIUM PRODUCTION, 1994 TO 2000/2001

By 1994, the area under opium poppy cultivation had expanded to 71,500 hectares, and production reached 3,400 tons. In 1995, the overall production of opium decreased by one third primarily because the bumper harvest of the previous year, coupled with dropping opium prices (which decreased by 30% in dollar terms), acted as a disincentive to cultivate. Increased law enforcement efforts by Iran apparently restricted Afghan opium exports and therefore contributed to the decline of opium production[32]. According to the UNDCP Annual Opium Poppy Survey of 1995 farmers reported that they would wait for prices to rise before selling the large stocks accumulated from the 1994 harvest. Another interesting finding from the 1995 Survey was that it was

in the irrigated districts where the reductions in the acreage of opium cultivation was most marked. These were also the areas where wheat yields were found to be high[33]. Production remained at roughly the 1995 levels until 1998.

In 1999, however, the production of opium increased dramatically to 4,600 tons, almost twice the average production of the previous four years. The area under cultivation increased by nearly a third, to 91,000 hectares. Amongst the factors fuelling the strong increase in cultivation were very high prices for opium, due to a poor 1998 harvest, and ideal weather condi- tions. Because the 1998 harvest was poor, farmers had experienced shortfalls in savings and credit payments, necessitating an increase in cultivation the following year. Most of the increase took place in Helmand, fol- lowed by Nangarhar, and a number of other provinces which had never before cultivated opium poppy. The value of the crop at farmgate prices at harvest time was estimated at US$251mn in 1999[34].

The international isolation of the Taleban regime over its violations of human rights, support of terrorism and increasing opium production led to the Security Council imposing sanctions on Afghanistan in October 1999[35]. A month earlier, in September, the Taleban issued a decree ordering all poppy farmers to reduce their culti- vation area by one third. The UNDCP survey indicated that the actual reduction achieved by the decree was about 10%. Total cultivation, however, fell in 2000 by 28% due to the added effects of a severe drought. According to UNDCP's Annual Opium Poppy Survey, 3,300 tons of opium were produced in Afghanistan in 2000, down from more than 4,600 tons in 1999. The drought, which has affected Afghanistan since early 2000, had a significant impact on the yield of opium poppy crops. The national average yield for poppy in the 2000 season was found to be 35.7kg/ha, down from 50.4 Kg/ha in 1999. The yield on rainfed poppy was only 18.5kg/ha.

There were 82,200 hectares of opium poppy under cul- tivation in the country in the 2000 season, representing a reduction in total poppy area under cultivation of just under 10% on the 1999 estimate of 91,000 hectares

---

c) The trade originates in the Afghan Transit Trade Agreement (ATTA) under which goods can be imported duty-free in sealed containers into Pakistan, for onward transmission to land-locked Afghanistan. This trade gradually developed in a reverse direction from the 1980s, with goods originating in the Persian Gulf and tran- siting Afghanistan. It is thus known as the transit trade. The infrastructure of the trade began to be used for drugs and arms, and came firmly under Taleban con- trol after 1996, when they consolidated their hold over practically all the country's roads, cities, airports and customs posts (see a detailed analysis of the transit trade in Rubin, op. cit. pp. 1793-95).

d) The Taleban movement grew out of the Afghan diaspora of the 1980s. The emigration or destruction of the elites, the collapse of the state and even the little public education it provided, created a vacuum. No education was available to young Pushtun refugees, who concentrated in the border provinces of Pakistan and Afghanistan. A network of madrasas (Islamic academies) dominated by ulema (Muslim priests) grew up to supply the education. Drawn from the conservative Deobandi tradition (a movement which began in 19th century India to combat modern and secular traditions in Islam; see Francis Robinson, Separatism among Indian Muslims, Cambridge University Press, 1975), these madrasas and ulema were supported by foreign aid from countries which sought to bolster anti-Soviet movements in the country. The social capital created in the madrasas banded together to create the Taleban movement, whose objective was to resist warlordism and corruption (see Rubin, op. cit., pp. 1794,1797, and W. Maley, Fundamentalism Reborn? Afghanistan and the Taleban, New York, St. Martins Press, 1998).

Afghanistan: Opium Poppy Cultivation, 1994

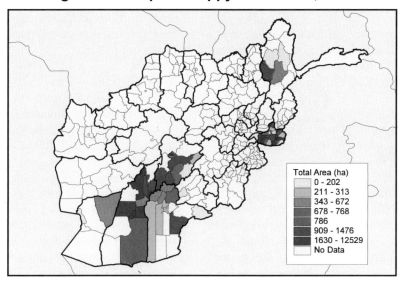

Afghanistan: Opium Poppy Cultivation, 1999

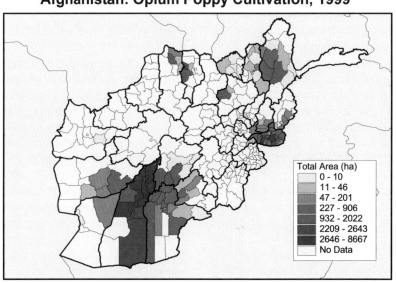

Afghanistan: Opium Poppy Cultivation, 2000

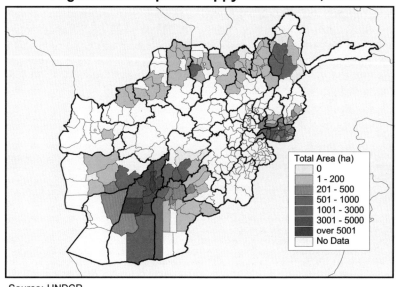

Source: UNDCP

Table 1: Opium Poppy Cultivation in Afghanistan, 1994-2000
(hectares)*

Province	1994	1995	1996	1997	1998	1999	2000	% of total cultivation	change 1999-2000
Helmand	29,579	29,753	24,909	29,400	30,673	44,552	42,853	51.90%	-1,699
Nangarhar	29,081	15,722	15,643	14,567	17,822	22,990	19,747	23.90%	-3,243
Oruzgan	6,211	2,573	7,777	4,587	4,288	4,479	4,331	5.20%	-148
Qandahar	4,034	2,461	3,160	4,521	5,602	6,032	3,427	4.20%	-2,605
Balkh			1,065	710	1,044	4,057	2,669	3.20%	-1,388
Badakhshan	1,714	2,970	3,230	2,902	2,817	2,684	2,458	3.00%	-226
Farah		9	630	568	171	787	1,509	1.80%	722
Kunar	115	152	19	-	75	288	786	1.00%	498
Jawzjan						2,593	746	0.90%	-1,847
Zabul	54		255	154	161	611	725	0.90%	114
Laghman	-	-		-	77	297	707	0.90%	410
Takhar						201	647	0.80%	446
Kunduz						38	489	0.60%	451
Herat							382	0.50%	382
Kabul						732	340	0.40%	-392
Nimroz	682	119	136	642	11	203	219	0.30%	16
Baghlan				328	929	1,005	199	0.20%	-806
Kapisa						5	104	0.10%	99
Samangan							54	0.10%	54
Logar	-	-	-	-	4	29	46	0.10%	17
Badghis							41	0.00%	41
Faryab							36	0.00%	36
Total	71470	53,759	56,824	58,379	63,674	91,583	82,515	100.00%	-9068

*blank = province not surveyed

Changes in opium poppy cultivation in Afghanistan 1999-2000

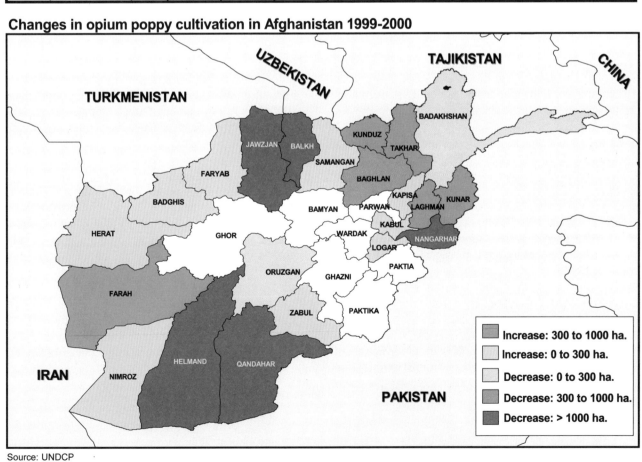

Source: UNDCP

37

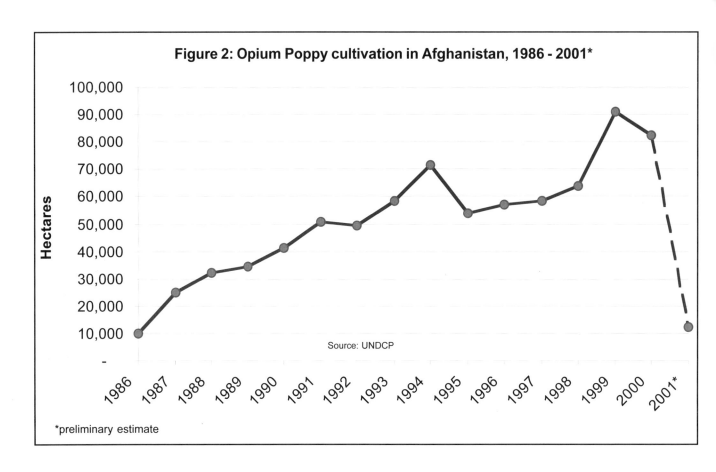

Figure 2: Opium Poppy cultivation in Afghanistan, 1986 - 2001*

Source: UNDCP

*preliminary estimate

(see Figure 2). Ninety two per cent of the opium cultivated in Afghanistan occurs in six provinces[e]. In 2000,
the top two provinces in terms of area under poppy were
Helmand and Nangahar. Helmand accounted for 52%
(42,900 ha) and Nangarhar for 24% (19,800 ha) of total
area under cultivation, and for 57% and 22% of national opium production respectively[43].

Significant reductions in the area under opium poppy
cultivation in 2000 occurred in Baghlan (80%), Balkh
(34%), Jawzjan (71%) and Quandahar (43%). With the
exception of Quandahar, all of these provinces had
reported opium under cultivation for a period of less than
four years. Three UNDCP target districts (as part of the
UNDCP Pilot Programme in Afghanistan) in Qandahar
province and one in Nangarhar province, recorded substantial declines for 2000. Balkh was poppy free until
1996, Baghlan until 1997 and Jawzjan until 1999. The
main provinces of cultivation, Helmand and Nangarhar,
also experienced reductions in total area under poppy
cultivation of 4% and 14% respectively[44]. Farmgate
prices for fresh opium fell in 2000 to an average of
US$30/kg[45]. The value of the entire crop of fresh opium
estimated at US$91 million, roughly one-third the value
of one year earlier.

On 27 July 2000, the Taleban supreme leader issued a
decree imposing a total ban on opium poppy cultivation
on the Islamic Emirate of Afghanistan. Early reports
from 2001 indicate that the Taleban ban is being
enforced vigilantly[46]. A preliminary assessment study in
February 2001, which serves as an interim report to
UNDCP's Annual Opium Poppy Survey, revealed that a
very large reduction of the area under cultivation had
occurred in Helmand and Nangahar, as well as in the
main poppy-growing districts in the provinces of
Oruzgan, Qandahar, Farah, Laghman, and Kunar.
These areas, covered by the preliminary assessment,
accounted for 86% of all opium poppy found in
Afghanistan 2000. If the reductions are as substantial as
they appear to be in the preliminary assessment, the
area under cultivation could go down by more than two-
thirds. It is unlikely, also, that this situation could be offset by changes in production in the so far un-assessed
provinces. They accounted for only 12,200 hectares
last year, including 3,105 hectares of cultivation in areas
under control of the Northern Alliance.

---

e) The Survey is carried out at the district level. The UNDCP Annual Opium Poppy Survey 2000 surveyed 125 out of the country's 344 districts. Out of the 125 districts surveyed, 123 were found to be cultivating poppy. However, the pattern of district divisions means that only ten of these districts account for 54% of the total
   national area, and 23 districts account for 73% of total national area. One district in Helmand province alone accounts for over 10% of national poppy area.

TRAFFICKING

Large scale seizures of opium have taken place in Afghanistan's neighbouring countries, notably Iran, since the early 1980s. Figure 3 shows how closely seizures of opiates in the ECO[f] countries correlate with the opium production levels in Afghanistan.

Afghanistan is the main source of opium, morphine and heroin in Iran, Pakistan, India and Central Asia, and of heroin in Europe. It is also the main source of heroin in some countries along the Arabian peninsula and eastern Africa[47]. There are two main routes for the opium trafficked from Afghanistan to European destinations. The first route, the so called "Balkan Route", follows a path which crosses Iran, Turkey, the Balkan states before heading into Europe. Sometimes there is a deviation of this route with drugs crossing the Mediterranean Sea into Italy. The second route grew in importance in the 1990s. Sometimes referred to as the "silk route" it crosses the northern border of Afghanistan

into the Central Asian Republics, then follows European and Asian trade routes - some dating back to the middle ages - into Russia and on through established trade routes to Europe.

The main destination of opiates trafficked from Afghanistan is Europe, including Turkey. Most of the morphine/heroin crossing Turkey is shipped along the Balkan route to final destinations in the European Union (EU) and the European Free Trade Association (EFTA). Markets for Afghanistan's opiate production have grown in eastern Europe – as an ever increasing portion of total heroin shipments are consumed in countries along the main trafficking routes[48]. In response to this, UNDCP and the international community are building a "security belt" around the country with the intention of limiting opiate trafficking.

Seizure statistics also indicate that Afghanistan has become increasingly involved in the actual manufacture of heroin over the last few years. Previously, the actual production of heroin and morphine in laboratories in

Table 2: Seizures of heroin as a percentage of all opiate seizures in Iran and Central Asia, 1995 and 1999

	1995	1999	Rate of annual growth
Iran			
heroin	2,075.0	6,030.0	31%
opiates	25,776.4	49,242.5	18%
heroin as a % of opiates	8%	12%	
Central Asia			
heroin	10.3	1,354.8	239%
opiates	355.9	2,308.0	60%
heroin as a % of opiates	3%	59%	

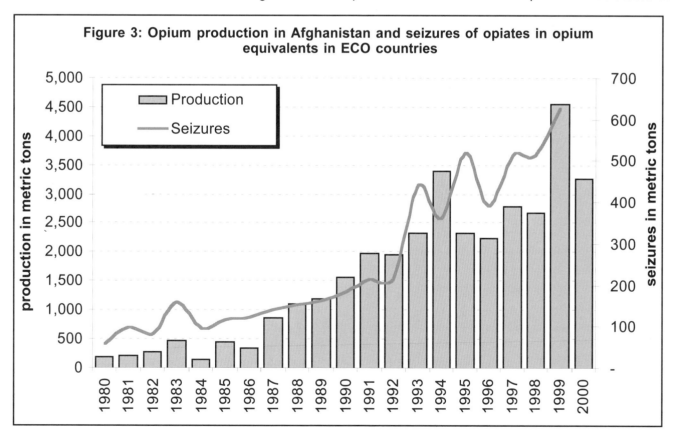

Figure 3: Opium production in Afghanistan and seizures of opiates in opium equivalents in ECO countries

f) ECO countries include: Afghanistan, Azerbaijan, Iran, Kazakhstan, Kyrgyzstan, Pakistan, Tajikistan, Turkey, Turkmenistan and Uzbekistan.

Afghanistan was quite rare. The country's opium used to be trafficked across its borders before being processed into heroin in laboratories outside the country, notably in Pakistan, in the border areas with Afghanistan, and in Turkey. This seems to be changing. Discoveries of laboratories in Afghanistan, as well as seizures in neighbouring countries of Central Asia and Iran also seem to confirm this trend. Table 2 shows how the proportion of heroin in opiate seizures has risen from 8% (1995) to 12%(1999) in Iran, and even more substantially, from 3% to 59% in the Central Asian Republics.

DRUG ABUSE

The abuse of drugs, which is a punishable criminal offence in Afghanistan, is a small but growing problem. While little is known of the actual extent of drug abuse, all available reports suggest that consumption is on the rise, although starting from low levels. In the past abuse was never a significant national problem. There is little historical evidence of traditional opium use among the Pashtuns. It did occur, however, among the Turkomans and Tajiks. Geographically, use of opium was mainly limited to areas in and around Badakshan. The prolonged war has, however, fundamentally altered some of the social norms which have thus far prevented large scale opium abuse. Opium was mainly eaten or smoked and heroin, when available, was usually smoked. There are now indications – such as the finding of significant numbers of hypodermic needles – that injecting drug use has been increasing recently, notably among refugees returning from camps in Pakistan. The increasing number of heroin laboratories in the country is also thought to have had an effect on the domestic abuse situation and could exacerbate it as higher quality heroin finds its way into a domestic market. White heroin of 85% purity has recently been identified in the country[49]. One of the main reasons given by the Taleban for their decree forbidding the planting of opium poppy was the fear of a rapid increase in abuse amongst the country's youth, notably in eastern Afghanistan[50].

OUTLOOK

Afghanistan is likely to remain one of the world's poorest and least developed countries for the foreseeable future. Twenty one years of protracted instability, war and political unrest have led to malnutrition, extreme poverty, illiteracy, and the world's fourth highest rate of child mortality[51]. Afghanistan's continuing war and resultant human development crisis have made it an insecure and threatening place for its roughly 23 million inhabitants[52] - half of whom are under 18 years of age[53]. Human development, according to the United Nations Development Programme's 1996 *Human Development Report*g, was almost the lowest in the

world, ranking number 169 out of the 175 countries covered in the report's Human Development Index.

There are indications that the country's development situation will deteriorate in the future. Approximately 12 million people have been affected by the severe drought (with three to four million severely affected) which began in Afghanistan at the beginning of 2000. The World Food Programme/Food and Agriculture Organisation's June 2000 Crop Assessment survey found that for the 2000/2001 harvest period there is an estimated shortfall in production of 2.3 million metric tons (or 57% of the national cereal requirement and double the 1999 deficit)[54]. The FAO estimates that 300,000 tons of wheat seed is planted annually in Afghanistan. In 2000 there was an estimated minimum deficit of 60,000 tons of seed as a result of either widespread production failure, forced consumption for food or poorly formed grains that will not germinate. In the autumn of 2000 it was thought that with no possibility of mobilizing more than 6000 tons of additional seed, upwards of 400,000 farmers missed the winter 2000 planting season due to lack of seed,[55] and it is now clear that many farmers and subsistence growers will not have enough seeds for the 2001 harvest. Daily wages for farm labourers have declined from seven kilograms of wheat per day to one kilograms per day[56]. Livestock herd sizes are down by as much as 50 to 75%. Households are thus expected to begin the 2001/2002 planting cycle with virtually no productive assets[57]. The worst drought in 30 years, the ongoing conflict and the deprivation and disease they cause will lead to continuing large scale population movements. More than 200,000 people were reported to have moved in the autumn of 2000. Many people will continue to flee to border areas or across borders, while the remainder could join the growing streams of people moving to already over-burdened urban areas[58]. The population remaining in the countryside is equally vulnerable to hunger and food shortages.

The very large potential decline in opium production revealed by the 2001 preliminary pre-assessment will have an effect on the amount of opium, heroin and morphine available on the international market, but it is too early to gauge its specific impact. Accumulated stocks from last year's harvest are bound to have a short-term effect on the market, but the extent of these stocks is unknown. There is some indication that prices are responding predictably to the contracting supply of fresh opium. According to the most recent price data available to UNDCP there was a dramatic increase in the price of opium between June 2000, when a kilogram sold for between US$35 and US$50, and February 2001, when a kilogram sold for between US$200 in Nangarhar and US$350 in Helmand. In the medium-term this could raise incentives for farmers to plant opium.

g) The last year for which statistical data was available.

In terms of the future, some indication can be drawn from looking backwards and reviewing the last two decades of opium production. Three observations, noted at the outset, are salient: poppy cultivation has grown in circumstances of endemic conflict and lack of effective government; the devastation of agriculture and economic infrastructure made opium production a viable alternative; and poppy cultivation gained widespread acceptance as a livelihood strategy among many rural households. Yet the outlook is contingent upon a good deal more than the "opium economy" in the country. Afghanistan's regional importance is still considerable. It was noted above that as opium production grew over the last twenty years, Afghanistan also became an open war economy, the lynchpin in a vast regional trade of arms, gemstones and many different kind of contraband. A World Bank study estimated this contraband trade to be worth $ 2.5 billion in 1997, equivalent to nearly half of Afghanistan's estimated GDP. The same study estimates that the Taleban derived at least US$ 75 million from taxes on this trade[59]. The value of the entire opium crop in 2000, at farm gate prices, was estimated to be $ 91 million[h]; Taleban taxes on it, even on the assumption that the traditional10% (*ushr*) and 20% (*zakat*) taxes were imposed, would have amounted to no more than $ 27 million,[60] which is a lot less than the taxes on the transit trade.

It follows, therefore, that Taleban losses from the stronger Security Council sanctions imposed as of January 2001[61], which also effect trade, would be greater than from tax losses resulting from the ban on opium cultivation. Sustaining the ban and the potential drop in opium production thus implies dealing simultaneously with the drug problem and the larger geo-strategic problem of Afghanistan. Supporting agricultural livelihoods, preventing displacement of opium cultivation and building a security belt around Afghanistan will need to be balanced with strategies to close down the war economy, which is both a cause and an effect of the endemic conflict in the country.

---

h) This is only a tiny portion of the final street price of the drugs. That price reflects the risk-premium that is added after the drugs leave the country of production, and enter the international trafficking chain (see UNDCP, *World Drug Report 1997*, Oxford University Press, pp. 122-142).

ENDNOTES

1. League of Nations, Report of the Second Opium Conference, Sub committee "B", 1924.

2. League of Nations, Permanent Central Opium Board, Pre-War Production and Distribution of Narcotics Drugs and their Raw Materials, Geneva, 1944.;O.C./Confidential/18 (3).; Statistiques relatives Opium brut (1926-37).;C.124.M.113.1940.XI. (O.C.1781.(1)), Annual Reports of Governments on the Traffic in Opium and other dangerous Drugs for the Year 1938.;CCP Rapports aux conseils pour 1947.

3. "Opium Production Throughout the World", *Bulletin on Narcotics*, No. 1, October 1949, United Nations, p.12.

4. *ibid*, p.12.

5. As in endnote 2 above.

6. E/3133, E/CN.7/354, Commission on Narcotic Drugs, Report of the Thirteenth Session, paras 290 to 314; also see summary of report in *Bulletin on Narcotics*, Vol. X. No. 4, October - December 1958, pp. 43-45.

7. Summary of report in *Bulletin on Narcotics*, Vol. IX, No. 4, October - December 1957, United Nations, p.61.

8. *Bulletin on Narcotics*, Vol. XIV, No.1, January - March 1962, p. 41.

9. Barnett R. Rubin, "The Political Economy of War and Peace in Afghanistan", *World Development*, Vol. 28., No. 10, 2000, p.1791.

10. *Report of the International Narcotics Control Board, 1970* (E/INCB/9); also see summary in *Bulletin on Narcotics*, Vol. XXIII, No. 3, July - September 1971, p. 33.

11. E/5082, E/CN.7/544, Commission on Narcotic Drugs, Report of the Twenty-Fourth Session, para 344; also see summary in *Bulletin on Narcotics*, Vol X1V, No. 1, January - March 1972.

12. *Report of the International Narcotics Control Board, 1972* (E/INCB/17) paras 63 - 70; see also summary in *Bulletin on Narcotics*, Vol XXV, No. 2, April-June 1973.

13. *Report of the International Narcotics Control Board, 1973* (E/INCB/21); see also summary in *Bulletin on Narcotics*, Vol XXVI, No 3, July-September 1974.

14. Rubin, *op. cit.*, p.1792.

15. *ibid.*, p1792.

16. UNDCP, *World Drug Report 2000*, Oxford University Press, London, 2000, p. 142.

17. *The Far East and Australasia 2000*, 31st Edition, Europa Publications Ltd, 2000, Surrey, p.73.

18. *Afghanistan Rehabilitation Strategy: Action Plan for Immediate Rehabilitation*, Volume IV, "A Report of the Agricultural and Alternative Cropping Expert," United Nations Development Programme, Kabul, Oct. 1993, p10.

19. *Afghanistan Rehabilitation Strategy, op. cit.*, Volume IV, p10.

20. *ibid.*

21. *ibid*, pp78-87.

22. *ibid.*, pp.9-33.

23. *ibid*, p.73.

24. *Afghanistan Rehabilitation Strategy*, Volume IV, p41.

25. Marek Sliwinski, *The Decimation of a People*, Orbis, Winter 1989, p53.

26. UNDCP, *World Drug Report 2000, op. cit.*, pp.142-43.

27. Rubin, *op. cit.*, p.1792.

28. *ibid.* p.1793.

29. Jonathan Goodhand, "From Holy War to Opium War," *Central Asian Survey*, 19 (2), pp. 271-272.

30. *Afghanistan Strategic Study #5*, p. 4, see full reference in endnote 32 below.

31. Rubin, op cit, p.1792.

32. UNDCP, *Afghanistan Opium Poppy Survey 1995*, p.iv

33. *ibid*, p.21.

34. UNDCP, *Global Illicit Drug Trends 2000*, p.48.

35. S/RES/1267 (1999), 15 October 1999; the sanctions were to come into effect from 14 November.

36. The information in this Box is drawn from four *UNDCP Afghanistan Strategic Studies*: *#3, The Role of Opium as a Source of Informal Credit; #4, Access to Labour: The Role of Opium in the Livelihood Strategies of Itinerant Harvesters Working in Helmand Province, Afghanistan; #5, An Analysis of the Process of Expansion of Opium Poppy to New Districts in Afghanistan; and #7, An Analysis of the Process of Expansion of Opium Poppy to New Districts in Afghanistan.*

37. See UNDCP *Afghanistan Opium Poppy Surveys of 1994 and 1995*, UNDCP, Islamabad. Also, Report of the Assessment Strategy and Programming Mission to Afghanistan May-July 1995, in particular, part IV, Report of the Agricultural and Alternative Cropping Expert.

38. *Afghanistan Rehabilitation Strategy: Action Plan for Immediate Rehabilitation*, Volume V, Infrastructure: Highways, Roads, Civil Aviation, Telecommunications, United Nations Development Programme, Kabul, Oct. 1993, p7.

39. For example, fieldwork completed as part of the study revealed that 95% of respondents from the Ghorak, Khakrez , Maiwand and Shinwar districts (in Nangarhar province) claimed that they had obtained loans during the previous 12 months; UNDCP *Afghanistan Strategic Study #3, op. cit.*, pp.3-4.

40. UNDCP *Afghanistan Strategic Study #5, op. cit.*, .p.3.

41. UNDCP, *Afghanistan Strategic Study #4, op. cit.*, p.7.

42. UNDCP, *Afghanistan Strategic Study #7,op. cit.*, p. 6.

43. UNDCP, *Annual Opium Poppy Survey 2000*

44. *ibid*, p.25

45. *ibid*,p.17.

46. UNDCP, *2001 Opium Poppy Pre-Assessment Survey*, February 2001.

47. UNDCP, *World Drug Report 2000*, Oxford University Press, London, p. 27.

48. UNDCP, *World Drug Report 2000, op cit*., p.41.

49. Information drawn from UNDCP Demand Reduction Support project in Afghanistan (AFG/97/C92).

50. *ibid*.

51. UNICEF, *State of the Worlds Children 2000*, United Nations, New York, 2000.p.29.

52. Estimates from the UNDP *Human Development Report 2000*, the World Bank *World Development Report 1999/2000* and the Taleban Central Statistics Administration, (cited in the Economist Intelligence Unit *Country Report Afghanistan*, August 2000) range from 21, 23 to 26 million respectively.

53. UNICEF, *op cit*, index tables.

54. World Food Programme, "Drought and Displacement in Afghanistan," 1 December 2000, p. 10.

55. General Assembly / Security Council, The situation in Afghanistan and its implications for international peace and security, Report of the Secretary General, A/55/393 - S/2000/875, p.6.

56. Economist Intelligence Unit, *Pakistan and Afghanistan Country Report*, Economist Intelligence Unit, London, p.36.

57. General Assembly / Security Council, *op cit*., p.6.

58. World Food Programme, Drought and Displacement in Afghanistan," 1 December 2000, p.2.

59. Z.F. Naqvi, *Afghanistan - Pakistan Trade Relations*, World Bank, Islamabad, 1999; also cited in Rubin, *op. cit*., p. 1802.

60. This follows the analysis in Rubin, *op. cit*., p. 1796, which uses UNDCP data for the 1999 opium crop.

61. S/RES/1333 (2000), 19 December 2000.

MYANMAR

HOW DID MYANMAR BECOME A MAJOR SUPPLIER OF ILLICIT OPIUM?

The Union of Myanmar (Union of Burma, prior to 1989[a]) was the second producer of illicit opiates in the world, after Afghanistan, during the 1990's, and is increasingly becoming a source of illicit amphetamine-type-stimulants since the mid-1990s. Relatively high levels of addiction and HIV-AIDS prevalence are some of the direct consequences of the illicit drug industry for Myanmar's population. Illicit drugs have also had a negative impact on Myanmar's internal political situation and external relations. To understand what lead the country to experience such a severe drug problem, a brief review of key historical factors is required.

The cultivation of opium poppy in the remote and rugged northeastern part[b] of today's Myanmar is believed to have been originally introduced by Chinese traders coming from the neighbouring province of Yunnan where opium poppy cultivation was regarded as common by Chinese historians in 1736[1]. While opium was used by hill tribes for its medicinal and recreational properties and had also spread to other groups of the Burmese society, it was still relatively uncommon by the beginning of the 19th century, mostly a habit of the lower classes, and was kept under control by the societal fabric and Buddhist morality. The increase in opium use and production to problematic levels in Burma is linked to the development of the international opium trade and the period of colonial rule in the 19th century (starting in 1824)[2].

Stimulated by the immediate proximity of expanding markets in China and Burma[c], opium production then started to increase in Yunnan province and northern Burma. After 1858, when China had to legalize opium imports, Chinese provincial authorities stopped discouraging local cultivation. By 1880, China was officially importing about as much as 20,000 metric tons of opium[3] annually, supplemented with unknown quantities produced locally, or smuggled from northern Burma. China then quickly became the first opium producer in the world — thereby reducing its opium imports — and,

by 1906, when official figures became available, the Chinese provinces of Szechwan and Yunnan were reportedly producing more than 19,000 metric tons of opium annually, more than half of China's total opium production of 35,364 metric tons for that year, which itself represented 85% of the 41,264 metric tons of non-medicinal opium produced in the world the same year[4]. The exact number of opium addicts in China at that time is unknown, but the national production alone would have been enough to supply more than 23 million daily opium users[d]. For comparison purposes, Myanmar's opium production in 2000 — also largely for the Chinese market — was estimated at 1,087 metric tons; the world illicit opium production at about 4,700 metric tons (one ninth of 1906's production); and the total number of opiate abusers in the world at 13.5 million.

By the time policy on opium use was reversed in Burma (1878) —"opium has become the scourge of this country", noted a British administrator[5]— the trend towards increasing use could no longer be easily curtailed and smuggling from Yunnan and northern Burma developed rapidly.

Opium poppy cultivation on the Burmese side further increased with the arrival in the Kokang and the Wa areas of Muslim Chinese opium growers migrating from the Yunnan province, following the end of their insurgency in 1873. By 1900, opium had become the dominant crop in the Kokang and the Wa regions and was spreading to adjacent areas[6].

When British rule was extended to northern Burma (1887) — which included states ruled by Shan, Kachin, and other groups, and thus the main opium growing areas — a system of "indirect rule"[e] in contrast to the approach taken for the rest of the country, was granted to the traditional leaders of these areas, which were considered too remote to be effectively controlled, in exchange for a formal acceptance of central government authority and the payment of an annual tribute.

---

a) Both names are used in this country profile, depending on the period to which the text refers.

b) Corresponding to today's Kachin State and Shan States (which include the Wa, Kokang and Kengtung traditional opium growing areas).

c) The use of opium in Burma was then promoted through a government-controlled monopoly.

d) Based on a average annual consumption of 1.5 kg of opium per daily user.

e) The indirect rule system was also used by the British colonial administration in other regions such as South Asia and West Africa.

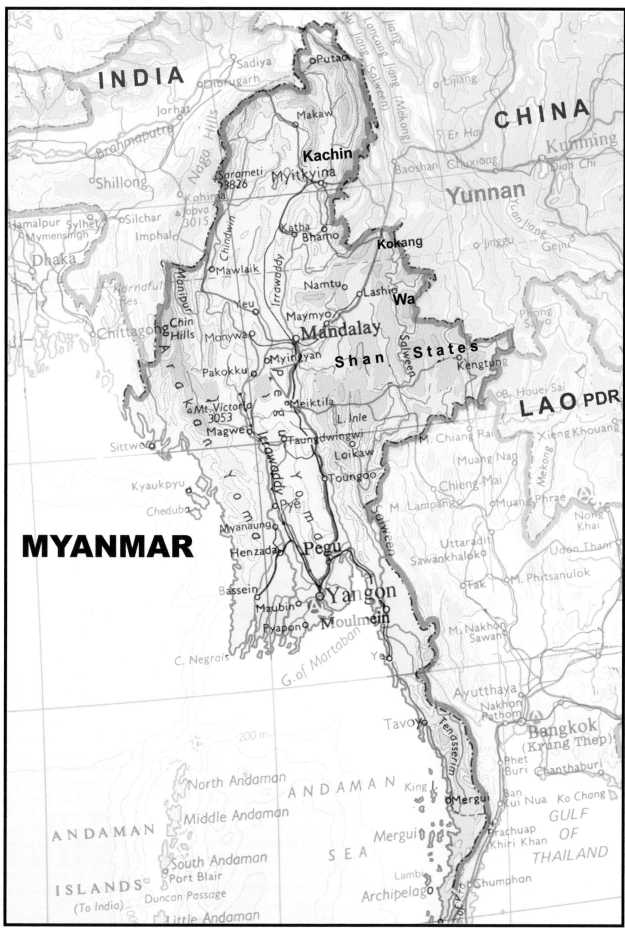

The autonomy thus guaranteed enabled local rulers to continue the opium trade and encouraged their sense of independence from the rest of the kingdom.

After the revolution of 1912 in China, the new Chinese government prohibited opium production. Its subsequent efforts to eliminate opium poppy cultivation in the Yunnan province lead another wave of Chinese opium poppy growers to move to Burma, in the Kachin and the Shan areas, where opium production further increased. The year 1912 also saw the adoption of the Hague Opium Convention, and the beginning of international pressures to control opium production. However, the authorities of British Burma felt it would be difficult to achieve in the Shan States and declared:

> "It is undesirable because opium is the main source of livelihood in many parts of the Shan States. It is impossible unless the whole of the Shan States, including the Wa country, which is at present under no administration at all, were taken under direct administration similar to that in the plains of Burma. The cost of introducing administration of this nature would be enormous and unremunerative, and problems would arise entailing armed interference on a large scale and a reversal of the existing policy of administration of the Shan States — problems of such magnitude as to be entirely incommensurate with the object to be achieved."[7]

Nevertheless, the government decided to make some attempts to control the opium production in Burma. In 1923, the Shan States Opium Order made the non-medical use of opium illegal in most of what had, by then, become the Federated Shan states. The Order, however, did not apply to the Trans-Salween States (areas located east of the Salween river and bordering China and northern Siam), where the largest growing areas like Kokang and Kengtung were located. Similarly, the ban on opium which was extended to the Kachin States in 1937 did not apply to the major growing area of the Hukawng Valley. Opium poppy cultivation therefore remained legal in all the main producing areas of Burma, namely: in the Kachin States, in the Trans-Salween States of the Shan States, in the Wa State and in the Naga Hills on the Indian border[f]. The dichotomy between the legality of opium cultivation on the one hand, and the illegality of opium outside of the production areas, even on the Burmese market, on the other hand, resulted in active smuggling, notably to the Yunnan and, increasingly, to the Siam markets. It is worth noting that it was not until the mid-1970s that a total ban on opium use and production was to be effectively and durably adopted in Burma.

After the independence of Burma in 1948, the unification of the country under the rule of a central government could not easily be achieved and a revolt of the ethnic minorities[g] erupted in 1959. Hostilities and armed clashes have, with various degrees of intensity, continued to this day[h]. Isolated and without outside support, the Shan separatist rebels turned to the opium trade to buy arms. Over time, the opium-arms cycle produced internal struggles — masked by political rhetoric — for the control of opium-producing territory among rival commanders, for whom the drug profits increasingly became more important than the political objectives they were initially meant to support. Over a period of twenty years, the opiate trade which fueled the rebellion, ended up fragmenting and consuming the Shan nationalist movement, reducing the rebel groups to mere instruments in the opiate business. This evolution complies with the theoretical model of civil war[i] recently developed by World Bank experts[8] which predicts that, beyond political motives (grievance), control of primary commodities (greed) is the most powerful explanatory factor for the development and continuation of rebellion, especially if an element of ethnic domination is present[j].

The grievance-greed dynamics apparently also played a significant role in the evolution of another major player in the opiate trade. In 1950, remnants of the defeated Chinese Nationalist (Kuomintang) army had started to regroup in the Burmese Shan states to prepare, with

---

f) John S. Calgue, a former Federated Shan States commissioner wrote in 1937: "The real point about opium in the Wa States and Kokang ... is that opium ... is the only thing produced which will pay for transport to a market where it can be sold. To suppress opium in Kokang and the Wa States without replacing it by a crop relatively valuable to its bulk, so that it would pay for transport, would be to reduce the people to the level of mere subsistence on what they could produce for food and wear themselves or to force them to migrate." (Quoted in Ronald D. Renard, *The Burmese Connection: Illegal Drugs and the Making of the Golden Triangle*, Boulder, London: Lynne Riener, 1996, p. 38). This problematic is still valid in many opium growing areas and is at the origin of the crop substitution approach, later improved as the alternative development method, that have been used to break the socioeconomic dependency of rural communities on opium poppy cultivation.

g) About 135 different ethnic groups are found in Myanmar, but no detailed census on ethnic minorities has been conducted since 1931 in Myanmar. In 1931 the Bamar (Burman) group represented 65% of the population, followed by the Karen (9%), the Shan (7%), the Chin (2%), the Mon (2%), the Kachin (1%) and the Wa (1%) (The Economist Intelligence Unit, Myanmar Country Profile, 1999-2000, 1999, p. 14). The Encyclopedia Britannica (in Nations of the World: Statistics, 2000) provides the following figures for 1983: Burman (69%), Shan (8.5%), Karen (6.2%), Rakhine (4.5%), Mon (2.4%), Chin (2.2%), Kachin (1.4%), other (5.8%).

h) Tensions eased after 1989 with the signing of cease-fires between the central government and most (17) of the armed ethnic groups.

i) The model is based on the analysis of data for 161 countries during the period 1960 to 1999.

j) According to the model, if the largest ethnic group represents between 45% and 90% of the population, the risk of internal conflict is doubled. In Myanmar, the main group represents more than 60% of the total population.

some outside support, an invasion of southern China (Yunnan). After three failed attempts, the Kuomintang turned westward and concentrated its efforts on the Shan States, which increasingly fell under its control, including the major opium producing areas of the Kokang, Wa and Kengtung states, and thereafter expanded opium production and trade in the area. During the same period, Yunnan's opium production was disappearing in the context of a vigorous anti-narcotics effort of the new Chinese government. Although the Kuomintang was finally pushed out of Burma by the Burmese army in 1961 and took refuge in northern Thailand, it continued to control a large share of the opiate trade in the region.

In 1962, when the Burmese army came to national power, the underground Burmese Communist Party joined forces with a number of ethnic minorities. Opposed to opium production at first, the communists eventually compromised. By the late 1970s, the Burmese Communist Party was the dominant rebel force in the Shan states and controlled an estimated 80% of all opium poppy fields.

When signing the United Nations Single Convention on Narcotics Drugs of 1961 — as authorized under articles 49 and 50 — Burma reserved the right to allow opium poppy cultivation to continue in the Kachin and the Shan States for a period of twenty years, which would presumably allow the implementation of a progressive elimination approach. However, around that same time, an important new drug market started to develop in southeast Asia with the presence of US troops sent to Vietnam. By some accounts, 10% to 15% of all GIs were using heroin in 1971. A committee established by the US government reported in 1973 that an estimated 34% of all the US troops in Vietnam had "commonly used" heroin[9]. Previously unknown in the region, refining of opium into heroin No. 4 developed on a large scale and, by the beginning of the 1970s, about thirty heroin laboratories were reportedly operating — mostly under the Kuomintang's control — near the border with Thailand.

While the Burmese Communist party was taking control of most of the production areas and the Kuomintang of heroin refining and trafficking routes, they were nevertheless confronted with the competing ambitions of autonomous local warlords. The most infamous was Khun Sa (also known as Chang Chi-Fu), a Chinese-Shan who, after learning the opium trade and guerilla techniques with the Kuomintang until 1961, then temporarily siding with the central government against the Communist party, created one of several Shan liberation groups and, in 1964, established an independent army in the Wa area, outside of the control of the Communist party. After a failed attempt to challenge the Kuomintang for the control of the opium trade in 1967, Khun Sa was captured by the Burmese military and jailed until 1974. When he returned to the opium busi-

ness in 1976, the Kuomintang had lost most of its former power and Khun Sa became a dominant force in the opiate trade. His position was later further strengthened by the collapse of the Burmese Communist Party during the second half of the 1980s. After military defeats inflicted by the Tatmadaw (Myanmar Armed Forces), the fate of the communist insurgency was sealed when their Kokang and Wa allies turned against them in March and April 1989 and signed cease-fire agreements with the government. Khun Sa and his 15,000 armed men were then the unrivaled masters of the opiate business in the Golden Triangle, until they, too, were defeated and surrendered to the Tatmadaw in 1995-96. Although the opiate business vacated by the Communist party and then Khun Sa was again at their entire disposal, the fragmented insurgent ethnic groups were also already engaged in a pacification/cooperation process with the central government which included narcotics control among its objectives. Possibly, the time was finally ripe to put an end to a century and a half of opiate business in northeastern Myanmar.

PRESENT SITUATION AND TRENDS IN MYANMAR'S ILLICIT DRUG MARKETS

Opium Production

The second largest country in southeast Asia after Indonesia, Myanmar has a relatively low population density of 69 inhabitants per square kilometer (Vietnam: 225, Thailand: 117) and almost half of the land area is covered with forests and rugged hilly terrain[10]. In 1983, the Shan state and the Kachin state had 11% (3.7 million) and 3% (0.9 million) of the country's population respectively, on an area as large as the United Kingdom, representing 23% and 13% of the country's total land area respectively (population density: 24 and 10 inhabitants per square kilometer respectively)[11]. Most of the opium poppy crop, grown and harvested during the September-March dry season, is found in the mountainous areas of the Shan plateau, which extends almost the entire length of the Shan state, from the Chinese border to the Thai border, and predominantly east of the Salween (Thanlwin) River, in the Kokang area, near the Chinese border; in the Wa region, south of Kokang and also bordering the Chinese border; and, further south, in the Kengtung area bordering China, Laos and Thailand. Together, it is estimated that the Wa and the Kokang areas now account for about 70% of Myanmar's opium production. Poppy fields are also found to a lesser extent in the Kachin, Chin and Kayah States and in the Saggaing Division. Opium poppy fields average half a hectare in size and are cultivated by small-scale farmers belonging to various hill-tribes. The government estimates that about 300,000 people depend on opium poppy cultivation as a cash-crop for their subsistence.

Note: Boundaries and names shown and designations used on this map do not imply official endorsement or acceptance by the United Nations.

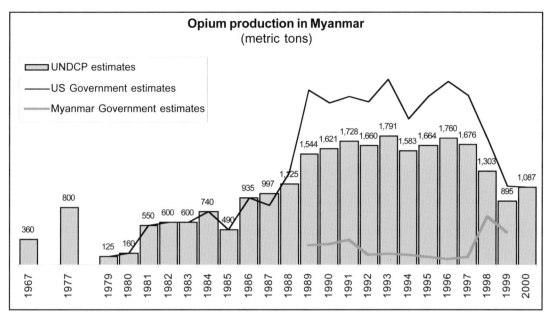

Figure 1. Sources: National Narcotics Intelligence Consumers Committee. The *NNIC Report 1985-1986*; U.S. Department of State, *1999 International Narcotics Control Strategy Report*, March 2000; Annual Report Questionnaire.

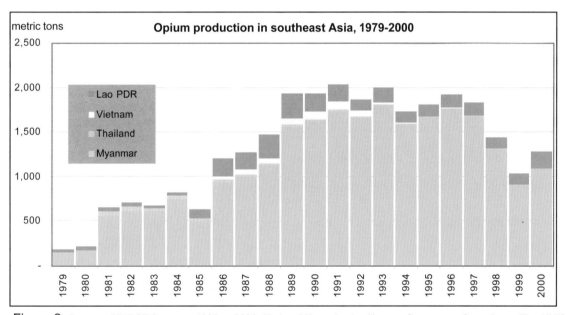

Figure 2. Sources: UNDCP for years 1986 to 2000; National Narcotics Intelligence Consumers Committee. The *NNIC Report 1985-1986* for prior years.

In 2000, the total area under opium poppy cultivation in Myanmar amounted to 108,700 hectares[k]. First in the world during the 1980s with an average quantity of about 700 metric tons of opium per year for the period 1981-1987, Myanmar's illicit opium production more than doubled to an annual average of 1,600 metric tons during the following ten years (1988-1997) (see Figure 1). Despite that increase, Afghanistan's production overtook Myanmar's in 1991, with an average production of about 2,100 metric tons per year during the period 1988-1997. From 1996 to 1999, opium poppy culti-

vation and opium production declined steadily in Myanmar, as a result of increased eradication and control efforts on the part of the government and local authorities, as well as unfavorable weather conditions. Even though the decline was halted in 2000, with an estimated 1,087 metric tons, Myanmar's 2000 opium output returned to levels recorded about a decade earlier (1988: 1,125 metric tons) and two decades earlier (1977: 800 metric tons). The sharp decrease recorded twenty years ago in 1979 and 1980 (125 and 160 metric tons respectively) was caused by a severe drought

---

k) According to the latest government data available, the area under opium poppy cultivation amounted to 61,200 hectares in 1998. However, government surveys have so far not covered all opium growing areas. UNDCP therefore relies on satellite-based data published by the US government, which reported 130,300 hectares under cultivation for the same year, and 108,700 ha for 2000 (U.S. Department of State, *International Narcotics Control Strategy Report*, March 2000 and March 2001).

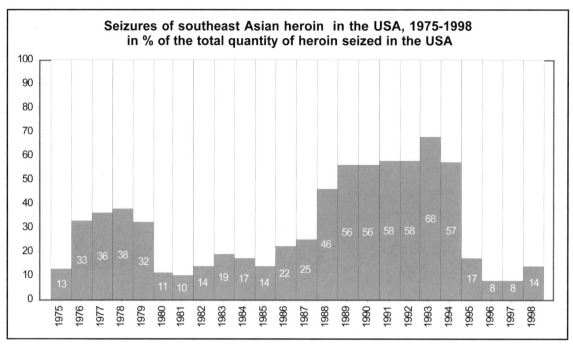

Figure 3. Source: U.S. Drug Enforcement Administration, Heroin signature programme 2000.

which played a catalytic role in the demise of southeast Asian heroin on the US market to the benefit of south-west Asian heroin (see Figure 3). After a seven-year return to first rank (1988-1994), southeast Asian heroin was largely replaced on the US market by heroin from south America and represented only 14% of the heroin seized in the USA in 1998 — against 68% in 1993[12]. As Myanmar was, on average, the source of about 80% of the opium produced annually in southeast Asia during the 1980s, and of about 90% during the 1990s, trends in southeast Asian heroin production and trafficking can essentially be identified with Myanmar's (see Figure 2).

Most of the opium which is not consumed locally is transformed into heroin in refineries operating deep in the forested areas under the protection of the armed groups that control the opium poppy cultivation areas. Precursor chemicals used in the transformation process — acetic anhydride is the main one — are smuggled mostly from China, India or Thailand. The general trend towards an increase in opiate production during the 1980s and 1990s was reflected in the evolution of inter-ceptions by law enforcement agencies (see Figure 4). From 1987 to 1998, the volume of opiates seized annu-ally in east and southeast Asia quadrupled, from 25 met-

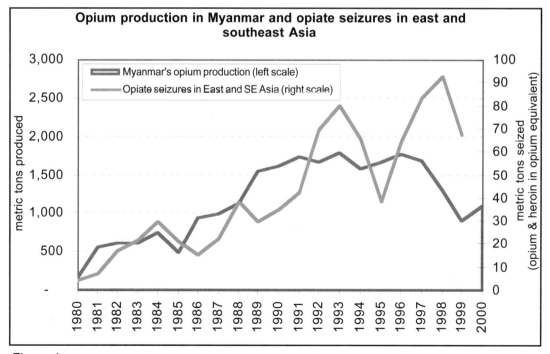

Figure 4. Source: UNDCP; Annual Report Questionnaire.

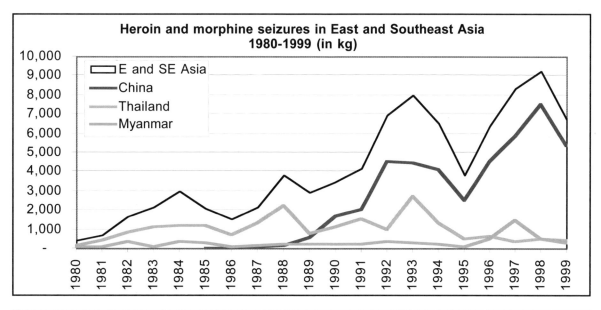

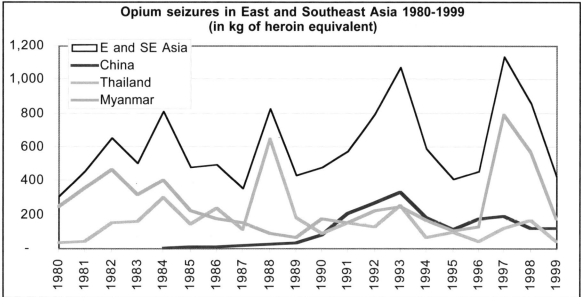

Figure 5. Source: UNDCP; Annual Report Questionnaire.

ric tons to 99 metric tons of opium equivalent. The trend was reversed in 1999, when the decline of opium production in the region started to be reflected in the level of opiate seizures in east and southeast Asia.

The overall trend masks however an important change in regional trafficking patterns. In 1994-95, the increased military pressure put on the Mong Tai Army in Myanmar, resulted in the surrender of its leader Khun Sa in December 1995-January 1996. As Khun Sa and his troops controlled most of Myanmar's heroin production, the southeast Asian heroin trade was temporarily disorganized and trafficking lines cut. This was reflected in heroin seizures data which show a large drop in 1995 in east and southeast Asia (see Figures 4 and 5). This fall was also reflected in the heroin seizures in the

USA: southeast Asian heroin represented 68% of the heroin seized in the USA in 1993; 58% in 1994 and only 17% in 1995 (see Figure 3). Khun Sa was linked with Hong Kong-based trafficking rings which used Thailand as a transit country. With the dismantling of Khun Sa's organization, trafficking was increasingly reoriented through China and taken over by smaller and less organized Chinese groups. Heroin seizures in China reflect this new trend with an increase of more than 300% from 1995 to 1998 (see Figure 5). Meanwhile, the level of heroin seizures in Thailand did not recover from the 1995 fall: in 1993, Thailand represented 33% of all heroin seizures in east and southeast Asia, but only 6% five years later in 1998. During the same period, China's share grew from 58% to 83%[l].

---

l) Opiate seizures in China started to increase after the adoption of a commercial trade agreement between Burma and China in 1986, and the subsequent increase in volume of trade and movement of persons across the China-Myanmar border. China's share in east and southeast Asian opiate seizures represented only 3% in 1987 (against 56% for Thailand).

Data for 1999 indicate a significant decline in seizures of heroin and heroin precursors in Yunnan province. The declining opium production in Myanmar is likely to have been a contributing factor, as well as changes in trafficking patterns (smaller consignments, rerouting of trafficking through less controlled areas and alternative routes in southern and western Myanmar, ... etc). The fact that law enforcement interventions have now been partly refocused on the growing trafficking of methamphetamine, and that more effective concealing methods seem to be used by traffickers, might also be contributing to the decline in the quantities of heroin seized on the Chinese side of the Myanmar-China border.

At the end of the 1990s, the main destinations for Myanmar's illicit opiates were neighbouring countries — China, in particular, now probably represents the largest outlet for Myanmar's illicit opiates[m] —, as well as countries from the Pacific Rim such as Australia — three to four tons of heroin (equivalent to 30 to 40 metric tons of opium) are estimated to enter Australia every year, with more than 80% coming from southeast Asia[13].

The positive outlook on the evolution of opium production in Myanmar is unfortunately offset by the emergence, in recent years, of large-scale production of amphetamine-type-stimulants (mostly methamphetamine) in the same areas that produce opium and heroin. Methamphetamine production seems to primarily occur in or near settlements that have a reliable supply of electricity. Precursor chemicals, ephedrine in particular, are imported from China and, more recently, also from India. In 1999, 75% of world stimulant seizures were made in east and southeast Asia, 48% in China and about 14% in Thailand. Thailand is one of the most buoyant markets for those substances and abuse of amphetamine-type stimulants, with a prevalence of 1.1 % among the population aged 15 and above, is now considered by Thai authorities a more serious problem than heroin use (0.6 % of the same age group).

DRUG ABUSE

Heroin use started to become a problem in Burma at the end of the 1960's, notably as a consequence of what drug control experts refer to as the "spill-over effect". Of the increasing quantities of heroin produced for the US troops in Vietnam, some started to find its way to the cities of Mandalay and Rangoon (Yangon, since 1988). Subsequently, the departure of the US troops in the early 1970s created surpluses which were increasingly sold on the Burmese market. Heroin use predominantly affected the younger generation, while opium was still preferred by older groups.

Data on present drug use in Myanmar is limited due to a lack of comprehensive epidemiological surveys. In 1999, 86,000 drug addicts were officially registered by the authorities. Given far higher prevalence rates reported from neighbouring states and very high levels of opiate abuse reported from some of the hill-tribes (allegedly reaching 10% and more of the population) in the opium producing areas, the overall level of opiate abusers in Myanmar is probably significantly higher than reflected in drug registry data (possibly as many as 300,000 users, about 0.9% of the population age 15 and above). Although reported cases in the drug registry are rising, authorities consider that the overall number of opiate abusers in Myanmar —in contrast to trends in neighbouring countries— is actually falling, a consequence of the decline in opium production.

Data from 1998 indicated that 91% of registered addicts abused opiates — 60% opium and 31% heroin. While no specific indications on the prevalence of use by drug types are available, heroin is known to be easily accessible at low cost in most areas of the country. A 1997 survey of treatment centres in Yangon indicated that 97% of the patients from the sample were heroin users. Like other Asian countries, Myanmar thus faces a general trend away from the traditional use of opium towards heroin abuse. Increasing seizures of amphetamine-type-stimulants confirms indications that the use of methamphetamine may also be becoming a serious problem. The same "spill-over effect" that triggered heroin use has likely been at work, generating a local consumption of amphetamine-type-stimulants produced in Myanmar. Other drugs used are morphine, pethidine, cough mixtures containing codein, marijuana, ephedrine and tranquilizers.

As far as the geographical distribution of drug abuse within the country is concerned, a rapid assessment survey conducted in 1995 identified five main areas with high prevalence of drug use: Yangon, Mandalay, the Sagaing Divisions and the Shan and Kachin States (the main urban centres, the mining areas and the northeastern border areas). Young males in the urban areas, seasonal workers in the mining sector and youth in the northeastern producing areas constitute the majority of the drug using population. Differences between regions also exist in terms of drug use patterns. Injecting use, as opposed to smoking or inhaling, is reported predominantly in urban, mining and border areas, where "shooting galleries" can be found. For a fee, addicts are administered heroin by a professional injector who uses the same injecting paraphernalia without sterilization for a large number of customers, increasing the risk of spreading HIV and other blood-borne infections.

---

m) In 1998 (with 7.5 tons) and in 1999 (with 5.4 tons) China seized the second largest quantity of heroin/morphine in the world, after Iran. Trafficking and consumption are mostly concentrated in Yunnan province, where 70% of all drug seizures made in China in 1998 took place (INTERPOL, *Heroin World Report 1999*, p.18).

DRUG USE AND HIV/AIDS

The first HIV/AIDS case in Myanmar was recorded in 1988 and an emerging epidemic was identified among injecting drug users. Largely as a direct consequence of drug use, Myanmar now has one of Asia's most severe epidemics of HIV infection[n]. The total number of people living with HIV/AIDS in Myanmar was estimated at 530,000 at the end of 1999, with a prevalence rate among adults of 1.99%[14]. In March 1999, 51% of the injecting drug users surveyed in the framework of the biyearly HIV sentinel surveillance conducted by the National AIDS programme were found to be HIV positive. The September 1999 site-specific survey reported the following regional differences for HIV infection among injecting drug users: Yangon, 39%; Mandalay, 88%; Taunggy (southern Shan States), 13%; Lashio (northern Shan State), 74%; Muse (northern Shan State), 92%; and Myitkyina (Kachin State), 77%. Overall, the Kachin and the Shan States are the areas most affected by HIV.

Myanmar's drug problem has contributed to the spread of HIV in the region. A study carried out in 1996-97 showed the role of heroin trafficking routes originating in Myanmar in the diffusion of HIV. Four different outbreaks of HIV-1 among injecting drug users in the region were linked to four different trafficking routes. Along those routes, molecular epidemiology enabled experts to clearly trace the diffusion of different HIV-1 subtypes. The first route went from Myanmar's eastern border to China's Yunnan Province; the second route from eastern Myanmar to Yunnan, going north and west, to Xinjiang Province; the third route from Myanmar and Laos, through northern Vietnam, to China Guangxi Province; and the fourth route from western Myanmar, across the Myanmar-India border to Manipur. The authors of the report concluded: "Single country narcotics and HIV programs are unlikely to succeed unless the regional narcotic-based economy is addressed."[15]

OUTLOOK

Since 1948, the history of Myanmar's opium producing areas has been characterized by war and violence. Insurgent groups with ideological and/or ethnic goals were *de facto* in control of these remote regions, maintaining a symbiotic relationship between drugs and rebellion: the proceeds of drug trafficking fuelled insurgence while the gun power of the insurgents protected drug production and trafficking, making it difficult to draw the line between politically motivated insurgence and illicit drug activity. The ethnic armies now present in drug producing areas are notably the United Wa State Army (UWSA, also now referred to as the Myanmar National Solidarity Party, MNSP)[o] and the Myanmar National Democratic Alliance army (MNDA-Kokang Chinese). Since 1989, the cease-fire agreements negotiated between seventeen of those groups[p] and the central government, which exchanged an end of insurgency for various degrees of political autonomy and development assistance, has considerably eased the situation in northeastern Myanmar and created a potential for the implementation of control measures in opium producing areas. A Progress of Border Areas and National Races Department created by the government after the cease-fire agreements was entrusted with the responsibility of economic and social development in the pacified areas.

At first, however, the autonomy granted under the agreements appeared to have stimulated production in the opium poppy growing areas (see Figure 1). Eventually, however, the strategy adopted by the government (the "State Peace and Development Council") apparently began to bear fruit as the 49% reduction in the area under opium poppy cultivation from 1996 to 1999 would suggest.

A drug-free zone was proclaimed in the Shan State East Special Region 4 (Mong Ma / Mongla) in 1997. An opium-free zone was also established in the Kachin

HIV/AIDS prevalence among adult popultion in Myanmar and neighbouring countries, end 1999							
India	Bangladesh	Thailand	Myanmar	China	Lao PDR	average SE-SW Asia	average W Europe
0.70%	0.02%	2.15%	1.99%	0.07%	0.50%	0.54%	0.23%

Source: UNAIDS, Report on the global HIV/AIDS epidemic, June 2000

---

n) Although it is not only spread by drug users, the start of the HIV epidemic in Myanmar is attributed to drug addicts using unsterilized needles.

o) The UWSA was created in 1989, after the collapse of the Communist Party of Burma which counted many Wa among its adherents.

p) With the Kokang armed group (MNDA) in Mar. 1989 (2,700 men), creation of northern Shan State special region 1; Wa (MNSP) Apr. 1989 (10,000 men) eastern Shan State special region 2; Shan/Akha/Lahu in Jun. 89 (3,300 men) eastern Shan State special region 4; Shan State Army in Sept. 89 (2,100 men) Shan special region 3; Kachin Defense Army in Jan. 91 (2,000 men) Northern Shan State special region 5; Pa-O National Organization Feb. 91 (1,400 men) Southern Shan State Special Region 6; Palaung State Liberation Army Apr. 91 (1,400 men) Northern Shan State Special Region 7: Kayan National Guard Feb. 92 (80 men); Kachin Independence Organization 92 (6,000 men) Kachin State Special Region 2; Kayinni National Development Party (now KNPP) Jan. 94 (7,800 men); Kayinni National People's Liberation Front May 94 (1,600 men) Kayah State Special Region 2; Kayan New Land Party Jul. 94 (1,500 men) Kayah State Special Region No 3; Shan State Nationalities People's Liberation Organization Oct. 94 (2,500 men); New Mon State Party Jun. 95 (7,800 men); Mong Tai Army (Khun Sa's private army) surrender in Jan. 96 (14,000 men); Burma Communist Party (Rakhine State) Apr. 97 (298 men). The pacification process continues to be pursued by the Tatmadaw. For instance, from January to September 2000, twenty-two groups (ranging from a few men to several hundreds, some remnants of, or seceding from, larger groups) have "returned to the legal fold". Source: Myanmar government, *Exchanging Arms for Peace*, 2000.

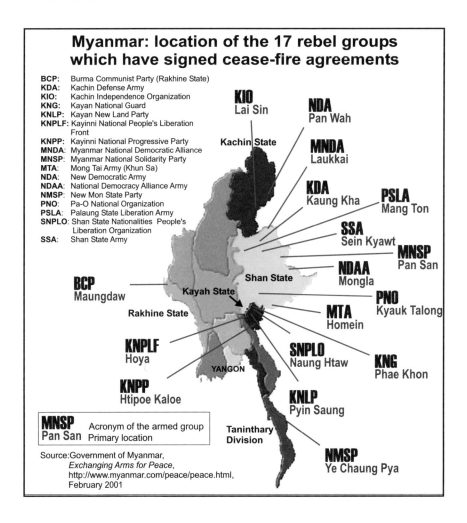

Myanmar: location of the 17 rebel groups which have signed cease-fire agreements

BCP: Burma Communist Party (Rakhine State)
KDA: Kachin Defense Army
KIO: Kachin Independence Organization
KNG: Kayan National Guard
KNLP: Kayan New Land Party
KNPLF: Kayinni National People's Liberation Front
KNPP: Kayinni National Progressive Party
MNDA: Myanmar National Democratic Alliance
MNSP: Myanmar National Solidarity Party
MTA: Mong Tai Army (Khun Sa)
NDA: New Democratic Army
NDAA: National Democracy Alliance Army
NMSP: New Mon State Party
PNO: Pa-O National Organization
PSLA: Palaung State Liberation Army
SNPLO: Shan State Nationalities People's Liberation Organization
SSA: Shan State Army

KIO Lai Sin
NDA Pan Wah
MNDA Laukkai
KDA Kaung Kha
PSLA Mang Ton
SSA Sein Kyawt
MNSP Pan San
NDAA Mongla
PNO Kyauk Talong
MTA Homein
KNG Phae Khon
SNPLO Naung Htaw
KNLP Pyin Saung
BCP Maungdaw
KNPLF Hoya
KNPP Htipoe Kaloe
NMSP Ye Chaung Pya

Kachin State
Shan State
Kayah State
Rakhine State
YANGON
Taninthary Division

MNSP Acronym of the armed group
Pan San Primary location

Source: Government of Myanmar,
Exchanging Arms for Peace,
http://www.myanmar.com/peace/peace.html,
February 2001

State and the government has announced plans to establish similar drug-free zones in the north of the Shan State, by the year 2000 in Special Region 1 (Kokang)[q], and by the year 2005 in Special Region 2 (Wa). In 1995, the Wa central Committee prepared a plan to eradicate opium poppy cultivation through a phased programme combining eradication and alternative development in the areas under their control. In 1999, the government decided to totally eliminate poppy cultivation in the country within a period of 15 years. The plan is scheduled to be implemented in the Shan State, the Kachin State, the Kayah State and the Chin State, through a succession of 5-year plans[16].

As part of their efforts to curb illicit opium poppy cultivation, the Myanmar government and the Wa authorities have also agreed and started to relocate large numbers of ethnic Wa, Akha, Lahu and Chinese from the hilly areas along the Sino-Myanmar border to flatter land in a southern area of the Shan states, along the Thai border area near Chiang Mai and Chang Rai.

However, ranked 125 out of 174 countries on the Human Development Index scale by UNDP[17], Myanmar faces serious financial constraints in the implementation of its socio-economic development and drug elimination strategies. Some limited bilateral assistance has been provided by countries such as China and Japan in the field of alternative development. UNDCP has also been providing alternative development assistance, through a five-year project in the Wa area, as well as through two smaller projects in the northern Wa area (Nam Tit) and the Kokang area (Laukkai).

With sanctions and criticism of its human right record since 1988, Myanmar can no longer receive loans and grants from international financial institutions. Bilateral as well as multilateral development assistance have also been almost entirely stopped. Joining the ASEAN in July 1997 has not yet had a significant economic impact on Myanmar and the financial crisis in Asia did not create a climate conducive to foreign investment during the end of the 1990s. Pockets of prosperous trading activities have however developed in recent years in the border areas, notably along the border with China[18], and the profits from drug smuggling (as well as from gems and timber) reinvested by some of the ethnic minority leaderships in infrastructure development appear to have become a significant complement

---

q) The target year for the Kokang area has now been changed to 2002.

to the limited financial allocations which the central government can provide for the development of the Shan States. Paradoxically, a form of money laundering might thus be one of the enabling factors of a diminishing reliance on opium-related income and of the progressive reduction in opium production recorded during the last few years.

However, it is doubtful whether the dependance of the eastern Shan State on drug production can be definitively broken as planned by the government without a quantitative jump in financial investments. As stated in the *International Narcotics Control Strategy Report* of the US government released in March 2001 : "... ultimately large-scale and long-term international aid, including development assistance and law-enforcement aid, will be needed to curb fundamentally and irre-

versibly drug production and trafficking in Burma".[19]

The sudden drop in the Afghan opium production in 2001 is likely to severely impact the world's opiate markets by creating supply shortages and price surges, particularly if it persists for more than a growing season. One of the main outlets for Afghanistan's heroin outside of southwest Asia has been the European market, but the history of drug control during the last thirty years provides evidence that opiate markets can rapidly shift from one source of illicit opiates to another. Myanmar is at present the only country where traffickers could find a potential to rapidly fill part of the heroin supply gap created by the evolution of the situation in Afghanistan. The resulting strong incentive to resume higher levels of opium production in the Shan states might create additional obstacles on the road to the elimination objective of the Myanmar Government.

ENDNOTES

1. Ronald D. Renard, *The Burmese Connection: Illegal Drugs and the Making of the Golden Triangle*, Boulder, London: Lynne Riener, 1996, p. 14.

2. United Nations Preliminary Joint Survey Team, 1992, Reprint,. *Report of the Preliminary Joint Survey Team on Opium Production and Consumption in the Union of Burma*, Thai-Yunnan Project Newsletter, no. 18: 8-16. Canberra: Australian National University Research School of Pacific Studies; Originally published in 1964.

3. Thomas D. Reins, *Reform, Nationalism and Internationalism: The Opium Suppression Movement in China and the Anglo-American Influence, 1900-1908*, Cambridge University Press, 1991, p. 115.

4. International Opium Commission, *Report of the International Opium Commission: Shanghai, China, February 1 to February 26*, 1909. It must be noted that no data was available on opium production in Burma.

5. Renard, *op cit*, p. 26.

6. *Ibid*. p. 29.

7. Government of Burma to Government of India, 27 December 1913. Enclosure 3 in no. 96. FO 415/8, pp. 85-88. In PRO. Quoted in Ronald D. Renard, *The Burmese Connection: Illegal Drugs and the Making of the Golden Triangle*, Boulder, London: Lynne Riener, 1996, p. 34.

8. Paul Collier and Anke Hoeffler, *Greed and Grievance in Civil War*, The World Bank Group, Policy Research Papers, no. 2355, May 2000

9. Paul B. Stares, *Global habit: the drug problem in a borderless world*, Washington DC: The Brookings Institution.1996. p. 26.

10. United Nations Statistics Division, http://www.un.org/Pubs/CyberSchoolBus/infonation/ e_infonation, 2000.

11. The Economist Intelligence Unit, *Myanmar Country Profile*, 1999-2000, 1999, p. 14.

12. US Drug Enforcement Administration, Heroin Signature Programme 2000.

13. INTERPOL, *Heroin World Report 1999*, p. 10.

14. UNAIDS, *Report on the global HIV/AIDS epidemic* - June 2000. http://www.unaids.org/ epidemic_update/report/index.html

15. Beyrer *et al*. *Overland heroin trafficking routes and HIV-1 spread in south and south-east Asia*, AIDS 2000, 14:75-83.

16. The plans are presented as follows by Myanmar's main daily newspaper: "In the first 5-year period, priority areas will be designated as 15 townships in northern Shan State, one township in eastern Shan State, and six townships in southern Shan State. In the second 5-year period, priority areas will be designated as 4 townships in Kachin State, 7 townships in northern Shan State, 7 townships in eastern Shan State, and three townships in southern Shan State. In the third 5-year period, priority areas will be designated as 5 townships in southern Shan State, 2 townships in Kayah State, and 2 townships in Chin State. The whole project covers 51 townships with total area of 55102.454 square miles inhabited by 3,817,199 people in 1,469 village-tracts. Eradication of poppy cultivation, control of narcotic drugs abuse, participation of local populace and cooperation with international organizations will be given priority.

Now, the Government is implementing the first 5-year project of the 15-year opium eradication plan which commenced in 1999-2000. Based on the 51 townships, production eradication, abuse elimination, law enforcement, people's participation and international relations will be targeted. The estimated costs of the plan are 33,588.14 million kyats and 150 million US dollars.

While the Government is taking measures for wiping out the drug menace, the Tatmadaw [the Army], Police Force, Customs Department and other organizations are taking action against the drug trafficking." (*The New Light of Myanmar*. Sunday, 9 July 2000).

17. United Nations Development Programme, *Human Development Report 2000*, New York, 2000.

18. The Economist Intelligence Unit, *op cit*, p. 29.

19. U.S. Department of State, Bureau for International Narcotics and Law Enforcement Affairs, *2000 International Narcotics Control Strategy Report*, March 2001.

ESTIMATES

PRODUCTION

OVERVIEW

Illicit cultivation of opium poppy and the coca bush are now mostly concentrated on the territories of two and three countries respectively. The year 2000 recorded a decline in global opium production and a stabilization in coca production. There is no reliable data on global cannabis cultivation, but 1999 seizure data showed a drastic increase that could possibly reflect a rise in global cannabis production.

OPIUM

Compared with 1999, the total area cultivated in opium poppy increased slightly, by about 3%, to reach 222,000 ha in 2000. However, global opium production decreased by 19%, to a level of about 4700 tons. The total increase in cultivation in 2000 is due to a 19,200 ha increase in cultivation in Myanmar, partly offset by a 8,400 ha decrease in Afghanistan and a 3,500 ha decrease in Lao PDR. The severe drought in Afghanistan reduced the yield of opium gum harvested per hectare in that country to 40 kg[a] in 2000 (from 50 kg in 1999), which was still four times higher than the 10 kg harvested per hectare in Myanmar.

In 2000, close to 50% of the global illicit opium poppy cultivation areas were located in Myanmar, 36% in Afghanistan, and 10% in other Asian countries (primarily Lao PDR, followed by Thailand and Pakistan). In the Americas, Colombia and Mexico accounted together for 4% of global cultivation.

Despite the larger cultivation area in Myanmar, 70% of global opium production still came from Afghanistan in 2000, against 23% from Myanmar. This discrepancy is due to a difference in opium varieties, weather conditions and growing methods, and is reflected in the yield differential mentioned above. The other Asian countries accounted for 5%, and Colombia and Mexico together remained relatively stable at 2%.

The ban on opium cultivation in Afghanistan for the 2000/2001 growing season is likely to result in a drastic reduction of both cultivation of poppy and production of opium in that country and, hence, at the global level. Myanmar will then certainly regain the first rank among opium producing areas it had during the 1980s.

COCA

Overall, the cultivation of coca bush, the production of coca leaf and the potential production of cocaine remained more or less stable in 2000. However, the overall stabilization is the result of diverging trends in the three main producing areas: (i) continued eradication in Bolivia brought the total cultivation area down to 14,600 ha in that country (which includes 12,000 ha of authorized cultivation under Bolivian law 1008 for traditional use); (ii) a decline of cultivation in Peru; (iii) some increase in Colombia, however at a slower pace than during the previous two years. New data for 1999 and 2000 recently released by the Colombian authorities shortly before the publication of this report are reflected in the following pages, along with data derived from US government surveys which was previously available and which can be used for reviewing the evolution of the situation over a longer period.

CANNABIS

In the absence of reliable information on global cannabis cultivation, seizures seem to confirm that cannabis continues to be widely cultivated and trafficked. More than 155 countries reported seizures of cannabis in 1999 and seizures of herbal cannabis increased by 35% from 1998 to 1999.

According to Interpol, "The indoor cultivation of cannabis continued to develop during the year, especially in the Netherlands, Canada and the United States. An increasing amount of cannabis from Colombia and Jamaica made its way to Europe during the year. The Central Asian Republics, where vast fields of cannabis cover several hundreds of thousands of hectares, remain for the time being a major source of supply for the illicit Russian market. Southern Africa (South Africa, Lesotho, Malawi and Swaziland) is also proving to be a region with a [large] production potential for herbal cannabis [...] and although most of the cannabis grown in this part of the world is intended for local consumption, large shipments are being sent to Europe and North America. Mexico [...] consolidated its position as the primary supplier of herbal cannabis to the United States, and Jamaica continued to supply large quantities of cannabis oil to Canada, either directly or through the United States."[b]

---

a) The unweighted average of yields in Afghanistan in 2000 was 35.7 kg/ha.

b) Interpol, World-wide cannabis traffic, March 2000 (http://www.interpol.int/Public/Drugs/cannabis/default.asp)

OPIUM

GLOBAL ILLICIT CULTIVATION OF OPIUM POPPY AND PRODUCTION OF OPIUM, 1988-2000

(UNDCP estimates)

	1988	1989	1990	1991	1992	1993	1994	1995	1996	1997	1998	1999	2000
CULTIVATION[1] IN HECTARES													
SOUTH-WEST ASIA													
Afghanistan	32,000	34,300	41,300	50,800	49,300	58,300	71,470	53,759	56,824	58,416	63,674	90,583	82,171
Pakistan	6,519	7,464	7,488	7,962	9,493	7,329	5,759	5,091	873	874	950	284	260
Subtotal	38,519	41,764	48,788	58,762	58,793	65,629	77,229	58,850	57,697	59,290	64,624	90,867	82,431
SOUTH-EAST ASIA													
Lao PDR	40,400	42,130	30,580	29,625	19,190	26,040	18,520	19,650	21,601	24,082	26,837	22,543	19,052
Myanmar	104,200	143,000	150,100	160,000	153,700	165,800	146,600	154,070	163,000	155,150	130,300	89,500	108,700
Thailand	2,811	2,982	1,782	3,727	3,016	998	478	168	368	352	716	702	890
Viet Nam [2]	12,000	14,000	18,000	17,000	12,199	4,268	3,066	1,880	1,743	340	442	442	
Subtotal	159,411	202,112	200,462	210,352	188,105	197,106	168,664	175,768	186,712	179,924	158,295	113,187	128,642
OTHER ASIAN COUNTRIES													
Combined	8,093	10,750	8,054	7,521	2,900	5,704	5,700	5,025	3,190	2,050	2,050	2,050	2,479
Total Asia	206,023	254,626	257,304	276,635	249,798	268,439	251,593	239,643	247,599	241,264	224,969	206,104	213,552
LATIN AMERICA													
Colombia [3]				1,160	6,578	5,008	15,091	5,226	4,916	6,584	7,350	6,500	6,500
Mexico [4]	5,001	6,600	5,450	3,765	3,310	3,960	5,795	5,050	5,100	4,000	5,500	3,600	1,900
Total Latin America	5,001	6,600	5,450	4,925	9,888	8,968	20,886	10,276	10,016	10,584	12,850	10,100	8,400
GRAND TOTAL	211,024	261,226	262,754	281,560	259,686	277,407	272,479	249,919	257,615	251,848	237,819	216,204	221,952
PRODUCTION IN METRIC TONS													
SOUTH-WEST ASIA													
Afghanistan	1,120	1,200	1,570	1,980	1,970	2,330	3,416	2,335	2,248	2,804	2,693	4,565	3,276
Pakistan	130	149	150	160	181	161	128	112	24	24	26	9	8
Subtotal	1,250	1,349	1,720	2,140	2,151	2,491	3,544	2,447	2,272	2,828	2,719	4,574	3,284
SOUTH-EAST ASIA													
Lao PDR	267	278	202	196	127	169	120	128	140	147	124	124	167
Myanmar	1,125	1,544	1,621	1,728	1,660	1,791	1,583	1,664	1,760	1,676	1,303	895	1,087
Thailand	17	31	20	23	14	17	3	2	5	4	8	8	6
Viet Nam	60	70	90	85	61	21	15	9	9	2	2	2	
Subtotal	1,469	1,923	1,933	2,032	1,862	1,998	1,721	1,803	1,914	1,829	1,437	1,029	1,260
OTHER ASIAN COUNTRIES													
Combined	8	57	45	45	-	4	90	78	48	30	30	30	38
Total Asia	2,727	3,329	3,698	4,217	4,013	4,493	5,355	4,328	4,234	4,687	4,186	5,633	4,582
LATIN AMERICA													
Colombia [3]				16	90	68	205	71	67	90	100	88	88
Mexico	67	66	62	41	40	49	60	53	54	46	60	43	21
Total Latin America	67	66	62	57	130	117	265	124	121	136	160	131	109
GRAND TOTAL	2,794	3,395	3,760	4,274	4,143	4,610	5,620	4,452	4,355	4,823	4,346	5,764	4,691
Potential HEROIN	279	340	376	427	414	461	562	445	436	482	435	576	469

[1] Potentially harvestable, after eradication.

[2] Due to small production, Viet Nam cultivation and production were included in the category "Other Asian countries" in 2000.

[3] According to the Government of Colombia, cultivation covered 7,350 ha and 6,500 ha and production amounted to 73 mt and 65 mt in 1998 and 1999 respectively. For 2000, no data available at time of publication. Data from previous year temporarely used.

[4] Sources: INCSR for cultivation data; Govt of Mexico for eradication data. As its survey system is under development, the Govt of Mexico indicates it can neither provide cultivation estimates nor endorse those published by UNDCP.

OPIUM POPPY CULTIVATION (1999-2000)

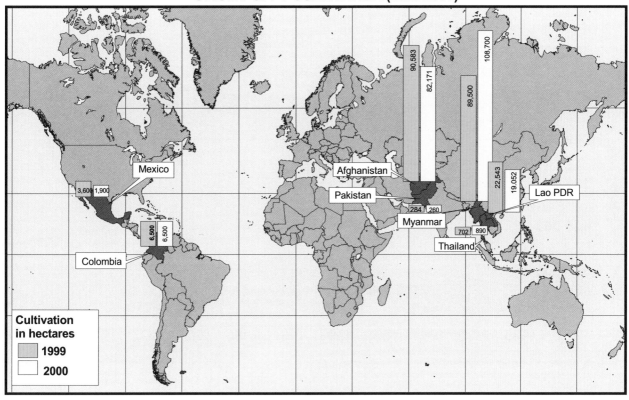

Mexico
3,600 1,900
Colombia
6,500 6,500
Afghanistan
Pakistan
284 260
Myanmar
Thailand 702 890
Lao PDR
90,583 82,171
108,700 89,500
22,543 19,052

Cultivation
in hectares
1999
2000

OPIUM PRODUCTION (1999-2000)

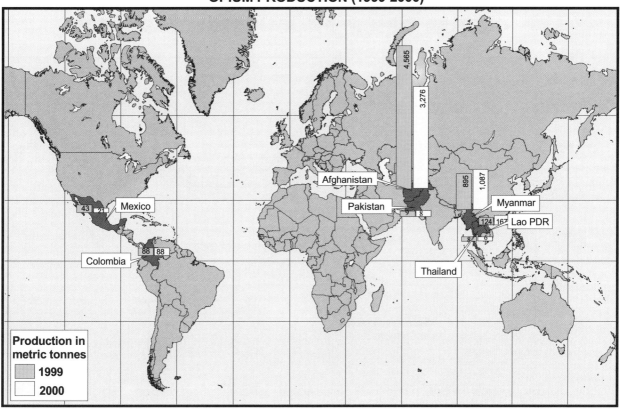

Mexico
43 21
Colombia
88 88
Afghanistan
Pakistan
9 8
Myanmar
Thailand
Lao PDR
124 167
6
4,565 3,276
895 1,087

Production in
metric tonnes
1999
2000

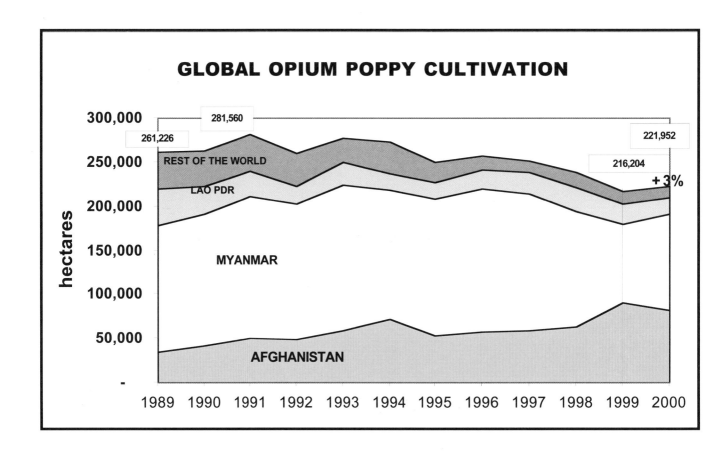

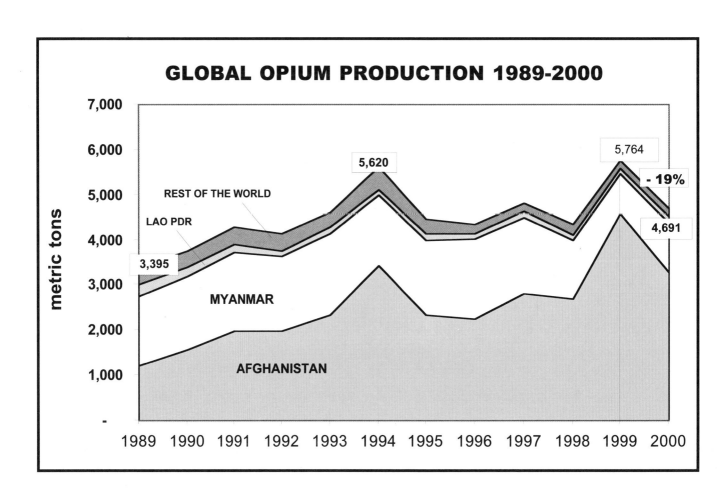

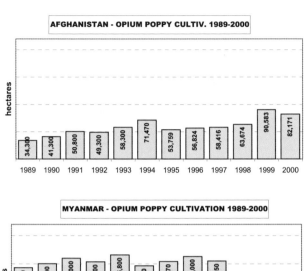

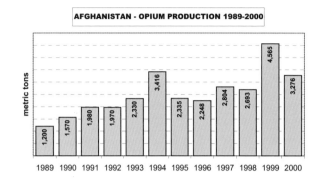

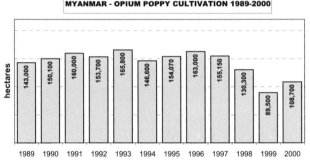

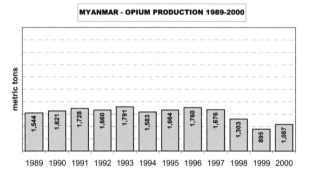

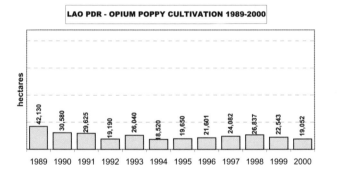

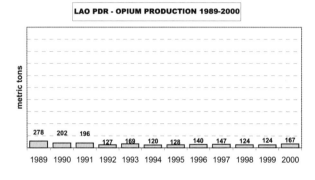

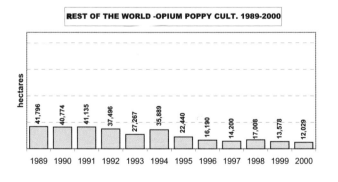

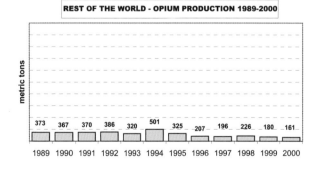

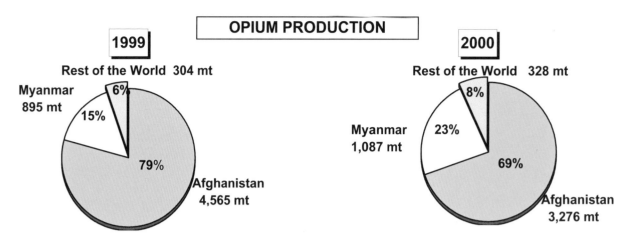

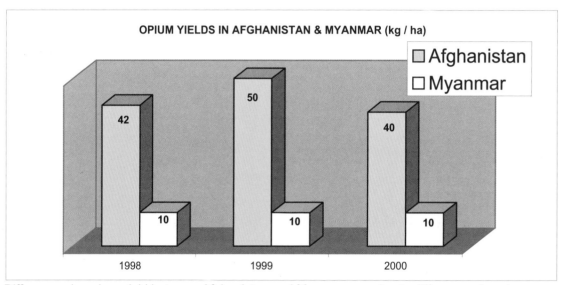

Differences in opium yield between Afghanistan and Myanmar are due to differences in opium poppy varieties and growing conditions. Variations of yields from year to year in the same country are mostlycaused by changes in weather conditions.

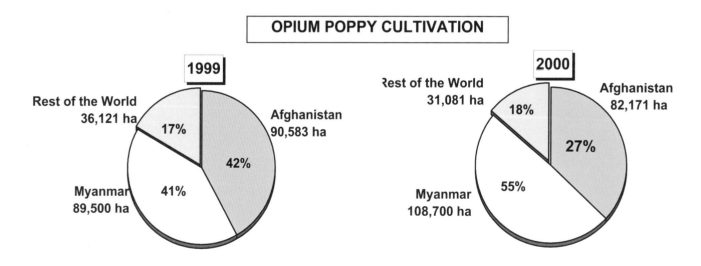

Afghanistan: Opium Poppy Cultivation, 2000

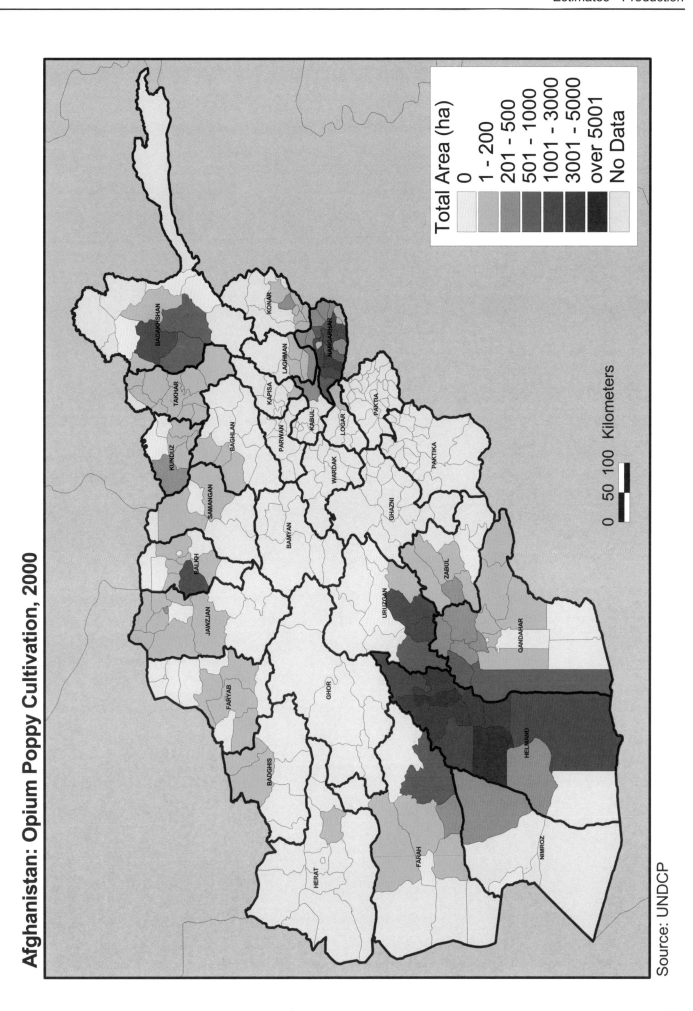

Total Area (ha)

0
1 - 200
201 - 500
501 - 1000
1001 - 3000
3001 - 5000
over 5001
No Data

0 50 100 Kilometers

Source: UNDCP

Lao PDR: Villages Cultivating Opium Poppy

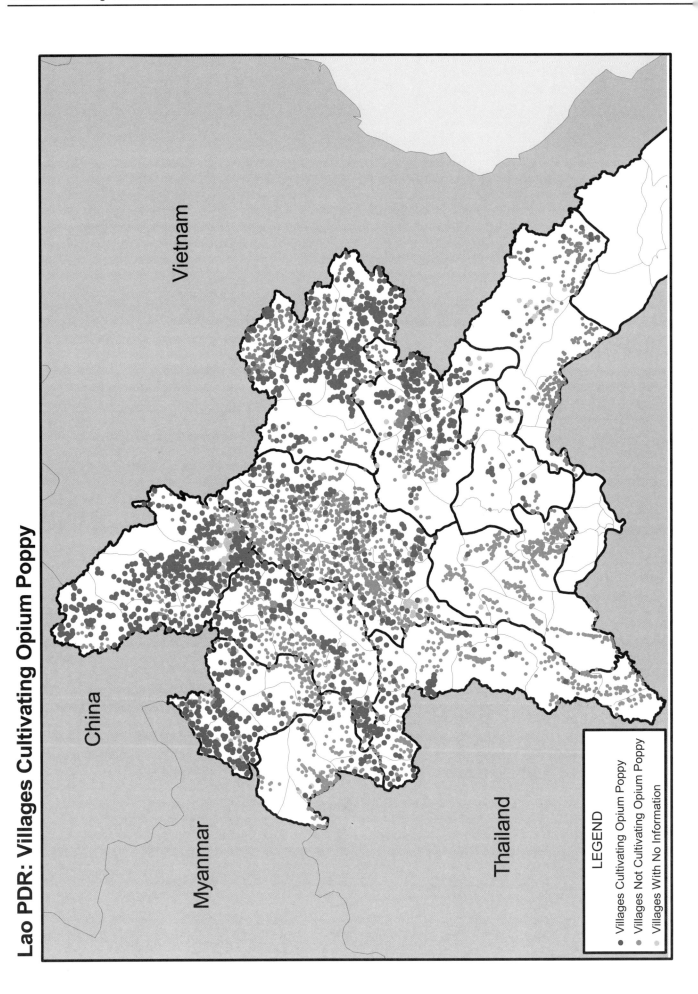

China

Vietnam

Myanmar

Thailand

LEGEND
• Villages Cultivating Opium Poppy
• Villages Not Cultivating Opium Poppy
• Villages With No Information

COCA

GLOBAL ILLICIT CULTIVATION OF COCA BUSH AND PRODUCTION OF COCA LEAF AND COCAINE, 1988-2000

	1988	1989	1990	1991	1992	1993	1994	1995	1996	1997	1998	1999	2000
CULTIVATION[1] OF COCA BUSH IN HECTARES (at end of reporting year)													
Bolivia [2]	48,900	52,900	50,300	47,900	45,300	47,200	48,100	48,600	48,100	45,800	38,000	21,800	14,600
Colombia (I) [3]	-	-	-	-	-	-	-	-	-	-	-	160,119	163,289
Colombia (II)	34,000	42,400	40,100	37,500	37,100	39,700	44,700	50,900	67,200	79,436	101,800	122,500	136,200
Peru	110,400	120,400	121,300	120,800	129,100	108,800	108,600	115,300	94,400	68,800	51,000	38,700	34,200
Total												220,619	212,089
	193,300	215,700	211,700	206,200	211,500	195,700	201,400	214,800	209,700	194,036	190,800	183,000	185,000
PRODUCTION OF DRY COCA LEAF IN METRIC TONS													
Bolivia	79,500	78,300	77,000	78,000	80,300	84,400	89,800	85,000	75,100	70,100	52,900	22,800	13,400
Colombia (I) [3]	-	-	-	-	-	-	-	-	-	-	-	260,995	266,161
Colombia (II)	25,840	33,072	45,313	45,000	44,891	45,258	67,497	80,931	108,864	129,481	165,934	195,000	220,000
Peru	187,700	186,300	196,900	222,700	223,900	155,500	165,300	183,600	174,700	130,600	95,600	69,200	54,400
Total												352,995	333,961
	293,040	297,672	319,213	345,700	349,091	285,158	322,597	349,531	358,664	330,181	314,434	287,000	287,800
POTENTIAL MANUFACTURE OF COCAINE IN METRIC TONS													
Bolivia	148	168	189	220	225	240	255	240	215	200	150	70	43
Colombia (I) [3][4]	-	-	-	-	-	-	-	-	-	-	-	680	695
Colombia (II)	51	64	92	88	91	119	201	230	300	350	435	520	580
Peru	327	373	492	525	550	410	435	460	435	325	240	175	145
Total												925	883
	527	604	774	833	866	769	891	930	950	875	825	765	768

[1] Potentially harvestable, after eradication

[2] Annual estimates include 12,000 hectares authorized by Bolivian law 1008

[3] Thanks to the new monitoring system of the Government of Colombia, new cultivation estimates are available starting in 1999 (Colombia (I)). It is important to note that, due to the use of different methodologies, the resulting data cannot be compared with data for previous years derived on US surveys (Colombia (II)). For more information provided by the Colombian authorities on their new monitoring system and resulting estimates, please see page 281. The month of reference was March for 1999 data and August for 2000 data.

[4] The Colombian authorities recently estimated that cocaine manufacture in Colombia could potentially have been as high as 947 tonnes in 2000.

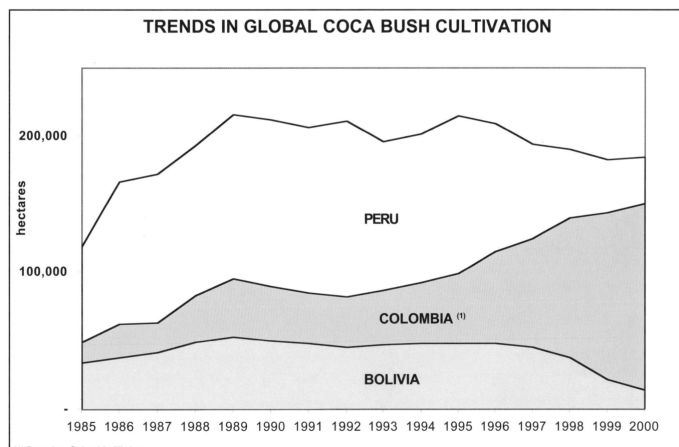

TRENDS IN GLOBAL COCA BUSH CULTIVATION

(1) Based on Colombia (II) data

COCA BUSH CULTIVATION (1999-2000)

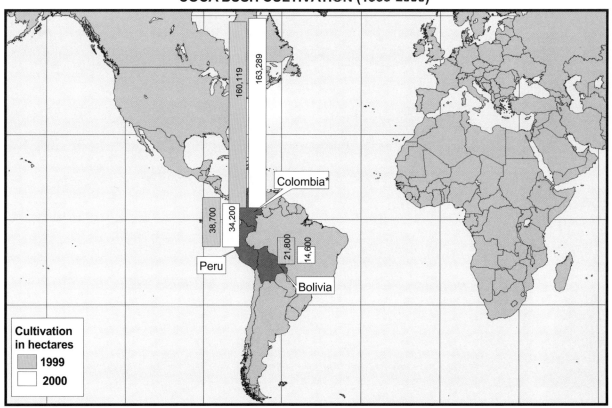

160,119 | 163,289

Colombia*

38,700 | 34,200

21,800 | 14,600

Peru

Bolivia

Cultivation in hectares
- 1999
- 2000

COCA LEAF PRODUCTION (1999-2000)

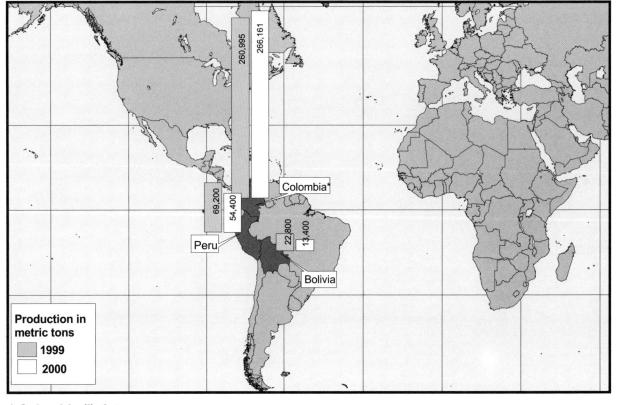

260,995 | 266,161

Colombia*

69,200 | 54,400

22,800 | 13,400

Peru

Bolivia

Production in metric tons
- 1999
- 2000

* Colombia (I) data

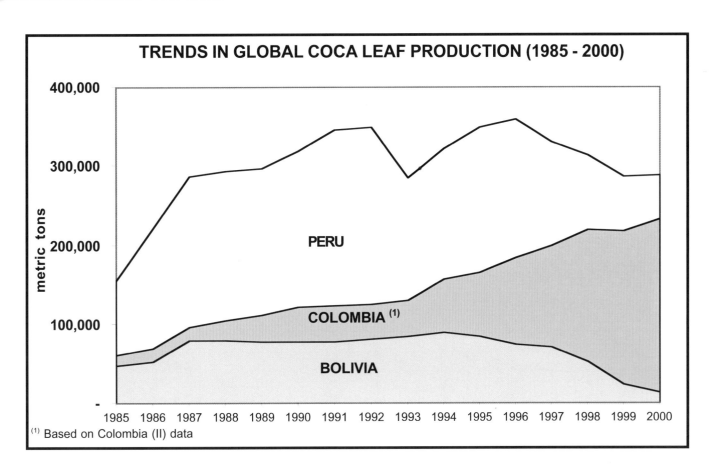

TRENDS IN GLOBAL COCA LEAF PRODUCTION (1985 - 2000)

(1) Based on Colombia (II) data

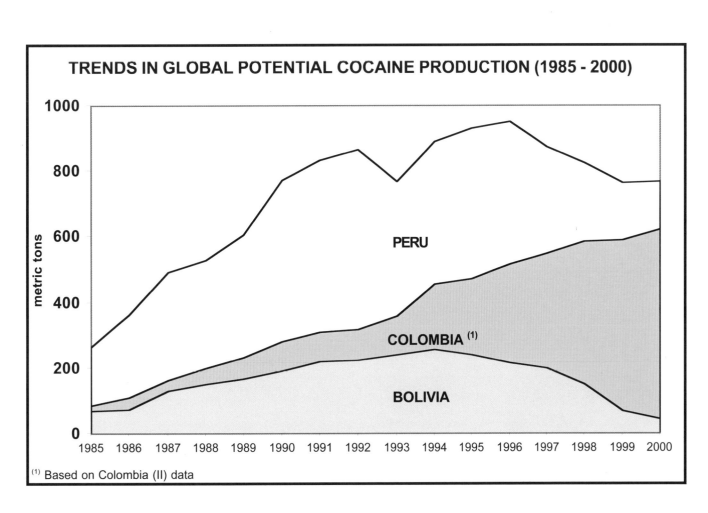

TRENDS IN GLOBAL POTENTIAL COCAINE PRODUCTION (1985 - 2000)

(1) Based on Colombia (II) data

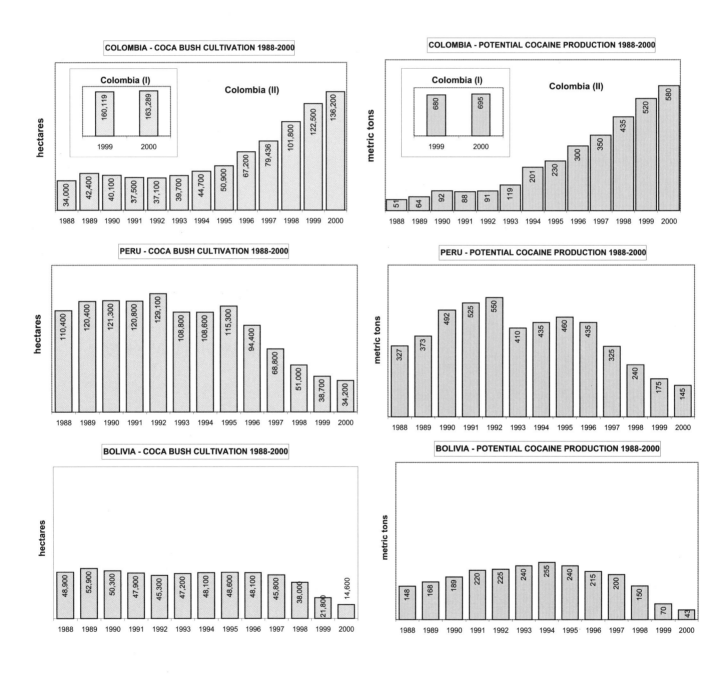

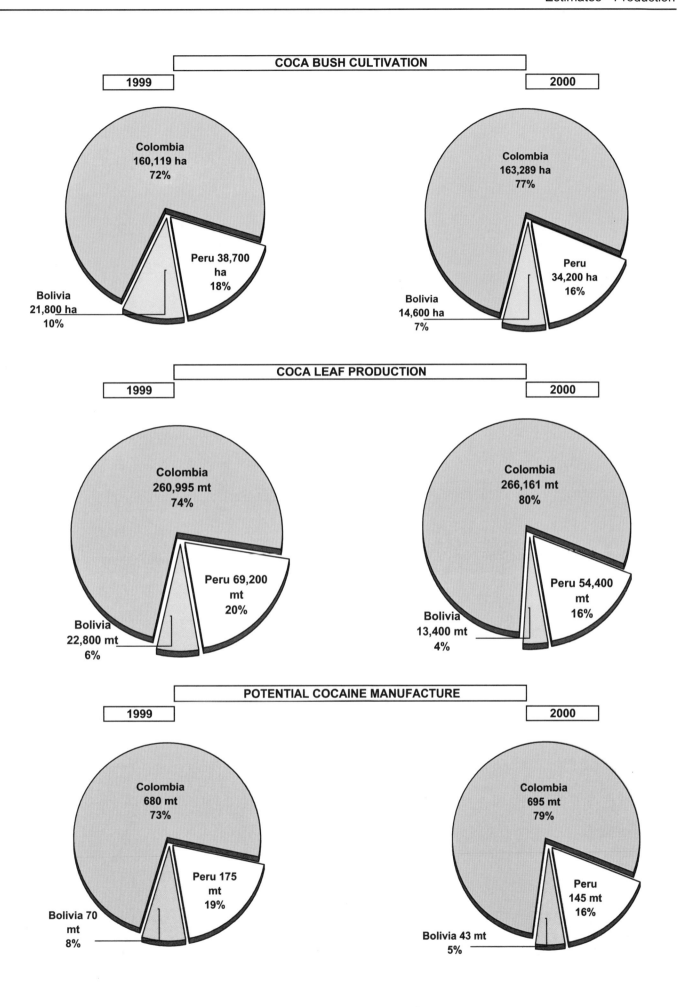

COCA BUSH CULTIVATION

1999 — 2000

Colombia 160,119 ha 72%
Peru 38,700 ha 18%
Bolivia 21,800 ha 10%

Colombia 163,289 ha 77%
Peru 34,200 ha 16%
Bolivia 14,600 ha 7%

COCA LEAF PRODUCTION

1999 — 2000

Colombia 260,995 mt 74%
Peru 69,200 mt 20%
Bolivia 22,800 mt 6%

Colombia 266,161 mt 80%
Peru 54,400 mt 16%
Bolivia 13,400 mt 4%

POTENTIAL COCAINE MANUFACTURE

1999 — 2000

Colombia 680 mt 73%
Peru 175 mt 19%
Bolivia 70 mt 8%

Colombia 695 mt 79%
Peru 145 mt 16%
Bolivia 43 mt 5%

ERADICATION REPORTED, 1991-2000
(in hectares)

	1991	1992	1993	1994	1995	1996	1997	1998	1999	2000
Opium poppy										
Afghanistan									400	121
Colombia	1,156	12,864	9,400	5,314	5,074	7,412	7,333	3,077	8,434	9,279
Mexico	9,342	11,222	13,015	10,959	15,389	14,671	17,732	17,449	15,461	15,717
Myanmar	873	4,228	160	1,041	3,310	1,938	3,093	3,172	9,824	1,643
Pakistan	440	977	856	463	-	867	654	2,194	1,197	1,704
Thailand	3,372	2,148	1,706	1,313	580	886	1,053	716	808	757
Vietnam	-	3,243	-	672	477	1,142	340	439	-	426
Coca bush										
Bolivia	5,486	5,149	2,400	1,100	5,493	7,512	7,000	11,620	15,353	7,653
Colombia	459	944	946	4,904	25,402	23,025	44,123	65,755	44,195	61,573
Peru	-	5,150	-	240	-	7,512	3,462	17,800	13,800	6,200
Cannabis plant										
Mexico	12,702	16,802	16,645	14,207	21,573	22,769	23,576	23,928	33,569	31,046

FARMGATE PRICES, 1990-2000

(in constant 2000 US$, per kilogram)

	1990	1991	1992	1993	1994	1995	1996	1997	1998	1999	2000
OPIUM											
Afghanistan	35	35	35	36	36	36	50	70	62	58	30
Pakistan	45	78	77	67	69	65	120	109	125	83	110
Lao, PDR	106	139	127	90	143	243	265	157	63	63	46
Myanmar	242	165	116	119	173	269	208	124	64	128	142
Colombia	2,360	2,264	1,369	591	587	540	585	432	370	198	340
COCA LEAF											
Bolivia	1.21	1.16	1.00	1.39	1.19	1.45	1.13	1.51	1.46	3.03	5.61
Colombia	n/a	n/a	n/a	n/a	n/a	n/a	n/a	n/a	n/a	n/a	n/a
Peru	0.92	1.69	2.80	2.14	2.64	1.24	0.66	0.77	1.41	2.10	2.70
COCA BASE											
Bolivia	727	526	509	827	771	914	583	683	757	1,333	1,850
Colombia	638	642	594	857	1,389	591	807	779	757	938	880
Peru	472	714	806	684	717	308	318	253	334	356	546

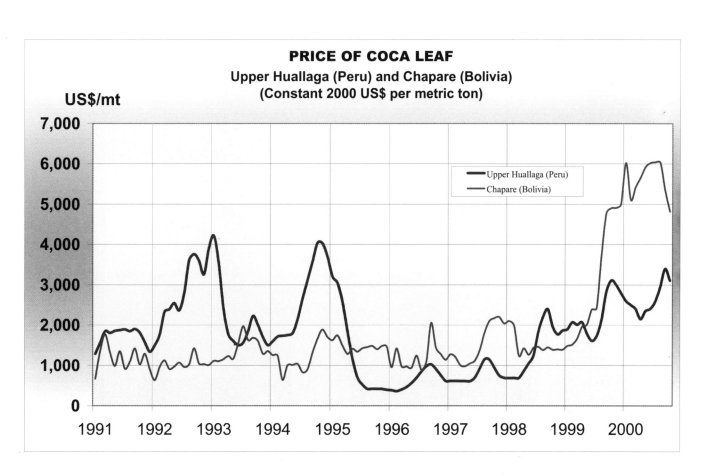

PRICE OF COCA LEAF
Upper Huallaga (Peru) and Chapare (Bolivia)
(Constant 2000 US$ per metric ton)

POTENTIAL VALUE OF 2000 FARMGATE PRODUCTION

(UNDCP estimates)

	Farmgate price US$ per kg	Production metric tons	Potential value millions of US$
OPIUM			
Myanmar	232	1,087	252
Afghanistan	28	3,276	91
Lao, PDR	46	167	8
Other Asia [1]		52	23
Colombia	340	88	30
Mexico [2]		21	4
Total opium		4,691	408
COCA BASE			
Colombia [3]	880	695	612
Peru	546	145	79
Bolivia	1,850	43	80
Total coca base		883	771
COMBINED POTENTIAL VALUE			1,179

[1] Including Pakistan, Thailand, Vietnam and other Asian countries; price is based on estimated average for these countries

[2] Farmgate price not available; value based on price in Colombia

[3] Based on production estimates Colombia (I)

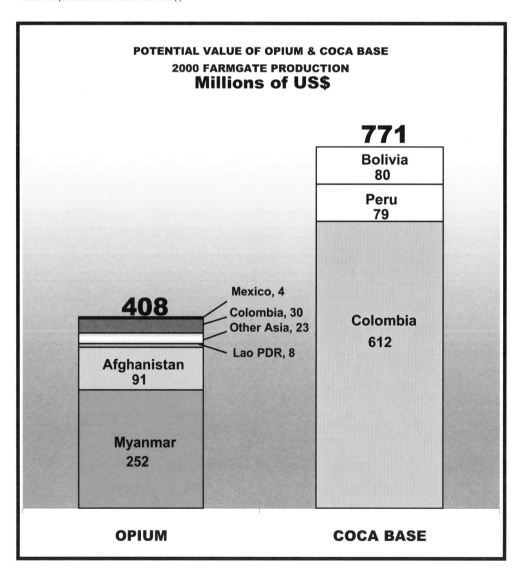

POTENTIAL VALUE OF OPIUM & COCA BASE
2000 FARMGATE PRODUCTION
Millions of US$

MANUFACTURE
SEIZURES OF ILLICIT LABORATORIES
REPORTED FOR 1998 - 1999
BY DRUG GROUP

Remark: For convenience, an attempt was made to group the reported estimates by drug categories. however, due to inconsistencies and gaps in the reporting, no overall analysis of the data set was performed. Numbers are presented as reported to UNDCP and should be interpreted with caution.

Source: Annual Report Questionnaire if not otherwise indicated

Country or Territory	Year	Name of drug seized	Number of laboratories (and quantity of drug) seized	Source
		OPIATE GROUP		
Africa				
East Africa				
Uganda	1998	Heroin	1 Lab.(1.302 kg)	ICPO
Subtotal East Africa			1 Lab.(1.302 kg)	
North Africa				
Algeria	1998	Heroin	1 Lab.(0.092 kg)	ICPO
Egypt	1999	Codeine	1 Lab.(0.030 lt.)	
Subtotal North Africa			2 Lab.(0.092 kg)(0.030 lt.)	
Southern Africa				
Zimbabwe	1998	Heroin	1 Lab.(0.740 kg)	ICPO
Subtotal Southern Africa			1 Lab.(0.740 kg)	
Total Africa			4 Lab.(2.134 kg)(0.030 lt.)	
Americas				
North America				
Canada	1998	Codeine and butalbital	81 Lab.(21456 u.)	
	1998	Codeine	337 Lab.(0.037 kg)(54.600 lt.)(836191 u.)	
	1998	Morphine	191 Lab.(0.036 kg)(27.580 lt.)(51139 u.)	
Mexico	1998	Heroin	1 Lab.(0.064 kg)	
	1999	Heroin	4 Lab.(6.817 kg)	
United States	1998	Heroin	1 Lab.	ICPO
Subtotal North America			615 Lab.(6.954 kg)(82.180 lt.)(908786 u.)	
South America				
Colombia	1998	Heroin and morphine	10 Lab.	INCSR
	1999	Heroin	10 Lab.	
Peru	1999	Opium	1 Lab.	
Subtotal South America			21 Lab.	
Total Americas			636 Lab.(6.954 kg)(82.180 lt.)(908786 u.)	
Asia				
Central Asia and Transcaucasian countries				
Georgia	1998	Heroin	1 Lab.(0.915 kg)	ICPO

Country or Territory	Year	Name of drug seized	Number of laboratories (and quantity of drug) seized	Source
Subtotal Central Asia and Transcaucasian countries			1 Lab.(0.915 kg)	
East and South-East Asia				
China (Hong Kong SAR)	1998	Heroin	11 Lab.	ICPO
	1999	Heroin	15 Lab.(73.850 kg)	
Malaysia	1998	Heroin no.3	5 Lab.(46.000 kg)	
Myanmar	1998	Heroin	21 Lab.(1363.270 kg)(2159.340 lt.)	
	1999	Opium	(205.250 kg)	
	1999	Morphine	(26.500 kg)	
	1999	Heroin	13 Lab.(42.290 kg)	
Thailand	1998	Heroin	1 Lab.(0.410 kg)	
Subtotal East and South-East Asia			66 Lab.(1757.570 kg)(2159.340 lt.)	
South Asia				
India	1998	Morphine	5 Lab.(3.000 kg)	
	1998	Heroin	4 Lab.(3.000 kg)	
	1999	Morphine		
	1999	Heroin	3 Lab.(36.000 kg)	
Subtotal South Asia			12 Lab.(42.000 kg)	
Total Asia			79 Lab.(1800.485 kg)(2159.340 lt.)	
Europe				
Eastern Europe				
Belarus	1998	Opium liquid	1 Lab.	
	1999	Opium liquid		
Lithuania	1998	Opium liquid	22 Lab.(29.000 lt.)	
	1999	Opium liquid	24 Lab.(75.086 lt.)	
Poland	1998	Polish heroin	210 Lab.(395.000 lt.)	
	1999	Polish heroin	170 Lab.(389.000 lt.)	
Republic of Moldova	1998	Opium liquid	17 Lab.(12.380 kg)	
	1999	Opium	69 Lab.	ICPO
Russian Federation	1999	Opium	341 Lab.	ICPO
	1999	Morphine	8 Lab.	ICPO
Ukraine	1998	Opium extract	1 Lab.(122.000 kg)	
	1999	Opium poppies	38 Lab.	ICPO
	1999	Opium	1 Lab.	ICPO
Subtotal Eastern Europe			902 Lab.(134.380 kg)(888.086 lt.)	
Western Europe				
France	1999	Heroin	1 Lab.(0.040 kg)	
Italy	1999	Morphine	1 Lab.	ICPO
Turkey	1998	Heroin	8 Lab.(223.666 kg)	
Subtotal Western Europe			10 Lab.(223.706 kg)	
Total Europe			912 Lab.(358.086 kg)(888.086 lt.)	
Opiate group			1631 Lab.(2167.659 kg)(3129.636 lt.)(908786 u.)	

COCA GROUP

Country or Territory	Year	Name of drug seized	Number of laboratories (and quantity of drug) seized	Source
Africa				
Southern Africa				
South Africa	1998	Cocaine (crack)	3 Lab.(6.000 kg)	
Subtotal Southern Africa			3 Lab.(6.000 kg)	
Total Africa			3 Lab.(6.000 kg)	
Americas				
Caribbean				
Dominica	1998	Cocaine	1 Lab.(29.615 kg)	ICPO
Subtotal Caribbean			1 Lab.(29.615 kg)	
Central America				
Costa Rica	1999	Cocaine (crack)		
Guatemala	1998	Cocaine	1 Lab.(63 u.)	
	1998	Cocaine (crack)	1 Lab.(276 u.)	
Subtotal Central America			2 Lab.(339 u.)	
North America				
United States	1998	Cocaine	2 Lab.	ICPO
	1999	Cocaine	1 Lab.	CICAD
Subtotal North America			3 Lab.	
South America				
Bolivia	1998	Cocaine base	1205 Lab.	INCSR
	1998	Cocaine	1 Lab.	INCSR
	1999	Cocaine base	925 Lab.(6904782.000 kg)	
	1999	Cocaine	12 Lab.(802226.000 kg)	
Brazil	1998	Cocaine	1 Lab.(229.000 kg)	
	1998	Cocaine (crack)	1 Lab.(181.000 kg)	
	1999	Cocaine	3 Lab.(80.000 kg)	
Colombia	1998	Cocaine base and cocaine	311 Lab.	INCSR
	1999	Cocaine	303 Lab.(985120.000 kg)	
Ecuador	1998	Cocaine	2 Lab.	INCSR
Peru	1998	Cocaine base and cocaine	14 Lab.	
	1999	Coca paste		
	1999	Cocaine		
Subtotal South America			2778 Lab.(8692618.000 kg)	
Total Americas			2784 Lab.(8692647.615 kg)(339 u.)	
Asia				
East and South-East Asia				
Indonesia	1998	Cocaine	1 Lab.(3.500 kg)	ICPO
Subtotal East and South-East Asia			1 Lab.(3.500 kg)	
Total Asia			1 Lab.(3.500 kg)	
Europe				
Western Europe				
Germany	1999	Cocaine (crack)	1 Lab.	
Italy	1998	Cocaine	1 Lab.(15.960 kg)	

Country or Territory	Year	Name of drug seized	Number of laboratories (and quantity of drug) seized	Source
Italy	1999	Coca paste	1 Lab.	ICPO
Spain	1998	Cocaine	5 Lab.(939.318 kg)	
	1999	Cocaine	6 Lab.(150.025 kg)	
Turkey	1999	Heroin	6 Lab.(930635.000 kg)	
Subtotal Western Europe			20 Lab.(931740.303 kg)	
Total Europe			20 Lab.(931740.303 kg)	
Coca group			2808 Lab.(9624397.418 kg)(339 u.)	

CANNABIS GROUP

Americas

Caribbean

Jamaica	1999	Cannabis oil	1 Lab.	ICPO
Subtotal Caribbean			1 Lab.	

Central America

Guatemala	1998	Cannabis herb	1 Lab.(51 u.)	
Subtotal Central America			1 Lab.(51 u.)	

North America

Canada	1998	Cannabis liquid	4 Lab.(17.000 kg)	
	1998	Cannabis resin	1 Lab.	CICAD
	1999	Cannabis	6 Lab.	
Subtotal North America			11 Lab.(17.000 kg)	
Total Americas			13 Lab.(17.000 kg)(51 u.)	

Asia

Central Asia and Transcaucasian countries

Kazakhstan	1999	Herbal cannabis		
Subtotal Central Asia and Transcaucasian countries				

South Asia

Nepal	1999	Cannabis herb		
	1999	Cannabis resin		
Subtotal South Asia				
Total Asia				
Cannabis group			13 Lab.(17.000 kg)(51 u.)	

AMPHETAMINE GROUP

Americas

North America

United States	1998	Amfetamine	5 Lab.	
	1999	Amfetamine	26 Lab.	
Subtotal North America			31 Lab.	
Total Americas			31 Lab.	

Asia

East and South-East Asia

Indonesia	1999	Amfetamine	1 Lab.	ICPO
Subtotal East and South-East Asia			1 Lab.	

Country or Territory	Year	Name of drug seized	Number of laboratories (and quantity of drug) seized	Source
Total Asia			1 Lab.	
Europe				
Eastern Europe				
Hungary	1998	Amfetamine	1 Lab.(3000 u.)	
Latvia	1998	Amfetamine	1 Lab.(1.700 lt.)	
Lithuania	1999	Amfetamine	1 Lab.	ICPO
Poland	1998	Amfetamine	4 Lab.(2.500 kg)	
	1999	Amfetamine	8 Lab.(5.000 kg)	
Subtotal Eastern Europe			15 Lab.(7.500 kg)(1.700 lt.)(3000 u.)	
Western Europe				
Denmark	1998	Amfetamine (with some metamfetamine)	1 Lab.(0.030 kg)	
	1999	Amfetamine	1 Lab.(17.500 kg)	
Germany	1998	Amfetamine (with some metamfetamine)	10 Lab.(0.714 kg)	
	1999	Amfetamine (with some metamfetamine)	4 Lab.(60.000 kg)(2000 u.)	
Netherlands	1999	Amfetamine	6 Lab.	
Spain	1998	Amfetamine	1 Lab.(10.000 kg)	
	1999	Amfetamine	3 Lab.(2.774 kg)	
Sweden	1998	Amfetamine	1 Lab.	
United Kingdom	1998	Amfetamine	6 Lab.(1000.000 kg)	
	1999	Amfetamine	10 Lab.(10000.000 kg)	
Subtotal Western Europe			43 Lab.(11091.018 kg)(2000 u.)	
Total Europe			58 Lab.(11098.518 kg)(1.700 lt.)(5000 u.)	
Oceania				
Oceania				
Australia	1998	Amfetamine	95 Lab.	Govt
Subtotal Oceania			95 Lab.	
Total Oceania			95 Lab.	
Amphetamine group			185 Lab.(11098.518 kg)(1.700 lt.)(5000 u.)	

COMBINED AMPHETAMINE, METHAMPHETAMINE AND ECSTASY GROUP

Country or Territory	Year	Name of drug seized	Number of laboratories (and quantity of drug) seized	Source
Asia				
East and South-East Asia				
Malaysia	1999	Metamfetamine and amfetamine	5 Lab.(0.440 kg)	
Subtotal East and South-East Asia			5 Lab.(0.440 kg)	
Total Asia			5 Lab.(0.440 kg)	
Europe				
Western Europe				
Netherlands	1999	ATS and ecstasy	5 Lab.	
Subtotal Western Europe			5 Lab.	

Country or Territory	Year	Name of drug seized	Number of laboratories (and quantity of drug) seized	Source
Total Europe			5 Lab.	
Combined amphetamine, methamphetamine and ecstasy group			10 Lab.(0.440 kg)	

METHAMPHETAMINE GROUP

Africa

<u>North Africa</u>

Egypt	1998	Metamfetamine (Maxiton Forte)	1 Lab.(15.347 lt.)	
	1999	Metamfetamine (Maxiton Forte)	1 Lab.(19.023 lt.)	
Subtotal North Africa			2 Lab.(34.370 lt.)	

<u>Southern Africa</u>

South Africa	1998	Metamfetamine	1 Lab.	
Subtotal Southern Africa			1 Lab.	
Total Africa			3 Lab.(34.370 lt.)	

Americas

<u>North America</u>

Canada	1998	Metamfetamine	2 Lab.	
	1999	Metamfetamine	12 Lab.	
Mexico	1998	Metamfetamine	6 Lab.(2.600 kg)	
	1999	Metamfetamine	13 Lab.	
United States	1998	Metamfetamine	1604 Lab.	
	1999	Metamfetamine	6894 Lab.	
Subtotal North America			8531 Lab.(145.508 kg)	
Total Americas			8531 Lab.(145.508 kg)	

Asia

<u>East and South-East Asia</u>

China	1999	Mefamfetamine	40 Lab.	ICPO
Korea (Republic of)	1999	Metamfetamine	2 Lab.(3.160 kg)	
Philippines	1999	Metamfetamine	3 Lab.(2.000 kg)	
Thailand	1998	Metamfetamine	12 Lab.(22.100 kg)(198924 u.)	
	1999	Mefamfetamine	16 Lab.	ICPO
Subtotal East and South-East Asia			73 Lab.(27.260 kg)(198924 u.)	

<u>Near and Middle East /South-West Asia</u>

Israel	1998	Metamfetamine	1 Lab.	
Subtotal Near and Middle East /South-West Asia			1 Lab.	
Total Asia			74 Lab.(27.260 kg)(198924 u.)	

Europe

<u>Eastern Europe</u>

Czech Republic	1998	Metamfetamine (pervitin)	19 Lab.(0.200 kg)	
	1999	Metamfetamine (pervitin)	27 Lab.(5.000 kg)	
Slovakia	1999	Metamfetamine	2 Lab.(2.000 kg)	
Ukraine	1998	Metamfetamine (pervitin)	7 Lab.(0.015 kg)	
Subtotal Eastern Europe			55 Lab.(7.215 kg)	

Country or Territory	Year	Name of drug seized	Number of laboratories (and quantity of drug) seized	Source
Total Europe			55 Lab.(7.215 kg)	

Oceania

<u>Oceania</u>

New Zealand	1998	Metamfetamine	1 Lab.	
	1999	Metamfetamine	6 Lab.	
Subtotal Oceania			7 Lab.	
Total Oceania			7 Lab.	
Methamphetamine group			8670 Lab.(179.983 kg)(34.370 lt.)(198924 u.)	

OTHER SYNTHETIC STIMULANTS

Americas

<u>North America</u>

Canada	1998	Other amfetamine analogues	1 Lab.	ICPO
	1999	Other Amphetamine Analogues (ex.MDA)	2 Lab.	ICPO
United States	1998	Methcathinone	6 Lab.	
	1999	Methcathinone	12 Lab.	
Subtotal North America			21 Lab.	
Total Americas			21 Lab.	

Asia

<u>Central Asia and Transcaucasian countries</u>

Kyrgyzstan	1999	Methcathinone (Ephedron)	2 Lab.(652.000 kg)	
Subtotal Central Asia and Transcaucasian countries			2 Lab.(652.000 kg)	
Total Asia			2 Lab.(652.000 kg)	

Europe

<u>Eastern Europe</u>

Bulgaria	1999	Methadone	1 Lab.(1.500 kg)	
Lithuania	1998	Methcathinone (Ephedron)	25 Lab.(0.812 lt.)	
	1999	Methcathinone (Ephedron)	1 Lab.	
Slovenia	1998	Fenetylline (Captagon)	1 Lab.(250 u.)	ICPO
	1999	Fenetylline (Captagon)	1 Lab.(345 u.)	
Ukraine	1999	Other Amphetamine Analogues (ex.MDA)	46 Lab.	ICPO
Subtotal Eastern Europe			75 Lab.(1.500 kg)(0.812 lt.)(595 u.)	

<u>Western Europe</u>

France	1998	Stimulants	1 Lab.(4.000 kg)	ICPO
Netherlands	1998	Synthetic Drugs	35 Lab.	
Turkey	1999	Fenetylline (Captagon)	1 Lab.(60000 u.)	
Subtotal Western Europe			37 Lab.(4.000 kg)(60000 u.)	
Total Europe			112 Lab.(5.500 kg)(0.812 lt.)(60595 u.)	
Other synthetic stimulants			135 Lab.(657.500 kg)(0.812 lt.)(60595 u.)	

DEPRESSANT GROUP

Africa

Country or Territory	Year	Name of drug seized	Number of laboratories (and quantity of drug) seized	Source
North Africa				
Algeria	1998	Barbiturate	1 Lab.(12815 u.)	ICPO
	1998	Benzodiazepam	1 Lab.(59396 u.)	ICPO
Subtotal North Africa			2 Lab.(72211 u.)	
Southern Africa				
South Africa	1998	Methaqualone	3 Lab.(18.000 kg)	
	1998	GHB	1 Lab.(53.000 lt.)	
Subtotal Southern Africa			4 Lab.(18.000 kg)(53.000 lt.)	
Total Africa			6 Lab.(18.000 kg)(53.000 lt.)(72211 u.)	
Asia				
South Asia				
India	1998	Methaqualone	2 Lab.(228.000 kg)	
Subtotal South Asia			2 Lab.(228.000 kg)	
Total Asia			2 Lab.(228.000 kg)	
Depressant group			8 Lab.(246.000 kg)(53.000 lt.)(72211 u.)	

HALLUCINOGEN GROUP

Americas				
North America				
Canada	1998	Phencyclidine (PCP)	2 Lab.	
	1998	LSD	1 Lab.	
	1999	Ketamine	1 Lab.	
United States	1998	Phencyclidine (PCP)	3 Lab.	
	1998	LSD	1 Lab.	
	1999	Phenecyclidine	1 Lab.	
	1999	LSD	1 Lab.	
Subtotal North America			10 Lab.	
Total Americas			10 Lab.	
Hallucinogen group			10 Lab.	

ECSTASY GROUP

Americas				
North America				
Canada	1998	MDA	1 Lab.	
	1998	MDMA (Ecstasy)	2 Lab.	
	1999	MDMA (Ecstasy)	8 Lab.	
United States	1998	MDMA (Ecstasy)	4 Lab.	
	1998	MDA	3 Lab.	
	1999	MDMA (Ecstasy)	20 Lab.	
Subtotal North America			38 Lab.	
Total Americas			38 Lab.	
Asia				
East and South-East Asia				
Indonesia	1999	MDMA/MDA	1 Lab.(0.848 kg)	

Country or Territory	Year	Name of drug seized	Number of laboratories (and quantity of drug) seized	Source
Malaysia	1999	MDMA (Ecstasy)	(2882 u.)	
Thailand	1999	MDMA (Ecstasy)	1 Lab.	HNLP
Subtotal East and South-East Asia			2 Lab.(0.848 kg)(2882 u.)	
Total Asia			2 Lab.(0.848 kg)(2882 u.)	
Europe				
Eastern Europe				
Ukraine	1998	MDMA (Ecstasy)	1 Lab.(6204 u.)	
Subtotal Eastern Europe			1 Lab.(6204 u.)	
Western Europe				
Belgium	1998	MDMA (Ecstasy)	2 Lab.	
	1999	MDMA (Ecstasy)	4 Lab.	
Germany	1998	MDMA	2 Lab.	
	1999	MDMA	1 Lab.	
Netherlands	1999	MDMA (Ecstasy)	24 Lab.	
Spain	1998	MDMA (Ecstasy)	1 Lab.(700 u.)	
United Kingdom	1999	MDMA (Ecstasy)	1 Lab.	
Subtotal Western Europe			35 Lab.(700 u.)	
Total Europe			36 Lab.(6904 u.)	
Ecstasy group			76 Lab.(0.848 kg)(9786 u.)	
		OTHER		
Africa				
North Africa				
Egypt	1999	Psychotropic substances	1 Lab.	
Subtotal North Africa			1 Lab.	
Total Africa			1 Lab.	
Asia				
East and South-East Asia				
Indonesia	1998	Psychotropic substances	3 Lab.	
Subtotal East and South-East Asia			3 Lab.	
Total Asia			3 Lab.	
Europe				
Eastern Europe				
Russian Federation	1998	Miscellaneous	1117 Lab.	Govt
Subtotal Eastern Europe			1117 Lab.	
Western Europe				
Belgium	1998	Psychotropic substances and narcotic drugs	26 Lab.	
Germany	1999	Phenethylamines	1 Lab.	
Spain	1998	Psychotropic substances	1 Lab.	
United Kingdom	1998	Phenethylamines	2 Lab.(1.000 kg)	

Country or Territory	Year	Name of drug seized	Number of laboratories (and quantity of drug) seized	Source
Subtotal Western Europe			30 Lab.(1.000 kg)	
Total Europe			1147 Lab.(1.000 kg)	
Other			1151 Lab.(1.000 kg)	
		UNSPECIFIED		
Americas				
South America				
Bolivia	1999	Unspecified	2087 Lab.	CICAD
Colombia	1999	Unspecified	316 Lab.	Govt
Peru	1999	Unspecified	51 Lab.	CICAD
Subtotal South America			2454 Lab.	
Total Americas			2454 Lab.	
Europe				
Western Europe				
Netherlands	1999	Unspecified	1 Lab.	
Subtotal Western Europe			1 Lab.	
Total Europe			1 Lab.	
Unspecified			2455 Lab.	

TRAFFICKING

OVERVIEW

Regional distribution

Based on 1999 seizure data[c], about a third of all drugs were seized in North America, a quarter in western Europe, a fifth in Asia and a tenth in South America. Africa accounted for six percent.

Drug ranking

Cannabis ranked first, both in terms of number of seizure cases and amounts seized. Large scale seizure cases of cocaine - notably when it is trafficked by sea - are more likely than of heroin or amphetamine-type stimulants. There were thirty-seven individual seizure cases of more than a metric ton of cocaine in 1999, but only two such cases for heroin and two for methamphetamine. As a result, during that year, the average amount per seizure case was: 1.9 kg for cocaine, 0.12 kg for heroin (less then a tenth) and only 0.06 kg for synthetic stimulants (about 3%). Local production and distribution of amphetamines reduces transport requirements and the possibilities of seizing the drugs while in transit.

One-year trend

The most significant increases in seizures in 1999 were reported for amphetamine-type stimulants (ATS), reflecting increasing levels of trafficking and of law enforcement activities in East and South-East Asia. As a consequence, the overall quantity of ATS seized more than doubled in 1999. Seizures of cannabis herb rose by a third on a year ear-

lier. Seizures of opiates, expressed in heroin equivalents, grew by 14%, largely reflecting the 1999 bumper harvest in Afghanistan. By contrast, global seizures of cocaine fell in 1999 by 6% on a year earlier, reflecting overall falling levels of coca leaf production and cocaine manufacture in the Andean region.

Ten-year trend

Similarly, over the 1990-99 period, the most significant rises in seizures were reported for synthetic drugs, notably the amphetamine-type stimulants (30% p.a. on average) and for depressants (23% p.a.). The latter are still mainly diverted from licit sources. The proportion of ATS in global seizure cases tripled from 1990 to 1999. Growth rates for the plant-based drugs were less significant (6% p.a. for marijuana, 5% p.a. for heroin, 4% p.a. for hashish and 3% p.a. for cocaine). As a consequence, the proportions of both cannabis and cocaine in global seizures declined. The proportions of opiates rose between 1990 and 1999, although they tended to remain stable during the second half of the 1990s. Due to increasing law enforcement efforts in countries bordering Afghanistan (notably in Iran and the Central Asian Republics), growth in opium and morphine seizures exceeded growth in heroin seizures. As a result of reduced seizures in the Andean countries, quantities of coca leaf seized declined over the 1990-99 period. A similar trend recorded for methaqualone is attributed to declining seizures in Asia (notably India) and in the countries of southern Africa.

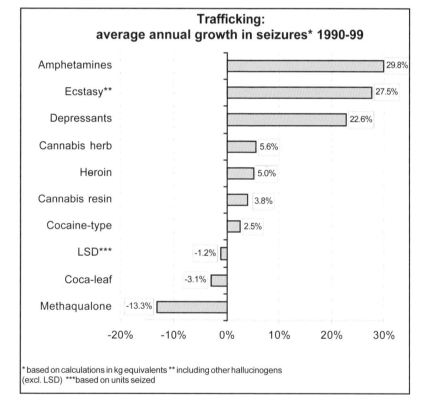

Trafficking:
average annual growth in seizures* 1990-99

Amphetamines	29.8%
Ecstasy**	27.5%
Depressants	22.6%
Cannabis herb	5.6%
Heroin	5.0%
Cannabis resin	3.8%
Cocaine-type	2.5%
LSD***	-1.2%
Coca-leaf	-3.1%
Methaqualone	-13.3%

*based on calculations in kg equivalents ** including other hallucinogens (excl. LSD) ***based on units seized

---

c) Seizure data converted into "units", see below for details.

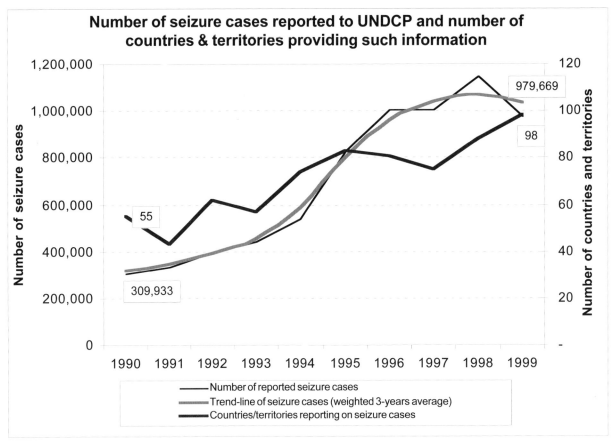

Number of seizure cases reported to UNDCP and number of countries & territories providing such information

Source: UNDCP, Annual Reports Questionnaire // DELTA

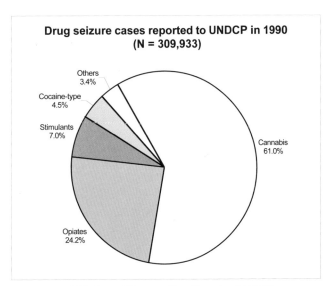

Drug seizure cases reported to UNDCP in 1990 (N = 309,933)

Source: UNDCP, Annual Reports Questionnaire // DELTA

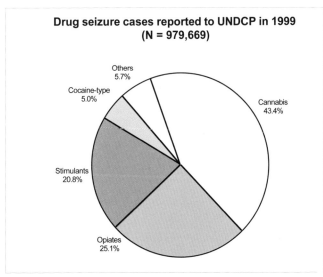

Drug seizure cases reported to UNDCP in 1999 (N = 979,669)

Source: UNDCP, Annual Reports Questionnaire // DELTA

Trafficking trends in units

Once amounts seized are transformed into 'standard units'[d] - an attempt to improve comparability - calculations suggest that global drug seizures were equivalent to some 23 billion units in 1999 (excl. seizures of plant seeds) up from 20 billion units in 1998 and 14 billion units in 1990. In per capita terms, amounts seized increased from about 2.5 units per inhabitant in 1990 to 4 in 1999. Such numbers are, of course, only very approximate and must therefore be treated with caution.

Almost two thirds of seizures made globally in 1999 and expressed in unit equivalents related to cannabis, 18% to cocaine, 10% to opiates and 8% to amphetamine-type stimulants (ATS). Those four drug categories thus accounted for 99% of global seizures.

Drug seizures in 1999, expressed in million units*, and in units per capita		Seizures in million units	in per cent of global	units seized per inhabitant
Americas	North America	7,328	32.0%	18.1
	Caribbean	317	1.4%	8.6
	South America	2,399	10.5%	7.0
	Central America	193	0.8%	5.4
Americas Total		10,237	45.8%	14.1
Europe	West Europe	6,401	28.0%	14.1
	East Europe	349	1.5%	1.0
Europe Total		6,750	29.5%	8.5
Oceania	Oceania	63	0.3%	2.2
Asia	Near and Middle East / South-West Asia	2,279	10.0%	6.7
	Central Asia and Transcaucasian countries	286	1.2%	4.0
	East and Southeast Asia	1,670	7.3%	0.8
	South Asia	169	0.7%	0.1
Asia Total		4,404	19.3%	1.2
Africa	Southern Africa	753	3.3%	6.9
	North Africa	501	2.2%	2.9
	West and Central Africa	118	0.5%	0.4
	East Africa	47	0.2%	0.3
	Africa Total	1,419	6.3%	1.9
Grand Total		22,874	100.0%	3.8

d) The calculation is based on reported seizures in unit terms (e.g. seizures of tablets) plus seizures in weight terms for which the following transformation ratios have been applied: 1 'unit' (dose) of cocaine = 100 mg; 1 unit of heroin or morphine = 100 mg; 1 unit of amphetamine or methamphetamine = 30 mg; 1 unit of MDMA (ecstasy), MDA, MDME etc. = 100 mg; 1 unit of cannabis herb = 500 mg; 1 unit of cannabis resin = 135 mg; 1 unit of LSD = 0.05 mg; 1 unit of methaqualone = 250 mg. The units are assumed to reflect a typical street dose at street purity.

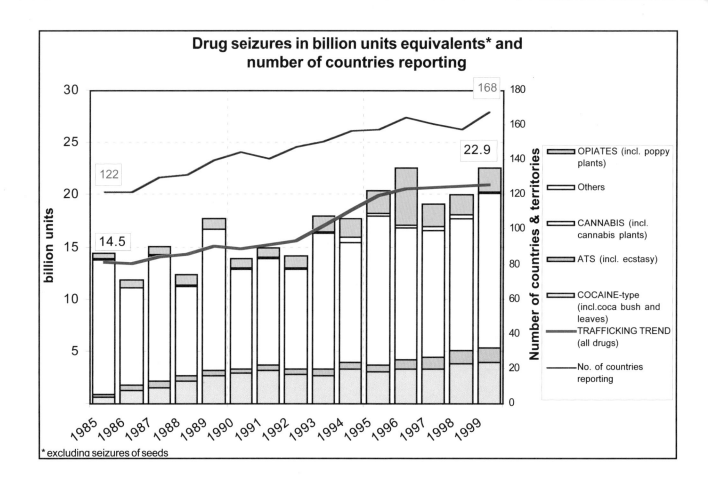

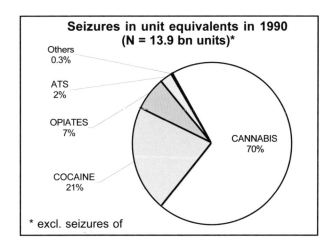

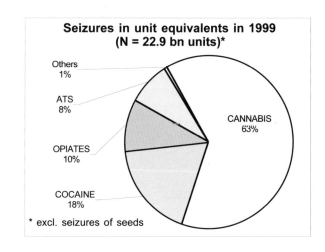

TRENDS IN WORLD SEIZURES - 1989-1999

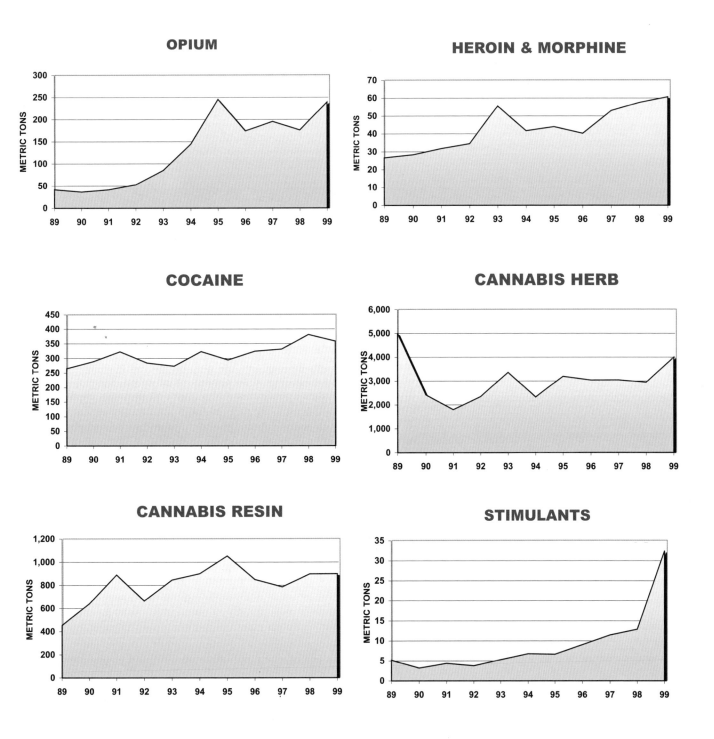

TRAFFICKING IN HEROIN AND MORPHINE

Combined global heroin and morphine seizures amounted to 61 tonnes in 1999. Trafficking in those two substances continues to be concentrated in Asia (71% of all seizures in 1999), reflecting both large-scale production in that region and increasing levels of consumption along transit routes. Heroin is primarily trafficked overland and seized on trucks. The most lucrative destination for opiates produced in Asia - notably in South-West Asia - is still western Europe. Even though trafficking and consumption in that region have both stagnated during the last few years, increasing levels of opiates appear to be smuggled and consumed along the main trafficking routes to western Europe. Two opposing trends characterized trafficking in Asia during 1999: an increase in and around South-West Asia and a decline in and around South-Eeast Asia.

The largest seizures of opiates in recent years were made, in the close vicinity of Afghanistan, by the Islamic Republic of Iran which accounted for 47% of the world's heroin and morphine seizures in 1999 (up from 44% in 1998 and 22% in 1990). Those levels reflect enforcement efforts in that country as well as increasing levels of opium production in Afghanistan during the 1990s,

and during 1999 in particular. Effects of that record year on trafficking continued to be felt in 2000, despite an almost 30% decline in Afghanistan's opium production for that year. Most of the opiates are seized in the Iranian provinces of Khorasan, neighbouring Afghanistan and Turkmenistan, and of Sistan - Baluchistan, bordering Pakistan.

Seizure data also provide some interesting insights into heroin manufacture patterns. In 1999, morphine represented 79% of the heroin/morphine seizures in Iran (down from 89% a year earlier), 22% in Turkey, and almost nothing in all the countries further along the Balkan route, as well as among EU and EFTA countries. This suggests that (i) manufacture of heroin out of morphine is increasing in Afghanistan and/or within the region (in the combined seizures of Iran, Pakistan and the countries of Central Asia, heroin accounted for 25% of heroin/morphine seizures in 1998 and 35% in 1999); (ii) while opiates mainly cross Iran in morphine form, they have been transformed into heroin when they leave Turkey.

The strongest increases in seizures over the last few years were reported by the Central Asian countries, signalling a diversification of trafficking routes through, and increased enforcement efforts in, that region. While

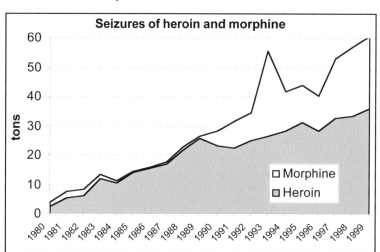

Source: UNDCP, Annual Reports Questionnaire / DELTA

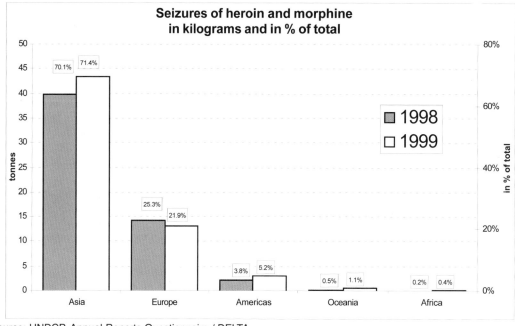

Source: UNDCP, Annual Reports Questionnaire / DELTA

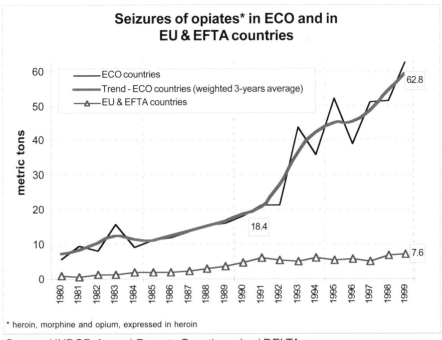

Seizures of opiates* in ECO and in EU & EFTA countries

metric tons

- ECO countries
- Trend - ECO countries (weighted 3-years average)
- EU & EFTA countries

62.8

18.4

7.6

1980 1981 1982 1983 1984 1985 1986 1987 1988 1989 1990 1991 1992 1993 1994 1995 1996 1997 1998 1999

* heroin, morphine and opium, expressed in heroin

Source: UNDCP, Annual Reports Questionnaire / DELTA

seizures of opiates (heroin, morphine and opium expressed in heroin equivalents) rose in Iran by 18% per year over the 1995-99 period, they increased more than four times faster in the countries of Central Asia (60% per year). In Tajikistan alone, heroin seizures rose exponentially, from 60 kg in 1997, to 271 kg in 1998, to 709 kg in 1999 and to 1.9 tons in 2000. The parallel decline in seizures of heroin and morphine in Turkey and in some of the East European countries along the Balkan route in 1999 are in line with this diversification of trafficking routes and the stronger role played by countries of Central Asia and of other CIS states as transit zones.

The bulk of opiate seizures take place in the immediate vicinity of Afghanistan, i.e. Iran, Pakistan, Turkey and in the countries of Central Asia. Expressed in heroin equivalents, the ECO countries seized 51 tons per year on average over the period 1995-99 (63 tons in 1999), the equivalent of 17.5 % of Afghanistan's annual opium har-

vest (293 tons per year, expressed in heroin equivalents over the same period). In comparison, the average of 6 tons of opiates seized annually (mostly heroin) in western Europe (EU and EFTA countries) corresponded to 2% of Afghanistan's annual harvest over the 1995-99 period expressed in heroin equivalents. Improved law enforcement efforts and thus rapidly growing seizures - seizures in the ECO countries more than tripled over the 1990-99 period - seem to have contributed to the stagnation of heroin trafficking and use in the West European markets (together with increased demand reduction efforts within Europe) in the 1990s despite growing levels of production in Afghanistan and the bumper harvests in 1999. While the aggregate amounts seized hardly changed in western Europe in 1999, they increased in Iran, Pakistan, Uzbekistan, Tajikistan, Kazakhstan and Kyrgyzstan as well as - in line with the supply push caused by Afghanistan's 1999 bumper harvest - in the Russian Federation, in India, Sri Lanka, the

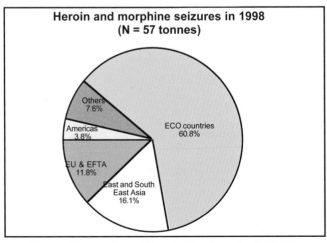

Heroin and morphine seizures in 1998
(N = 57 tonnes)

Others 7.6%
Americas 3.8%
EU & EFTA 11.8%
East and South East Asia 16.1%
ECO countries 60.8%

Source: UNDCP, Annual Reports Questionnaire / DELTA

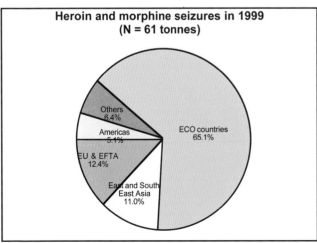

Heroin and morphine seizures in 1999
(N = 61 tonnes)

Others 6.4%
Americas 5.1%
EU & EFTA 12.4%
East and South East Asia 11.0%
ECO countries 65.1%

Source: UNDCP, Annual Reports Questionnaire / DELTA

countries of the Arabian peninsula as well as in countries of eastern and western Africa, which are used as transshipment points to camouflage heroin deliveries to Europe.

Seizures of heroin and morphine alone (i.e. excluding opium) amounted to 40 tons among ECO member states in 1999, equivalent to 65% of global seizures, up from 61% a year earlier and 55% in 1990. The share of EU and EFTA countries in global heroin and morphine seizures, the world's largest market of opiates in economic terms, remained unchanged at 12%. The ECO countries, the EU & EFTA countries and the countries of eastern Europe, all of which are predominantly supplied by opiates manufactured out of Afghan opium production, were responsible for 80% of global heroin and morphine seizures in 1999, almost identical with Afghanistan's share in global opium production in that year (79%).

By contrast, seizures of heroin and morphine in East and South-East Asia fell from 16% of global seizures in 1998 to 11% in 1999, reflecting the reduction of production in Myanmar , the world's second largest producer of opiates. Declines in seizures were reported by China, Thailand, Malaysia, Indonesia, Singapore as well as by Myanmar. The bulk of the opiates produced in Myanmar continues to be trafficked to China, increasingly for local consumption and transshipments to Hong Kong, SAR. Smaller amounts are trafficked to Thailand and other countries in the region. In 1999, 80% of all seizures in the region took place in China, 6% in Thailand, 4% in Myanmar and 4% in Hong Kong, SAR. The importance of Thailand as a transshipment zone fell in the 1990s while trafficking via China gained in importance. In 1990 China accounted for 48% of the heroin and morphine seizures in the region and Thailand for 33%. Some of the South-East Asian heroin is still destined for the US market, trafficked from South-East Asia, notably via Hong Kong, SAR and Canada or via Thailand. The share of South-East Asian heroin on the US market fell from 68% in 1993 to 14% in 1999. South-East Asian heroin plays an even smaller role in Europe, accounting usually for around 10% or less of the market. By contrast, most of the heroin encountered in the markets of the Oceania region originate in South-East Asia. As in East and South-East Asia, heroin seizures in the Oceania region seem to have declined in

1999, as indicated by declines in New Zealand and Australia (based on partial seizure data from customs and federal police; the complete data set, available only for the fiscal year July 1998-June 1999, still shows an increase as compared to the previous fiscal year 1997-98).

Seizure data for the Americas, comprising two opium and heroin producers of regional importance, Colombia and Mexico, have generally shown upward trends in recent years, increasing their share in global seizures of heroin and morphine from 3% in 1990 to 4% in 1998 and to 5% in 1999. Increases in 1999 were reported from Mexico, Colombia, Venezuela, Ecuador, Central America, the Caribbean as well as Argentina in the very south and Canada in the very north. The situation is less clear for the USA, the largest heroin market in the Americas, as some official sources indicate an increase while others show a decline. Differences in coverage (fiscal year / calendar year; federal seizures / all seizures) may explain the divergence. In any case, when compared to European ones, US seizures of heroin and morphine are relatively small, representing only one sixth of the seizures made in EU & EFTA countries, or one tenth of all European seizures, an indication that trafficking in heroin is still far more widespread in Europe than in the USA. Most of the heroin now found on the US market is identified by the US authorities as originating in Latin America (65% Colombia; 17% Mexico) while, during the first half of the 1990s, South-East Asia was the main source. Most of the Mexican heroin is destined for the western and southern parts of the USA, while the east coast is dominated by Colombian heroin, reflecting a similar partition of the market as observed for cocaine.

The bulk of heroin in Europe, as mentioned earlier, comes from South-West Asia. Various West European countries report that the share of South-West Asian opiates is between two thirds and 90% (median 80%) of the seizures they make. As in previous years, the largest seizures in Europe took place in Turkey (34% of all European heroin and morphine seizures in 1999). In 1999, the largest seizures among the EU & EFTA countries were in the UK (31%), followed by Italy (17%), Spain (15%), Germany (11%) and the Netherlands (10%). Overall seizures of opiates in western Europe increased slightly in 1999.

Seizures of heroin and morphine in North America and Europe in 1999 in tonnes and in % of global seizures

Source: UNDCP, Annual Reports Questionnaire /DELTA

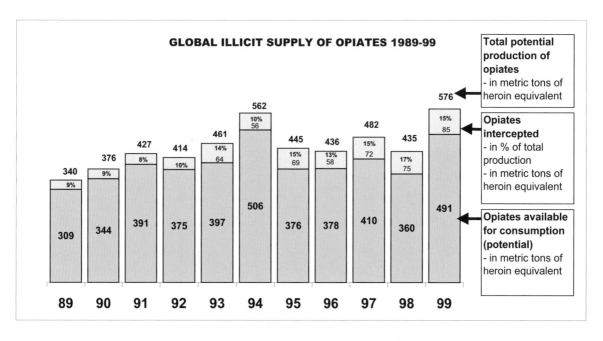

GLOBAL ILLICIT SUPPLY OF OPIATES 1989-99

Total potential production of opiates
- in metric tons of heroin equivalent

Opiates intercepted
- in % of total production
- in metric tons of heroin equivalent

Opiates available for consumption (potential)
- in metric tons of heroin equivalent

(opiates intercepted = combined seizures of opium, heroin and morphine, in metric tons of heroin equivalent)

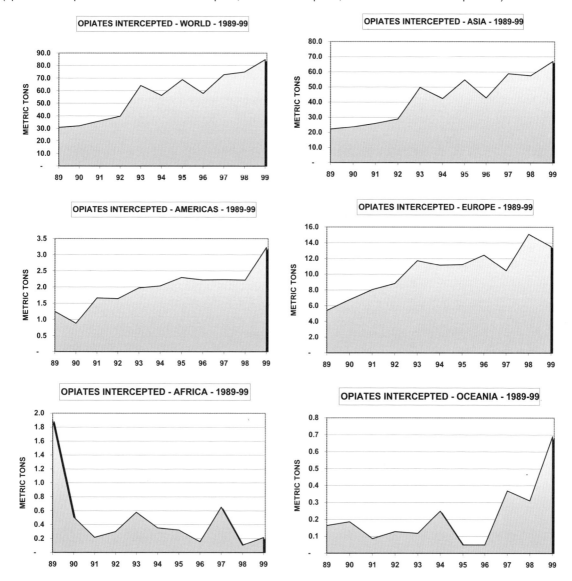

GLOBAL SEIZURES OF OPIUM 1989-99

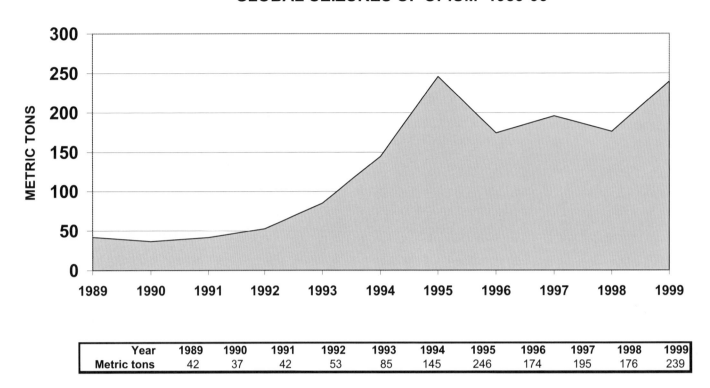

Year	1989	1990	1991	1992	1993	1994	1995	1996	1997	1998	1999
Metric tons	42	37	42	53	85	145	246	174	195	176	239

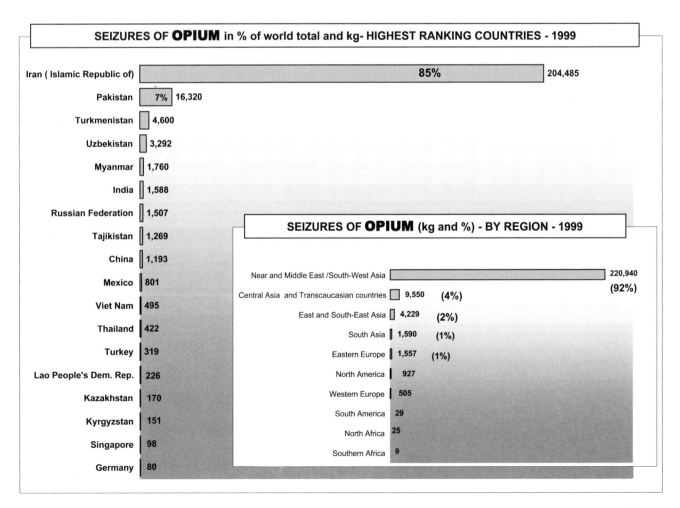

SEIZURES OF OPIUM in % of world total and kg- HIGHEST RANKING COUNTRIES - 1999

Iran (Islamic Republic of)	85% — 204,485
Pakistan	7% 16,320
Turkmenistan	4,600
Uzbekistan	3,292
Myanmar	1,760
India	1,588
Russian Federation	1,507
Tajikistan	1,269
China	1,193
Mexico	801
Viet Nam	495
Thailand	422
Turkey	319
Lao People's Dem. Rep.	226
Kazakhstan	170
Kyrgyzstan	151
Singapore	98
Germany	80

SEIZURES OF OPIUM (kg and %) - BY REGION - 1999

Near and Middle East /South-West Asia	220,940 (92%)
Central Asia and Transcaucasian countries	9,550 (4%)
East and South-East Asia	4,229 (2%)
South Asia	1,590 (1%)
Eastern Europe	1,557 (1%)
North America	927
Western Europe	505
South America	29
North Africa	25
Southern Africa	9

Seizures of opium in Asia 1999 (Only highest ranking countries represented)

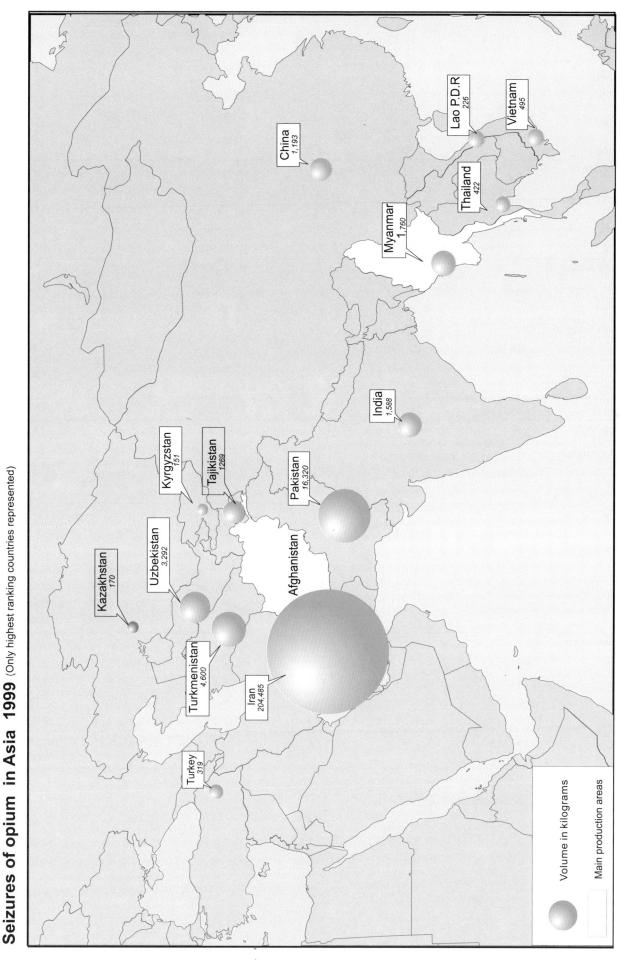

China
1,193

Lao P.D.R
226

Vietnam
495

Thailand
422

Myanmar
1,760

India
1,588

Kyrgyzstan
151

Tajikistan
1269

Pakistan
16,320

Kazakhstan
170

Uzbekistan
3,292

Afghanistan

Turkmenistan
4,600

Iran
204,485

Turkey
319

Volume in kilograms

Main production areas

Note: The boundaries and names shown and the designations used on this map do not imply official endorsement or acceptance by the United Nations

Region/country or territory	Opium (raw and prepared)					
	1994	**1995**	**1996**	**1997**	**1998**	**1999**
AFRICA						
East Africa						
United Republic of Tanzania	0.150 kg	0.130 kg	No Report	No Report	No Report	No Report
Sub-Total	0.150 kg	0.130 kg				
North Africa						
Algeria	0.358 kg [ICPO]	0.008 kg [INCB]	No Report	No Report	No Report	No Report
Egypt	49.380 kg	16.956 kg	16.272 kg	31.156 kg	25.894 kg	24.702 kg
Tunisia	0.029 kg	13.000 kg	No Report	No Report	No Report	No Report
Sub-Total	49.767 kg	29.964 kg	16.272 kg	31.156 kg	25.894 kg	24.702 kg
Southern Africa						
Zambia	No Report	0.195 kg [ICPO]	2.344 kg [ICPO]	0.102 kg [ICPO]	6.770 kg [Govt]	8.622 kg
Sub-Total		0.195 kg	2.344 kg	0.102 kg	6.770 kg	8.622 kg
West and Central Africa						
Gabon	No Report	No Report	0.001 kg [ICPO]	No Report	No Report	No Report
Niger	No Report	No Report	No Report	No Report	No Report	0.013 kg [ICPO]
Sub-Total			0.001 kg			0.013 kg
Total region	49.917 kg	30.289 kg	18.617 kg	31.258 kg	32.664 kg	33.337 kg
AMERICAS						
Central America						
Panama	No Report	5.730 kg	No Report	No Report	No Report	No Report
Sub-Total		5.730 kg				
North America						
Canada	16.964 kg	1.431 kg	1.150 kg	11.925 kg	61.310 kg	57.000 kg 10061 u.
Mexico	149.002 kg	222.914 kg	196.421 kg	342.081 kg	149.064 kg	801.180 kg
United States	No Report	42.076 kg	61.925 kg	39.010 kg	No Report	68.970 kg
Sub-Total	165.966 kg	266.421 kg	259.496 kg	393.016 kg	210.374 kg	927.150 kg 10061 u.
South America						
Argentina	No Report	[ICPO]	No Report	No Report	No Report	No Report
Colombia	128.019 kg	144.163 kg	102.772 kg	121.550 kg	99.950 kg	29.203 kg
Peru	580.650 kg	23.809 kg	No Report	No Report	11.528 kg	No Report
Sub-Total	708.669 kg	167.972 kg	102.772 kg	121.550 kg	111.478 kg	29.203 kg
Total region	874.635 kg	440.123 kg	362.268 kg	514.566 kg	321.852 kg	956.353 kg 10061 u.
ASIA						
Central Asia and Transcaucasian countries						
Armenia	6.400 kg	9.128 kg [ICPO]	1.906 kg	2.054 kg	No Report	2.032 kg [Govt]
Azerbaijan	12.396 kg [ICPO]	254.902 kg [Govt]	39.039 kg [ICPO]	83.328 kg [ICPO]	48.541 kg	52.218 kg
Georgia	No Report	No Report	17.593 kg [ICPO]	No Report	No Report	14.700 kg [ICPO]

Source: Annual Report Questionnaire if not otherwise indicated

Opium (raw and prepared)

Region/country or territory	1994	1995	1996	1997	1998	1999
ASIA						
Central Asia and Transcaucasian countries						
Kazakhstan	434.742 kg	245.000 kg	500.000 kg [Govt]	1000.000 kg [Govt]	296.574 kg	170.236 kg
Kyrgyzstan	No Report	726.890 kg	1489.684 kg	1639.476 kg	171.872 kg	151.174 kg
Tajikistan	243.600 kg [F.O.]	1571.400 kg [F.O.]	3405.000 kg	3455.510 kg [F.O.]	1190.400 kg	1269.278 kg [F.O.]
Turkmenistan	650.000 kg [Govt]	No Report	No Report	1410.000 kg [Govt]	1412.000 kg [Govt]	4600.000 kg [F.O.]
Uzbekistan	226.387 kg	834.788 kg	1865.000 kg [Govt]	2364.167 kg	1935.315 kg	3292.342 kg
Sub-Total	1573.525 kg	3642.108 kg	7318.222 kg	9954.535 kg	5054.702 kg	9551.979 kg
East and South-East Asia						
Cambodia	1.170 kg [ICPO]	19.000 kg [Govt]	No Report	15.006 kg [ICPO]	No Report	No Report
China	1778.080 kg [INCB]	1110.000 kg	1745.000 kg	1880.000 kg	1215.000 kg	1193.000 kg [ICPO]
China (Hong Kong SAR)	9.401 kg	8.000 kg [Govt]	12.800 kg	3.400 kg	No Report	0.100 kg
Indonesia	2.602 kg	0.030 kg	0.030 kg	No Report	0.030 kg [HNLP]	3.097 kg [HNLP]
Japan	33.739 kg	32.823 kg	31.106 kg	39.061 kg	19.811 kg	7.688 kg
Korea (Republic of)	2.998 kg [Govt]	7.141 kg	0.567 kg	6.805 kg	1.035 kg	3.064 kg
Lao People's Dem. Rep.	293.300 kg	695.500 kg [Govt]	199.001 kg [Govt]	200.100 kg [Govt]	No Report	225.800 kg [HNLP]
Macau	0.055 kg [INCB]	No Report	No Report	No Report	No Report	No Report
Malaysia	69.050 kg [Govt]	155.089 kg	2.640 kg [Govt]	150.311 kg	32.747 kg	21.066 kg
Myanmar	1688.594 kg	1060.718 kg	1300.002 kg	7883.975 kg	5705.881 kg	1759.538 kg
Singapore	2.296 kg	80.487 kg	28.464 kg	1.545 kg	22.781 kg	98.144 kg
Thailand	606.350 kg [Govt]	927.461 kg [ICPO]	381.322 kg [ICPO]	1150.582 kg	1631.124 kg	421.939 kg
Viet Nam	1410.000 kg [Govt]	No Report	839.850 kg [ICPO]	No Report	No Report	495.350 kg [F.O.]
Sub-Total	5897.635 kg	4096.249 kg	4540.782 kg	11330.790 kg	8628.408 kg	4228.786 kg
Near and Middle East /South-West Asia						
Bahrain	0.049 kg	No Report	No Report	0.007 kg	0.014 kg [ICPO]	0.323 kg [ICPO]
Iran (Islamic Republic of)	117095.000 kg	126554.000 kg	149577.000 kg	162413.953 kg	154453.563 kg [Govt]	204485.000 kg [Govt]
Iraq	No Report	No Report	1.000 kg	4.815 kg	No Report	No Report
Israel	0.137 kg	(1	0.003 kg	5.100 kg	0.556 kg	0.005 kg [ICPO]
Jordan	No Report	0.018 kg	43.350 kg	22.671 kg	No Report	61.700 kg
Kuwait	25.260 kg	30.380 kg [INCB]	40.804 kg [ICPO]	11.710 kg [ICPO]	4.720 kg	14.000 kg [INCB]
Lebanon	15.965 kg	7.000 kg	3.000 kg	7.625 kg	No Report	44.226 kg
Oman	No Report	0.877 kg	12.000 kg [INCB]	0.060 kg [INCB]	No Report	No Report
Pakistan	14662.909 kg [Govt]	109420.398 kg [ICPO]	7422.772 kg [ICPO]	7300.000 kg [Govt]	5021.712 kg	16319.918 kg
Qatar	0.327 kg	2.267 kg	0.340 kg	0.962 kg [ICPO]	0.030 kg [ICPO]	0.100 kg [ICPO]
Saudi Arabia	74.057 kg	155.768 kg	23.038 kg [ICPO]	16.127 kg [ICPO]	16.721 kg [(2]	No Report
Syrian Arab Republic	0.974 kg [ICPO]	No Report	No Report	6.003 kg	1.200 kg	5.876 kg
United Arab Emirates	161.318 kg	61.612 kg	16.269 kg	3.822 kg	9.717 kg	8.389 kg
Sub-Total	132036.000 kg	236232.300 kg	157139.500 kg	169792.800 kg	159508.300 kg	220939.500 kg

Source: Annual Report Questionnaire if not otherwise indicated

Opium (raw and prepared)

Region/country or territory	1994	1995	1996	1997	1998	1999
ASIA						
South Asia						
Bangladesh	8.225 kg	No Report	0.073 kg	No Report	No Report	0.072 kg [F.O.]
India	2256.000 kg	1349.000 kg	2876.000 kg [Govt]	3316.000 kg	2031.000 kg	1588.000 kg
Nepal	4.477 kg	0.206 kg	0.441 kg	No Report	0.950 kg	1.440 kg
Sri Lanka	1.172 kg	0.082 kg	0.145 kg	1571 u.	0.020 kg	0.008 kg
Sub-Total	2269.874 kg	1349.288 kg	2876.659 kg	3316.000 kg 1571 u.	2031.970 kg	1589.520 kg
Total region	141777.000 kg	245320.000 kg	171875.200 kg	194394.200 kg 1571 u.	175223.300 kg	236309.800 kg
EUROPE						
Eastern Europe						
Albania	No Report	No Report	No Report	No Report	No Report	0.026 kg [ICPO]
Belarus	882.000 kg	88.542 kg	No Report	1.124 kg [INCB]	0.001 kg	0.033 kg
Bulgaria	No Report	0.371 kg	0.080 kg	8.240 kg	1.970 kg	4.466 kg
Croatia	0.014 kg	0.007 kg	[1]	0.001 kg	[1]	0.103 kg
Czech Republic	No Report	No Report	1.000 kg	No Report	No Report	No Report
Estonia	No Report	No Report	0.001 kg [ICPO]	No Report	No Report	No Report
FYR of Macedonia	No Report	9.964 kg	2.003 kg [ICPO]	No Report	19.985 kg	12.239 kg [ICPO]
Hungary	0.080 kg [INCB]	0.075 kg [INCB]	No Report	No Report	No Report	2.149 kg
Latvia	No Report	No Report	0.001 kg	0.230 kg	0.755 kg	0.005 kg
Lithuania	1.266 kg	3.114 kg	0.278 kg	0.236 kg	0.101 kg	0.190 kg
Republic of Moldova	0.119 kg [ICPO]	1.384 kg [ICPO]	No Report	20.000 kg	No Report	28.000 kg [ICPO]
Romania	0.193 kg	1.003 kg	1.442 kg	2.488 kg [ICPO]	0.728 kg	2.470 kg
Russian Federation	784.230 kg [ICPO]	1156.900 kg	1400.500 kg	222.706 kg	1803.700 kg [F.O.]	1506.966 kg
Slovenia	0.001 kg	No Report	No Report	No Report	No Report	No Report
Ukraine	No Report	23.000 kg [ICPO]	194.528 kg	No Report	No Report	No Report
Yugoslavia	0.007 kg	No Report	No Report	No Report	No Report	No Report
Sub-Total	1667.910 kg	1284.360 kg	1599.833 kg	255.025 kg	1827.240 kg	1556.647 kg
Western Europe						
Austria	64.885 kg	1.766 kg	17.667 kg	9.041 kg	10.447 kg	33.646 kg
Belgium	0.674 kg	0.023 kg	No Report	No Report	0.011 kg	0.200 kg
Cyprus	0.062 kg	0.030 kg	0.654 kg	1.913 kg	0.021 kg	0.062 kg
Denmark	4.500 kg [INCB]	No Report	0.052 kg	0.105 kg	5.428 kg	0.330 kg
Finland	0.286 kg	0.077 kg	0.254 kg	No Report	0.007 kg	No Report
France	3.087 kg [INCB]	1.005 kg	4.326 kg	2.696 kg	3.194 kg	0.503 kg
Germany	35.500 kg	14.534 kg	45.387 kg	41.656 kg	286.074 kg	79.500 kg
Greece	0.085 kg	0.409 kg	0.235 kg	2.559 kg	No Report	46.208 kg [ICPO]
Italy	0.289 kg 15 u.	0.103 kg	0.617 kg	9.821 kg 54 u.	2.895 kg	0.401 kg [ICPO]
Netherlands	0.333 kg [ICPO]	6.000 kg [ICPO]	No Report	No Report	1.034 kg [2]	No Report
Norway	2.840 kg	0.024 kg	1.288 kg	0.023 kg	2.498 kg	1.661 kg

Source: Annual Report Questionnaire if not otherwise indicated

Opium (raw and prepared)

Region/country or territory	1994	1995	1996	1997	1998	1999
EUROPE						
Western Europe						
Portugal	No Report	No Report	No Report	0.012 kg	0.001 kg	No Report
Spain	45.732 kg	0.007 kg	2.857 kg	26.287 kg	0.002 kg	1.080 kg
Sweden	9.328 kg	7.728 kg	30.679 kg	7.709 kg 139 u.	15.641 kg	9.867 kg
Switzerland	1.072 kg	0.131 kg	0.168 kg	0.042 kg	0.015 kg	0.775 kg
Turkey	91.189 kg	121.547 kg	233.000 kg	93.356 kg	141.665 kg	318.624 kg
United Kingdom	11.200 kg	5.500 kg	11.400 kg	17.800 kg	54.263 kg	37.700 kg [NCIS]
Sub-Total	271.062 kg 15 u.	158.884 kg	348.584 kg	213.020 kg 193 u.	523.196 kg	530.557 kg
Total region	1938.972 kg 15 u.	1443.244 kg	1948.417 kg	468.045 kg 193 u.	2350.436 kg	2087.204 kg
OCEANIA						
Oceania						
Australia	No Report	0.118 kg [3 687 u.	8.072 kg	2.095 kg	No Report	3.000 kg [INCB]
New Zealand	0.034 kg [ICPO]	0.192 kg [INCB]	No Report	0.016 kg [INCB]	0.006 kg	No Report
Sub-Total	0.034 kg	0.310 kg 687 u.	8.072 kg	2.111 kg	0.006 kg	3.000 kg
Total region	0.034 kg	0.310 kg 687 u.	8.072 kg	2.111 kg	0.006 kg	3.000 kg
TOTAL	144640.600 kg 15 u.	247233.900 kg 687 u.	174212.600 kg	195410.100 kg 1764 u.	177928.300 kg	239389.700 kg 10061 u.

1) Small quantity. 2) Including other opiates. 3) Fiscal year

Source: Annual Report Questionnaire if not otherwise indicated

Region/country or territory	Opium (liquid)					
	1994	1995	1996	1997	1998	1999
AFRICA						
East Africa						
Mauritius	No Report		No Report	No Report	No Report	No Report
Sub-Total						
North Africa						
Egypt	0.670 lt.	1.022 lt.	0.017 lt.	0.009 lt.	0.030 lt.	(1
Sub-Total	0.670 lt.	1.022 lt.	0.017 lt.	0.009 lt.	0.030 lt.	
Total region	0.670 lt.	1.022 lt.	0.017 lt.	0.009 lt.	0.030 lt.	
AMERICAS						
South America						
Peru	No Report	No Report	36.921 kg	No Report	No Report	66.088 kg
Sub-Total			36.921 kg			66.088 kg
Total region			36.921 kg			66.088 kg
ASIA						
Central Asia and Transcaucasian countries						
Armenia	No Report	No Report	No Report	No Report	2.000 kg	No Report
Azerbaijan	1.250 kg ICPO	No Report	No Report	No Report	No Report	No Report
Kazakhstan	No Report	No Report	No Report	No Report	1.265 kg	No Report
Kyrgyzstan	No Report	No Report	No Report	15000 u.	No Report	No Report
Sub-Total	1.250 kg			15000 u.	3.265 kg	
East and South-East Asia						
Indonesia	No Report	No Report	No Report	No Report	0.030 kg	3.097 kg
Japan	0.050 kg	No Report	5.912 lt.	No Report	0.130 lt.	No Report
Macau	0.055 kg	No Report	No Report	No Report	No Report	No Report
Myanmar	0.361 kg	5.134 kg	No Report	1027.685 kg	383.251 kg	332.495 kg
Sub-Total	0.466 kg	5.134 kg	5.912 lt.	1027.685 kg	383.281 kg 0.130 lt.	335.592 kg
Near and Middle East /South-West Asia						
Lebanon	No Report	No Report	No Report	No Report	35.840 kg	No Report
Oman	0.025 kg	No Report	No Report	No Report	No Report	No Report
United Arab Emirates	0.670 kg	No Report	No Report	No Report	No Report	No Report
Sub-Total	0.695 kg				35.840 kg	
Total region	2.411 kg	5.134 kg	5.912 lt.	1027.685 kg 15000 u.	422.386 kg 0.130 lt.	335.592 kg
EUROPE						
Eastern Europe						
Belarus	42.114 kg	No Report	82.196 kg	No Report	330.882 kg	244.034 kg (2
Croatia	No Report	No Report	No Report	2.000 lt.	8.600 lt.	No Report
Estonia	No Report	No Report	20.701 lt. ICPO	No Report	19.200 kg 293 u.	0.276 kg 61 u.

Source: Annual Report Questionnaire if not otherwise indicated

Region/country or territory	Opium (liquid)					
	1994	1995	1996	1997	1998	1999
EUROPE						
Eastern Europe						
Latvia	No Report	43.000 kg 22000 u.	89.000 lt.	0.133 lt.	64.800 kg	17.300 kg
Lithuania	25.595 lt.	53.217 lt.	96.085 lt.	86.000 lt.	49.490 lt.	190.000 lt.
Poland	8.000 kg	No Report	No Report	No Report	No Report	No Report
Republic of Moldova	No Report	No Report	27.104 kg	No Report	13.480 kg	No Report
Ukraine	No Report	No Report	No Report	171.200 kg	127.000 kg	No Report
Sub-Total	50.114 kg 25.595 lt.	43.000 kg 53.217 lt. 22000 u.	109.300 kg 205.786 lt.	171.200 kg 88.133 lt.	555.362 kg 58.090 lt. 293 u.	261.610 kg 190.000 lt. 61 u.
Western Europe						
Denmark	No Report	0.061 kg	0.005 kg	0.030 kg	0.004 kg	2.640 kg
Norway	No Report	0.026 kg 1 u.	No Report	No Report	No Report	No Report
Spain	No Report	0.050 kg	No Report	No Report	No Report	No Report
Sweden	3.550 kg	No Report	No Report	No Report	0.326 lt.	16.000 lt.
Sub-Total	3.550 kg	0.137 kg 1 u.	0.005 kg	0.030 kg	0.004 kg 0.326 lt.	2.640 kg 16.000 lt.
Total region	53.664 kg 25.595 lt.	43.137 kg 53.217 lt. 22001 u.	109.305 kg 205.786 lt.	171.230 kg 88.133 lt.	555.366 kg 58.416 lt. 293 u.	264.250 kg 206.000 lt. 61 u.
OCEANIA						
Oceania						
Australia	No Report	0.082 kg [3] 2.000 lt.	0.080 kg	1.630 kg	No Report	No Report
Sub-Total		0.082 kg 2.000 lt.	0.080 kg	1.630 kg		
Total region		0.082 kg 2.000 lt.	0.080 kg	1.630 kg		
TOTAL	56.075 kg 26.265 lt.	48.353 kg 56.239 lt. 22001 u.	146.306 kg 211.715 lt.	1200.545 kg 88.142 lt. 15000 u.	977.752 kg 58.576 lt. 293 u.	665.930 kg 206.000 lt. 61 u.

1) Small quantity. 2) Includes liquid heroin (1.160kg) 3) Fiscal year

Source: Annual Report Questionnaire if not otherwise indicated

Opium (plant,capsule)

Region/country or territory	1994	1995	1996	1997	1998	1999
AFRICA						
North Africa						
Egypt	138828496 u.	17621796 u.	3639320832 u.	No Report	0.352 kg	14.552 kg
Tunisia	0.210 kg 1972 u.	13.000 kg [ICPO]	No Report	No Report	No Report	No Report
Sub-Total	0.210 kg 138830500 u.	13.000 kg 17621800 u.	3639321000 u.		0.352 kg	14.552 kg
West and Central Africa						
Niger	No Report	No Report	No Report	No Report	0.040 kg [ICPO]	No Report
Sao Tome and Principe	No Report	No Report	No Report	0.300 kg	No Report	0.300 kg
Sub-Total				0.300 kg	0.040 kg	0.300 kg
Total region	0.210 kg 138830500 u.	13.000 kg 17621800 u.	3639321000 u.	0.300 kg	0.392 kg	14.852 kg
AMERICAS						
Central America						
Guatemala	No Report	No Report	No Report	2.600 kg [Govt] 69119 u.	114238 u.	23100 u.
Sub-Total				2.600 kg 69119 u.	114238 u.	23100 u.
North America						
Canada	No Report	0.480 kg	4.757 kg	18 u.	2.016 kg	15000 u.
United States	37.555 kg	No Report	No Report	50.685 kg 0.109 lt.	No Report	No Report
Sub-Total	37.555 kg	0.480 kg	4.757 kg	50.685 kg 0.109 lt. 18 u.	2.016 kg	15000 u.
South America						
Argentina	No Report	No Report	301 u. [Govt]	2.470 kg	408 u.	No Report
Colombia	7000 u.	76117504 u.	75000 u.	104818496 u.	No Report	No Report
Ecuador	No Report	No Report	No Report	No Report	100873 u.	No Report
Peru	No Report	0.444 kg	534.253 kg	1754 u.	964 u.	63703.614 kg
Sub-Total	7000 u.	0.444 kg 76117500 u.	534.253 kg 75301 u.	2.470 kg 104820200 u.	102245 u.	63703.610 kg
Total region	37.555 kg 7000 u.	0.924 kg 76117500 u.	539.010 kg 75301 u.	55.755 kg 0.109 lt. 104889400 u.	2.016 kg 216483 u.	63703.610 kg 38100 u.
ASIA						
Central Asia and Transcaucasian countries						
Armenia	17.910 kg	7.735 kg [ICPO]	76.826 kg	4.460 kg	18.725 kg	No Report
Azerbaijan	75263.000 kg [ICPO]	95000.000 kg [Govt]	No Report	38750.000 kg [ICPO]	6.200 kg	No Report

Source: Annual Report Questionnaire if not otherwise indicated

Region/country or territory	1994	1995	1996	1997	1998	1999
			Opium (plant,capsule)			

ASIA

Central Asia and Transcaucasian countries

Region/country or territory	1994	1995	1996	1997	1998	1999
Georgia	No Report	No Report	19.168 kg [ICPO]	No Report	7.500 kg [ICPO]	No Report
Kazakhstan	No Report	No Report	335.719 kg [ICPO]	No Report	113.895 kg	No Report
Kyrgyzstan	No Report	1.372 kg	No Report	No Report	No Report	No Report
Uzbekistan	1773.146 kg	936.381 kg	863.767 kg [ICPO]	118.285 kg	54.496 kg	No Report
Sub-Total	77054.060 kg	95945.490 kg	1295.480 kg	38872.750 kg	200.816 kg	

East and South-East Asia

Region/country or territory	1994	1995	1996	1997	1998	1999
China	No Report	21313.000 kg	No Report	No Report	No Report	No Report
China (Hong Kong SAR)	No Report	No Report	No Report	No Report	No Report	32 u.
Indonesia	No Report	No Report	No Report	1620 u.	0.030 kg	No Report
Japan	11700 u.	8240 u.	No Report	6803 u.	0.063 kg 6807 u.	No Report
Korea (Republic of)	45677 u. [Govt]	235896 u.	72645 u.	24301 u.	21944 u.	No Report
Malaysia	No Report	No Report	No Report	321 u.	No Report	No Report
Thailand	177.760 kg [Govt]	115.880 kg [Govt]	No Report	205.234 kg	No Report	312.837 kg
Viet Nam	No Report	1418.000 kg [ICPO]	No Report	919.000 kg [ICPO]	1.100 kg [ICPO]	No Report
Sub-Total	177.760 kg 57377 u.	22846.880 kg 244136 u.	72645 u.	1124.234 kg 33045 u.	1.193 kg 28751 u.	312.837 kg 32 u.

Near and Middle East /South-West Asia

Region/country or territory	1994	1995	1996	1997	1998	1999
Kuwait	843 u.	23.509 kg [ICPO]	No Report	No Report	No Report	No Report
Saudi Arabia	225.000 kg	No Report	0.038 kg [ICPO]	No Report	No Report	No Report
United Arab Emirates	176 u.	No Report	No Report	129 u.	No Report	No Report
Yemen	No Report	No Report	No Report	No Report	[ICPO]	No Report
Sub-Total	225.000 kg 1019 u.	23.509 kg	0.038 kg	129 u.		

South Asia

Region/country or territory	1994	1995	1996	1997	1998	1999
India	No Report	10.000 kg [ICPO]	No Report	No Report	No Report	No Report
Nepal	562 u.	No Report	No Report	0.693 kg [ICPO]	No Report	No Report
Sub-Total	562 u.	10.000 kg		0.693 kg		
Total region	77456.810 kg 58958 u.	118825.900 kg 244136 u.	1295.518 kg 72645 u.	39997.670 kg 33174 u.	202.009 kg 28751 u.	312.837 kg 32 u.

EUROPE

Eastern Europe

Region/country or territory	1994	1995	1996	1997	1998	1999
Belarus	No Report	1470.000 kg	1792.000 kg	327.744 kg [INCB]	1621.000 kg	1056.000 kg
Bulgaria	61.270 kg	18.560 kg	48.500 kg	No Report	No Report	No Report
Croatia	13.010 kg	0.006 kg [ICPO] 1500 u.	No Report	769 u.	3504 u.	6206 u.
Estonia	No Report	No Report	135.428 kg [ICPO]	165.800 kg	36.011 kg 111 u.	No Report
Latvia	No Report	216.000 kg 432000 u.	0.180 kg	218.000 kg	192.000 kg	30.200 kg

Source: Annual Report Questionnaire if not otherwise indicated

Region/country or territory	Opium (plant,capsule)					
	1994	1995	1996	1997	1998	1999
EUROPE						
Eastern Europe						
Lithuania	1020.000 kg	976.000 kg	1652.000 kg	1291.000 kg	1525.000 kg	744.000 kg
Poland	8010.000 kg	1100.000 kg	1000.000 kg	8500.000 kg	4000.000 kg	3553.000 kg
Republic of Moldova	249.722 kg [ICPO]	4397.587 kg [ICPO]	No Report	597.000 kg	406.550 kg	No Report
Russian Federation	22932.871 kg [ICPO]	22864.600 kg	19469.801 kg	853.019 kg	16511.359 kg	18366.055 kg
Slovenia	23 u.	No Report	No Report	No Report	No Report	No Report
Ukraine	171.900 kg [ICPO]	199.200 kg [ICPO] 36797 u.	No Report	34003.262 kg	26632.801 kg	No Report
Sub-Total	32458.770 kg 23 u.	31241.950 kg 470297 u.	24097.910 kg	45955.820 kg 769 u.	50924.720 kg 3615 u.	23749.260 kg 6206 u.
Western Europe						
Austria	2.252 kg	8.560 kg	1103.859 kg	1.193 kg	9.367 kg	9.349 kg
Finland	No Report	No Report	No Report	No Report	1.000 kg	No Report
Greece	2743 u.	106 u.	130 u.	640 u.	No Report	No Report
Italy	27767 u.	5034 u.	No Report	1448 u.	5991 u.	No Report
Norway	0.346 kg	252.792 kg	No Report	0.115 kg	0.070 kg	No Report
Portugal	No Report	No Report	150 u.	No Report	28848 u.	351 u.
Spain	5193.915 kg	75867.000 kg	11185.998 kg	862.112 kg	4.800 kg	1003.004 kg
Sweden	37.454 kg	0.782 kg	No Report	(1	No Report	3615 u.
Turkey	No Report	1508 u.	No Report	No Report	No Report	No Report
Sub-Total	5233.967 kg 30510 u.	76129.130 kg 6648 u.	12289.860 kg 280 u.	863.420 kg 2088 u.	15.237 kg 34839 u.	1012.353 kg 3966 u.
Total region	37692.740 kg 30533 u.	107371.100 kg 476945 u.	36387.770 kg 280 u.	46819.250 kg 2857 u.	50939.960 kg 38454 u.	24761.610 kg 10172 u.
OCEANIA						
Oceania						
Australia	1100 u. (2	0.037 kg (2 105 u.	0.001 kg	0.095 kg	No Report	No Report
New Zealand	4912 u. [ICPO]	2715 u. [Govt]	No Report	No Report	20249 u.	338 u.
Sub-Total	6012 u.	0.037 kg 2820 u.	0.001 kg	0.095 kg	20249 u.	338 u.
Total region	6012 u.	0.037 kg 2820 u.	0.001 kg	0.095 kg	20249 u.	338 u.
TOTAL	115187.300 kg 138933000 u.	226210.900 kg 94463200 u.	38222.290 kg 3639469000 u.	86873.060 kg 0.109 lt. 104925400 u.	51144.380 kg 303937 u.	88792.910 kg 48642 u.

1) Including depressants. 2) Fiscal year

Source: Annual Report Questionnaire if not otherwise indicated

Opium (poppy seed)

Region/country or territory	1994	1995	1996	1997	1998	1999
AFRICA						
North Africa						
Egypt	1267.515 kg	2655.578 kg		No Report	No Report	180.022 kg
Sub-Total	1267.515 kg	2655.578 kg				180.022 kg
Total region	1267.515 kg	2655.578 kg				180.022 kg
AMERICAS						
Central America						
Guatemala	No Report	No Report	No Report	0.014 kg [Govt]	2.003 kg	54.886 kg 121 u.
Sub-Total				0.014 kg	2.003 kg	54.886 kg 121 u.
North America						
Canada	No Report	0.004 kg	0.045 kg	0.014 kg	No Report	0.000 kg
Mexico	1369.020 kg	2134.422 kg	1155.152 kg	587.028 kg	702.055 kg	749.985 kg
Sub-Total	1369.020 kg	2134.426 kg	1155.197 kg	587.042 kg	702.055 kg	749.985 kg
South America						
Argentina	No Report	No Report	No Report	No Report	30.000 kg	No Report
Colombia	969.000 kg	208.911 kg	No Report	411.200 kg	12.600 kg	49.945 kg
Peru	20.227 kg	0.148 kg	No Report	No Report	1.047 kg	193.739 kg
Sub-Total	989.227 kg	209.059 kg		411.200 kg	43.647 kg	243.684 kg
Total region	2358.247 kg	2343.485 kg	1155.197 kg	998.256 kg	747.705 kg	1048.555 kg 121 u.
ASIA						
Central Asia and Transcaucasian countries						
Armenia	No Report	No Report	No Report	2.330 kg	No Report	0.117 kg
Azerbaijan	No Report	No Report	No Report	No Report	No Report	2577.008 kg
Georgia	No Report	No Report	No Report	No Report	No Report	83.500 kg [ICP]
Kazakhstan	1812.000 kg	No Report	No Report	No Report	No Report	141.159 kg
Kyrgyzstan	No Report	No Report	32392 u.	No Report	No Report	No Report
Turkmenistan	No Report	No Report	No Report	No Report	No Report	17996.000 kg [F.C]
Uzbekistan	No Report	0.200 kg	No Report	No Report	No Report	61.400 kg [ICP]
Sub-Total	1812.000 kg	0.200 kg	32392 u.	2.330 kg		20859.180 kg
East and South-East Asia						
China	No Report	No Report	29754.000 kg	No Report	No Report	No Report
Japan	No Report	No Report	12425 u.	No Report	No Report	28256 u.
Korea (Republic of)	No Report	No Report	No Report	0.036 kg	No Report	28268 u.
Thailand	No Report	No Report	No Report	No Report	60.393 kg	No Report
Sub-Total			29754.000 kg 12425 u.	0.036 kg	60.393 kg	56524 u.
Near and Middle East /South-West Asia						
Bahrain	2.531 kg	0.003 kg	0.020 kg	No Report	No Report	1.200 kg [ICP]

Source: Annual Report Questionnaire if not otherwise indicated

Opium (poppy seed)

Region/country or territory	1994	1995	1996	1997	1998	1999
ASIA						
Near and Middle East /South-West Asia						
Kuwait	No Report	No Report	No Report	No Report	No Report	13.695 kg [ICPO]
Lebanon	No Report	No Report	No Report	No Report	10.000 kg	59.000 kg
Saudi Arabia	No Report	No Report	No Report	No Report	No Report	5.697 kg [ICPO]
United Arab Emirates	0.750 kg	No Report	No Report	No Report	No Report	0.122 kg
Sub-Total	3.281 kg	0.003 kg	0.020 kg		10.000 kg	79.714 kg
South Asia						
Sri Lanka	No Report	17.900 kg	58.250 kg	No Report	No Report	No Report
Sub-Total		17.900 kg	58.250 kg			
Total region	1815.281 kg	18.103 kg	29812.270 kg 44817 u.	2.366 kg	70.393 kg	20938.900 kg 56524 u.
EUROPE						
Eastern Europe						
Croatia	No Report	No Report	14.000 kg	No Report	No Report	0.002 kg
Czech Republic	No Report	No Report	No Report	No Report	No Report	91.400 kg
Estonia	No Report	No Report	No Report	No Report	No Report	128.934 kg 249 u.
Republic of Moldova	No Report	No Report	2264.000 kg	No Report	No Report	706.000 kg [ICPO]
Ukraine	No Report	No Report	No Report	No Report	No Report	133.000 kg [ICPO]
Sub-Total			2278.000 kg			1059.336 kg 249 u.
Western Europe						
Finland	No Report	No Report	No Report	6.518 kg	0.220 kg	No Report
Italy	No Report	No Report	15919 u.	No Report	No Report	[ICPO]
Norway	No Report	No Report	41.100 kg	No Report	No Report	0.008 kg 49 u.
Portugal	No Report	No Report	0.035 kg	No Report	No Report	No Report
Sub-Total			41.135 kg 15919 u.	6.518 kg	0.220 kg	0.008 kg 49 u.
Total region			2319.135 kg 15919 u.	6.518 kg	0.220 kg	1059.344 kg 298 u.
OCEANIA						
Oceania						
Australia	No Report	No Report	No Report	1.410 kg	No Report	No Report
Sub-Total				1.410 kg		
Total region				1.410 kg		
TOTAL	5441.043 kg	5017.166 kg	33286.600 kg 60736 u.	1008.550 kg	818.318 kg	23226.820 kg 56943 u.

Source: Annual Report Questionnaire if not otherwise indicated

GLOBAL SEIZURES OF HEROIN & MORPHINE 1998-99

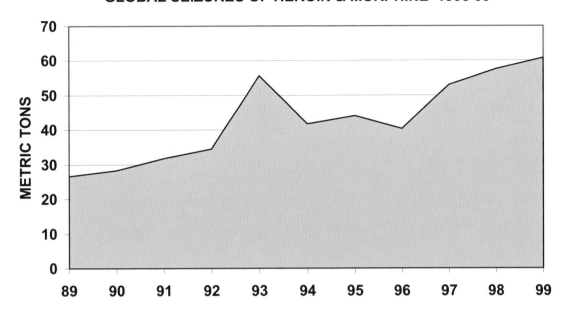

Year	89	90	91	92	93	94	95	96	97	98	99
Metric tons	27	28	32	35	56	42	44	40	53	58	61

SEIZURES OF **HEROIN** (and morphine) in % of world total and kg- HIGHEST RANKING COUNTRIES - 1999

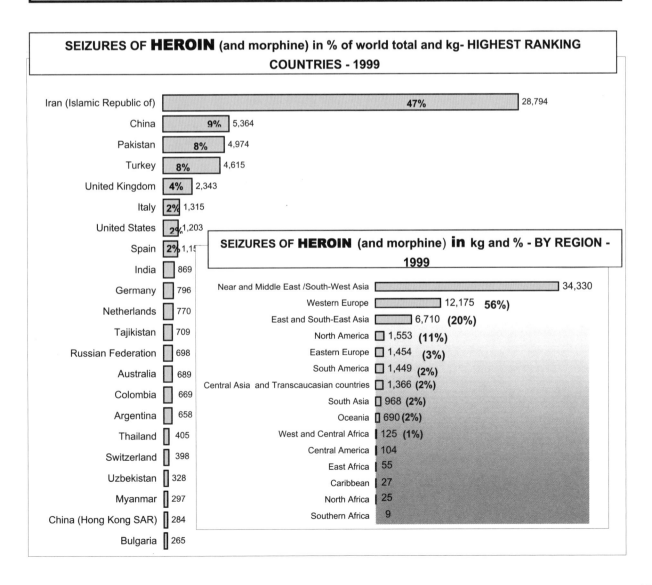

Country	%	kg
Iran (Islamic Republic of)	47%	28,794
China	9%	5,364
Pakistan	8%	4,974
Turkey	8%	4,615
United Kingdom	4%	2,343
Italy	2%	1,315
United States	2%	1,203
Spain	2%	1,15
India		869
Germany		796
Netherlands		770
Tajikistan		709
Russian Federation		698
Australia		689
Colombia		669
Argentina		658
Thailand		405
Switzerland		398
Uzbekistan		328
Myanmar		297
China (Hong Kong SAR)		284
Bulgaria		265

SEIZURES OF **HEROIN** (and morphine) in kg and % - BY REGION - 1999

Region	kg	%
Near and Middle East /South-West Asia	34,330	56%
Western Europe	12,175	
East and South-East Asia	6,710	(20%)
North America	1,553	(11%)
Eastern Europe	1,454	(3%)
South America	1,449	(2%)
Central Asia and Transcaucasian countries	1,366	(2%)
South Asia	968	(2%)
Oceania	690	(2%)
West and Central Africa	125	(1%)
Central America	104	
East Africa	55	
Caribbean	27	
North Africa	25	
Southern Africa	9	

Heroin and morphine trafficking 1998-1999: extent and trends (countries reporting seizures of more than 0.01 tons (10 kg))

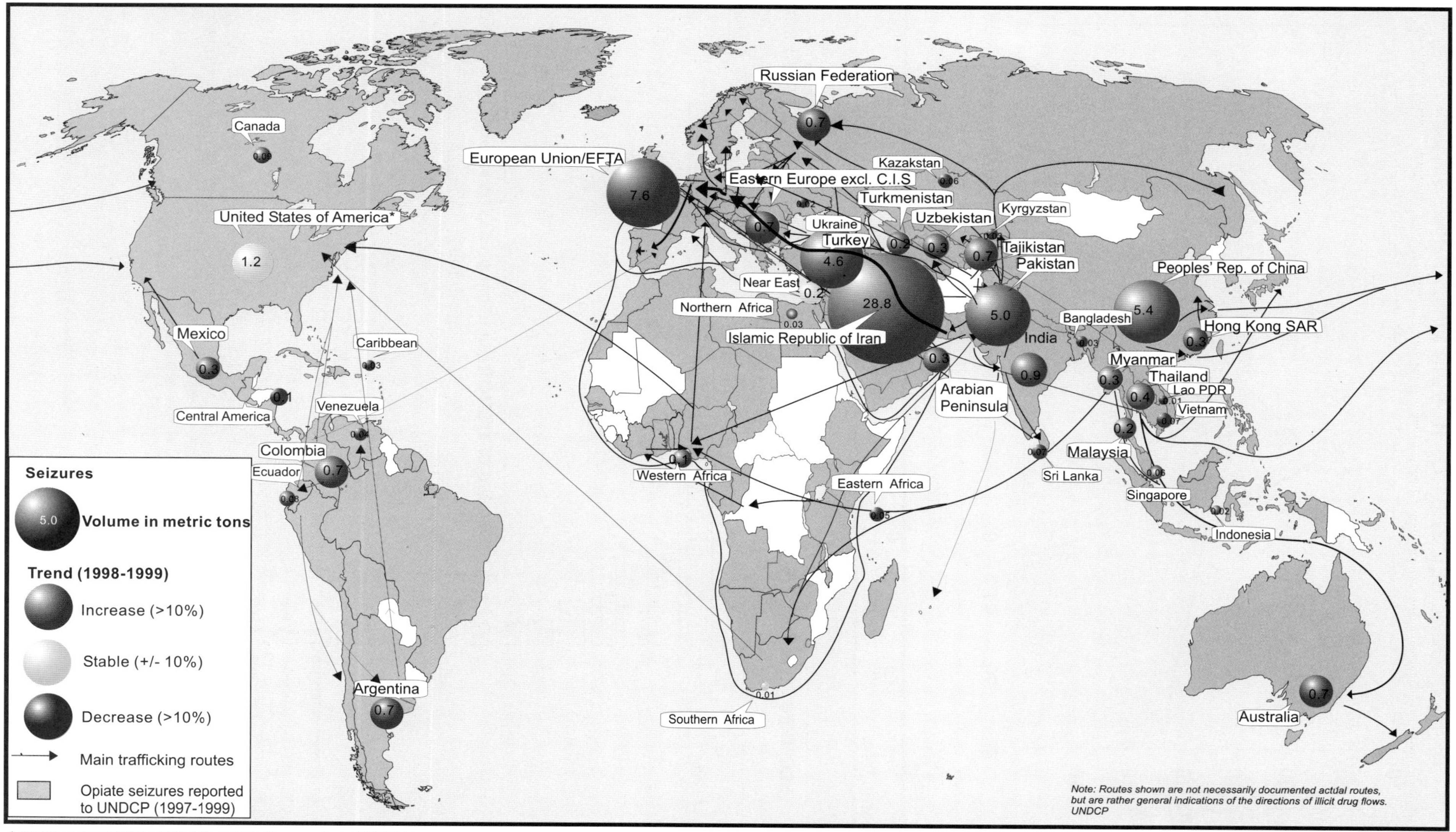

Note: Routes shown are not necessarily documented actual routes, but are rather general indications of the directions of illicit drug flows. UNDCP

Seizures

Volume in metric tons

5.0

Trend (1998-1999)

Increase (>10%)

Stable (+/- 10%)

Decrease (>10%)

Main trafficking routes

Opiate seizures reported to UNDCP (1997-1999)

* some increase according to ARQ data, some decline according to ONDCP data.

Note: The boundaries and names shown and the designations used on this map do not imply official endorsement or acceptance by the United Nations.

Labels on map: Peoples Rep. of China, Hong Kong SAR, Thailand, Vietnam, Lao PDR, Myanmar, Indonesia, Bangladesh, Singapore, Malaysia, Sri Lanka, Australia, Kyrgyzstan, Tajikistan, Pakistan, India, Kazakhstan, Uzbekistan, Turkmenistan, Arabian Peninsula, Russian Federation, Eastern Europe excl. C.I.S, Ukraine, Turkey, Islamic Republic of Iran, Eastern Africa, Near East, Northern Africa, Western Africa, Southern Africa, European Union/EFTA, Caribbean, Venezuela, Colombia, Ecuador, Argentina, Canada, United States of America*, Central America, Mexico

	Heroin					
Region/country or territory	1994	1995	1996	1997	1998	1999

AFRICA
East Africa

Burundi	0.191 kg [ICPO]	No Report	0.800 kg [Govt]	No Report	No Report	0.006 kg [ICPO] 260 u.
Ethiopia	10.265 kg	3.616 kg	27.472 kg [ICPO]	36.112 kg	8.987 kg	12.582 kg
Kenya	22.781 kg	29.032 kg	15.492 kg	7.787 kg	9.954 kg	17.459 kg
Madagascar	No Report	0.863 kg [INCB]	No Report	No Report	No Report	0.005 kg [ICPO]
Mauritius	6.523 kg	0.790 kg	5.235 kg	6.920 kg	6.060 kg	3.067 kg
Rwanda	No Report	No Report	2.520 kg [Govt]	No Report	No Report	No Report
Uganda	2.800 kg [Govt]	1.519 kg [Govt]	2.722 kg	No Report	1.302 kg	14.170 kg
United Republic of Tanzania	1.325 kg	2.827 kg	No Report	4.852 kg	2.745 kg	7.583 kg
Sub-Total	43.885 kg	38.647 kg	54.241 kg	55.671 kg	29.048 kg	54.872 kg 260 u.

North Africa

Algeria	1.626 kg [INCB]	0.105 kg [INCB]	0.222 kg [ICPO]	No Report	0.256 kg [ICPO]	0.002 kg
Egypt	86.844 kg 0.201 lt.	48.195 kg	48.256 kg	51.222 kg 224.500 lt.	24.416 kg 0.266 lt.	23.627 kg
Libyan Arab Jam.	No Report	No Report	No Report	No Report	4.809 kg	No Report
Morocco	1.545 kg	7.152 kg	0.362 kg 6 u.	0.318 kg [Govt]	1.282 kg	0.437 kg
Tunisia	0.703 kg	5.000 kg	4.575 kg [ICPO]	0.308 kg [ICPO]	0.474 kg	1.391 kg
Sub-Total	90.718 kg 0.201 lt.	60.452 kg	53.415 kg 6 u.	51.848 kg 224.500 lt.	31.237 kg 0.266 lt.	25.457 kg

Southern Africa

Angola	No Report	0.023 kg [ICPO]	No Report	0.010 kg [ICPO]	No Report	(1
Botswana	No Report	0.469 kg [INCB]	No Report	0.228 kg [ICPO]	No Report	No Report
Lesotho	No Report	No Report	No Report	No Report	No Report	0.500 kg [ICPO]
Malawi	No Report	No Report	No Report	No Report	0.200 kg	0.500 kg
Namibia	No Report	No Report	No Report	No Report	No Report	0.003 kg [ICPO]
South Africa	24.745 kg	5.942 kg	0.811 kg	1.548 kg	5.383 kg	7.435 kg [ICPO]
Swaziland	No Report	0.449 kg [INCB]	0.002 kg [ICPO]	1.041 kg [ICPO]	0.010 kg	0.097 kg
Zambia	No Report	152.617 kg [ICPO]	0.939 kg [ICPO]	No Report	No Report	0.369 kg
Zimbabwe	7.058 kg [INCB]	0.294 kg [ICPO]	0.032 kg [ICPO]	No Report	0.740 kg	No Report
Sub-Total	31.803 kg	159.794 kg	1.784 kg	2.827 kg	6.333 kg	8.904 kg

West and Central Africa

Benin	1.998 kg [GSR]	5.162 kg [GSR]	2.271 kg [GSR]	0.143 kg [GSR]	0.888 kg	18.670 kg [GSR]
Burkina Faso	9.000 kg [ICPO]	No Report	1.144 kg [Govt]	222.000 kg [Govt]	No Report	No Report
Cameroon	No Report	No Report	No Report	No Report	2.150 kg	0.400 kg
Chad	0.070 kg	No Report	0.500 kg [Govt]	No Report	No Report	1.800 kg [ICPO]
Congo	0.450 kg [Govt]	No Report	No Report	0.070 kg	No Report	No Report
Côte d'Ivoire	0.047 kg	5.416 kg	4.531 kg	0.538 kg	0.060 kg	1.889 kg 16 u. 19 u.

Source: Annual Report Questionnaire if not otherwise indicated

Heroin

Region/country or territory	1994	1995	1996	1997	1998	1999
AFRICA						
West and Central Africa						
Democratic Republic of the Congo	No Report	No Report	2.654 kg [Govt]	No Report	No Report	No Report
Gabon	0.430 kg [ICPO]	No Report	0.005 kg [ICPO]	No Report	No Report	0.106 kg [ICPO]
Gambia	No Report	No Report	0.084 kg [ICPO]	0.088 kg [ICPO]	0.590 kg [ICPO]	0.039 kg
Ghana	0.153 kg	5.570 kg	3.850 kg [F.O]	0.005 kg	18.023 kg	21.020 kg
Mali	0.034 kg [INCB]	0.250 kg [ICPO]	2.710 kg [Govt]	No Report	No Report	No Report
Mauritania	0.037 kg [ICPO]	No Report	0.173 kg [Govt]	0.005 kg [GSR]	0.005 kg [GSR]	No Report
Niger	0.630 kg [ICPO]	0.032 kg [ICPO]	0.100 kg [ICPO]	0.100 kg [ICPO]	0.412 kg [ICPO]	No Report
Nigeria	91.650 kg	30.265 kg [Govt]	19.379 kg [ICPO]	10.490 kg	5.840 kg [Govt]	81.035 kg
Senegal	77.530 kg [ICPO]	15.088 kg [ICPO]	7.830 kg [F.O]	No Report	0.234 kg [ICPO]	0.071 kg [ICPO] 382 u.
Sierra Leone	0.002 kg [Govt]	0.003 kg [Govt]	0.002 kg	No Report	No Report	No Report
Togo	No Report	No Report	0.027 kg	81.601 kg [Govt]	No Report	No Report
Sub-Total	182.031 kg	61.786 kg	45.260 kg	315.040 kg	28.202 kg 16 u.	125.030 kg 401 u.
Total region	348.437 kg 0.201 lt.	320.679 kg	154.700 kg 6 u.	425.386 kg 224.500 lt.	94.820 kg 0.266 lt. 16 u.	214.263 kg 661 u.
AMERICAS						
Caribbean						
Aruba	9.480 kg [INCB]	4.590 kg [ICPO]	No Report	3.298 kg [INCB]	No Report	5.679 kg [ICPO]
Bahamas	0.540 kg	No Report	No Report	No Report	No Report	No Report
Barbados	No Report	No Report	No Report	No Report	No Report	3.230 kg [HONLC]
Bermuda	0.367 kg [ICPO]	0.109 kg [INCB]	0.100 kg	0.398 kg	No Report	0.836 kg
Cuba	No Report	No Report	1.630 kg	0.700 kg [ICPO]	No Report	3.200 kg [F.O.]
Dominican Republic	No Report	2.912 kg	12.158 kg	11.328 kg	6.891 kg	11.909 kg
Jamaica	0.343 kg [INCB]	0.230 kg [INCB]	0.600 kg [ICPO]	No Report	No Report	No Report
Netherlands Antilles	No Report	No Report	No Report	No Report	No Report	2.000 kg [INCB]
Trinidad Tobago	No Report	No Report	0.719 kg [ICPO]	No Report	No Report	No Report
Sub-Total	10.730 kg	7.841 kg	15.207 kg	15.724 kg	6.891 kg	26.854 kg
Central America						
Costa Rica	16.990 kg	9.730 kg	18.000 kg [CICAD]	26.000 kg [CICAD]	13.500 kg	2.400 kg
El Salvador	No Report	No Report	No Report	2.151 kg [ICPO]	0.697 kg [ICPO]	0.099 kg
Guatemala	No Report	No Report	13.479 kg	17.420 kg [Govt]	3.650 kg	53.000 kg
Honduras	4.000 kg [INCB]	No Report	No Report	No Report	No Report	No Report
Nicaragua	No Report	1.000 kg [INCB]	1.000 kg	2.000 kg	No Report	2.000 kg [CICAD]
Panama	8.018 kg	29.613 kg	10.047 kg	33.307 kg	22.825 kg	46.456 kg
Sub-Total	29.008 kg	40.343 kg	42.526 kg	80.878 kg	40.672 kg	103.955 kg

Source: Annual Report Questionnaire if not otherwise indicated

Region/country or territory	Heroin					
	1994	1995	1996	1997	1998	1999
AMERICAS						
North America						
Canada	62.172 kg	106.439 kg	83.000 kg	95.000 kg	22.295 kg 0.176 lt. 994 u.	88.000 kg 91 u.
Mexico	297.465 kg	203.177 kg	363.457 kg	114.903 kg	120.896 kg	260.191 kg
United States	1293.600 kg Govt	1337.100 kg	1366.300 kg	1542.000 kg	1580.700 kg Govt	1200.000 kg 437 u.
Sub-Total	1653.237 kg	1646.716 kg	1812.757 kg	1751.903 kg	1723.891 kg 0.176 lt. 994 u.	1548.191 kg 528 u.
South America						
Argentina	No Report	ICPO	No Report	38.580 kg	31.040 kg	7.962 kg
Bolivia	No Report	No Report	No Report	No Report	0.760 kg	No Report
Brazil	12.788 kg INCB	0.006 kg	No Report	No Report	0.950 kg	No Report
Colombia	95.399 kg	145.023 kg	80.772 kg	129.735 kg	239.154 kg	514.592 kg
Ecuador	2.321 kg	34.950 kg	80.980 kg	53.096 kg	58.248 kg	80.559 kg
Suriname	No Report	No Report	No Report	No Report	0.030 kg	No Report
Uruguay	No Report	1.601 kg	No Report	No Report	No Report	No Report
Venezuela	14.590 kg	80.945 kg	56.002 kg	16.086 kg CICAD	No Report	41.514 kg
Sub-Total	125.098 kg	262.525 kg	217.754 kg	237.497 kg	330.182 kg	644.627 kg
Total region	1818.073 kg	1957.425 kg	2088.244 kg	2086.002 kg	2101.636 kg 0.176 lt. 994 u.	2323.627 kg 528 u.
ASIA						
Central Asia and Transcaucasian countries						
Armenia	No Report	No Report	0.171 kg	0.429 kg	0.065 kg	0.191 kg
Azerbaijan	0.097 kg ICPO	0.124 kg Govt	0.098 kg ICPO	0.170 kg ICPO	4.332 kg	4.018 kg
Georgia	No Report	No Report	0.310 kg ICPO	No Report	0.083 kg ICPO	2.300 kg ICPO
Kazakhstan	0.026 kg	No Report	No Report	43.000 kg Govt	24.196 kg	54.264 kg
Kyrgyzstan	No Report	0.199 kg	30.000 kg Govt	4.404 kg	24.732 kg	26.870 kg
Tajikistan	No Report	No Report	6.350 kg	60.000 kg	271.471 kg	708.820 kg
Turkmenistan	12.000 kg Govt	No Report	No Report	1948.000 kg Govt	495.000 kg Govt	240.000 kg F.O.
Uzbekistan	1.849 kg	10.060 kg	18.000 kg Govt	70.269 kg	194.679 kg	324.843 kg
Sub-Total	13.972 kg	10.383 kg	54.929 kg	2126.272 kg	1014.558 kg	1361.306 kg
East and South-East Asia						
Brunei Darussalam	0.028 kg	0.013 kg	0.032 kg	0.001 kg	0.003 kg	No Report
Cambodia	6.000 kg ICPO	80.000 kg Govt	No Report	16.000 kg ICPO	No Report	No Report
China	4086.088 kg INCB	2375.000 kg	4347.000 kg	5477.000 kg	7358.000 kg	5364.000 kg ICPO
China (Hong Kong SAR)	446.086 kg	411.000 kg Govt	309.100 kg	202.200 kg	209.000 kg Govt	284.001 kg 0.003 lt.
Indonesia	42.801 kg	1.709 kg 20 u.	1.709 kg 20 u.	20.433 kg	27.761 kg	14.049 kg

Source: Annual Report Questionnaire if not otherwise indicated

Region/country or territory	Heroin					
	1994	1995	1996	1997	1998	1999

ASIA

East and South-East Asia

Japan	10.229 kg	7.741 kg	3.974 kg	5.990 kg	3.947 kg	2.150 kg
Korea (Republic of)	1.987 kg Govt	3.626 kg	1.791 kg	0.599 kg	2.126 kg	0.342 kg
Lao People's Dem. Rep.	44.900 kg	49.650 kg Govt	16.200 kg Govt	72.300 kg Govt	No Report	14.750 kg HNLP
Macau	0.842 kg	0.370 kg INCB	0.348 kg ICPO	0.231 kg ICPO	2.217 kg ICPO	1.000 kg INCB
Malaysia	212.200 kg Govt	119.259 kg	240.734 kg Govt	276.154 kg	289.664 kg	200.937 kg
Myanmar	233.459 kg	72.609 kg	504.603 kg	1401.079 kg	403.805 kg	273.193 kg
Philippines	23.000 kg	No Report	1.534 kg	3.014 kg ICPO	1.741 kg ICPO	0.022 kg
Singapore	67.838 kg	50.232 kg	121.291 kg	82.613 kg	141.852 kg	56.730 kg
Thailand	1295.250 kg Govt	517.790 kg Govt	597.650 kg ICPO	323.287 kg	507.769 kg	405.034 kg
Viet Nam	15.400 kg Govt	20.500 kg ICPO	54.750 kg ICPO	24.300 kg ICPO	60.000 kg ICPO	66.663 kg F.O.
Sub-Total	6486.107 kg	3709.499 kg 20 u.	6200.717 kg 20 u.	7905.201 kg	9007.884 kg	6682.871 kg 0.003 lt.

Near and Middle East /South-West Asia

Bahrain	2.354 kg	2.126 kg	12.703 kg	4.165 kg	3.982 kg ICPO	2.856 kg ICPO
Iran (Islamic Republic of)	865.000 kg	2075.000 kg	804.500 kg	1986.042 kg	2894.462 kg Govt	6030.000 kg Govt
Iraq	No Report	No Report	No Report	No Report	8.300 kg	No Report
Israel	117.616 kg	94.445 kg	80.404 kg	75.100 kg	137.800 kg	111.830 kg ICPO
Jordan	9.100 kg 429 u.	5.646 kg	67.387 kg	82.449 kg	52.397 kg	41.397 kg
Kuwait	3.175 kg	7.286 kg INCB	47.525 kg ICPO	23.590 kg ICPO	21.601 kg	35.000 kg INCB
Lebanon	18.172 kg	20.723 kg	50.771 kg	2.361 kg	3.093 kg	8.149 kg
Oman	0.104 kg	6.271 kg	8.000 kg INCB	0.756 kg INCB	No Report	54.109 kg
Pakistan	6443.677 kg Govt	10760.100 kg ICPO	5872.105 kg ICPO	6156.000 kg ICPO	3363.723 kg	4973.711 kg
Qatar	0.274 kg	0.189 kg	0.338 kg	No Report	1.480 kg ICPO	0.108 kg ICPO
Saudi Arabia	112.402 kg	324.147 kg	483.416 kg ICPO	115.667 kg ICPO	63.107 kg	No Report
Syrian Arab Republic	8.169 kg ICPO	16.560 kg	9.783 kg	12.264 kg	36.204 kg	57.659 kg
United Arab Emirates	47.205 kg	76.479 kg	21.635 kg	35.767 kg	34.450 kg	65.909 kg
Yemen	4.605 kg Govt	No Report	No Report	No Report	0.027 kg ICPO	No Report
Sub-Total	7631.853 kg 429 u.	13388.970 kg	7458.567 kg	8494.160 kg	6620.626 kg	11380.730 kg

South Asia

Bangladesh	12.872 kg	No Report	16.800 kg	No Report	No Report	28.840 kg F.O.
India	1011.000 kg	1681.000 kg	1257.000 kg Govt	1332.000 kg	655.000 kg	839.000 kg
Maldives	0.037 kg	0.023 kg	No Report	No Report	1.142 kg	0.357 kg
Nepal	17.119 kg	7.320 kg	9.989 kg	No Report	9.041 kg	1.550 kg
Sri Lanka	22.090 kg	40.332 kg	39.815 kg	55.015 kg	56.942 kg	68.500 kg
Sub-Total	1063.118 kg	1728.675 kg	1323.604 kg	1387.015 kg	722.125 kg	938.247 kg

Source: Annual Report Questionnaire if not otherwise indicated

Region/country or territory	Heroin					
	1994	1995	1996	1997	1998	1999
ASIA						
Total region	15195.050 kg 429 u.	18837.530 kg 20 u.	15037.820 kg 20 u.	19912.650 kg	17365.190 kg	20363.150 kg 0.003 lt.
EUROPE						
Eastern Europe						
Albania	No Report	No Report	No Report	No Report	No Report	7.122 kg [ICPO]
Belarus	3.400 kg	1.696 kg	No Report	0.635 kg [INCB]	0.907 kg	1.977 kg
Bosnia Herzegovina	No Report	No Report	No Report	No Report	5.469 kg [ICPO]	1.125 kg [ICPO]
Bulgaria	363.408 kg	199.379 kg	248.265 kg	322.691 kg	219.632 kg	265.249 kg
Croatia	12.070 kg	38.294 kg	2.273 kg	3.040 kg	50.095 kg	13.232 kg
Czech Republic	62.349 kg	5.000 kg	20.125 kg	21.442 kg	240.000 kg	108.380 kg
Estonia	No Report	No Report	No Report	No Report	0.091 kg 129 u.	0.518 kg 1269 u.
FYR of Macedonia	No Report	110.340 kg	29.339 kg [ICPO]	No Report	91.672 kg	16.375 kg [ICPO]
Hungary	812.319 kg [INCB]	568.075 kg [INCB]	319.205 kg	206.160 kg [Govt]	634.613 kg	172.703 kg
Latvia	No Report	No Report	No Report	0.011 kg	0.098 kg	0.768 kg
Lithuania	No Report	0.026 kg	No Report	0.089 kg	0.423 kg	0.923 kg
Poland	64.300 kg	66.354 kg	43.189 kg	142.812 kg	67.405 kg	44.947 kg
Republic of Moldova	559.106 kg [INCB]	0.006 kg [ICPO]	No Report	10.000 kg	No Report	No Report
Romania	348.975 kg	54.484 kg	103.347 kg	117.922 kg [ICPO]	412.327 kg	63.630 kg
Russian Federation	8.800 kg [Govt]	6.500 kg	18.100 kg	24.027 kg	442.900 kg	695.085 kg
Slovakia	3.657 kg	120.950 kg [INCB]	11.000 kg [INCB]	90.450 kg	13.671 kg	5.808 kg
Slovenia	13.810 kg	18.152 kg [ICPO]	24.571 kg	29.828 kg	46.106 kg	32.270 kg
Ukraine	No Report	9.502 kg [ICPO]	4.025 kg	3.728 kg	8.940 kg	21.530 kg [WIB]
Yugoslavia	31.785 kg	No Report	No Report	15.425 kg [ICPO]	No Report	No Report
Sub-Total	2283.979 kg	1198.758 kg	823.439 kg	988.260 kg	2234.349 kg 129 u.	1451.642 kg 1269 u.
Western Europe						
Andorra	0.007 kg [ICPO]	0.014 kg [ICPO]	No Report	0.005 kg [ICPO]	0.003 kg [ICPO]	0.013 kg
Austria	80.220 kg	47.015 kg	81.326 kg	102.138 kg	118.213 kg	78.914 kg
Belgium	136.865 kg	129.399 kg	133.000 kg	55.000 kg	75.790 kg	73.537 kg
Cyprus	0.999 kg	No Report	0.004 kg	No Report	0.035 kg	2.193 kg
Denmark	29.000 kg [INCB]	37.400 kg	61.400 kg	37.900 kg	55.136 kg	96.040 kg
Finland	1.557 kg	16.117 kg	6.450 kg	2.532 kg	1.965 kg	2.884 kg
France	661.032 kg [Govt]	498.629 kg	617.241 kg	415.453 kg	343.783 kg	203.313 kg
Germany	1590.498 kg	933.384 kg	898.191 kg	722.211 kg	685.920 kg	796.400 kg
Gibraltar	No Report	No Report	0.001 kg	No Report	0.011 kg 1 u.	0.021 kg 2 u.
Greece	284.884 kg 25 u.	172.814 kg 20 u.	193.656 kg 38 u.	146.311 kg 38 u.	232.110 kg 6 u.	98.401 kg 10 u.
Iceland	0.002 kg	No Report	No Report	No Report	No Report	0.001 kg
Ireland	4.649 kg [ICPO]	6.400 kg [ICPO]	10.800 kg	8.184 kg	36.963 kg	15.921 kg

Source: Annual Report Questionnaire if not otherwise indicated

Heroin

Region/country or territory	1994	1995	1996	1997	1998	1999
EUROPE						
Western Europe						
Italy	1151.227 kg 5363 u.	939.520 kg 6144 u.	1251.432 kg	470.335 kg 5360 u.	703.335 kg 3069 u.	1313.708 kg [ICPO]
Liechtenstein	27.741 kg	0.006 kg	9.303 kg	18.680 kg	No Report	14.388 kg
Luxembourg	0.906 kg	13.248 kg	2.934 kg	2.525 kg	3.592 kg	1.914 kg
Malta	0.568 kg	2.130 kg	2.658 kg	4.535 kg	0.498 kg	1.724 kg
Monaco	0.005 kg	0.001 kg	0.003 kg	0.011 kg	[(2]	No Report
Netherlands	246.000 kg [INCB]	351.000 kg [ICPO]	361.000 kg [ICPO]	190.400 kg	2072.000 kg 963 u.	770.000 kg
Norway	26.326 kg	48.390 kg	74.080 kg	55.509 kg	37.347 kg	45.810 kg
Portugal	89.038 kg	65.507 kg	46.697 kg	57.389 kg	96.666 kg	76.417 kg
Spain	824.391 kg	546.005 kg	537.219 kg	479.450 kg	444.243 kg	1159.297 kg
Sweden	20.961 kg	31.884 kg 0.004 lt.	39.621 kg	11.509 kg	70.927 kg 0.011 lt.	63.009 kg 0.509 lt.
Switzerland	224.600 kg	212.686 kg	405.732 kg	209.261 kg	403.680 kg	397.527 kg
Turkey	2171.698 kg	3456.458 kg	4422.000 kg	3509.851 kg	4651.486 kg	3605.123 kg
United Kingdom	744.200 kg	1394.600 kg	1070.100 kg	2234.900 kg	1345.804 kg	2341.700 kg [NCIS]
Sub-Total	8317.375 kg 5388 u.	8902.606 kg 0.004 lt. 6164 u.	10224.850 kg 38 u.	8734.089 kg 5398 u.	11379.510 kg 0.011 lt. 4039 u.	11158.260 kg 0.509 lt. 12 u.
Total region	10601.350 kg 5388 u.	10101.360 kg 0.004 lt. 6164 u.	11048.290 kg 38 u.	9722.349 kg 5398 u.	13613.860 kg 0.011 lt. 4168 u.	12609.900 kg 0.509 lt. 1281 u.
OCEANIA						
Oceania						
Australia	248.499 kg [(3]	49.425 kg [(3] 0.105 lt. 8 u.	46.604 kg 278 u.	365.370 kg	298.690 kg [Govt (4]	689.000 kg [INCB]
New Zealand	0.334 kg [ICPO]	0.083 kg [Govt]	1.000 kg [INCB]	0.171 kg [INCB]	10.859 kg	0.544 kg
Sub-Total	248.833 kg	49.508 kg 0.105 lt. 8 u.	47.604 kg 278 u.	365.541 kg	309.549 kg	689.544 kg
Total region	248.833 kg	49.508 kg 0.105 lt. 8 u.	47.604 kg 278 u.	365.541 kg	309.549 kg	689.544 kg
TOTAL	28211.740 kg 0.201 lt. 5817 u.	31266.500 kg 0.109 lt. 6192 u.	28376.650 kg 342 u.	32511.920 kg 224.500 lt. 5398 u.	33485.060 kg 0.453 lt. 5178 u.	36200.480 kg 0.512 lt. 2470 u.

1) Small quantity. 2) Including depressants. 3) Fiscal year 4) Provisional figures.

Source: Annual Report Questionnaire if not otherwise indicated

Region/country or territory	Morphine					
	1994	1995	1996	1997	1998	1999
AFRICA						
East Africa						
Ethiopia	2 u.	0.008 lt. ICPO	No Report	No Report	0.001 kg 6 u.	No Report
Mauritius	1.102 kg	No Report	No Report	No Report	No Report	No Report
United Republic of Tanzania	No Report	No Report	No Report	0.283 kg	No Report	0.020 kg
Sub-Total	1.102 kg 2 u.	0.008 lt.		0.283 kg	0.001 kg 6 u.	0.020 kg
North Africa						
Egypt	0.020 lt.	0.012 lt.	0.024 lt.	0.001 kg	(1	0.007 kg
Morocco	No Report		0.110 kg	0.318 kg	0.997 kg	No Report
Sub-Total	0.020 lt.	0.012 lt.	0.110 kg 0.024 lt.	0.319 kg	0.997 kg	0.007 kg
Southern Africa						
Mozambique	No Report	No Report	No Report	No Report	No Report	0.085 kg ICPO
Swaziland	No Report	0.001 kg ICPO	No Report	No Report	No Report	No Report
Zambia	No Report	0.500 kg ICPO	No Report	No Report	3.200 kg Govt	0.028 kg
Sub-Total		0.501 kg			3.200 kg	0.113 kg
West and Central Africa						
Benin	No Report	No Report	No Report	No Report	3.190 kg	No Report
Nigeria	No Report	No Report	0.019 kg ICPO	0.130 kg	No Report	No Report
Sub-Total			0.019 kg	0.130 kg	3.190 kg	
Total region	1.102 kg 0.020 lt. 2 u.	0.501 kg 0.020 lt.	0.129 kg 0.024 lt.	0.732 kg	7.388 kg 6 u.	0.140 kg
AMERICAS						
Caribbean						
Cuba	No Report	No Report	23 u.	No Report	No Report	No Report
Dominican Republic	0.831 kg	No Report	No Report	No Report	No Report	No Report
Sub-Total	0.831 kg		23 u.			
Central America						
Guatemala	No Report	No Report	No Report	0.720 kg Govt	No Report	No Report
Sub-Total				0.720 kg		
North America						
Canada	0.095 kg 1.616 lt.	0.044 kg 0.532 lt.	0.100 kg 0.172 lt. 329 u.	1.076 kg 2468 u.	1.662 kg 0.433 lt. 1166 u.	1.000 kg 1.016 lt. 1826 u.
Mexico	No Report	3.002 kg	No Report	2.068 kg	No Report	1.130 kg
United States	39.204 kg	0.121 kg	0.081 kg 482 u.	0.006 lt. 560 u.	No Report	3.134 kg 998 u.

Source: Annual Report Questionnaire if not otherwise indicated

Region/country or territory	1994	1995	1996	1997	1998	1999
Morphine						

AMERICAS

North America

Sub-Total	39.299 kg	3.167 kg	0.181 kg	3.144 kg	1.662 kg	5.264 kg
	1.616 lt.	0.532 lt.	0.172 lt.	0.006 lt.	0.433 lt.	1.016 lt.
			811 u.	3028 u.	1166 u.	2824 u.

South America

Argentina	No Report	ICPO	No Report	No Report	No Report	650.000 kg
Brazil	No Report	No Report	No Report	No Report	No Report	0.150 kg
Chile	No Report	80 u.	No Report	No Report	29 u.	1 u.[ICPO]
Colombia	85.746 kg	290.240 kg	94.120 kg	87.122 kg	79.111 kg	154.023 kg
Peru	No Report	0.002 kg	0.001 kg	No Report	No Report	No Report
Sub-Total	85.746 kg	290.242 kg	94.121 kg	87.122 kg	79.111 kg	804.173 kg
		80 u.			29 u.	1 u.
Total region	125.876 kg	293.409 kg	94.302 kg	90.986 kg	80.773 kg	809.437 kg
	1.616 lt.	0.532 lt.	0.172 lt.	0.006 lt.	0.433 lt.	1.016 lt.
		80 u.	834 u.	3028 u.	1195 u.	2825 u.

ASIA

Central Asia and Transcaucasian countries

Armenia	171 u.	1.177 kg[ICPO]	12 u.	3 u.	(1	No Report
Azerbaijan	0.260 kg[ICPO]	No Report	No Report	No Report	No Report	0.085 kg
Georgia	No Report	No Report	0.022 kg[ICPO]	No Report	No Report	0.003 kg[ICPO]
			0.057 lt.			
			1659 u.			
Kazakhstan	1.167 kg	No Report	No Report	No Report	4.172 kg	1.493 kg
Kyrgyzstan	No Report	7.840 kg	21 u.	No Report	No Report	No Report
Uzbekistan	No Report	No Report	No Report	8 u.	0.030 kg	3.400 kg[ICPO]
Sub-Total	1.427 kg	9.017 kg	0.022 kg	11 u.	4.202 kg	4.981 kg
	171 u.		0.057 lt.			
			1692 u.			

East and South-East Asia

China	No Report	113.000 kg	178.000 kg	358.000 kg	146.000 kg	No Report
China (Hong Kong SAR)	0.194 kg	No Report	17.300 kg	No Report	No Report	(1
Indonesia	0.701 kg	0.002 kg	0.002 kg	0.320 kg	No Report	3.174 kg
						202 u.
Japan	0.006 kg	No Report	0.835 kg	0.011 kg	0.363 kg	0.002 kg
				1.107 lt.	0.002 lt.	
				229 u.	146 u.	
Korea (Republic of)	2.998 kg[INCB]	No Report	No Report	No Report	No Report	No Report
Lao People's Dem. Rep.	8.000 kg	No Report	No Report	No Report	No Report	No Report
Macau	No Report	0.273 kg[INCB]	No Report	No Report	No Report	No Report
Malaysia	27.940 kg[ICPO]	0.007 kg	No Report	No Report	No Report	No Report
Myanmar	0.004 kg	No Report	No Report	45.728 kg	95.087 kg	24.001 kg
				200 u.		

Source: Annual Report Questionnaire if not otherwise indicated

Region/country or territory	1994	1995	1996	1997	1998	1999
			Morphine			

ASIA

East and South-East Asia

Region/country or territory	1994	1995	1996	1997	1998	1999
Thailand	No Report	0.630 kg [Govt]	No Report	0.005 kg	No Report	0.200 kg [ICPO]
Viet Nam	3.000 kg [Govt]	3.000 kg [ICPO]	12937 u. [ICPO]	No Report	No Report	No Report
Sub-Total	42.843 kg	116.912 kg	196.137 kg 12937 u.	404.064 kg 1.107 lt. 429 u.	241.450 kg 0.002 lt. 146 u.	27.377 kg 202 u.

Near and Middle East /South-West Asia

Region/country or territory	1994	1995	1996	1997	1998	1999
Iran (Islamic Republic of)	12902.000 kg	11046.000 kg	10430.000 kg	18949.754 kg	22291.102 kg [Govt]	22764.000 kg [Govt]
Israel	No Report	0.041 kg	0.005 kg 25 u.	No Report	No Report	0.028 kg [ICPO]
Kuwait	No Report	No Report	0.007 kg [ICPO]	No Report	No Report	34.813 kg [ICPO]
Lebanon	No Report	317.077 kg	No Report	No Report	No Report	No Report
Oman	No Report	No Report	No Report	No Report	No Report	1.006 kg
Qatar	No Report	No Report	No Report	0.133 kg [ICPO]	No Report	No Report
Saudi Arabia	No Report	No Report	No Report	No Report	No Report	149.491 kg [ICPO]
United Arab Emirates	No Report	No Report	No Report	No Report	0.018 kg	0.030 kg
Sub-Total	12902.000 kg	11363.120 kg	10430.010 kg 25 u.	18949.890 kg	22291.120 kg	22949.370 kg

South Asia

Region/country or territory	1994	1995	1996	1997	1998	1999
India	51.000 kg 44500 u.	4.000 kg	4.000 kg [Govt]	128.000 kg	19.000 kg	30.000 kg
Nepal	No Report	No Report	No Report	11.126 kg [ICPO]	No Report	No Report
Sub-Total	51.000 kg 44500 u.	4.000 kg	4.000 kg	139.126 kg	19.000 kg	30.000 kg
Total region	12997.270 kg 44671 u.	11493.050 kg	10630.170 kg 0.057 lt. 14654 u.	19493.080 kg 1.107 lt. 440 u.	22555.770 kg 0.002 lt. 146 u.	23011.720 kg 202 u.

EUROPE

Eastern Europe

Region/country or territory	1994	1995	1996	1997	1998	1999
Belarus	No Report	3.617 kg	No Report	0.001 kg [INCB]	0.154 kg	0.005 kg
Bulgaria	No Report	4.895 kg	No Report	4.000 kg	No Report	16 u.
Croatia	No Report	103 u.	17 u.	No Report	79 u.	652 u.
Estonia	No Report	No Report	0.508 lt. [ICPO]	[2]	0.003 kg 5 u.	No Report
Hungary	No Report	6.400 kg [INCB]	0.209 kg	0.686 kg [Govt]	No Report	0.200 kg
Latvia	No Report	0.030 kg 30 u.	No Report	No Report	No Report	No Report
Lithuania	0.001 kg	0.250 kg	0.365 lt.	No Report	No Report	No Report
Republic of Moldova	No Report	No Report	No Report	31 u.	No Report	No Report
Romania	288 u.	51 u.	74 u.	71 u. [ICPO]	86 u.	132 u.

Source: Annual Report Questionnaire if not otherwise indicated

Region/country or territory	Morphine					
	1994	**1995**	**1996**	**1997**	**1998**	**1999**
EUROPE						
Eastern Europe						
Russian Federation	19.353 kg [ICPO]	3.500 kg	45.141 kg	6.037 kg 8 u.	15.000 kg [F.O.]	2.427 kg
Slovakia	No Report	No Report	No Report	No Report	3 u.	
Sub-Total	19.354 kg 288 u.	18.692 kg 184 u.	45.350 kg 0.873 lt. 91 u.	10.724 kg 110 u.	15.157 kg 173 u.	2.632 kg 800 u.
Western Europe						
Austria	0.532 kg	0.434 kg	0.815 kg	0.327 kg	1.522 kg	0.328 kg
Belgium	7.754 kg	19.080 kg	No Report	10.000 kg	0.098 kg	
Denmark	0.146 kg [INCB]	1.062 kg	0.981 kg	1.560 lt.	3.000 kg	No Report
Finland	0.009 kg	0.002 kg	0.066 kg 2422 u.	0.005 kg	No Report	0.910 kg 60 u.
France	1.956 kg [INCB]	0.095 kg	0.080 kg	0.020 kg	0.088 kg	1.566 kg
Greece	0.207 kg	0.005 kg	0.004 kg	No Report	No Report	No Report
Ireland	No Report	979 u. [ICPO]	1261 u.	0.003 kg 528 u.	0.004 kg	90 u. [ICPO]
Italy	0.283 kg 46 u.	0.021 kg 1 u.	0.042 kg	0.095 kg 9 u.	2.270 kg 12 u.	1.314 kg [ICPO]
Norway	0.001 kg	0.255 kg 1149 u.	No Report	0.011 kg	0.008 kg 33 u.	0.001 kg 1219 u.
Portugal	No Report	No Report	11 u.	No Report	0.005 kg	85 u.
Spain	No Report	No Report	74 u.	8 u.	3 u.	13 u.
Sweden	0.005 kg 129 u.	0.006 kg 0.327 lt.	0.170 kg	0.003 kg 104 u.	0.154 lt.	0.011 kg 0.202 lt. 120 u.
Switzerland	No Report	0.099 kg [ICPO]	0.040 kg	No Report	0.054 kg	0.537 kg
Turkey	302.269 kg	939.271 kg	1157.000 kg	662.816 kg	754.494 kg	1010.328 kg
United Kingdom	31.400 kg	2.000 kg	1.600 kg	0.400 kg	41.251 kg	1.300 kg [NCIS]
Sub-Total	344.562 kg 175 u.	962.330 kg 0.327 lt. 2129 u.	1160.798 kg 3768 u.	673.680 kg 1.560 lt. 649 u.	802.794 kg 0.154 lt. 48 u.	1016.295 kg 0.202 lt. 1587 u.
Total region	363.916 kg 463 u.	981.022 kg 0.327 lt. 2313 u.	1206.148 kg 0.873 lt. 3859 u.	684.404 kg 1.560 lt. 759 u.	817.951 kg 0.154 lt. 221 u.	1018.927 kg 0.202 lt. 2387 u.
OCEANIA						
Oceania						
Australia	No Report	0.013 kg [(3] 61 u.	1.086 kg 56 u.	2.049 kg	No Report	No Report
New Zealand	0.018 kg [ICPO] 318 u.	0.002 kg [INCB] 0.002 lt.	No Report	1.422 kg [INCB]	1.166 kg	0.312 kg
Sub-Total	0.018 kg 318 u.	0.015 kg 0.002 lt. 61 u.	1.086 kg 56 u.	3.471 kg	1.166 kg	0.312 kg

Source: Annual Report Questionnaire if not otherwise indicated

Region/country or territory	Morphine					
	1994	1995	1996	1997	1998	1999
OCEANIA						
Total region	0.018 kg	0.015 kg	1.086 kg	3.471 kg	1.166 kg	0.312 kg
	318 u.	0.002 lt.	56 u.			
		61 u.				
TOTAL	13488.180 kg	12767.990 kg	11931.840 kg	20272.670 kg	23463.050 kg	24840.540 kg
	1.636 lt.	0.881 lt.	1.126 lt.	2.673 lt.	0.589 lt.	1.218 lt.
	45454 u.	2454 u.	19403 u.	4227 u.	1568 u.	5414 u.

1) Small quantity. 2) Including depressants. 3) Fiscal year

Source: Annual Report Questionnaire if not otherwise indicated

Region/country or territory	1994	1995	1996	1997	1998	1999
Other opiates						

AFRICA

East Africa

Region/country or territory	1994	1995	1996	1997	1998	1999
Mauritius	793 u.	0.229 kg	No Report	26 u. [ICPO]	No Report	No Report
Sub-Total	793 u.	0.229 kg		26 u.		
North Africa						
Egypt	No Report	30.904 lt.	[1]	No Report	No Report	No Report
Sub-Total		30.904 lt.				
Total region	793 u.	0.229 kg 30.904 lt.		26 u.		

AMERICAS

Caribbean

Region/country or territory	1994	1995	1996	1997	1998	1999
Cayman Islands	No Report	No Report	No Report	No Report	No Report	0.003 kg [ICPO]
Dominican Republic	No Report	No Report	No Report	No Report	No Report	8.000 kg [ICPO]
Sub-Total						8.003 kg
North America						
Canada	0.551 kg	0.140 kg 3055 u.	1.355 kg 2524 u.	0.912 kg 0.301 lt. 4826 u.	1.446 kg 0.093 lt. 8880 u.	0.594 kg 8805 u.
United States	No Report	0.072 kg 19431 u.	6.112 kg 72075 u.	No Report	No Report	9338 u. [ICPO] [2]
Sub-Total	0.551 kg	0.212 kg 22486 u.	7.467 kg 74599 u.	0.912 kg 0.301 lt. 4826 u.	1.446 kg 0.093 lt. 8880 u.	0.594 kg 18143 u.
South America						
Chile	No Report	No Report	No Report	No Report	25 u.	No Report
Colombia	2.000 kg	No Report	No Report	No Report	No Report	3.500 kg [2]
Peru	No Report	No Report	No Report	No Report	No Report	38.693 kg [ICPO]
Sub-Total	2.000 kg				25 u.	42.193 kg
Total region	2.551 kg	0.212 kg 22486 u.	7.467 kg 74599 u.	0.912 kg 0.301 lt. 4826 u.	1.446 kg 0.093 lt. 8905 u.	50.790 kg 18143 u.

ASIA

Central Asia and Transcaucasian countries

Region/country or territory	1994	1995	1996	1997	1998	1999
Armenia	No Report	No Report	50 u.	No Report	No Report	0.017 kg [ICPO]
Georgia	No Report	No Report	30.150 kg [ICPO] 3980 u.	No Report	No Report	25.003 kg [ICPO] [3]
Kazakhstan	4.606 kg	416.000 kg	No Report	No Report	3.219 kg	7.944 kg
Kyrgyzstan	No Report	1.642 kg	7.484 kg	No Report	No Report	No Report
Tajikistan	No Report	No Report	66.000 kg	No Report	No Report	No Report
Uzbekistan	No Report	7.225 kg	0.169 kg [ICPO]	0.019 kg	No Report	No Report
Sub-Total	4.606 kg	424.867 kg	103.803 kg 4030 u.	0.019 kg	3.219 kg	32.964 kg

Source: Annual Report Questionnaire if not otherwise indicated

Region/country or territory	Other opiates					
	1994	1995	1996	1997	1998	1999

ASIA

East and South-East Asia

Region/country or territory	1994	1995	1996	1997	1998	1999
Brunei Darussalam	72.893 lt. 5085 u.	488.235 lt.	309.272 lt. 3714 u.	85.173 kg 554 u.	0.057 kg 474 u.	12.970 lt. 2377 u.
China (Hong Kong SAR)	No Report	0.150 kg [ICPO]	No Report	No Report	No Report	187 u. [(3]
Indonesia	No Report	138 u.	No Report	No Report	7179 u.	564 u. [ICPO (2]
Japan	0.001 kg	0.029 kg 177 u.	0.004 kg 88 u.	0.141 kg 1809 u.	0.006 kg 0.030 lt. 5557 u.	0.005 kg
Macau	No Report	No Report	159 u. [ICPO]	64 u. [ICPO]	8.000 lt. [ICPO] 45 u.	No Report
Malaysia	No Report	No Report	No Report	No Report	No Report	18453 u.
Myanmar	No Report	No Report	No Report	194.377 kg	No Report	555.000 kg 121.000 lt.
Singapore	87 u.	163 u.	525 u.	136 u.	301 u.	0.438 kg [(3]
Thailand	No Report	No Report	No Report	No Report	No Report	381.600 lt. [ICPO (2]
Viet Nam	No Report	No Report	1.400 kg [ICPO]	No Report	No Report	No Report
Sub-Total	0.001 kg 72.893 lt. 5172 u.	0.179 kg 488.235 lt. 478 u.	1.404 kg 309.272 lt. 4486 u.	279.691 kg 2563 u.	0.063 kg 8.030 lt. 13556 u.	555.443 kg 515.570 lt. 21581 u.

Near and Middle East /South-West Asia

Region/country or territory	1994	1995	1996	1997	1998	1999
Iran (Islamic Republic of)	No Report	No Report	No Report	255.065 kg	No Report	No Report
Israel	No Report	No Report	No Report	No Report	No Report	2.121 lt. [ICPO (2] 7 u.
Jordan	No Report	No Report	1349.464 kg	894.738 kg	No Report	No Report
Kuwait	No Report	0.051 kg [ICPO]	No Report	No Report	No Report	No Report
Qatar	No Report	No Report	0.016 kg 42 u.	No Report	No Report	No Report
Syrian Arab Republic	No Report	No Report	No Report	No Report	No Report	No Report 17 u.
Sub-Total		0.051 kg	1349.480 kg 42 u.	1149.803 kg		32.102 kg 2.121 lt. 24 u.

South Asia

Region/country or territory	1994	1995	1996	1997	1998	1999
Bangladesh	62252 u.	No Report	85903 u.	No Report	No Report	No Report
Nepal	No Report	No Report	No Report	4971 u. [ICPO]	3676 u.	No Report
Sub-Total	62252 u.		85903 u.	4971 u.	3676 u.	
Total region	4.607 kg 72.893 lt. 67424 u.	425.097 kg 488.235 lt. 478 u.	1454.687 kg 309.272 lt. 94461 u.	1429.513 kg 7534 u.	3.282 kg 8.030 lt. 17232 u.	620.509 kg 517.691 lt. 21605 u.

Source: Annual Report Questionnaire if not otherwise indicated

121

Region/country or territory	Other opiates					
	1994	1995	1996	1997	1998	1999
EUROPE						
Eastern Europe						
Bosnia Herzegovina	No Report	No Report	No Report	No Report	1 u. ICPO	No Report
Bulgaria	No Report	4.330 kg	No Report	No Report	No Report	No Report
Estonia	No Report	No Report	73.529 lt. ICPO	23.332 lt.	No Report	2 u.
FYR of Macedonia	No Report	No Report	No Report	No Report	No Report	3.988 kg ICPO 2.250 lt. 135 u.
Hungary	No Report	No Report	No Report	No Report	438 u.	120 u. ICPO (3
Latvia	No Report	No Report	No Report	0.134 kg	No Report	No Report
Lithuania	No Report	No Report	0.001 kg	No Report	13 u.	0.210 kg 92 u.
Poland	223.000 kg	76.000 kg	2801.000 kg	1004.000 lt.	395.000 lt.	389.000 lt. (4
Republic of Moldova	283 u. ICPO	No Report	No Report	1000 u.	2100 u.	682 u. ICPO
Romania	No Report	No Report	No Report	No Report	19494 u.	26 u. (3
Russian Federation	No Report	No Report	106.400 kg	4.925 kg 11 u.	167.700 kg F.O.	54.575 kg
Slovakia	No Report	No Report	No Report	No Report	922 u.	278 u.
Slovenia	No Report	No Report	No Report	No Report	No Report	0.552 lt.
Ukraine	No Report	No Report	486.500 kg	No Report	No Report	11600 u. ICPO (2
Sub-Total	223.000 kg 283 u.	80.330 kg	3393.901 kg 73.529 lt.	5.059 kg 1027.332 lt. 1011 u.	167.700 kg 395.000 lt. 22968 u.	58.773 kg 391.802 lt. 12935 u.
Western Europe						
Andorra	No Report	2 u. ICPO	No Report	No Report	No Report	No Report
Austria	0.719 kg	0.035 kg	0.477 kg	0.083 kg	No Report	No Report
Belgium	0.032 kg	0.021 kg 1092 u.	No Report	No Report	0.109 kg	9.100 kg ICPO 0.200 lt. 307500 u.
Cyprus	No Report	No Report	No Report	No Report	No Report	55 u. ICPO
Denmark	No Report	338 u. ICPO	No Report	No Report	6.000 kg	No Report
Finland	No Report	No Report	No Report	No Report	No Report	46 u. ICPO
France	No Report	No Report	No Report	No Report	No Report	521 u. ICPO (3
Germany		No Report	No Report	No Report	No Report	No Report
Gibraltar	No Report	No Report	No Report	No Report	No Report	8 u. ICPO (3
Greece	0.089 kg 3784 u.	0.035 kg 4672 u.	0.280 kg 5089 u.	2.308 kg 15322 u.	1.529 kg 6774 u.	0.132 kg 7795 u.
Ireland	No Report	No Report	No Report	No Report	No Report	0.320 kg ICPO (3 579 u.
Italy	0.499 kg 1733 u.	0.100 kg 1 u.	0.170 kg	0.002 kg 7 u.	0.554 kg 7538 u.	2.426 kg ICPO (3
Luxembourg	No Report	No Report	No Report	No Report	No Report	0.180 lt. ICPO (3

Source: Annual Report Questionnaire if not otherwise indicated

Other opiates

Region/country or territory	1994	1995	1996	1997	1998	1999
EUROPE						
Western Europe						
Malta	No Report	No Report	No Report	No Report	77 u.	No Report
Monaco	No Report	0.001 kg	No Report	No Report	No Report	No Report
Netherlands	No Report	No Report	No Report	No Report	No Report	50.000 kg [3] 445.000 lt. 186437 u.
Norway	5797 u.	6454 u.	No Report	No Report	No Report	0.017 kg 9657 u.
Portugal	No Report	No Report	No Report	21 u.	35 u.	21 u.
Spain	No Report	No Report	373 u.	1159 u.	No Report	966 u. [ICPO]
Sweden	No Report	No Report	No Report	No Report	0.003 kg	0.053 kg 783 u.
					1.312 lt.	
Switzerland	No Report	No Report	4305 u.	0.010 kg	No Report	5006 u.
Turkey	No Report	No Report	No Report	No Report	No Report	34090 u. [ICPO] [3]
United Kingdom				1.000 kg 1.000 lt. 1 u.	0.064 kg	No Report
Sub-Total	1.339 kg 11314 u.	0.192 kg 12559 u.	0.927 kg 9767 u.	3.403 kg 1.000 lt. 16510 u.	8.259 kg 1.312 lt. 14424 u.	62.048 kg 445.380 lt. 553464 u.
Total region	224.339 kg 11597 u.	80.522 kg 12559 u.	3394.828 kg 73.529 lt. 9767 u.	8.462 kg 1028.332 lt. 17521 u.	175.959 kg 396.312 lt. 37392 u.	120.821 kg 837.182 lt. 566399 u.
OCEANIA						
Oceania						
Australia	No Report	0.002 kg [5] 4 u.	0.115 kg	[1]	22.243 kg [Govt 6]	6.792 kg [Govt 6]
New Zealand	550 u. [ICPO]	207 u. [ICPO]	No Report	No Report	No Report	0.100 kg
Sub-Total	550 u.	0.002 kg 211 u.	0.115 kg		22.243 kg	6.892 kg
Total region	550 u.	0.002 kg 211 u.	0.115 kg		22.243 kg	6.892 kg
TOTAL	231.497 kg 72.893 lt. 80364 u.	506.062 kg 519.139 lt. 35734 u.	4857.097 kg 382.801 lt. 178827 u.	1438.887 kg 1028.633 lt. 29907 u.	202.930 kg 404.435 lt. 63529 u.	766.91 kg 1354.873 lt. 606147 u.

1) Small quantity. 2) Codeine 3) Methadone 4) Polish heroin (also called "compot") 5) Fiscal year 6) Provisional figures.

Source: Annual Report Questionnaire if not otherwise indicated

TRAFFICKING IN COCAINE

Following strong increases throughout the 1980s, trafficking in cocaine, as reflected in seizure data, stabilized during the 1990s, and even declined slightly in 1999. Seizures remained concentrated in the Americas (about 88% of global seizures in 1999) and to a lesser extent in Europe (about 12% of global seizures).

Regional distribution : The year 1999 was characterized by an overall decline of seizures in the Americas, notably in the Andean region, in Central America and in the Caribbean, reflecting a decline in coca leaf production and cocaine manufacture. However, cocaine seizures in the USA, the world's largest cocaine market, increased in 1999, although within the range of fluctuations observed in recent years (according to preliminary figures, US seizures fell again in 2000). It should be noted that the higher US seizures in 1999 did not reflect an increase in consumption, as cocaine use in that country was even reported to have fallen among the general population.

Seizures declined in Africa and in Asia, possibly as a result of a lesser use of those regions as transit routes to Europe, where, by contrast, the quantity of cocaine intercepted was on the increase, in line with reports of rising availability and consumption.

While North American cocaine seizures as a percentage of global cocaine seizures remained more or less stable at around 47% over the 1990-99 period, the share of European seizures rose from 6% in 1990 to 12% in 1999. Despite those trends, cocaine seizures in North America are still almost four times larger than in western Europe. The US alone accounted for 37% of global cocaine seizures in 1999, three times the amounts reported in western Europe. The largest seizures in western Europe, as in previous years, were reported in Spain and the Netherlands (41% and 24% of all West European seizures, respectively), which continue to be the main entry points of cocaine into the European Union.

After the USA, Colombia has been reporting the largest seizures of cocaine in the world in recent years. Despite a reduction in the quantities it intercepted in 1999, Colombia still accounted for 18% of global cocaine seizures in 1999 (more than western Europe) and for more than 75% of the quantities seized by the three main coca producing countries in the Andean region (Peru 14%; Bolivia 9%). This pattern reflects both the enforcement efforts by the authorities in the three Andean countries as well as the extent of cocaine manufacture and trafficking in the region. Taken together, the three Andean countries seized 83 tonnes in 1999, equivalent to 9% of the estimated global cocaine production.

Preliminary data show that seizures of cocaine-related substances in Colombia might have doubled in 2000, from 64 tonnes (1999) to 121 tonnes (2000), including 95 tonnes of cocaine hydrochloride, generally referred to as 'cocaine'. Most of the large seizures were made in ports along the Pacific coast.

Trafficking routes: US authorities report that close to 90% of the cocaine found on the US market in 1999 originated in, or transited through, Colombia. Seizure

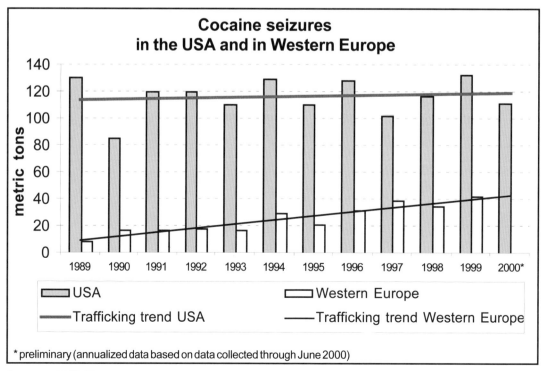

* preliminary (annualized data based on data collected through June 2000)

Sources: UNDCP, Annual Reports Questionnaire / DELTA, DEA

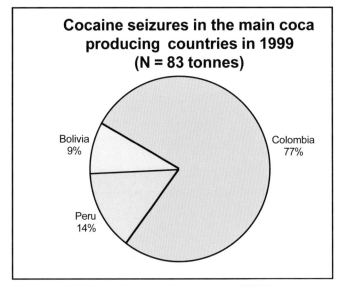

Cocaine seizures in the main coca producing countries in 1999 (N = 83 tonnes)

Colombia 77%
Peru 14%
Bolivia 9%

Source: UNDCP Annual Reports Questionnaire / DELTA

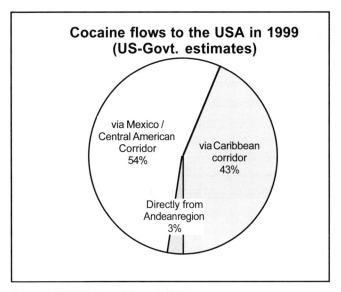

Cocaine flows to the USA in 1999 (US-Govt. estimates)

via Mexico / Central American Corridor 54%
via Caribbean corridor 43%
Directly from Andeanregion 3%

Source: ONDCP, Annual Report, 2001.

data indicate that the bulk of consignments of cocaine continued to be despatched from the Andean region to North America and western Europe by sea, often in containerized freight, but also as deck cargo. Mexican authorities reported a marked increase in shipments of cocaine along the Pacific coast during 1999.

Latin American countries intercepted 182 tons of cocaine in 1999, equivalent to a fifth (20%) of global cocaine manufacture (925 tons in 1999). Almost half of those seizures were made in the three main coca producing countries of the Andean region. Excluding those three countries, half of the remaining Latin American cocaine seizures were concentrated in Mexico and in the countries of Central America in 1999, and a quarter in the Caribbean countries and Venezuela. That distribution supports the thesis that, in the late 1990s, the Central American/Mexican corridor was more important for trafficking than the Caribbean corridor. Brazil, Chile and Argentina accounted for 13% of the seizures, reflecting the existence of local markets and the use of a number of alternative routes by traffickers. Although trafficking outside the two main corridors to the US market is frequently destined for Europe - either directly or via southern or western Africa - some of the quantities seized along those routes were also destined for North America.

According to US intelligence information, Colombia based drug trafficking organisations continue to dominate the cocaine trade, although Mexico based trafficking organizations are playing an increasing role in the US. According to the same sources, while Colombian trafficking organisations continue to control wholesale cocaine distribution in the populated northeastern parts of that country, Mexico based trafficking organisations would now be predominant in the western and midwestern states.

Significant increases in cocaine seizures in 1999 were reported by Mexico, Venezuela, Ecuador and Brazil. In Chile and Argentina they tended to remain stable, reflecting stagnating or falling levels of cocaine manufacture in Bolivia and Peru. Seizures in Central America and the Caribbean region were declining.

In the case of Europe, shipments of cocaine have tended to come directly from the producer countries. Transshipment through countries neighbouring the producing areas seem however to play a growing role (Caribbean countries, Venezuela and Brazil, in particular), along more habitual transit points in southern and western Africa (mostly linked to Brazil). In Spain, Europe's main entry point for cocaine, 48% of all seizures in 1999 were linked to direct shipments from

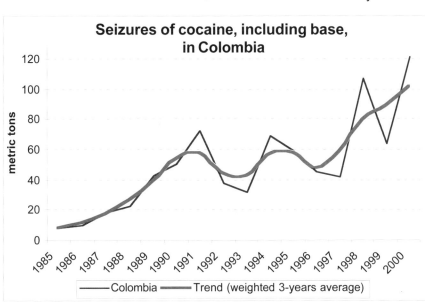

Seizures of cocaine, including base, in Colombia

Colombia — Trend (weighted 3-years average)

Source: UNDCP Annual Reports Questionnaire / DELTA

Cocaine trafficking in Latin America in 1999		
Country reporting	**Main source(s) of cocaine**	**Main destination(s)**
Colombia	domestic, Bolivia, Peru	USA, Europe, Mexico
Peru	domestic	USA, Europe, Asia
Bolivia	domestic (92%); Peru (8%)	Mexico, Chile, Argentina, Brazil, Colombia, Paraguay
Mexico	Colombia	USA
Central America	Colombia (70%-100%)	Mexico, USA
Venezuela	Colombia	USA, Europe
Caribbean	Colombia (around 90%), via other Caribbean and via Venezuela	USA
Ecuador	Colombia (80%), Peru (20%)	Australia, USA, Europe, Asia
Brazil	Colombia	USA; Guyana and Suriname (mainly for Europe)
Argentina	Bolivia (75%), Colombia (20%), Peru (5%)	Europe, North America
Uruguay	Bolivia (90%), Colombia (10%)	Europe
Paraguay	Bolivia and Peru	Europe, Africa
Source: UNDCP, Annual Reports Questionnaire / DELTA.		

Colombia, 11% had transited Brazil and 2.5 % Venezuela. Forty percent of the cocaine seized in Germany the same year came directly from Colombia and 15% via Central America. In France, 68% of the cocaine seized had been shipped directly from Colombia and 2% from Peru. In the UK and in Belgium, 90% of the cocaine originated in Colombia and the rest came from Peru and Bolivia.

For West Europe as a whole, individual seizures reported over the period January 1998 - June 2000 indicate that 31% of the cocaine seized was obtained in Central America, 17% in the Caribbean region, 16% and 12%, respectively, was directly obtained from Colombia and Peru, 8% transited Brazil and 3% transited Venezuela. Less than 1% was directly purchased in Bolivia. During the first six months of 2000, more cocaine was directly imported into western Europe from Colombia (39%) and/or shipped via the Caribbean region (19%), via Venezuela (7%) and via Suriname (4%). Cocaine obtained in Central America, by contrast, lost in importance (4%), and so did direct shipments from Peru and Bolivia (1% each), probably reflecting lower volumes of cocaine production in these countries.

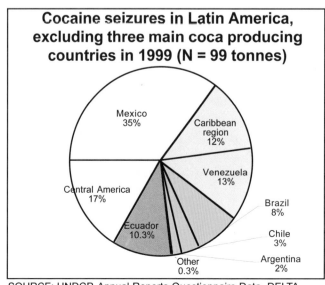

Cocaine seizures in Latin America, excluding three main coca producing countries in 1999 (N = 99 tonnes)

SOURCE: UNDCP, Annual Reports Questionnaire Data, DELTA

GLOBAL ILLICIT SUPPLY OF COCAINE IN 1999

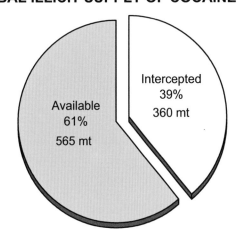

Available
61%
565 mt

Intercepted
39%
360 mt

BASED ON A TOTAL PRODUCTION OF 925 mt

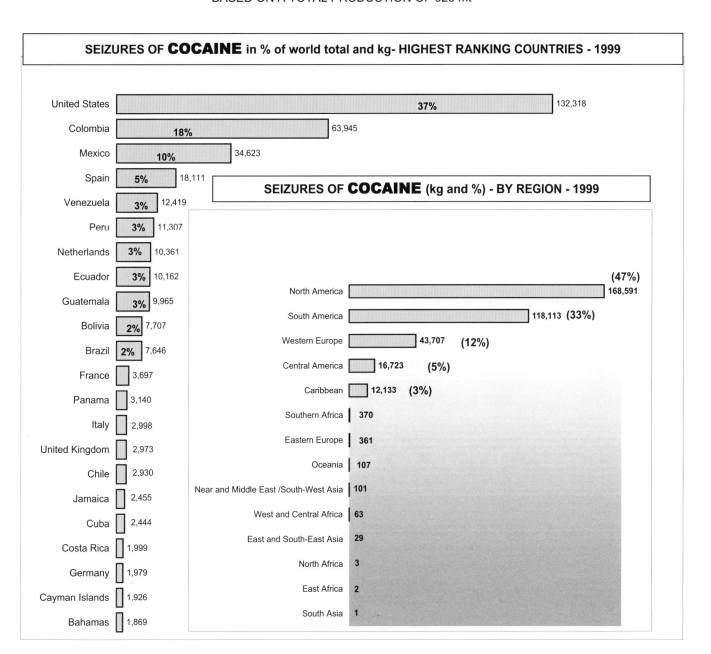

SEIZURES OF **COCAINE** in % of world total and kg- HIGHEST RANKING COUNTRIES - 1999

Country	%	kg
United States	37%	132,318
Colombia	18%	63,945
Mexico	10%	34,623
Spain	5%	18,111
Venezuela	3%	12,419
Peru	3%	11,307
Netherlands	3%	10,361
Ecuador	3%	10,162
Guatemala	3%	9,965
Bolivia	2%	7,707
Brazil	2%	7,646
France		3,697
Panama		3,140
Italy		2,998
United Kingdom		2,973
Chile		2,930
Jamaica		2,455
Cuba		2,444
Costa Rica		1,999
Germany		1,979
Cayman Islands		1,926
Bahamas		1,869

SEIZURES OF **COCAINE** (kg and %) - BY REGION - 1999

Region	kg	%
North America	168,591	(47%)
South America	118,113	(33%)
Western Europe	43,707	(12%)
Central America	16,723	(5%)
Caribbean	12,133	(3%)
Southern Africa	370	
Eastern Europe	361	
Oceania	107	
Near and Middle East /South-West Asia	101	
West and Central Africa	63	
East and South-East Asia	29	
North Africa	3	
East Africa	2	
South Asia	1	

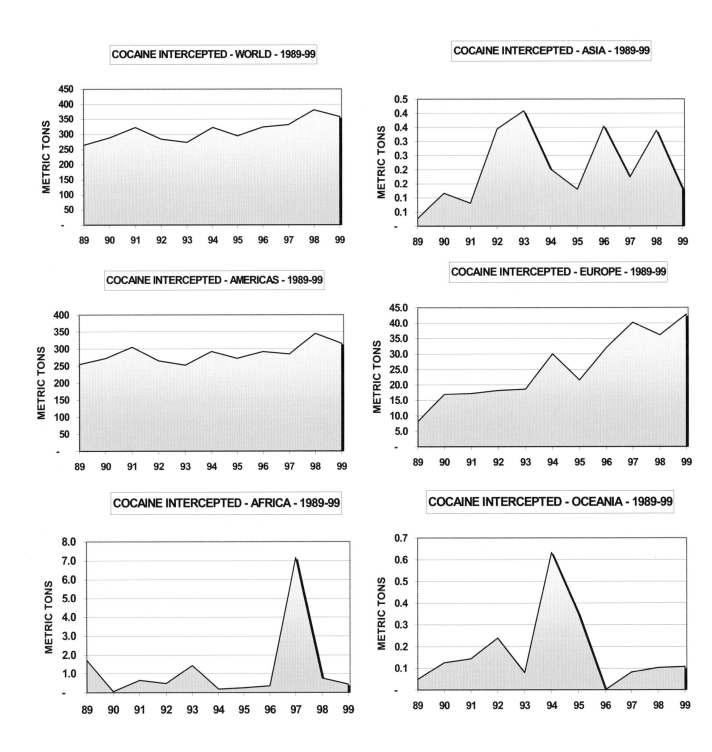

Cocaine trafficking 1998-1999: extent and trends (countries reporting seizures of more than 0.01 tons (10 kg))

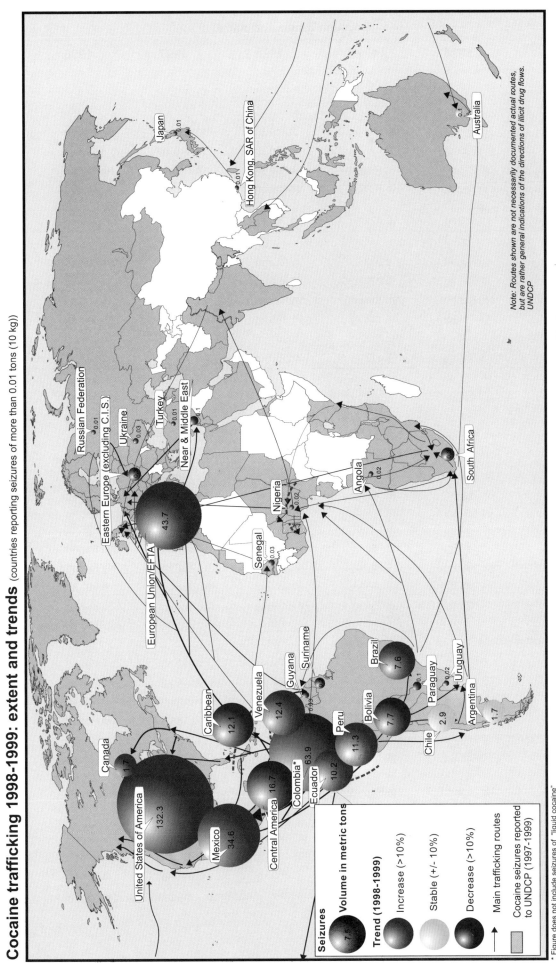

Note: Routes shown are not necessarily documented actual routes, but are rather general indications of the directions of illicit drug flows.
UNDCP

Seizures

Volume in metric tons

7.5

Trend (1998-1999)

Increase (>10%)

Stable (+/- 10%)

Decrease (>10%)

Main trafficking routes

Cocaine seizures reported to UNDCP (1997-1999)

* Figure does not include seizures of "liquid cocaine"
Note: The boundaries and names shown and the designations used on this map do not imply official endorsement or acceptance by the United Nations.

Cocaine (base and salts)

Region/country or territory	1994	1995	1996	1997	1998	1999
AFRICA						
East Africa						
Burundi	No Report	No Report	3.819 kg [Govt]	No Report	No Report	No Report
Kenya	0.065 kg	0.422 kg	3.440 kg	0.410 kg	1.240 kg	0.110 kg
Uganda	No Report	No Report	4.000 kg	No Report	No Report	0.412 kg
United Republic of Tanzania	No Report	No Report	No Report	0.200 kg	No Report	1.161 kg
Sub-Total	0.065 kg	0.422 kg	11.259 kg	0.610 kg	1.240 kg	1.683 kg
North Africa						
Algeria	No Report	0.003 kg [INCB]	No Report	No Report	No Report	No Report
Egypt	1.204 kg	0.220 kg	0.934 kg	0.914 kg	1.860 kg	0.792 kg
Libyan Arab Jam.	No Report	No Report	No Report	No Report	0.136 kg	No Report
Morocco	2.324 kg	6.294 kg	91.195 kg	6055.550 kg	30.111 kg	1.742 kg
Tunisia	[(1]	No Report	0.001 kg [ICPO]	0.047 kg [ICPO]	0.127 kg	0.017 kg [ICPO]
Sub-Total	3.528 kg	6.517 kg	92.130 kg	6056.511 kg	32.234 kg	2.551 kg
Southern Africa						
Angola	No Report	8.902 kg [ICPO]	64.360 kg [Govt]	536.000 kg [ICPO]	38.007 kg [ICPO]	15.901 kg
Botswana	No Report	0.407 kg [INCB]	3.000 kg [ICPO]	0.982 kg [ICPO]	0.700 kg [ICPO]	1.696 kg [ICPO]
Lesotho	No Report	No Report	No Report	2.346 kg [ICPO]	No Report	0.632 kg [ICPO]
Malawi	No Report	No Report	No Report	No Report	1.500 kg	1.200 kg
Mozambique	No Report	No Report	No Report	No Report	2.134 kg [ICPO]	0.385 kg [ICPO]
Namibia	No Report	0.595 kg	5.953 kg	23.932 kg [INCB]	2.110 kg	No Report
South Africa	69.561 kg	187.765 kg	106.629 kg	151.519 kg	635.908 kg	345.549 kg [ICPO]
					3825 u.	12940 u.
Swaziland	0.421 kg [INCB]	2.766 kg [INCB]	6.745 kg [ICPO]	9.650 kg [ICPO]	No Report	3.609 kg
Zambia	No Report	1.761 kg [ICPO]	4.443 kg [ICPO]	6.498 kg [ICPO]	No Report	1.116 kg
Zimbabwe	4.343 kg [INCB]	0.088 kg [ICPO]	0.597 kg [ICPO]	No Report	0.501 kg	0.166 kg
Sub-Total	74.325 kg	202.284 kg	191.727 kg	730.927 kg	680.860 kg	370.254 kg
					3825 u.	12940 u.
West and Central Africa						
Benin	0.008 kg [GSR]	6.962 kg [GSR]	3.189 kg [GSR]	0.015 kg [GSR]	0.628 kg	No Report
Burkina Faso	3.000 kg [ICPO]	No Report	0.260 kg [F.O]	278.000 kg [Govt]	No Report	No Report
Cameroon	No Report	0.225 kg [ICPO]	No Report	No Report	3.780 kg	No Report
Chad	No Report	No Report	No Report	No Report	No Report	0.015 kg [ICPO]
Congo	0.120 kg [Govt]	0.008 kg	No Report	No Report	No Report	No Report
Côte d'Ivoire	0.132 kg	2.863 kg	33.147 kg	22.028 kg	19.015 kg	9.287 kg
						16 u.
Democratic Republic of the Congo	No Report	No Report	1.101 kg [Govt]	No Report	No Report	No Report
Equatorial Guinea	0.060 kg	No Report	No Report	No Report	No Report	No Report
Gabon	0.116 kg [ICPO]	0.087 kg [ICPO]	0.022 kg [ICPO]	No Report	No Report	0.216 kg [ICPO]
Gambia	No Report	0.070 kg [ICPO]	0.880 kg [ICPO]	0.057 kg [ICPO]	0.074 kg [ICPO]	0.060 kg

Source: Annual Report Questionnaire if not otherwise indicated

Cocaine (base and salts)

Region/country or territory	1994	1995	1996	1997	1998	1999
AFRICA						
West and Central Africa						
Ghana	0.920 kg [F.O]	5.370 kg [F.O]	0.785 kg	6.350 kg [F.O]	5.035 kg	7.062 kg
Mali	0.015 kg [INCB]	No Report	4.300 kg [Govt]	No Report	No Report	No Report
Mauritania	0.037 kg [ICPO]	No Report	0.334 kg [Govt]	No Report	No Report	No Report
Niger	0.002 kg [ICPO]	No Report	0.020 kg [ICPO]	28.866 kg [ICPO]	0.233 kg [ICPO]	No Report
Nigeria	90.760 kg	15.908 kg [Govt]	6.160 kg [ICPO]	31.900 kg [CICAD]	9.260 kg [Govt]	15.064 kg
Sao Tome and Principe	No Report	No Report	No Report	0.100 kg	No Report	0.100 kg
Senegal	11.834 kg [ICPO]	7.940 kg [F.O]	8.110 kg [F.O]	No Report	5.321 kg [ICPO]	31.564 kg [ICPO] 110 u.
Sierra Leone	0.003 kg [Govt]	4.000 kg [Govt]	0.002 kg	No Report	No Report	No Report
Togo	No Report	No Report	1.081 kg	13.873 kg [Govt]	No Report	No Report
Sub-Total	107.007 kg	43.433 kg	59.391 kg	381.189 kg	43.346 kg	63.368 kg 126 u.
Total region	184.925 kg	252.656 kg	354.507 kg	7169.237 kg	757.680 kg 3825 u.	437.856 kg 13066 u.
AMERICAS						
Caribbean						
Anguilla	342.000 kg [NAPOL]	75.000 kg [INCB]	289.000 kg [NAPOL]	0.003 kg 8 u.	0.108 kg	0.020 kg [F.O.]
Antigua and Barbuda	73.000 kg	115.312 kg [INCB]	5.000 kg [INCB]	156.600 kg [ICPO]	1.000 kg [F.O.]	21.000 kg [F.O.]
Aruba	146.378 kg [INCB]	151.295 kg [ICPO]	203.000 kg [NAPOL]	408.307 kg [INCB]	794.000 kg [NAPOL]	467.857 kg [ICPO]
Bahamas	491.543 kg	392.000 kg [NAPOL]	115.000 kg [NAPOL]	2579.040 kg [ICPO]	3343.054 kg	1869.090 kg [ICPO]
Barbados	250.402 kg [ICPO]	247.000 kg [INCB]	37.000 kg [INCB]	88.050 kg [INCB]	35.000 kg [NAPOL]	132.760 kg [HONL(]
Bermuda	58.364 kg [WCO]	40.185 kg [INCB]	24.662 kg	4.516 kg	4.330 kg	8.076 kg
British Virgin Islands	457.000 kg [NAPOL]	1194.020 kg [ICPO]	1765.000 kg [NAPOL]	838.000 kg [NAPOL]	20.000 kg [NAPOL]	432.000 kg [F.O.]
Cayman Islands	3.855 kg [INCB]	143.000 kg [NAPOL]	2219.090 kg	1054.000 kg 319 u.	1195.142 kg 1824 u.	1926.129 kg
Cuba	238.408 kg [Govt]	371.501 kg [INCB]	7923.373 kg	1443.796 kg [ICPO]	669.000 kg [NAPOL]	2444.000 kg [F.O.]
Dominica	3.341 kg [ICPO]	7.000 kg [F.O.]	2.947 kg	101.000 kg [F.O.]	29.000 kg [F.O.]	82.769 kg [ICPO]
Dominican Republic	2888.278 kg	4391.092 kg	1341.300 kg	1234.206 kg	2341.916 kg	1075.953 kg
Grenada	9.186 kg 792 u.	3.533 kg 611 u.	9.000 kg [F.O.]	6.995 kg [INCB]	26.500 kg	43.000 kg [F.O.]
Haiti	716.000 kg [NAPOL]	1357.000 kg [NAPOL]	956.000 kg [NAPOL]	2100.000 kg [NAPOL]	1272.000 kg [NAPOL]	436.000 kg
Jamaica	124.730 kg [INCB]	570.007 kg [INCB]	253.530 kg [ICPO] 2321 u.	414.680 kg [ICPO] 6296 u.	2455.000 kg [F.O.]	2455.340 kg [ICPO] 3543 u.
Montserrat	60.000 kg [NAPOL]	0.058 kg [INCB]	No Report	0.130 kg 1 u.	No Report	No Report
Netherlands Antilles	906.200 kg [WCO]	111.000 kg [NAPOL]	710.000 kg [NAPOL]	850.340 kg [INCB]	639.000 kg [NAPOL]	18.000 kg [F.O.]
Saint Kitts and Nevis	No Report	5.809 kg [INCB] 13 u.	0.000 kg [F.O.]	150.000 kg [F.O.]	1.000 kg [F.O.]	1.000 kg [CICAD]

Source: Annual Report Questionnaire if not otherwise indicated

Cocaine (base and salts)

Region/country or territory	1994	1995	1996	1997	1998	1999
AMERICAS						
Caribbean						
Saint Lucia	17.525 kg	27.247 kg	19.800 kg	7.782 kg	78.137 kg	133.000 kg [CICAD]
Saint Vincent and the Grenadines	6.100 kg [F.O.]	13.000 kg [F.O.]	2.000 kg [F.O.]	1.000 kg [F.O.]	13.000 kg [F.O.]	15.300 kg [F.O.]
Trinidad Tobago	390.970 kg	95.000 kg [NAPOL]	179.380 kg [ICPO]	71.000 kg [CICAD]	77.680 kg	137.000 kg [CICAD]
Turks and Caicos Islands	44.059 kg [ICPO]	20.000 kg [INCB]	400.000 kg	1.500 kg	2075.000 kg	3.000 kg
US Virgin Islands	No Report	No Report	No Report	No Report	No Report	432.028 kg [ICPO]
Sub-Total	7227.340 kg 792 u.	9330.058 kg 624 u.	16455.080 kg 2321 u.	11510.950 kg 6624 u.	15069.870 kg 1824 u.	12133.320 kg 3543 u.
Central America						
Belize	142.594 kg	845.000 kg [NAPOL]	720.000 kg [CICAD]	2691.000 kg [CICAD]	1221.000 kg [NAPOL]	38.615 kg [ICPO]
Costa Rica	1411.170 kg 16657 u.	1170.241 kg 39225 u.	1872.719 kg 45327 u.	7857.000 kg [ICPO] 52170 u.	7387.140 kg 102844 u.	1998.720 kg 56514 u.
El Salvador	No Report	65.000 kg [CICAD]	99.000 kg [CICAD]	234.431 kg [ICPO]	45.256 kg [ICPO]	38.649 kg
Guatemala	1900.000 kg [Govt]	956.000 kg [Govt]	3950.870 kg	5098.466 kg [Govt] 17 u.	9217.070 kg	9964.788 kg
Honduras	930.035 kg [INCB]	408.851 kg 32 u.	3275.000 kg [CICAD]	2187.673 kg 209 u.	No Report	709.000 kg [CICAD] 662 u.
Nicaragua	1337.754 kg [Govt]	1506.889 kg [INCB]	398.444 kg 3531 u.	2790.200 kg 7109 u.	4750.265 kg 21235 u.	833.000 kg [CICAD]
Panama	5176.570 kg	7168.556 kg	8617.621 kg	15177.250 kg	11828.085 kg	3139.889 kg
Sub-Total	10898.120 kg 16657 u.	12120.540 kg 39257 u.	18933.650 kg 48858 u.	36036.020 kg 59505 u.	34448.820 kg 124079 u.	16722.660 kg 57176 u.
North America						
Canada	8357.264 kg	3597.730 kg	3123.467 kg	2090.000 kg 312 u.	562.983 kg 0.007 lt.	1650.518 kg 0.407 lt. 19 u.
Mexico	22116.509 kg	22708.227 kg	23835.203 kg	34952.070 kg	22597.072 kg	34622.600 kg
United States	129543.000 kg [Govt]	110842.203 kg	128725.102 kg [Govt]	102000.000 kg [Govt]	117000.000 kg [Govt]	132318.000 kg
Sub-Total	160016.800 kg	137148.200 kg	155683.800 kg	139042.100 kg 312 u.	140160.100 kg 0.007 lt.	168591.100 kg 0.407 lt. 19 u.
South America						
Argentina	2236.412 kg	3416.080 kg	2451.250 kg [Govt]	5192.570 kg	1766.900 kg	1660.776 kg
Bolivia	10021.000 kg [Govt]	8496.641 kg [ICPO]	8305.000 kg [CICAD]	13688.938 kg	10101.940 kg	7707.008 kg
Brazil	12027.765 kg [ICPO]	5814.857 kg	4070.504 kg	4309.378 kg	6560.414 kg	7646.103 kg
Chile	1226.452 kg	2900.355 kg	2962.098 kg	2660.720 kg	2952.471 kg	2930.000 kg [CICAD]
Colombia	69592.000 kg 2652.000 lt.	59030.000 kg [Govt]	45779.000 kg [Govt]	42044.000 kg	107480.000 kg	63945.000 kg [(2] 36411.949 lt.
Ecuador	1789.941 kg	4284.400 kg	9533.970 kg	3697.160 kg	3854.229 kg	10161.831 kg
Guyana	76.000 kg [NAPOL]	51.115 kg	91.503 kg	66.005 kg [ICPO]	3222.000 kg [NAPOL]	37.319 kg [ICPO]
Paraguay	290.000 kg [WCO]	58.634 kg	47.490 kg	77.083 kg	222.352 kg	95.058 kg

Source: Annual Report Questionnaire if not otherwise indicated

Cocaine (base and salts)

Region/country or territory	1994	1995	1996	1997	1998	1999
AMERICAS						
South America						
Peru	10633.690 kg	22660.852 kg	19694.666 kg	8795.617 kg	9936.968 kg	11307.116 kg
Suriname	219.000 kg [NAPOL]	63.616 kg	1412.690 kg	116.099 kg	283.444 kg	185.000 kg [CICAD]
Uruguay	19.451 kg	231.719 kg	84.793 kg	27.968 kg [Govt]	23.604 kg	18.698 kg
Venezuela	6034.990 kg	6650.185 kg	5906.451 kg	16741.000 kg [CICAD]	8159.000 kg [CICAD]	12418.839 kg
Sub-Total	114166.700 kg 2652.000 lt.	113658.500 kg	100339.400 kg	97416.550 kg	154563.300 kg	118112.700 kg 36411.950 lt.
Total region	292308.900 kg 2652.000 lt. 17449 u.	272257.200 kg 39881 u.	291411.900 kg 51179 u.	284005.600 kg 66441 u.	344242.100 kg 0.007 lt. 125903 u.	315559.800 kg 36412.360 lt. 60738 u.
ASIA						
Central Asia and Transcaucasian countries						
Armenia	No Report	No Report	0.004 kg	No Report	No Report	No Report
Azerbaijan	No Report	No Report	No Report	No Report	No Report	0.005 kg
Georgia	No Report	No Report	0.002 kg [ICPO]	No Report	No Report	0.002 kg [ICPO]
Kazakhstan	No Report	No Report	No Report	No Report	20.000 kg	0.035 kg
Turkmenistan	No Report	No Report	No Report	No Report	1.000 kg [Govt]	No Report
Sub-Total			0.006 kg		21.000 kg	0.042 kg
East and South-East Asia						
Cambodia	No Report	11.000 kg [ICPO]	No Report	No Report	No Report	No Report
China	9.368 kg [ICPO]	No Report	No Report	No Report	No Report	No Report
China (Hong Kong SAR)	12.251 kg	1.800 kg [Govt]	13.900 kg	31.300 kg	167.700 kg [Govt]	11.990 kg
Indonesia	4.374 kg	0.113 kg	0.388 kg	3.301 kg	4.748 kg	0.500 kg
Japan	19.996 kg	36.623 kg	37.110 kg	25.455 kg	20.846 kg	10.349 kg
Korea (Republic of)	0.039 kg [Govt]	No Report	0.766 kg	11.218 kg	2.080 kg	2.251 kg
Mongolia	No Report	No Report	No Report	No Report	No Report	2.800 kg [ICPO]
Philippines	9.420 kg	1.421 kg	1.593 kg	1.000 kg [ICPO]	1.080 kg [ICPO]	0.227 kg
Singapore	No Report	No Report	No Report	No Report	1.050 kg	No Report
Thailand	No Report	1.009 kg [HNLP]	2.264 kg [HNLP]	2.426 kg	3.555 kg	0.619 kg [ICPO]
Viet Nam	No Report	2.000 kg [ICPO]	No Report	No Report	No Report	No Report
Sub-Total	55.448 kg	53.966 kg	56.021 kg	74.700 kg	201.059 kg	28.736 kg
Near and Middle East /South-West Asia						
Iran (Islamic Republic of)	No Report	No Report	No Report	1.700 kg	No Report	No Report
Israel	24.329 kg	14.091 kg	73.339 kg	43.700 kg	99.800 kg	28.229 kg [ICPO]
Jordan	0.007 kg	0.016 kg	1.100 kg	No Report	0.940 kg	1.912 kg
Kuwait	No Report	0.051 kg [INCB]	0.016 kg [ICPO]	0.010 kg [ICPO]	0.003 kg	No Report
Lebanon	111.641 kg	12.736 kg	166.690 kg	4.804 kg	11.898 kg	32.013 kg
Pakistan	No Report	No Report	No Report	No Report	0.100 kg	1.100 kg
Saudi Arabia	9.645 kg	4.311 kg	11.809 kg [ICPO]	0.347 kg [ICPO]	2.202 kg	4.908 kg [ICPO]

Source: Annual Report Questionnaire if not otherwise indicated

Region/country or territory	Cocaine (base and salts)					
	1994	1995	1996	1997	1998	1999
ASIA						
Near and Middle East /South-West Asia						
Syrian Arab Republic	0.011 kg [ICPO]	5.135 kg	1.673 kg	0.240 kg	0.236 kg	32.102 kg
United Arab Emirates	No Report	0.002 kg	40.008 kg	No Report	0.146 kg	0.840 kg
Sub-Total	145.633 kg	36.342 kg	294.635 kg	50.801 kg	115.325 kg	101.104 kg
South Asia						
Bangladesh	0.050 kg	No Report	No Report	No Report	No Report	No Report
India	1.580 kg	40.000 kg	3.000 kg [Govt]	24.000 kg	1.000 kg	1.000 kg [ICPO]
Nepal	No Report	No Report	No Report	24.000 kg [ICPO]	No Report	No Report
Sri Lanka	No Report	No Report	0.050 kg	No Report	No Report	No Report
Sub-Total	1.630 kg	40.000 kg	3.050 kg	48.000 kg	1.000 kg	1.000 kg
Total region	202.711 kg	130.308 kg	353.712 kg	173.501 kg	338.384 kg	130.882 kg
EUROPE						
Eastern Europe						
Albania	No Report	No Report	No Report	No Report	No Report	2.159 kg [ICPO]
Belarus	No Report	No Report	No Report	2.074 kg [INCB]	No Report	No Report
Bosnia Herzegovina	No Report	No Report	No Report	No Report	0.009 kg [ICPO]	No Report
Bulgaria	0.467 kg	7.605 kg	21.515 kg	2.011 kg	685.585 kg	17.010 kg
Croatia	9.228 kg	0.056 kg	1.525 kg	563.009 kg	6.426 kg	1.807 kg
Czech Republic	23.658 kg	51.720 kg	23.358 kg	66.828 kg	42.000 kg	140.800 kg
Estonia	No Report	No Report	No Report	0.006 kg	2.565 kg 71 u.	0.128 kg 139 u.
FYR of Macedonia	No Report	No Report	13.744 kg [ICPO]	No Report	0.040 kg	2.955 kg [ICPO]
Hungary	26.843 kg [INCB]	18.683 kg [INCB]	4.985 kg	6.995 kg [Govt]	26.385 kg	121.147 kg
Latvia	No Report	0.012 kg 24 u.	0.012 kg	0.024 kg 0.895 lt.	0.063 kg	1.915 kg
Lithuania	No Report	1.720 kg	1.056 kg	2.049 kg	10.133 kg	0.275 kg
Poland	525.700 kg	383.232 kg	31.378 kg	15.501 kg	21.157 kg	20.082 kg
Romania	No Report	16.090 kg	712.611 kg	69.556 kg [ICPO]	1.203 kg	9.670 kg
Russian Federation	1.257 kg [ICPO]	44.800 kg [ICPO]	73.800 kg	70.825 kg	100.340 kg	12.749 kg
Slovakia	No Report	25.709 kg [INCB]	No Report	9.580 kg [ICPO]	1.642 kg	2.508 kg
Slovenia	1.909 kg	3.241 kg [ICPO]	0.830 kg	3.573 kg	3.522 kg	1.580 kg
Ukraine	6.400 kg [ICPO]	No Report	No Report	625.010 kg	250.586 kg	26.263 kg [ICPO]
Yugoslavia	0.779 kg	No Report	No Report	No Report	No Report	No Report
Sub-Total	596.241 kg	552.868 kg 24 u.	884.814 kg	1437.041 kg 0.895 lt.	1151.656 kg 71 u.	361.048 kg 139 u.
Western Europe						
Andorra	0.026 kg [ICPO]	0.026 kg [ICPO]	No Report	0.108 kg [ICPO]	0.064 kg [ICPO]	0.060 kg
Austria	52.679 kg	55.259 kg	72.794 kg	86.902 kg	99.140 kg	63.377 kg
Belgium	479.425 kg	576.183 kg	838.000 kg	3329.000 kg	2088.312 kg	1761.709 kg
Cyprus	4.934 kg	2.500 kg	0.004 kg	0.020 kg	0.018 kg	5.361 kg

Source: Annual Report Questionnaire if not otherwise indicated

Cocaine (base and salts)

Region/country or territory	1994	1995	1996	1997	1998	1999
EUROPE						
Western Europe						
Denmark	29.900 kg [INCB]	110.100 kg	32.000 kg	58.000 kg	44.133 kg	24.200 kg
Finland	0.037 kg	0.040 kg	0.072 kg	0.121 kg	1.987 kg	1.703 kg
France	4742.591 kg [Govt]	873.578 kg	1752.702 kg	860.599 kg	1076.000 kg	3697.372 kg
Germany	767.348 kg	1846.020 kg	1378.435 kg	1721.189 kg	1133.243 kg	1979.100 kg
Gibraltar	No Report	No Report	0.035 kg	0.098 kg	0.007 kg 7 u.	0.026 kg
Greece	115.253 kg	8.978 kg	155.254 kg	16.734 kg	283.971 kg	45.485 kg 8 u.
Iceland	0.316 kg	0.143 kg	No Report	No Report	No Report	0.955 kg
Ireland	0.046 kg [ICPO]	21.800 kg [ICPO]	642.000 kg	11.044 kg	334.230 kg	85.553 kg
Italy	6656.938 kg 749 u.	2556.579 kg 364 u.	2147.347 kg	1639.542 kg 887 u.	2143.804 kg 1341 u.	2997.611 kg [ICPO] 14 u.
Liechtenstein	0.342 kg	0.503 kg	0.010 kg	1.065 kg	0.151 kg	0.003 kg
Luxembourg	15.459 kg	0.525 kg	12.891 kg	8.983 kg	5.995 kg	0.327 kg
Malta	0.380 kg	0.163 kg	0.171 kg	0.301 kg	0.058 kg	1.366 kg
Monaco	0.006 kg	0.016 kg	0.003 kg	0.001 kg	0.012 kg	0.056 kg [ICPO]
Netherlands	8200.000 kg [INCB]	4896.000 kg [ICPO]	8067.000 kg [ICPO]	6743.600 kg	11452.000 kg 1935 u.	10361.000 kg
Norway	4.903 kg	3.798 kg	24.140 kg	4.633 kg	93.020 kg	60.477 kg
Portugal	1719.413 kg	2115.835 kg	811.568 kg	3162.641 kg	624.949 kg	822.560 kg
San Marino	0.024 kg	No Report	No Report	No Report	No Report	No Report
Spain	4016.291 kg	6897.023 kg	13742.901 kg	18418.760 kg	11687.623 kg	18110.883 kg
Sweden	28.839 kg	4.036 kg	28.702 kg	33.920 kg	18.505 kg	413.945 kg 1.944 lt. 430 u.
Switzerland	295.360 kg	262.092 kg	255.677 kg	349.435 kg	251.616 kg	288.013 kg
Turkey	21.216 kg	75.668 kg	13.000 kg	9.637 kg	604.880 kg	13.153 kg
United Kingdom	2261.500 kg	672.100 kg	1219.300 kg	2350.200 kg	2985.323 kg [(3]	2972.700 kg [NCIS]
Sub-Total	29413.230 kg 749 u.	20978.960 kg 364 u.	31194.010 kg	38806.530 kg 887 u.	34929.040 kg 3283 u.	43707.000 kg 1.944 lt. 452 u.
Total region	30009.470 kg 749 u.	21531.830 kg 388 u.	32078.820 kg	40243.570 kg 0.895 lt. 887 u.	36080.700 kg 3354 u.	44068.040 kg 1.944 lt. 591 u.
OCEANIA						
Oceania						
Australia	632.000 kg [(4]	348.038 kg [(4]	1.764 kg 24 u.	81.944 kg	103.162 kg [Govt (5]	107.000 kg [INCB]
New Zealand	0.066 kg [ICPO]	0.081 kg [Govt]	No Report	0.037 kg [INCB]	0.015 kg	0.454 kg
Tonga	No Report	No Report	No Report	0.001 kg [INCB]	No Report	No Report
Sub-Total	632.066 kg	348.119 kg	1.764 kg 24 u.	81.982 kg	103.177 kg	107.454 kg

Source: Annual Report Questionnaire if not otherwise indicated

Region/country or territory	Cocaine (base and salts)					
	1994	**1995**	**1996**	**1997**	**1998**	**1999**
OCEANIA						
Total region	632.066 kg	348.119 kg	1.764 kg 24 u.	81.982 kg	103.177 kg	107.454 kg
TOTAL	323338.100 kg 2652.000 lt. 18198 u.	294520.200 kg 40269 u.	324200.700 kg 51203 u.	331673.800 kg 0.895 lt. 67328 u.	381522.000 kg 0.007 lt. 133082 u.	360304.100 kg 36414.300 lt. 74395 u.

1) Small quantity. 2) Include 4,737 gallons coca base liquid and 4,882 gallons cocaine liquid 3) Included in cannabis seeds. 4) Fiscal year 5) Provisional figures.

Source: Annual Report Questionnaire if not otherwise indicated

Coca leaf

Region/country or territory	1994	1995	1996	1997	1998	1999
AMERICAS						
Central America						
Guatemala	No Report	No Report	28903 u.	No Report	No Report	No Report
Panama	No Report	60.573 kg [ICPO]	No Report	No Report	No Report	No Report
Sub-Total		60.573 kg	28903 u.			
North America						
Canada	0.178 kg [ICPO]	No Report	No Report	0.192 kg	No Report	0.316 kg
United States	0.035 kg	No Report	No Report	No Report	No Report	58.436 kg
Sub-Total	0.213 kg			0.192 kg		58.752 kg
South America						
Argentina	59120.000 kg	54749.930 kg	56853.820 kg [Govt]	49754.102 kg	47847.961 kg	68492.192 kg
Bolivia	127868.000 kg [ICPO]	76710.000 kg [CICAD]	No Report	No Report	110400.250 kg	64026.360 kg
Brazil	0.766 kg [ICPO]	0.027 kg	No Report	0.035 kg	No Report	No Report
Chile	173.935 kg	21.720 kg	4.867 kg	No Report	No Report	No Report
Colombia	491270.000 kg	394216.000 kg	686018.000 kg	117817.000 kg	340564.000 kg	307783.000 [(1]
Ecuador	No Report	No Report	No Report	No Report	0.050 kg	5000 u.
Peru	25000.188 kg	40092.949 kg	99104.242 kg	146824.953 kg	132209.875 kg	34792.500 kg
Uruguay	0.142 kg [Govt]	No Report	No Report	No Report	No Report	No Report
Venezuela	900 u.	No Report	No Report	No Report	No Report	No Report
Sub-Total	703433.000 kg 900 u.	565790.600 kg	841980.900 kg	314396.100 kg	631022.100 kg	475094.100 kg 5000 u.
Total region	703433.200 kg 900 u.	565851.200 kg	841980.900 kg 28903 u.	314396.300 kg	631022.100 kg	475152.800 kg 5000 u.
ASIA						
Central Asia and Transcaucasian countries						
Armenia	No Report	No Report	No Report	No Report	0.163 kg	No Report
Sub-Total					0.163 kg	
East and South-East Asia						
Japan	0.096 kg	No Report	No Report	No Report	No Report	No Report
Sub-Total	0.096 kg					
Near and Middle East /South-West Asia						
Bahrain	No Report	No Report	0.012 kg	No Report	No Report	No Report
Iraq	No Report	No Report	No Report	No Report	No Report	
Sub-Total			0.012 kg			
Total region	0.096 kg		0.012 kg		0.163 kg	
EUROPE						
Western Europe						
France	0.160 kg [ICPO]	0.510 kg	0.005 kg	No Report	No Report	11.133 kg

Source: Annual Report Questionnaire if not otherwise indicated

Coca leaf

Region/country or territory	1994	1995	1996	1997	1998	1999
EUROPE						
Western Europe						
Greece	No Report	0.150 kg	No Report	No Report	No Report	No Report
Italy	No Report	0.388 kg 73 u.	1.660 kg	No Report	0.049 kg	0.109 kg [ICPO]
Norway	No Report	No Report	No Report	No Report	0.001 kg	3.420 kg
Portugal	No Report	No Report	No Report	0.043 kg	0.020 kg	No Report
Sweden	0.536 kg	0.273 kg	1.054 kg	No Report	No Report	No Report
Sub-Total	0.696 kg	1.321 kg 73 u.	2.719 kg	0.043 kg	0.070 kg	14.662 kg
Total region	0.696 kg	1.321 kg 73 u.	2.719 kg	0.043 kg	0.070 kg	14.662 kg
OCEANIA						
Oceania						
Australia	No Report	0.049 kg [(2]	0.019 kg	0.590 kg	No Report	No Report
New Zealand	0.258 kg [ICPO]	No Report	No Report	No Report	0.019 kg	0.011 kg
Sub-Total	0.258 kg	0.049 kg	0.019 kg	0.590 kg	0.019 kg	0.011 kg
Total region	0.258 kg	0.049 kg	0.019 kg	0.590 kg	0.019 kg	0.011 kg
TOTAL	703434.300 kg 900 u.	565852.600 kg 73 u.	841983.700 kg 28903 u.	314396.900 kg	631022.400 kg	475167.320 kg 5000 u.

1) Do not include 9702 gallons (36726 litres) of coca leaf in process 2) Fiscal year

Source: Annual Report Questionnaire if not otherwise indicated

TRAFFICKING IN CANNABIS

In 1999, as in previous years, cannabis remained by far the most widely trafficked drug worldwide. Trafficking in cannabis herb continues to be more widespread than trafficking in cannabis resin although, in some regions, cannabis resin is more popular than cannabis herb. While 192 countries and territories reported seizures of cannabis herb in 1999, 144 reported seizures of cannabis resin, and 81 reported seizures of cannabis oil (the overall amount of cannabis oil seizures is however hardly noticeable if compared to cannabis herb and resin).

The production of cannabis resin continues to be concentrated, mainly in north Africa (notably Morocco), South-West Asia (notably Afghanistan and Pakistan) and, to a lesser extent, in Central Asia and Nepal. Given the geographic concentration of production, trafficking patterns in cannabis resin therefore resemble those encountered for other plant based drugs such as heroin or cocaine. By contrast, centres of cannabis herb production can be found almost all over the globe. Most trafficking activities relating to cannabis herb are thus either local in nature (within the same country) and/or affect mainly (neighbouring) countries within the same region, such as cannabis herb from Mexico (and to a lesser extent from Canada) to the USA, from Paraguay to Brazil and Argentina, from Afghanistan to Tajikistan and Kazakhstan, from Albania to Greece and Italy, from the Netherlands to neighbouring countries in western Europe, from Cambodia to Thailand, from Malawi to other countries of southern Africa, etc. Nonetheless, there are also some important overseas exports, such as cannabis herb from various countries in western Africa, southern Africa (notably South Africa), South-East Asia (notably Thailand) and south America (notably Colombia) to West Europe, or from South Africa or Jamaica to North America.

The global quantities of cannabis resin seized remained basically stable in 1999, while seizures of cannabis herb increased. Overall, cannabis seizures (herb and resin together) were thus rising, reaching a higher level than in the early 1990s, but falling short of the high levels reported in the early 1980s (mainly from south American countries).

Trafficking in cannabis herb

Trafficking in cannabis herb intensified in 1999, notably in the Americas, which represented close to 80% of global seizures. North America alone represented two thirds of global cannabis herb seizures. Increases in cannabis herb seizures were reported from a majority of countries in the Americas, including Mexico, the USA and Canada in North America, countries in the Caribbean, as well as most countries of South America, including Paraguay and Brazil which, together with Colombia, have been the main sources of cannabis herb originating in South America.

The next largest seizures of cannabis herb were in Africa, notably in South Africa and in a number of other countries of southern and eastern Africa, including Swaziland and Malawi, of western Africa (including Nigeria) and of northern Africa (mainly Egypt). The level of seizures increased in most countries of southern and eastern Africa but declined or remained stable in northern and western Africa.

The overall decline in European seizures was mainly due to falling seizures in countries of West Europe, reversing the upward trend that prevailed until the mid 1990s. The reversal reflects a stabilization of consumption (at higher levels than before) as well as some shift in the focus of law enforcement activities towards other drugs (an explanation which may also be partly responsible for the decline in cannabis herb seizures reported from Australia). By contrast, trafficking in cannabis in the countries of the former Soviet Union continues to expand. In other East European countries trafficking appears to have stabilized.

Data from Asia show mixed results as well : there have been increases of seizures in Central Asia and in South-East Asia, while declines have been reported from South Asia.

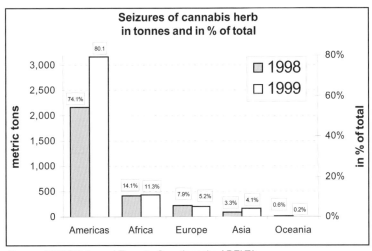

Source: UNDCP, Annual Reports Questionnaire / DELTA

GLOBAL SEIZURES OF CANNABIS HERB 1989-99

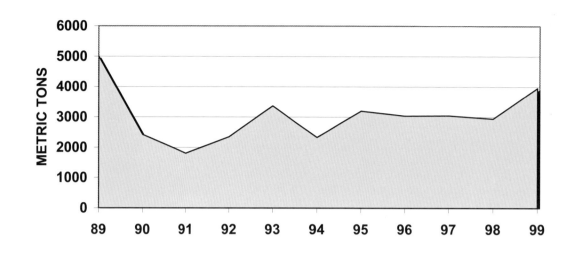

Year	1989	1990	1991	1992	1993	1994	1995	1996	1997	1998	1999
Metric tons	5,005	2,422	1,802	2,351	3,366	2,329	3,200	3,039	3,048	2,942	3,959

SEIZURES OF CANNABIS HERB in % of world total and kg- HIGHEST RANKING COUNTRIES - 1999

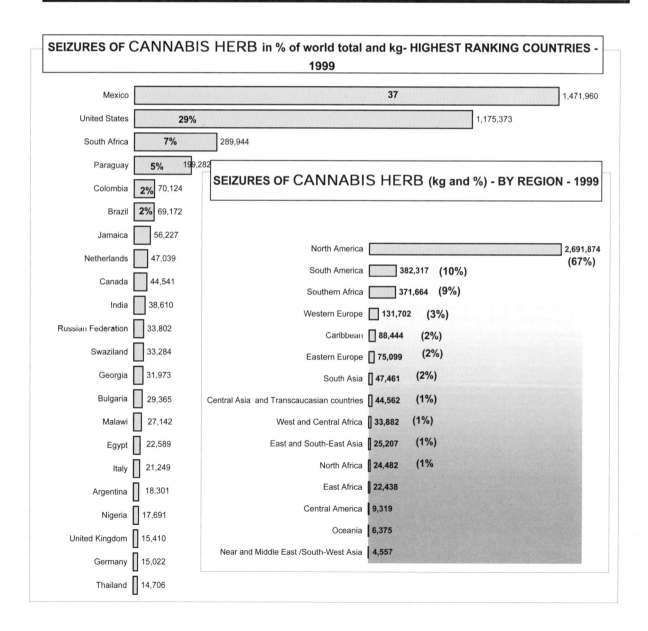

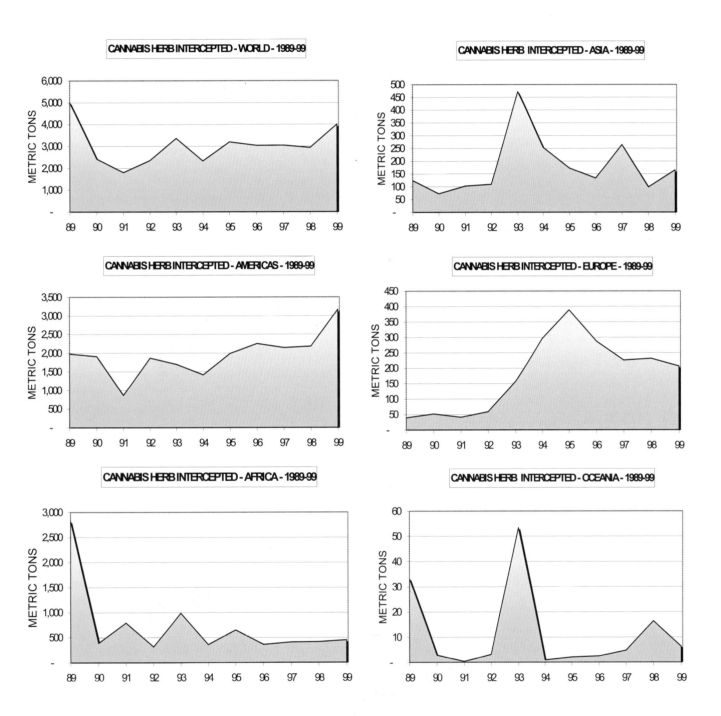

Cannabis herb trafficking 1998-1999: extent and trends (countries reporting seizures of more than 0.1 tons (100 kg))

Note: Routes shown are not necessarily documented actual routes, but are rather general indications of the directions of illicit drug flows. UNDCP

Japan 0.6
Philippines
New Zealand 0.3
Australia 6
Lao PDR
Viet Nam 0.1
Malaysia
Indonesia
Thailand 15
Myanmar
Bangladesh 0.7
Nepal 0.3
India 39
Sri Lanka 4
Kazakhstan
Kyrgyzstan
Tajikistan 0.6
Uzbekistan 0.5
Russian Federation 34
Eastern Europe (excluding C.I.S)
Belarus
Ukraine 0.4
Turkey 5
Syria 0.8
Iraq 0.3
Israel 3
Egypt 23
37
Ethiopia
Uganda 6
Kenya 9
Tanzania 6
Madagascar 3
Mozambique 9
Swaziland 33
Lesotho 7
Malawi 27
Zambia 7
Zimbabwe 1.2
Botswana 0.3
Namibia
Angola 3
South Africa 290
Chad
Cameroon 2
Niger
Nigeria 18
1.4
Ghana
Cote d'Ivoire 7
Senegal
Tunisia
European Union/EFTA 126
4
3

Brazil 69
Uruguay 0.5
Paraguay 199
Argentina 18
Bolivia
Chile 2
Peru
Ecuador
Colombia 70
Venezuela 13
Guyana
Suriname 0.2
Caribbean 88
Central America 9
United States of America 1,175
Canada 45
Mexico 1,473

Seizures
Volume in metric tons
100

Trend (1998-1999)
Increase (>10%)
Stable (+/- 10%)
Decrease (>10%)

Main trafficking routes
Cannabis herb seizures reported to UNDCP (1997-99)

<u>Note</u>: The boundaries and names shown and the designations used on this map do not imply official endorsement or acceptance by the United Nations.

Cannabis herb

Region/country or territory	1994	1995	1996	1997	1998	1999
AFRICA						
East Africa						
Burundi	424.820 kg [ICPO]	No Report	No Report	No Report	No Report	45.847 kg [ICPO]
Djibouti	No Report	105.505 kg [ICPO]	No Report	No Report	No Report	No Report
Ethiopia	667.547 kg	312.240 kg [ICPO]	2.117 kg [ICPO]	135.346 kg	331.561 kg	807.364 kg
Kenya	4146.212 kg	2547.673 kg	8238.000 kg	11250.000 kg	2375.240 kg	8762.033 kg
Madagascar	No Report	2452.000 kg [INCB]	3320.000 kg [INCB]	510.460 kg [INCB]	No Report	1265.332 kg [ICPO]
Mauritius	3.385 kg	4.088 kg	8.792 kg	18435.000 kg	3.090 kg	5.592 kg
Seychelles	0.595 kg	0.813 kg [INCB]	0.162 kg [ICPO]	No Report	2.056 kg [ICPO]	1.005 kg
Uganda	7910.560 kg [Govt]	No Report	258.810 kg	No Report	5530.000 kg	5530.000 kg [ICPO]
United Republic of Tanzania	No Report	4011.652 kg	No Report	82539.539 kg	4617.862 kg	6021.273 kg [ICPO]
Sub-Total	13153.120 kg	9433.971 kg	11827.880 kg	112870.300 kg	12859.810 kg	22438.450 kg
North Africa						
Algeria	39.355 kg [ICPO]	1475.252 kg [INCB]	0.036 kg [ICPO]	No Report	58.300 kg [ICPO]	No Report
Egypt	No Report	No Report	6608.687 kg	10185.538 kg	31078.387 kg	22588.505 kg
Morocco	34200.285 kg	35807.871 kg	38521.145 kg	27955.979 kg	37160.879 kg	No Report
Sudan	No Report	No Report	1202.812 kg [ICPO]	No Report	No Report	No Report
Tunisia	1.084 kg	3.865 kg	0.066 kg [ICPO]	18.163 kg [ICPO]	2.000 kg	1893.381 kg [ICPO]
Sub-Total	34240.730 kg	37286.990 kg	46332.750 kg	38159.680 kg	68299.560 kg	24481.890 kg
Southern Africa						
Angola	No Report	2223.228 kg [ICPO]	63.850 kg [Govt]	518.006 kg [ICPO]	1.975 kg [ICPO]	2829.167 kg
Botswana	29.347 kg [ICPO]	1349.000 kg [INCB]	1588.198 kg [ICPO]	1446.153 kg [ICPO]	1186.000 kg [ICPO]	1229.000 kg [ICPO]
Lesotho	4864.190 kg	No Report	15390.089 kg [Govt]	10472.073 kg [ICPO]	21583.824 kg [ICPO]	7243.697 kg [ICPO]
Malawi	4863.814 kg [ICPO]	39911.254 kg	8453.497 kg	10320.105 kg	5201.971 kg	27141.583 kg
Mozambique	No Report	No Report	No Report	184.024 kg [ICPO]	462.000 kg [ICPO]	894.406 kg [ICPO]
Namibia	No Report	No Report	No Report	298.830 kg [INCB]	361.395 kg	282.363 kg
South Africa	268652.000 kg	238813.203 kg	203353.953 kg	171929.328 kg	197116.297 kg	289943.561 kg [ICPO]
Swaziland	3522.842 kg [INCB]	No Report	440.485 kg [ICPO]	11302.505 kg [ICPO]	5943.293 kg	33283.707 kg
Zambia	No Report	4291.498 kg [ICPO]	7794.402 kg [ICPO]	11176.308 kg [ICPO]	3256.366 kg [Govt]	7000.653 kg
Zimbabwe	1085.885 kg [Govt]	3934.594 kg [ICPO]	2428.647 kg [ICPO]	4667.320 kg [ICPO]	6117.086 kg	1816.001 kg
Sub-Total	283018.100 kg	290522.800 kg	239513.100 kg	222314.600 kg	241230.200 kg	371664.200 kg
West and Central Africa						
Benin	230.510 kg [GSR]	42.898 kg [GSR]	44.404 kg [GSR]	26.862 kg [GSR]	611.077 kg [GSR]	25.138 kg [GSR]
Burkina Faso	305.059 kg [ICPO]	No Report	2967.410 kg [F.O]	2402.734 kg [Govt]	No Report	No Report
Cameroon	491.280 kg [ICPO]	9.678 kg [ICPO]	581.870 kg [ICPO]	No Report	112.875 kg	1154.560 kg
Central African Republic	No Report	100.000 kg [Govt]	No Report	No Report	57.551 kg [ICPO]	No Report
Chad	575.000 kg	No Report	435.200 kg [Govt]	No Report	No Report	686.000 kg [ICPO]
Congo	478.008 kg	No Report	No Report	No Report	No Report	1.000 kg
Côte d'Ivoire	634.134 kg	535.683 kg	1482.549 kg	853.871 kg	898.960 kg	1650.189 kg

Source: Annual Report Questionnaire if not otherwise indicated

Region/country or territory	Cannabis herb					
	1994	**1995**	**1996**	**1997**	**1998**	**1999**

AFRICA

West and Central Africa

Region/country or territory	1994	1995	1996	1997	1998	1999
Democratic Republic of the Congo	No Report	No Report	1.066 kg ^{Govt}	No Report	No Report	No Report
Equatorial Guinea	No Report	1.500 kg ^{INCB}	No Report	3.500 kg ^{INCB}	24.000 kg 6 u.	26.000 kg 46 u.
Gabon	80.469 kg ^{ICPO}	90.843 kg ^{ICPO}	160.189 kg ^{ICPO}	24.255 kg ^{ICPO}	114.336 kg ^{ICPO}	45.648 kg ^{ICPO}
Gambia	No Report	286.587 kg ^{ICPO}	11.164 kg ^{ICPO}	566.971 kg ^{ICPO}	376.145 kg ^{ICPO}	No Report
Ghana	4225.530 kg $^{F.O}$	209506.859 kg	8294.190 kg $^{F.O}$	1409.470 kg $^{F.O}$	4375.098 kg	4080.049 kg
Mali	288.775 kg ^{INCB}	94.256 kg ^{INCB}	80.000 kg ^{Govt}	404.270 kg ^{ICPO}	No Report	No Report
Mauritania	29.010 kg ^{ICPO}	No Report	6765.170 kg $^{F.O}$	92.006 kg ^{GSR}	17.200 kg ^{GSR}	No Report
Niger	722.937 kg ^{ICPO}	690.933 kg ^{ICPO}	777.384 kg ^{ICPO}	499.887 kg ^{ICPO}	682.173 kg ^{ICPO}	1356.162 kg ^{ICPO}
Nigeria	19732.660 kg	15258.000 kg ^{Govt}	18604.000 kg ^{ICPO}	15904.721 kg	16170.500 kg ^{Govt}	17691.014 kg
Saint Helena	No Report	No Report	No Report	3.009 kg	0.183 kg	No Report
Sao Tome and Principe	No Report	No Report	No Report	0.200 kg	No Report	No Report
Senegal	1391.875 kg ^{ICPO}	34391.570 kg $^{F.O}$	24803.230 kg $^{F.O}$	13627.390 kg $^{F.O}$	39652.000 kg $^{F.O}$	7165.830 kg ^{ICPO}
Sierra Leone	684.308 kg ^{Govt}	397.562 kg ^{Govt}	No Report	No Report	No Report	No Report
Togo	No Report	No Report	156.848 kg	1066.189 kg ^{Govt}	No Report	No Report
Sub-Total	29869.560 kg	311406.400 kg	65164.670 kg	36885.330 kg	93092.090 kg 6 u.	33881.590 kg 46 u.
Total region	360281.500 kg	648650.100 kg	362838.400 kg	410230.000 kg	415481.700 kg 6 u.	452466.100 kg 46 u.

AMERICAS

Caribbean

Region/country or territory	1994	1995	1996	1997	1998	1999
Anguilla	No Report	90.000 kg ^{INCB}	No Report	0.644 kg	5.037 kg	8.300 kg $^{F.O.}$
Antigua and Barbuda	4374.000 kg	219.574 kg ^{INCB}	1210.000 kg ^{INCB}	No Report	105.000 kg $^{F.O.}$	75.000 kg $^{F.O.}$
Aruba	30.104 kg ^{INCB}	215.793 kg ^{ICPO}	No Report	12850.000 kg ^{INCB}	No Report	141.647 kg ^{ICPO} 51 u.
Bahamas	1419.432 kg	No Report	No Report	3759.010 kg ^{ICPO}	2591.065 kg	3609.011 kg ^{ICPO}
Barbados	222.050 kg ^{INCB}	73.483 kg ^{ICPO}	3118.000 kg ^{INCB} 118 u.	1132.027 kg ^{INCB}	1650.000 kg ^{CICAD}	333.580 kg ^{HONL}
Bermuda	361.023 kg ^{ICPO}	79.480 kg ^{INCB}	107.050 kg	91.800 kg	91.800 kg	87.067 kg
British Virgin Islands	No Report	235.533 kg ^{ICPO}	No Report	No Report	No Report	354.000 kg $^{F.O.}$
Cayman Islands	1728.000 kg ^{INCB}	No Report	3188.018 kg	3422.073 kg 427 u.	4063.009 kg 650 u.	5100.371 kg
Cuba	1195.598 kg ^{Govt}	4482.138 kg ^{INCB}	3931.682 kg	7625.278 kg ^{ICPO}	No Report	5512.000 kg $^{F.O.}$
Dominica	740.693 kg ^{ICPO}	422.000 kg $^{F.O.}$	136.249 kg	404.000 kg $^{F.O.}$	361.000 kg $^{F.O.}$	105.000 kg $^{F.O.}$
Dominican Republic	7088.400 kg	1055.700 kg	245.900 kg	800.660 kg	110.298 kg	184.333 kg
Grenada	297.008 kg 1167 u.	1167 u.	191.000 kg $^{F.O.}$	123.199 kg ^{INCB}	84.000 kg	217.000 kg $^{F.O.}$
Haiti	46 u. ^{CICAD}	114 u. ^{CICAD}	No Report	4455.000 kg ^{CICAD}	24 u. ^{CICAD}	71.030 kg

Source: Annual Report Questionnaire if not otherwise indicated

Region/country or territory	Cannabis herb					
	1994	1995	1996	1997	1998	1999
AMERICAS						
Caribbean						
Jamaica	33565.000 kg [ICPO]	54697.828 kg [INCB]	41262.699 kg [ICPO]	24728.730 kg [ICPO]	22740.000 kg [F.O.]	56226.940 kg [ICPO]
Montserrat	No Report	2.000 kg [INCB]	No Report	3.285 kg 14090 u.	No Report	2.680 kg [ICPO]
Netherlands Antilles	No Report	No Report	No Report	1553.310 kg [INCB]	No Report	541.000 kg [F.O.]
Saint Kitts and Nevis	6.000 kg [F.O.]	3.185 kg [INCB]	5.000 kg [INCB]	67.000 kg [F.O.]	31.000 kg [F.O.]	16.000 kg [CICAD]
Saint Lucia	182.296 kg	102.327 kg	326.048 kg	621.684 kg	363.663 kg	267.000 kg [CICAD]
Saint Vincent and the Grenadines	1710.000 kg [F.O.]	3630.000 kg [F.O.]	1227.000 kg [F.O.]	527.000 kg [F.O.]	1321.000 kg [F.O.]	7188.000 kg [F.O.]
Trinidad Tobago	7249.000 kg [(1]	3210.000 kg [CICAD]	11408.526 kg [ICPO]	1430.000 kg [CICAD]	3483.545 kg	8287.000 kg [CICAD]
Turks and Caicos Islands	14.377 kg [ICPO]	9.701 kg [INCB]	25.000 kg	22.000 kg	8.000 kg	68.500 kg
US Virgin Islands	No Report	No Report	No Report	No Report	No Report	48.123 kg [ICPO]
Sub-Total	60182.980 kg 1213 u.	68528.750 kg 1281 u.	66382.170 kg 118 u.	63616.700 kg 14517 u.	37008.410 kg 674 u.	88443.590 kg 51 u.
Central America						
Belize	196.525 kg	15.000 kg [CICAD]	184.000 kg [CICAD]	263.000 kg [CICAD]	No Report	392.250 kg [ICPO]
Costa Rica	107.370 kg 781 u.	63.119 kg 263 u.	387.053 kg	107.000 kg [CICAD]	469.340 kg	1693.550 kg
El Salvador	No Report	133.000 kg [CICAD]	650.000 kg [CICAD]	971.247 kg [ICPO]	291.202 kg [ICPO]	604.581 kg
Guatemala	1760.000 kg [Govt]	1011.000 kg [Govt]	16388.295 kg	256.222 kg [Govt]	193.970 kg	814.212 kg
Honduras	399.048 kg [INCB]	489.650 kg	472.000 kg [CICAD]	2.147 kg	1293.000 kg [CICAD]	1583.000 kg [CICAD]
Nicaragua	401.000 kg [Govt]	459.482 kg [INCB]	853.961 kg	285.198 kg	613.027 kg	754.000 kg [CICAD]
Panama	122.310 kg	316.913 kg	18125.553 kg	14102.055 kg	16536.006 kg	3477.268 kg
Sub-Total	2986.253 kg 781 u.	2488.164 kg 263 u.	37060.860 kg	15986.870 kg	19396.550 kg	9318.860 kg
North America						
Canada	95630.953 kg	149265.422 kg	176673.000 kg	50624.000 kg	27299.990 kg 8 u.	44541.000 kg 52 u.
Mexico	529933.276 kg	780169.060 kg	1015755.538 kg	1038470.414 kg	1062143.980 kg	1471959.958 kg
United States	474971.813 kg [Govt]	627945.688 kg	638661.313 kg	684745.375 kg	799000.875 kg [Govt]	1175373.000 kg
Sub-Total	1100536.000 kg	1557380.000 kg	1831090.000 kg	1773840.000 kg	1888445.000 kg 8 u.	2691874.000 kg 52 u.
South America						
Argentina	2596.928 kg	5149.620 kg	8893.190 kg [Govt]	13709.620 kg	10920.230 kg	18301.339 kg
Bolivia	144.000 kg [Govt]	12.942 kg [ICPO]	175.000 kg [CICAD]	No Report	320.150 kg	2160.389 kg
Brazil	18836.545 kg [ICPO]	11730.796 kg	22430.588 kg	31828.432 kg	28982.492 kg	69171.506 kg
Chile	1676.600 kg	3788.305 kg	912.634 kg	784.430 kg	2238.325 kg	2105.000 kg [CICAD]
Colombia	207712.000 kg	206260.000 kg	238943.000 kg	178132.000 kg [Govt]	70025.000 kg	70124.000 kg
Ecuador	160.932 kg	13946.000 kg	175.240 kg	224.206 kg	17734.697 kg	2976.910 kg

Source: Annual Report Questionnaire if not otherwise indicated

Cannabis herb

Region/country or territory	1994	1995	1996	1997	1998	1999
AMERICAS						
South America						
Guyana	No Report	1007.115 kg	196.225 kg	186.157 kg [ICPO]	No Report	413.652 kg [ICPO]
Paraguay	12755.573 kg [ICPO]	Э7566.281 kg	43325.414 kg	17218.105 kg	80077.914 kg	199282.319 kg
Peru	404.210 kg	6442.813 kg	No Report	20910.326 kg	19880.324 kg	4055.732 kg
Suriname	No Report	41.732 kg	42.916 kg	No Report	104.754 kg	177.000 kg [CICAD]
Uruguay	30.996 kg [Govt]	97.008 kg	269.675 kg [Govt]	25601.006 kg [Govt]	424.778 kg	493.783 kg
Venezuela	9988.527 kg	13684.607 kg	2983.943 kg	No Report	4500.000 kg [CICAD]	13055.778 kg
Sub-Total	254306.300 kg	359727.200 kg	318347.800 kg	288594.300 kg	235208.700 kg	382317.400 kg
Total region	1418012.000 kg 1994 u.	1988124.000 kg 1544 u.	2252881.000 kg 118 u.	2142038.000 kg 14517 u.	2180059.000 kg 682 u.	3171954.000 kg 103 u.
ASIA						
Central Asia and Transcaucasian countries						
Armenia	132.000 kg	33.412 kg [ICPO]	90.245 kg	No Report	0.888 kg	46.675 kg [Govt]
Azerbaijan	77.214 kg [ICPO]	203.208 kg [Govt]	10.950 kg [ICPO]	37.475 kg [ICPO]	40.287 kg	55.395 kg
Georgia	No Report	No Report	642.088 kg [ICPO]	No Report	No Report	31972.800 kg [ICPO]
Kazakhstan	3503.689 kg [(2]	No Report	6800.000 kg [Govt]	11800.000 kg [Govt]	716.236 kg	10481.505 kg
Kyrgyzstan	No Report	No Report	560.065 kg	110.190 kg	No Report	1716.475 kg
Tajikistan	2700.000 kg [Govt]	9.922 kg [F.O.]	22.000 kg [F.O.]	336.311 kg [F.O.]	323.331 kg [F.O.]	No Report
Uzbekistan	1130.233 kg	862.631 kg	512.910 kg [ICPO]	374.496 kg	358.558 kg	288.689 kg
Sub-Total	7543.136 kg	1109.173 kg	8638.258 kg	12658.470 kg	1439.300 kg	44561.540 kg
East and South-East Asia						
Brunei Darussalam	0.549 kg	0.500 kg	1.132 kg	0.139 kg	3.288 kg	0.364 kg
Cambodia	1034.000 kg [ICPO]	1085.000 kg [Govt]	No Report	53751.000 kg [ICPO]	No Report	No Report
China	460.000 kg [F.O.]	466.000 kg	4876.000 kg	2408.000 kg	5079.000 kg	No Report
China (Hong Kong SAR)	3248.523 kg	1052.400 kg [Govt]	8822.700 kg	1002.100 kg	585.000 kg [Govt]	24.727 kg
Indonesia	1331.039 kg	443.856 kg	443.856 kg	715.735 kg	1071.862 kg	3741.068 kg
Japan	665.160 kg	208.051 kg	172.659 kg	155.246 kg	120.884 kg	565.904 kg
Korea (Republic of)	118.481 kg [Govt]	164.516 kg	44.434 kg	59.548 kg	32.751 kg	39.442 kg
Lao People's Dcm. Rep.	115.000 kg	5197.000 kg [Govt]	1896.300 kg [Govt]	7026.000 kg [Govt]	No Report	2187.000 kg [HNLP]
Macau	1.155 kg	0.922 kg [INCB]	21.690 kg [ICPO]	5.519 kg [ICPO]	1.661 kg [ICPO]	3.000 kg [INCB]
Malaysia	717.040 kg [Govt]	15.985 kg	1425.728 kg [Govt]	3889.132 kg	1781.010 kg	2064.498 kg
Mongolia	No Report	No Report	No Report	No Report	No Report	5.000 kg [ICPO]
Myanmar	306.624 kg	245.766 kg	263.786 kg	288.034 kg	380.970 kg	274.282 kg
Philippines	10844.283 kg	2212.710 kg	2044.572 kg	2226.894 kg [ICPO]	No Report	1187.870 kg
Singapore	38.372 kg	54.222 kg [(2]	70.868 kg	4363.452 kg	21.831 kg [(2]	7.432 kg [(2]
Thailand	8820.000 kg [Govt]	19880.000 kg [Govt]	16720.000 kg [Govt]	9141.927 kg	5581.840 kg	14706.198 kg
Viet Nam	2137.000 kg [Govt]	578.700 kg [ICPO]	581.100 kg [ICPO]	7986.000 kg [ICPO]	379.000 kg [ICPO]	400.100 kg [F.O.]
Sub-Total	29837.230 kg	31605.630 kg	37384.830 kg	93018.730 kg	15039.100 kg	25206.890 kg

Source: Annual Report Questionnaire if not otherwise indicated

Cannabis herb

Region/country or territory	1994	1995	1996	1997	1998	1999
ASIA						
Near and Middle East /South-West Asia						
Bahrain	0.696 kg	0.681 kg	6.529 kg	7.382 kg	0.041 kg [ICPO]	0.042 kg [ICPO]
Iraq	No Report	No Report	No Report	No Report	No Report	270.000 kg [INCB]
Israel	320.553 kg	3207.091 kg	1075.181 kg	10635.000 kg	3581.000 kg	3400.000 kg [ICPO]
Jordan	1.597 kg	No Report	1.040 kg	0.106 kg	No Report	62.525 kg [ICPO]
Kuwait	No Report	0.403 kg [INCB]	124.623 kg [ICPO]	28.580 kg [ICPO]	0.246 kg	[ICPO]
Lebanon	256.000 kg	No Report	No Report	No Report	No Report	1.379 kg
Oman	0.046 kg	No Report	No Report	No Report	No Report	0.269 kg
Pakistan	20087.170 kg [Govt]	No Report	No Report	No Report	No Report	No Report
Qatar	0.015 kg	0.042 kg	0.027 kg	No Report	146.250 kg [ICPO]	3.297 kg [ICPO]
Syrian Arab Republic	1128.567 kg [ICPO]	1662.884 kg	No Report	1714.635 kg	231.795 kg	819.058 kg
United Arab Emirates	0.457 kg	No Report	No Report	No Report	0.095 kg	0.341 kg
Yemen	No Report	No Report	No Report	0.569 kg [ICPO]	11.350 kg [ICPO]	No Report
Sub-Total	21795.100 kg	4871.101 kg	1207.400 kg	12386.270 kg	3970.777 kg	4556.911 kg
South Asia						
Bangladesh	788.650 kg	No Report	121.939 kg	No Report	No Report	724.070 kg [F.O.]
India	187896.000 kg	121873.000 kg	62992.000 kg [Govt]	30866.000 kg	68221.000 kg	38610.000 kg
Maldives	0.371 kg	No Report	No Report	No Report	0.001 kg	0.022 kg
Nepal	2482.470 kg	5521.151 kg	2271.923 kg	2040.894 kg [ICPO]	6409.669 kg	4064.650 kg
Sri Lanka	3803.361 kg	7997.900 kg	20332.385 kg	63338.734 kg	3450.686 kg	4062.421 kg
Sub-Total	194970.900 kg	135392.000 kg	85718.240 kg	146245.600 kg	78081.360 kg	47461.160 kg
Total region	254146.300 kg	172978.000 kg	132948.700 kg	264309.100 kg	98530.530 kg	121786.500 kg
EUROPE						
Eastern Europe						
Albania	No Report	No Report	No Report	No Report	No Report	4395.156 kg [ICPO]
Belarus	13.000 kg	112.000 kg	56.000 kg	90.802 kg [INCB]	No Report	425.000 kg
Bosnia Herzegovina	No Report	No Report	No Report	No Report	44.980 kg [ICPO]	59.144 kg [ICPO]
Bulgaria	440.067 kg	93.902 kg	5475.649 kg	227.440 kg	1527.562 kg	29365.000 kg
Croatia	52.955 kg	35.013 kg	40.651 kg	135.868 kg	20342.877 kg	200.898 kg
Czech Republic	1.887 kg	No Report	11900.000 kg [Govt]	5.403 kg	5.500 kg	111.200 kg
Estonia	No Report	No Report	1.236 kg [ICPO]	3.439 kg	4.789 kg 358 u.	1.468 kg 491 u.
FYR of Macedonia	No Report	10.107 kg	130.619 kg [ICPO]	No Report	1136.752 kg	698.098 kg [ICPO]
Hungary	104.409 kg [INCB]	88.178 kg [ICPO]	3.084 kg	2140.000 kg [Govt]	42.930 kg	65.725 kg
Latvia	No Report	11.000 kg 24200 u.	793.000 kg	22.000 kg	2.480 kg	231.200 kg
Lithuania	27.312 kg	1.437 kg	0.826 kg	8.063 kg	30.357 kg	25.667 kg
Poland	164.000 kg	2086.572 kg	2631.156 kg	62.476 kg	62.146 kg	847.901 kg
Republic of Moldova	30.206 kg [ICPO]	229.690 kg [ICPO]	906.510 kg	435.500 kg	No Report	416.000 kg [ICPO]

Source: Annual Report Questionnaire if not otherwise indicated

Region/country or territory	**Cannabis herb**					
	1994	**1995**	**1996**	**1997**	**1998**	**1999**

EUROPE

Eastern Europe

Region/country or territory	1994	1995	1996	1997	1998	1999
Romania	1228.851 kg	4.589 kg	1737.213 kg	40.186 kg [ICPO]	7.478 kg	4.530 kg [ICPO]
Russian Federation	19936.000 kg [ICPO]	20141.900 kg	18967.801 kg	22976.000 kg	23510.650 kg	33801.919 kg
Slovakia	2.903 kg	10.402 kg [ICPO]	24.000 kg [INCB]	865.615 kg	12539.934 kg	156.000 kg
Slovenia	55.189 kg	29.914 kg [ICPO]	34.596 kg	47.555 kg	2772.604 kg	249.156 kg
Ukraine	No Report	3141.000 kg [ICPO]	1279.200 kg	No Report	No Report	4045.000 kg [WIB (3]
Sub-Total	22056.780 kg	25995.710 kg 24200 u.	43981.540 kg	27060.350 kg	62031.040 kg 358 u.	75099.070 kg 491 u.

Western Europe

Region/country or territory	1994	1995	1996	1997	1998	1999
Andorra	0.072 kg [ICPO]	1.122 kg [INCB]	2.000 kg [INCB]	1.892 kg [ICPO]	0.116 kg [ICPO]	0.046 kg
Austria	240.554 kg	458.775 kg	270.659 kg	668.071 kg	1211.031 kg	341.402 kg
Belgium	34737.551 kg	38103.508 kg	56791.000 kg	39072.000 kg	2463.270 kg	2914.749 kg
Cyprus	0.626 kg	13.100 kg	5.915 kg	17.582 kg	128.905 kg	30.108 kg
Denmark	10655.000 kg [ICPO]	No Report	No Report	. No Report	No Report	52.830 kg
Finland	4.367 kg	No Report	3.152 kg	12.153 kg	8.014 kg	18.167 kg
France	2095.708 kg [Govt]	3055.964 kg	31279.678 kg	3452.210 kg	3521.790 kg	3382.205 kg
Germany	21659.766 kg	10436.227 kg	6108.577 kg	4167.282 kg	14897.189 kg	15021.800 kg
Gibraltar	No Report	No Report	0.026 kg	(4	0.084 kg	0.028 kg
Greece	462.069 kg	931.587 kg	2565.959 kg 542 u.	12409.776 kg 482 u.	17510.434 kg	12038.938 kg 10 u.
Iceland	20.235 kg	10.929 kg	49.000 kg [INCB]	No Report	No Report	0.503 kg
Ireland	65.459 kg [ICPO]	77.500 kg [ICPO]	2.400 kg	34.824 kg	38.909 kg	68.290 kg
Italy	803.339 kg 1091 u.	473.248 kg 999 u.	5722.201 kg	45011.035 kg 2675 u.	38785.988 kg 1192 u.	21248.982 kg [ICPO]
Liechtenstein	No Report	0.022 kg	25.919 kg	1.530 kg	No Report	No Report
Luxembourg	292.577 kg	0.961 kg	16.460 kg	34.387 kg	4.956 kg	3.932 kg
Malta	5.300 kg	0.224 kg	7217.046 kg	0.163 kg	0.069 kg	0.161 kg
Monaco	0.005 kg	0.008 kg	0.011 kg	0.028 kg	0.032 kg	0.013 kg [ICPO]
Netherlands	190476.781 kg [ICPO]	275035.000 kg [ICPO]	82232.000 kg [ICPO]	31513.199 kg [(2]	55463.000 kg	47039.000 kg [ICPO]
Norway	3.589 kg	19444.568 kg	70.000 kg	44.095 kg	88.172 kg	16.471 kg
Portugal	32.694 kg	159.892 kg	35.971 kg	72.240 kg	7.115 kg	65.766 kg
San Marino	0.024 kg	No Report	No Report	No Report	No Report	No Report
Spain	0.642 kg	16.720 kg	13267.759 kg	24890.311 kg	412.866 kg	761.342 kg
Sweden	80.963 kg	26.105 kg	148.423 kg	30.705 kg	98.431 kg	28.228 kg 4 u.
Switzerland	84.689 kg	221.822 kg	3559.769 kg	6634.843 kg	13163.982 kg	7800.229 kg
Turkey	(5	No Report	No Report	No Report	No Report	5458.350 kg [ICPO]
United Kingdom	11578.900 kg	13871.500 kg	34189.102 kg	31120.199 kg	21660.666 kg	15410.048 kg [ICPO] 20 u.
Sub-Total	273300.900 kg 1091 u.	362338.800 kg 999 u.	243563.000 kg 542 u.	199188.500 kg 3157 u.	169465.000 kg 1192 u.	131701.600 kg 34 u.

Source: Annual Report Questionnaire if not otherwise indicated

Region/country or territory	1994	1995	1996	1997	1998	1999
Cannabis herb						

EUROPE

| Total region | 295357.700 kg 1091 u. | 388334.500 kg 25199 u. | 287544.600 kg 542 u. | 226248.900 kg 3157 u. | 231496.100 kg 1550 u. | 206800.700 kg 525 u. |

OCEANIA

Oceania

Australia	No Report	1393.269 kg [6] 117 u.	1747.722 kg 1922 u.	4398.986 kg [7]	15996.628 kg Govt [3]	5874.000 kg INCB
Fiji	5.000 kg	16.986 kg ICPO	6.989 kg	No Report	No Report	45.618 kg ICPO
New Caledonia	No Report	No Report	138.000 kg INCB	133.610 kg INCB	No Report	132.000 kg INCB
New Zealand	908.925 kg ICPO	700.000 kg Govt	455.000 kg INCB	285.012 kg	389.182 kg [7]	323.649 kg
Tonga	No Report	No Report	150.000 kg Govt	0.297 kg INCB	No Report	No Report
Sub-Total	913.925 kg	2110.255 kg 117 u.	2497.711 kg 1922 u.	4817.905 kg	16385.810 kg	6375.267 kg
Total region	913.925 kg	2110.255 kg 117 u.	2497.711 kg 1922 u.	4817.905 kg	16385.810 kg	6375.267 kg
TOTAL	2328711.000 kg 3085 u.	3200197.000 kg 26860 u.	3038710.000 kg 2582 u.	3047644.000 kg 17674 u.	2941953.000 kg 2238 u.	3959383.000 kg 674 u.

1) Including cannabis plants. 2) Including cannabis resin. 3) Provisional figures. 4) Including depressants. 5) Included in cannabis resin. 6) Fiscal year 7) Including cannabis resin, liquid cannabis.

Source: Annual Report Questionnaire if not otherwise indicated

Trafficking in cannabis resin

Compared to 1998, trafficking in cannabis resin remained basically unchanged in 1999. As in previous years, about three quarters of all cannabis resin seizures were in Europe, mostly West Europe. Seizures in western Europe, the Near and Middle East (including countries of South-West Asia) and North Africa accounted for 97% of global seizures of cannabis resin in 1999.

Authorities in West Europe report that between 60% and 90% of the cannabis resin seized came from Morocco.

The main other sources are Pakistan and Afghanistan. Pakistan is cited as the main source for cannabis resin found in the markets of Turkey, eastern and southern Africa and Canada. Pakistan itself has identified Afghanistan as its main source of cannabis resin. The main sources of cannabis resin seized in the Russian Federation are located in Central Asia, notably Kyrgyzstan. Nepal is the main external source for cannabis resin found in India. Lebanon, next to Pakistan, is cited as a source for cannabis resin found in the countries of the Near East.

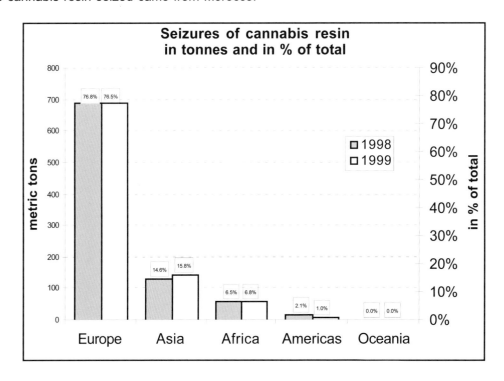

150

GLOBAL SEIZURES OF CANNABIS RESIN 1989-99

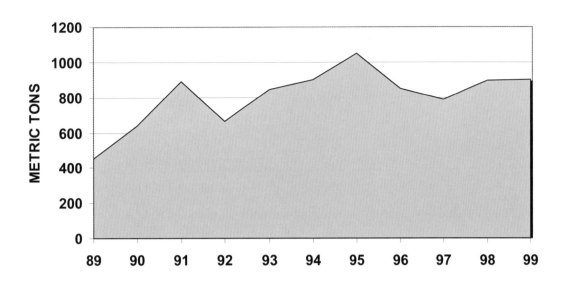

Year	1989	1990	1991	1992	1993	1994	1995	1996	1997	1998	1999
Metric tons	454	641	890	665	846	901	1,053	851	787	899	900

SEIZURES OF **CANNABIS RESIN** in % of world total and kg- HIGHEST RANKING COUNTRIES - 1999

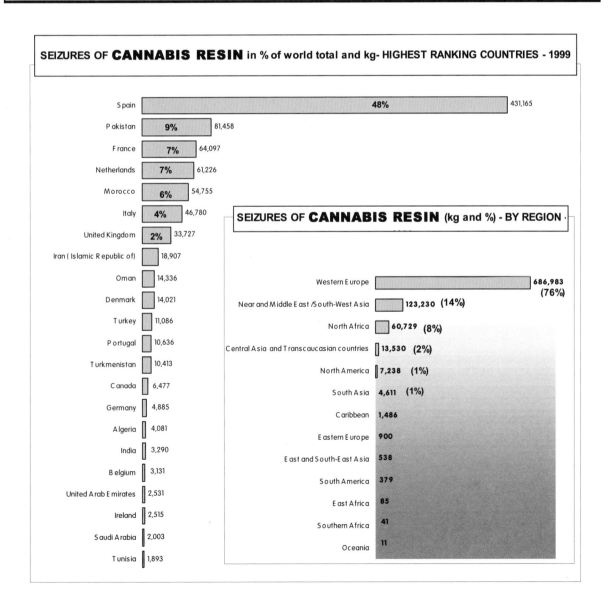

SEIZURES OF **CANNABIS RESIN** (kg and %) - BY REGION

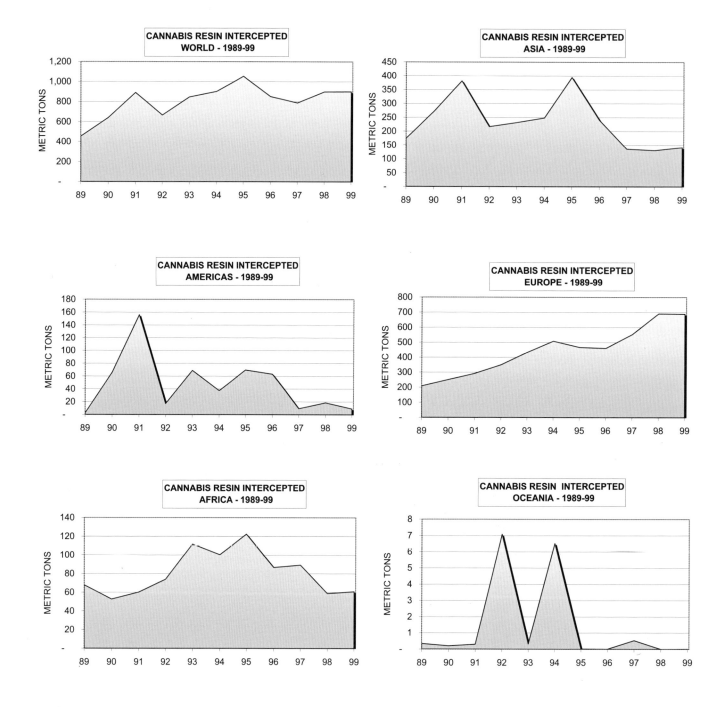

Cannabis resin trafficking 1998-1999: extent and trends (countries reporting seizures of more than 0.1 tons (100 kg))

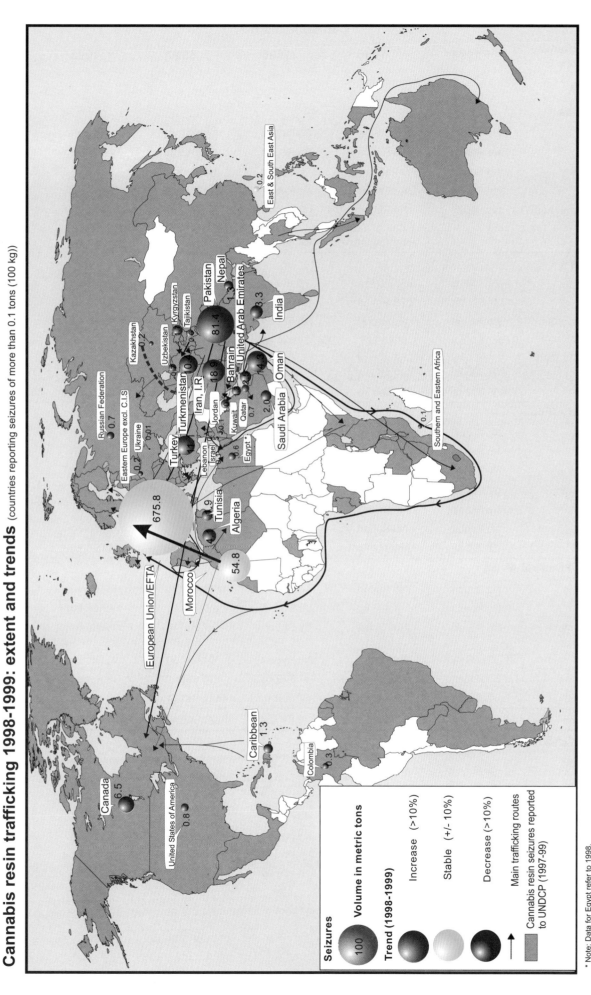

East & South East Asia
0.2

Pakistan
Nepal
1.3

United Arab Emirates
India
3.3

Kyrgyzstan
Tajikistan
0.9
Kazakhstan
0.2
Uzbekistan
81.4
0.1

Bahrain
18.9
0.1
Oman
4.3

Russian Federation
0.7
Turkmenistan
Iran, I.R
Jordan
Kuwait
Qatar
0.7
Saudi Arabia
2.0

Eastern Europe excl. C.I.S
Ukraine
0.01
0.2
Turkey
1.1
Lebanon
Israel
0.6
Egypt*
Southern and Eastern Africa
0.1

675.8

9
Tunisia
Algeria

54.8

European Union/EFTA
Morocco
4

Caribbean
1.3

Colombia
0.3

Canada
6.5

United States of America
0.8

Seizures

Volume in metric tons
100

Trend (1998-1999)

Increase (>10%)

Stable (+/- 10%)

Decrease (>10%)

Main trafficking routes

Cannabis resin seizures reported
to UNDCP (1997-99)

* Note: Data for Egypt refer to 1998.
Note: The boundaries and names shown and the designations used on this map do not imply official endorsement or acceptance by the United Nations

Cannabis resin

Region/country or territory	1994	1995	1996	1997	1998	1999
AFRICA						
East Africa						
Kenya	No Report	5707.000 kg	19633.000 kg	7.007 kg	No Report	3.200 kg [ICPO]
Mauritius	No Report	No Report	No Report	No Report	0.130 kg	[(1]
Seychelles	No Report	4.452 kg [INCB]	6.600 kg [ICPO]	No Report	1.073 kg [Govt]	72.883 kg
Uganda	No Report	No Report	No Report	No Report	25.000 kg	8.797 kg
United Republic of Tanzania	No Report	No Report	No Report	No Report	42.162 kg	No Report
Sub-Total		5711.452 kg	19639.600 kg	7.007 kg	68.365 kg	84.880 kg
North Africa						
Algeria	1169.408 kg [ICPO]	1920.609 kg [INCB]	712.160 kg [ICPO]	No Report	1217.179 kg [ICPO]	4080.662 kg
Egypt	1744.977 kg	1026.860 kg [Govt]	No Report	441.588 kg	628.434 kg	No Report
Libyan Arab Jam.	No Report	No Report	No Report	No Report	471.955 kg	No Report
Morocco	97047.578 kg	110245.328 kg	64769.098 kg	71887.469 kg	55519.734 kg	54755.235 kg
Tunisia	297.306 kg	170.198 kg	555.162 kg [ICPO]	201.074 kg [ICPO]	806.324 kg	1893.381 kg
Sub-Total	100259.300 kg	113363.000 kg	66036.420 kg	72530.130 kg	58643.630 kg	60729.280 kg
Southern Africa						
Lesotho	No Report	2979.000 kg [ICPO]	No Report	3.942 kg [ICPO]	No Report	No Report
Malawi	No Report	No Report	No Report	No Report	3.000 kg	3.000 kg
Mozambique	No Report	No Report	No Report	12000.000 kg [ICPO]	14.160 kg [ICPO]	11.000 kg [ICPO]
South Africa	27.078 kg	7.858 kg	1.068 kg	2.150 kg	20.568 kg	22.612 kg [ICPO]
Zambia	No Report	258.219 kg [ICPO]	15.724 kg [ICPO]	40.269 kg [ICPO]	3.111 kg [Govt]	4.201 kg
Zimbabwe	No Report	No Report	No Report	No Report	3.191 kg	No Report
Sub-Total	27.078 kg	3245.077 kg	16.792 kg	12046.360 kg	44.030 kg	40.813 kg
West and Central Africa						
Burkina Faso	No Report	No Report	No Report	4647.000 kg [Govt]	No Report	No Report
Gambia	No Report	0.013 kg [ICPO]	No Report	0.048 kg [ICPO]	0.420 kg [ICPO]	0.007 kg
Sao Tome and Principe	No Report	No Report	No Report	4.000 kg	No Report	No Report
Senegal	2.100 kg [ICPO]	No Report	No Report	No Report	No Report	No Report
Sierra Leone	No Report	No Report	987.000 kg	No Report	No Report	No Report
Sub-Total	2.100 kg	0.013 kg	987.000 kg	4651.048 kg	0.420 kg	0.007 kg
Total region	100288.400 kg	122319.500 kg	86679.810 kg	89234.540 kg	58756.440 kg	60854.980 kg
AMERICAS						
Caribbean						
Antigua and Barbuda	No Report	1.850 kg [INCB]	33.000 kg [INCB]	1944.900 kg [ICPO]	No Report	1000.000 kg [CICAD]
Aruba	No Report	No Report	No Report	0.004 kg [INCB]	No Report	No Report
Bahamas	2.381 kg	No Report	No Report	5.030 kg [ICPO]	16.082 kg	2.095 kg [ICPO]
Barbados	No Report	992.250 kg [ICPO]	No Report	No Report	No Report	1.270 kg [HONL(]
Bermuda	0.543 kg [ICPO]	0.430 kg [INCB]	0.975 kg	0.609 kg	0.609 kg	171.002 kg

Source: Annual Report Questionnaire if not otherwise indicated

154

Cannabis resin

Region/country or territory	1994	1995	1996	1997	1998	1999
AMERICAS						
Caribbean						
Cayman Islands	27.027 kg [INCB]	No Report	0.104 kg	No Report	No Report	No Report
Cuba	No Report	No Report	35.503 kg	No Report	No Report	66.200 kg [F.O.]
Dominica	508 u. [ICPO]	No Report	No Report	No Report	No Report	0.015 kg [ICPO]
Dominican Republic	0.018 kg	0.044 kg	0.003 kg	No Report	No Report	184.000 kg [ICPO]
Jamaica	No Report	No Report	172.680 kg [ICPO]	67.590 kg [ICPO]	No Report	61.450 kg [ICPO]
Netherlands Antilles	No Report	No Report	No Report	0.354 kg [INCB] [(2]	No Report	No Report
Saint Lucia	0.058 kg	0.032 kg	No Report		No Report	No Report
Trinidad Tobago	No Report	No Report	No Report	No Report	2725.305 kg	No Report
Sub-Total	30.027 kg 508 u.	994.606 kg	242.265 kg	2018.487 kg	2741.996 kg	1486.032 kg
Central America						
Honduras	No Report	No Report	No Report	No Report	No Report	1027 u. [CICAD]
Sub-Total						1027 u.
North America						
Canada	36368.996 kg	40369.469 kg	24655.000 kg	6178.000 kg	15925.320 kg 0.002 lt. 97 u.	6477.000 kg 1.000 lt. 5 u.
Mexico	42.885 kg	13477.191 kg	8.795 kg	115.155 kg	1.743 kg	0.329 kg
United States	783.000 kg [Govt]	14636.800 kg	38205.000 kg	1072.600 kg	No Report	761.000 kg
Sub-Total	37194.880 kg	68483.460 kg	62868.800 kg	7365.755 kg	15927.060 kg 0.002 lt. 97 u.	7238.330 kg 1.000 lt. 5 u.
South America						
Argentina	0.210 kg	[ICPO]	6.720 kg [Govt]	0.060 kg	1.880 kg	5006 u.
Brazil	1.432 kg [INCB]	6.340 kg	8.509 kg	12.160 kg	No Report	37.550 kg
Chile	0.044 kg	No Report	No Report	No Report	No Report	No Report
Colombia	73.390 kg	12.510 kg	13.000 kg [Govt]	7.000 kg	No Report	338.000 kg
Falkland Islands	No Report	No Report	No Report	0.122 kg	No Report	0.063 kg
Guyana	No Report	0.001 kg	No Report	No Report	No Report	No Report
Paraguay	0.874 kg [ICPO]	0.475 kg	0.880 kg	1.780 kg	3.702 kg	2.337 kg
Suriname	No Report	No Report	No Report	No Report	0.529 kg	No Report
Uruguay	No Report	No Report	0.100 kg [Govt]	No Report	No Report	1.136 kg
Sub-Total	75.950 kg	19.326 kg	29.209 kg	21.122 kg	6.111 kg	379.085 kg 5006 u.
Total region	37300.860 kg 508 u.	69497.400 kg	63140.270 kg	9405.364 kg	18675.170 kg 0.002 lt. 97 u.	9103.447 kg 1.000 lt. 6038 u.
ASIA						
Central Asia and Transcaucasian countries						
Armenia	No Report	8.536 kg [ICPO]	0.516 kg	No Report	No Report	0.178 kg [ICPO]
Azerbaijan	No Report	No Report	No Report	No Report	23.256 kg	0.832 kg

Source: Annual Report Questionnaire if not otherwise indicated

Cannabis resin

Region/country or territory	1994	1995	1996	1997	1998	1999
ASIA						
Central Asia and Transcaucasian countries						
Georgia	No Report	No Report	8.568 kg [ICPO]	No Report	No Report	0.003 kg [ICPO]
Kazakhstan	(3	1555.000 kg	1500.000 kg [Govt]	4100.000 kg [Govt]	298.635 kg	145.462 kg
Kyrgyzstan	No Report	86.432 kg	No Report	No Report	1498.000 kg [F.O.]	1717.000 kg [F.O.]
Tajikistan	0.320 kg [F.O.]	81.300 kg [F.O.]	64.000 kg [F.O.]	630.311 kg [F.O.]	726.449 kg [F.O.]	560.000 kg [F.O.]
Turkmenistan	1000.000 kg [Govt]	No Report	No Report	No Report	22249.000 kg [Govt]	10413.000 kg [F.O.]
Uzbekistan	242.987 kg	394.247 kg	144.502 kg [ICPO]	316.055 kg	No Report	694.000 kg [F.O.]
Sub-Total	1243.307 kg	2125.515 kg	1717.586 kg	5046.366 kg	24795.340 kg	13530.480 kg
East and South-East Asia						
China (Hong Kong SAR)	80.034 kg	20.100 kg [Govt]	27.900 kg	38.900 kg	No Report	14.376 kg
Indonesia	No Report	0.546 kg	2.050 kg	No Report	0.690 kg / 230 u.	300.005 kg [HNLP]
Japan	96.980 kg	130.670 kg	145.143 kg	107.421 kg	214.560 kg	200.297 kg
Korea (Republic of)	No Report	No Report	No Report	0.635 kg	0.884 kg	1.963 kg
Macau	No Report	No Report	4.237 kg [ICPO]	No Report	0.995 kg [ICPO]	No Report
Malaysia	No Report	965.027 kg	No Report	No Report	No Report	No Report
Philippines	126.593 kg	5.789 kg	0.031 kg	0.283 kg [ICPO]	No Report	No Report
Singapore	7.869 kg	(3	No Report	No Report	No Report	0.350 kg [ICPO]
Thailand	No Report	No Report	No Report	45.169 kg	20.592 kg	121.220 kg
Sub-Total	311.476 kg	1122.132 kg	179.361 kg	192.408 kg	237.721 kg / 230 u.	638.210 kg
Near and Middle East /South-West Asia						
Bahrain	0.001 kg	No Report	No Report	0.012 kg	1.036 kg [ICPO]	1263.049 kg [ICPO]
Iran (Islamic Republic of)	7618.000 kg	15854.000 kg	13063.000 kg	11095.789 kg	14376.000 kg [Govt]	18907.000 kg [Govt]
Iraq	5.995 kg	No Report	No Report	No Report	No Report	No Report
Israel	3047.374 kg	206.117 kg	83.578 kg	133.000 kg	60.900 kg	70.000 kg [ICPO]
Jordan	1726.205 kg / 633 u.	2910.915 kg	No Report	No Report	166.737 kg	112.410 kg
Kuwait	125.370 kg	631.571 kg [INCB]	3.668 kg [ICPO]	0.530 kg [ICPO]	214.103 kg	972.878 kg [ICPO]
Lebanon	39872.074 kg	3760.152 kg	4908.757 kg	1876.281 kg	2492.609 kg	76.698 kg
Oman	816.662 kg	308.948 kg	1500.000 kg [INCB]	1979.000 kg [INCB]	No Report	14335.695 kg
Pakistan	189252.188 kg [Govt]	357690.531 kg [ICPO]	192837.469 kg [ICPO]	107000.000 kg [ICPO]	65909.234 kg	81458.142 kg
Qatar	42.247 kg	No Report	No Report	361.692 kg [ICPO]	374.526 kg [ICPO]	680.869 kg [ICPO]
Saudi Arabia	1972.470 kg	1809.704 kg	3531.225 kg [ICPO]	1321.285 kg [ICPO]	2357.874 kg	2003.000 kg [ICPO]
Syrian Arab Republic	No Report	No Report	1569.293 kg	No Report	No Report	819.580 kg [ICPO]
United Arab Emirates	1792.568 kg	2545.060 kg	1377.591 kg	3505.585 kg	7087.219 kg	2530.511 kg
Yemen	4.243 kg [Govt]	No Report	No Report	No Report	No Report	No Report
Sub-Total	246275.400 kg / 633 u.	385717.000 kg	218874.600 kg	127273.200 kg	93040.230 kg	123229.800 kg

Source: Annual Report Questionnaire if not otherwise indicated

Cannabis resin						
Region/country or territory	**1994**	**1995**	**1996**	**1997**	**1998**	**1999**

ASIA
South Asia

Bangladesh	12.250 kg	No Report	7.206 kg	No Report	No Report	0.700 kg [F.O.]
India	No Report	3629.000 kg [ICPO]	6520.000 kg [Govt]	3281.000 kg	10106.000 kg	3290.000 kg
Maldives	No Report	No Report	No Report	No Report	No Report	0.004 kg
Nepal	501.273 kg	2133.428 kg	1917.372 kg	No Report	2585.887 kg	1319.993 kg
Sri Lanka	0.771 kg	1.397 kg [ICPO]	11027.420 kg	17.756 kg	No Report	[(1]
Sub-Total	514.294 kg	5763.825 kg	19472.000 kg	3298.756 kg	12691.890 kg	4610.697 kg
Total region	248344.500 kg 633 u.	394728.500 kg	240243.500 kg	135810.700 kg	130765.200 kg	142009.200 kg 230 u.

EUROPE
Eastern Europe

Belarus	6.338 kg	0.288 kg	14.519 kg	5.380 kg [INCB]	0.509 kg	1.949 kg
Bulgaria	No Report	No Report	8995.840 kg	533.570 kg	0.680 kg	0.010 kg
Croatia	5.853 kg	3.281 kg	3.104 kg	3.257 kg	2.878 kg	6.555 kg
Czech Republic	499.341 kg	5.000 kg	2.806 kg	0.324 kg	No Report	1.200 kg
Estonia	No Report	No Report	4.462 kg [ICPO]	0.316 kg	0.133 kg 52 u.	1.191 kg 191 u.
FYR of Macedonia	No Report	No Report	2.534 kg [ICPO]	No Report	1164.005 kg	0.090 kg [ICPO]
Hungary	24.419 kg [INCB]	0.618 kg [INCB]	816.215 kg	21.739 kg [Govt]	6.803 kg	5.242 kg
Latvia	No Report	1.500 kg 1500 u.	1.497 kg	0.646 kg	3.150 kg	0.685 kg
Lithuania	0.140 kg	6.470 kg	0.249 kg	0.078 kg	3.780 kg	1.054 kg
Poland	17.000 kg	10001.341 kg	5.253 kg	628.000 kg	8.176 kg	49.203 kg
Republic of Moldova	0.529 kg [ICPO]	0.828 kg [ICPO]	0.209 kg	No Report	228.000 kg	No Report
Romania	350.547 kg	36.457 kg	4851.528 kg	1309.792 kg [ICPO]	1.673 kg	43.530 kg
Russian Federation	428.668 kg [ICPO]	458.100 kg	650.500 kg	887.500 kg [Govt]	1588.700 kg	710.895 kg
Slovakia	0.612 kg	No Report	No Report	0.038 kg	0.015 kg	No Report
Slovenia	0.280 kg	No Report	5.438 kg	0.938 kg	1.958 kg	64.622 kg
Ukraine	208.200 kg [ICPO]	51.013 kg [ICPO]	20.816 kg	9.500 kg	6150.100 kg	14.000 kg [WIB (4]
Yugoslavia	3.994 kg	No Report	No Report	No Report	No Report	No Report
Sub-Total	1545.921 kg	10564.900 kg 1500 u.	15374.970 kg	3401.078 kg	9160.560 kg 52 u.	900.226 kg 191 u.

Western Europe

Andorra	24.511 kg [ICPO]	2.075 kg [ICPO]	No Report	No Report	1.372 kg [ICPO]	1.422 kg
Austria	147.535 kg	238.282 kg	247.039 kg	243.909 kg	124.718 kg	109.996 kg
Belgium	25165.980 kg	32582.146 kg	49899.000 kg	8980.000 kg	817.622 kg	3130.812 kg [ICPO]
Cyprus	14.983 kg	33.200 kg	29.905 kg	3.413 kg	1.201 kg	7.291 kg
Denmark	9433.020 kg [WCO]	2414.100 kg	1772.400 kg	467.100 kg	1572.455 kg	14021.300 kg
Finland	64.325 kg	147.514 kg	99.444 kg	197.659 kg	160.972 kg	492.316 kg
France	55889.934 kg [Govt]	39203.449 kg	35575.816 kg	51664.367 kg	52176.426 kg	64096.665 kg
Germany	4032.954 kg	3809.261 kg	3246.536 kg	7327.560 kg	6109.549 kg	4885.200 kg

Source: Annual Report Questionnaire if not otherwise indicated

Cannabis resin

Region/country or territory	1994	1995	1996	1997	1998	1999
EUROPE						
Western Europe						
Gibraltar	No Report	No Report	481.431 kg	655.882 kg	163.862 kg	30.171 kg
Greece	5692.813 kg	287.730 kg	830.319 kg	6825.727 kg	30.817 kg	55.819 kg
Iceland	No Report	0.305 kg	No Report	No Report	No Report	41.622 kg
Ireland	1460.722 kg [ICPO]	15529.000 kg [ICPO]	1933.000 kg	1247.244 kg	3179.178 kg	2514.975 kg
Italy	18128.277 kg 961 u.	14921.714 kg 1376 u.	5939.923 kg	14740.517 kg 1954 u.	15412.128 kg 711 u.	46780.319 kg [ICPO]
Liechtenstein	0.196 kg	0.158 kg	0.082 kg	0.008 kg	2.770 kg	No Report
Luxembourg	24.420 kg	11.275 kg	14.419 kg	0.868 kg	1.974 kg	1.270 kg
Malta	1.147 kg	0.941 kg	1.067 kg	1.788 kg	25.116 kg	1.606 kg
Monaco	0.186 kg	0.079 kg	0.651 kg	0.170 kg	0.396 kg	0.111 kg [ICPO]
Netherlands	43299.258 kg [ICPO]	79985.000 kg [ICPO]	11378.000 kg [ICPO]	No Report	70696.000 kg	61226.000 kg [ICPO] 3274 u.
Norway	456.904 kg	501.173 kg	641.000 kg	904.059 kg	1874.136 kg	1254.762 kg
Portugal	40392.699 kg	6334.287 kg	5324.091 kg	9621.183 kg	5747.793 kg	10636.075 kg
San Marino	0.028 kg	No Report	No Report	No Report	No Report	No Report
Spain	219176.141 kg	197024.047 kg	247745.094 kg	315328.000 kg [ICPO]	428236.375 kg	431165.280 kg
Sweden	355.568 kg	494.300 kg	304.112 kg	627.994 kg	390.930 kg	1065.387 kg 26 u.
Switzerland	447.754 kg	585.496 kg	676.736 kg	653.467 kg	1837.480 kg	651.548 kg
Turkey	31218.000 kg [5]	17359.648 kg	12294.000 kg	10439.201 kg	9434.290 kg	11085.546 kg
United Kingdom	51430.102 kg	44607.000 kg	66936.703 kg	118849.203 kg	82837.533 kg	33727.243 kg [ICPO] 194 u.
Sub-Total	506857.400 kg 961 u.	456072.200 kg 1376 u.	445370.800 kg	548779.300 kg 1954 u.	680835.200 kg 3985 u.	686982.800 kg 220 u.
Total region	508403.300 kg 961 u.	466637.100 kg 2876 u.	460745.800 kg	552180.400 kg 1954 u.	689995.800 kg 4037 u.	687883.000 kg 411 u.
OCEANIA						
Oceania						
Australia	6521.073 kg [5]	17.283 kg [6] 30 u.	9.195 kg 246 u.	537.289 kg	No Report	10.000 kg [INCB]
New Caledonia	No Report	No Report	No Report	0.003 kg [INCB]	No Report	No Report
New Zealand	0.623 kg [ICPO]	0.707 kg [Govt]	No Report	2.198 kg [INCB]	3.632 kg	0.676 kg
Sub-Total	6521.696 kg	17.990 kg 30 u.	9.195 kg 246 u.	539.490 kg	3.632 kg	10.676 kg
Total region	6521.696 kg	17.990 kg 30 u.	9.195 kg 246 u.	539.490 kg	3.632 kg	10.676 kg
TOTAL	900858.800 kg 2102 u.	1053201.000 kg 2906 u.	850818.600 kg 246 u.	787170.500 kg 1954 u.	898196.200 kg 0.002 lt. 4364 u.	899861.300 kg 1.000 lt. 6449 u.

1) Small quantity. 2) Including depressants. 3) Included in cannabis herb. 4) Provisional figures. 5) Including cannabis herb. 6) Fiscal year

Source: Annual Report Questionnaire if not otherwise indicated

Region/country or territory	Cannabis oil					
	1994	1995	1996	1997	1998	1999
AFRICA						
East Africa						
Kenya	No Report	No Report	No Report	No Report	No Report	4.057 kg
Sub-Total						4.057 kg
North Africa						
Algeria	0.091 kg [ICPO]	No Report	No Report	No Report	No Report	No Report
Morocco	10.625 kg	7.054 kg	4.295 kg	1.060 kg [Govt]	14.473 kg	19.000 lt.
Sub-Total	10.716 kg	7.054 kg	4.295 kg	1.060 kg	14.473 kg	19.000 lt.
Southern Africa						
Zimbabwe	No Report	No Report	2.000 kg [ICPO]	No Report	No Report	No Report
Sub-Total			2.000 kg			
West and Central Africa						
Benin	No Report	No Report	No Report	No Report	26.863 kg	No Report
Sub-Total					26.863 kg	
Total region	10.716 kg	7.054 kg	6.295 kg	1.060 kg	41.336 kg	4.057 kg 19.000 lt.
AMERICAS						
Caribbean						
Antigua and Barbuda	0.740 kg	No Report	No Report	No Report	No Report	No Report
Aruba	No Report	No Report	No Report	No Report	No Report	0.002 kg [ICPO]
Bahamas	29.257 kg	No Report	No Report	0.020 kg [ICPO]	No Report	104.089 kg [ICPO]
Barbados	No Report	0.170 kg [ICPO]	No Report	No Report	No Report	No Report
Cayman Islands	No Report	No Report	No Report	46.036 kg 2 u.	No Report	No Report
Cuba	No Report	No Report	38.722 kg	No Report	No Report	No Report
Haiti	No Report	No Report	No Report		11.000 kg [CICAD]	No Report
Jamaica	1595.065 kg [ICPO]	No Report	263.420 kg [ICPO]	383.820 kg [ICPO]	No Report	371.490 kg [ICPO]
Trinidad Tobago	No Report	No Report	No Report	1430.000 kg [CICAD]	No Report	No Report
Sub-Total	1625.062 kg	0.170 kg	302.142 kg	1859.876 kg 2 u.	11.000 kg	475.581 kg
Central America						
Panama	No Report	No Report	No Report	No Report	No Report	11.360 lt.
Sub-Total						11.360 lt.
North America						
Canada	502.415 kg 4.435 lt.	589.275 kg 21.827 lt.	802.115 kg 114.667 lt.	824.000 kg	524.937 kg 20.166 lt. 2 u.	434.000 kg 55.302 lt. 6 u.
United States	525.216 kg	779.528 kg	248.289 kg	No Report	No Report	490.685 kg
Sub-Total	1027.631 kg 4.435 lt.	1368.803 kg 21.827 lt.	1050.404 kg 114.667 lt.	824.000 kg	524.937 kg 20.166 lt. 2 u.	924.685 kg 55.302 lt. 6 u.

Source: Annual Report Questionnaire if not otherwise indicated

	Cannabis oil					
Region/country or territory	1994	1995	1996	1997	1998	1999

AMERICAS

South America

Chile	No Report	No Report	No Report	No Report	No Report	0.025 kg [ICPO]
Colombia	32.000 lt.	30.210 lt.	199.250 lt.	8.000 lt.	No Report	No Report
Venezuela	No Report	No Report	No Report	8003.000 kg [CICAD]	No Report	No Report
Sub-Total	32.000 lt.	30.210 lt.	199.250 lt.	8003.000 kg 8.000 lt.		0.025 kg
Total region	2652.693 kg 36.435 lt.	1368.973 kg 52.037 lt.	1352.546 kg 313.917 lt.	10686.880 kg 8.000 lt. 2 u.	535.937 kg 20.166 lt. 2 u.	1400.291 kg 66.662 lt. 6 u.

ASIA

Central Asia and Transcaucasian countries

Armenia	No Report	No Report	No Report	No Report	22.353 kg	0.002 kg [ICPO]
Azerbaijan	No Report	No Report	3.378 kg [ICPO]	1.793 kg [ICPO]	No Report	No Report
Georgia	No Report	No Report	0.002 kg [ICPO]	No Report	No Report	No Report
Kyrgyzstan	No Report	No Report	No Report	603.554 kg	1569.238 kg	No Report
Sub-Total			3.380 kg	605.347 kg	1591.591 kg	0.002 kg

East and South-East Asia

Indonesia	0.075 kg	0.545 kg [ICPO]	0.546 kg	4.017 kg	No Report	300.005 kg
Japan	2.700 kg	0.900 kg	0.081 lt.	0.143 lt.	3.750 kg	0.002 kg 0.002 lt.
Korea (Republic of)	No Report	No Report	No Report	0.027 kg	No Report	No Report
Thailand	12.003 kg [Govt]	No Report	32.766 kg [ICPO]	No Report	No Report	No Report
Sub-Total	14.778 kg	1.445 kg	33.312 kg 0.081 lt.	4.044 kg 0.143 lt.	3.750 kg	300.007 kg 0.002 lt.

Near and Middle East /South-West Asia

Iran (Islamic Republic of)	No Report	No Report	No Report	No Report	No Report	68.000 kg [ICPO]
Israel	0.007 kg	No Report	No Report	No Report	No Report	No Report
Jordan	No Report	No Report	No Report	0.145 kg	No Report	No Report
Lebanon	1001.000 kg	No Report	6.000 kg	58.000 kg	No Report	No Report
Sub-Total	1001.007 kg		6.000 kg	58.145 kg		68.000 kg

South Asia

Maldives	0.264 kg	0.018 kg	No Report	No Report	No Report	0.001 kg
Nepal	No Report	2.000 kg	No Report	1342.492 kg [ICPO]	No Report	2.100 kg
Sub-Total	0.264 kg	2.018 kg		1342.492 kg		2.101 kg
Total region	1016.049 kg	3.463 kg	42.692 kg 0.081 lt.	2010.028 kg 0.143 lt.	1595.341 kg	370.110 kg 0.002 lt.

EUROPE

Eastern Europe

Albania	No Report	No Report	No Report	No Report	No Report	13.000 lt. [ICPO]
Belarus	No Report	0.300 kg [ICPO]	No Report	No Report	No Report	0.002 kg
Bulgaria	No Report	No Report	No Report	No Report	No Report	0.100 kg

Source: Annual Report Questionnaire if not otherwise indicated

Region/country or territory	Cannabis oil					
	1994	1995	1996	1997	1998	1999
EUROPE						
Eastern Europe						
Croatia	No Report	No Report	No Report	No Report	0.008 kg	No Report
Romania	No Report	36.183 kg [ICPO]	No Report	No Report	No Report	No Report
Russian Federation	51.988 kg [ICPO]	45.200 kg	42.200 kg	No Report	102.900 kg [F.O.]	141.344 kg
Slovenia	10.000 kg	No Report	No Report	No Report	No Report	No Report
Ukraine	No Report	0.015 kg [ICPO]	No Report	No Report	No Report	No Report
Sub-Total	61.988 kg	81.698 kg	42.200 kg		102.908 kg	141.446 kg 13.000 lt.
Western Europe						
Austria	6.792 kg	0.168 kg	0.228 kg	3.164 kg	No Report	No Report
Belgium	[(1]		No Report	No Report	No Report	5.000 kg
Cyprus	No Report	No Report	No Report	No Report	No Report	30.294 kg
Denmark	0.050 kg [ICPO]	0.200 kg	2.420 kg	0.123 kg	0.008 kg	3.910 kg
France	28.846 kg [Govt]	10.802 kg	5.238 kg	5.442 kg	0.592 kg	1.690 kg
Germany	1.434 kg	2.834 kg	1.786 kg	3.510 kg	0.538 kg	2.300 kg
Greece	No Report	0.090 kg [ICPO]	No Report	No Report	No Report	0.200 kg [ICPO]
Italy	9.690 kg 10 u.	1.328 kg 9 u.	0.217 kg	6.259 kg 6 u.	0.635 kg 3 u.	6.772 kg [ICPO]
Liechtenstein	0.186 kg	No Report	No Report	No Report	No Report	No Report
Monaco	No Report	No Report	No Report	0.029 lt.	No Report	No Report
Netherlands	No Report	No Report	No Report	No Report	0.012 kg 150.000 lt.	1.000 lt.
Norway	0.759 kg	0.002 kg [ICPO]	0.052 kg	0.308 kg	0.034 kg	0.026 kg
Portugal	No Report	No Report	No Report	No Report	No Report	0.001 kg
Spain	59.292 kg	No Report	962 u.	0.705 lt.	74.970 lt.	2346 u.
Sweden	0.250 kg	No Report	0.091 kg	0.019 kg	No Report	0.006 kg
Switzerland	7.007 kg	1.911 kg	1.710 kg	8.607 kg	1.541 kg	0.609 kg
Turkey	No Report	292.000 kg	No Report	No Report	63.411 kg	No Report
United Kingdom	11.800 kg	5.600 kg	17.500 kg	26.600 kg	7.366 kg	No Report
Sub-Total	126.106 kg 10 u.	314.935 kg 9 u.	29.242 kg 962 u.	54.032 kg 0.734 lt. 6 u.	74.137 kg 224.970 lt. 3 u.	50.808 kg 1.000 lt. 2346 u.
Total region	188.094 kg 10 u.	396.633 kg 9 u.	71.442 kg 962 u.	54.032 kg 0.734 lt. 6 u.	177.045 kg 224.970 lt. 3 u.	192.254 kg 14.000 lt. 2346 u.
OCEANIA						
Oceania						
Australia	No Report	0.891 kg [(2] 0.002 lt.	1.095 kg 40 u.	4.945 kg	No Report	No Report
New Zealand	3.478 kg [ICPO]	3.400 kg [Govt]	No Report	No Report	4.159 kg	0.026 kg
Sub-Total	3.478 kg	4.291 kg 0.002 lt.	1.095 kg 40 u.	4.945 kg	4.159 kg	0.026 kg

Source: Annual Report Questionnaire if not otherwise indicated

Region/country or territory	Cannabis oil					
	1994	**1995**	**1996**	**1997**	**1998**	**1999**
OCEANIA						
Total region	3.478 kg	4.291 kg 0.002 lt.	1.095 kg 40 u.	4.945 kg	4.159 kg	0.026 kg
TOTAL	3871.030 kg 36.435 lt. 10 u.	1780.414 kg 52.039 lt. 9 u.	1474.070 kg 313.998 lt. 1002 u.	12756.940 kg 8.877 lt. 8 u.	2353.818 kg 245.136 lt. 5 u.	1966.738 kg 99.664 lt. 2352 u.

1) Including cannabis resin, liquid cannabis. 2) Fiscal year

Source: Annual Report Questionnaire if not otherwise indicated

Cannabis plant						
Region/country or territory	1994	1995	1996	1997	1998	1999

AFRICA

East Africa

Ethiopia	46.465 kg	40.762 kg	No Report	No Report	No Report	No Report
Kenya	No Report	No Report	No Report	5.565 kg 2226 u.	No Report	No Report
Mauritius	18002 u.	36417 u.	22066 u.	41316 u.	43294 u.	45444 u.
Seychelles	No Report	No Report	No Report	No Report	No Report	30.700 kg
Uganda	12000 u. [Govt]	No Report	4000 u.	No Report	9411 u.	35000 u.
United Republic of Tanzania	300.350 kg	No Report	No Report	No Report	No Report	6021.273 kg
Sub-Total	346.815 kg 30002 u.	40.762 kg 36417 u.	26066 u.	5.565 kg 43542 u.	52705 u.	6051.973 kg 80444 u.

North Africa

Egypt	8264115 u.	51153272 u.	231482720 u.	63542820 u.	35150384 u.	No Report
Morocco	6315.926 kg	No Report	No Report	No Report	No Report	No Report
Tunisia	47 u.	No Report	No Report	No Report	No Report	No Report
Sub-Total	6315.926 kg 8264162 u.	51153270 u.	231482700 u.	63542820 u.	35150380 u.	

Southern Africa

Angola	No Report	200.000 kg [ICPO] 2000 u.	No Report	No Report	No Report	5733 u.
Lesotho	201 u.	2001 u. [ICPO]	2625 u. [Govt]	No Report	No Report	No Report
Malawi	No Report	31364.082 kg 731580 u.	22959 u.	1116.725 kg 8313 u.	6371.045 kg	9428.350 kg
Namibia	No Report	No Report	No Report	No Report	No Report	25 u.
South Africa	7182906.000 kg	1188018.000 kg	69450.977 kg	243565.688 kg	784201.063 kg	No Report
Swaziland	No Report	4195.609 kg [INCB]	No Report	No Report	7517.000 kg	2528136 u.
Zimbabwe	960 u. [Govt]	26.474 kg [ICPO]	No Report	No Report	300.000 kg	165 u. 2936 u.
Sub-Total	7182906.000 kg 1161 u.	1223804.000 kg 735581 u.	69450.980 kg 25584 u.	244682.400 kg 8313 u.	798389.100 kg 2936 u.	9428.350 kg 2534059 u.

West and Central Africa

Congo	No Report	36.742 kg [(1]	No Report	3435.000 kg	No Report	10.000 kg [(1]
Côte d'Ivoire	No Report	No Report	502 u.	No Report	200 u.	No Report
Gabon	184 u. [ICPO]	37 u. [ICPO]	No Report	No Report	No Report	No Report
Gambia	No Report	No Report	No Report	No Report	No Report	834.982 kg
Ghana	No Report	No Report	[(2]	No Report	No Report	No Report
Nigeria	No Report	137.962 kg [ICPO]	No Report	No Report	1712580.000 kg [Govt]	No Report
Saint Helena	No Report	No Report	No Report	18 u.	17 u.	17 u.
Sub-Total	184 u.	174.704 kg 37 u.	502 u.	3435.000 kg 18 u.	1712580.000 kg 217 u.	844.982 kg 17 u.

Source: Annual Report Questionnaire if not otherwise indicated

163

Region/country or territory	Cannabis plant					
	1994	1995	1996	1997	1998	1999
AFRICA						
Total region	7189569.000 kg 8295509 u.	1224020.000 kg 51925300 u.	69450.980 kg 231534900 u.	248123.000 kg 63594690 u.	2510969.000 kg 35206240 u.	16325.310 kg 2614520 u.
AMERICAS						
Caribbean						
Anguilla	No Report	No Report	No Report	48 u.	40 u.	No Report
Antigua and Barbuda	323 u.	No Report	No Report	No Report	No Report	23384 u. [CICAD]
Bahamas	No Report	No Report	No Report	No Report	99 u.	No Report
Barbados	No Report	No Report	No Report	No Report	400 u. [CICAD]	81 u. [HONLC]
Bermuda	No Report	No Report	53 u.	871 u.	No Report	268 u.
Cuba	No Report	No Report	3517 u.	No Report	No Report	No Report
Dominica	45855 u. [ICPO]	No Report	176713 u.	No Report	No Report	55120 u. [CICAD]
Dominican Republic	226 u.	29 u.	110 u.	116 u.	346 u.	1991 u.
Grenada	20857 u.	1804.154 kg	No Report	No Report	6212.000 kg	12086 u. [CICAD]
Jamaica	No Report	No Report	No Report	6858.300 kg [ICPO]	No Report	No Report
Saint Kitts and Nevis	25000 u. [CICAD]	No Report	32926 u. [CICAD]	126293 u. [CICAD]	36000 u. [CICAD]	63911 u. [CICAD]
Saint Lucia	81923 u.	259456 u.	163893 u.	26037 u.	69200 u.	18047 u. [CICAD]
Saint Vincent and the Grenadines	No Report	No Report	No Report	No Report	1500 u. [CICAD]	4760 u. [CICAD]
Trinidad Tobago	1842500 u.	No Report	No Report	No Report	2869850 u.	4415958 u. [CICAD]
Sub-Total	2016684 u.	1804.154 kg 259485 u.	377212 u.	6858.300 kg 153365 u.	6212.000 kg 2977435 u.	4595606 u.
Central America						
Belize	12777 u.	134925 u. [CICAD]	87546 u. [CICAD]	294712.000 kg [CICAD]	202803 u. [CICAD]	270136 u. [CICAD]
Costa Rica	229363 u.	389222 u.	110002 u.	No Report	733089 u.	2153645 u.
El Salvador	No Report	No Report	No Report	No Report	No Report	4688 u.
Guatemala	No Report	971250 u. [Govt]	1052845 u.	587096 u. [Govt]	576060 u.	594378 u.
Honduras	No Report	2729915 u.	2309.000 kg [CICAD]	337322 u.	No Report	133680 u. [CICAD]
Nicaragua	99254 u. [Govt]	No Report	53528.000 kg	24239.000 kg	833943 u.	13569 u. [CICAD]
Panama	No Report	No Report	No Report	No Report	No Report	25102 u.
Sub-Total	341394 u.	4225312 u.	55837.000 kg 1250393 u.	318951.000 kg 924418 u.	2345895 u.	3195198 u.
North America						
Canada	No Report	274150 u.	No Report	776288 u.	1025808 u.	1304477 u.
United States	15961.803 kg	24562.629 kg	676866.375 kg [Govt]	No Report	No Report	497.366 kg
Sub-Total	15961.800 kg	24562.630 kg 274150 u.	676866.400 kg	776288 u.	1025808 u.	497.366 kg 1304477 u.
South America						
Argentina	342 u.	No Report	2152 u. [Govt]	458 u.	1296 u.	1222 u.
Bolivia	No Report	No Report	No Report	3450.000 kg	No Report	No Report

Source: Annual Report Questionnaire if not otherwise indicated

Region/country or territory	Cannabis plant					
	1994	1995	1996	1997	1998	1999

AMERICAS

South America

Brazil	No Report	2532461 u.	1523.200 kg	2884811 u.	3371112 u.	3462158 u.
Chile	41692 u.	72787 u.	94481 u.	34263 u.	956.942 kg 759 u.	No Report
Colombia	8000 u.	280000 u.	37.000 kg	No Report	No Report	No Report
Ecuador	No Report	No Report	336 u.	1 u.	126 u.	0.339 kg
Falkland Islands	No Report	No Report	No Report	No Report	1 u.	No Report
Guyana	No Report	9988.000 kg	52181.000 kg	18993.000 kg [ICPO]	No Report	No Report
Paraguay	No Report	2106125.000 kg	749412.500 kg	2009500 u.	1415875.000 kg	3769000 u.
Peru	No Report	No Report	150481.219 kg	140700.000 kg	No Report	5418.300 kg
Suriname	No Report	35.000 kg	35.000 kg	65.838 kg	500 u.	No Report
Uruguay	12 u.	17 u.	16 u. [Govt]	No Report	No Report	No Report
Venezuela		94 u.	No Report	No Report	No Report	No Report
Sub-Total	50046 u.	2116148.000 kg 2885359 u.	953669.900 kg 96985 u.	163208.800 kg 4929033 u.	1416832.000 kg 3373794 u.	5418.639 kg 7232380 u.
Total region	15961.800 kg 2408124 u.	2142515.000 kg 7644306 u.	1686373.000 kg 1724590 u.	489018.200 kg 6783104 u.	1423044.000 kg 9722932 u.	5916.005 kg 16327660 u.

ASIA

Central Asia and Transcaucasian countries

Armenia	No Report	15000.000 kg [ICPO]	No Report	No Report	24.218 kg	No Report
Azerbaijan	No Report	255000.000 kg [Govt]	No Report	507380.000 kg [ICPO]	489000.000 kg	405669.000 kg
Kazakhstan	[3]	8329.000 kg	No Report	No Report	200.077 kg	1869.000 kg
Kyrgyzstan	No Report	525.718 kg	No Report	No Report	No Report	No Report
Uzbekistan	No Report	30 u.	No Report	18.930 kg	663.316 kg	238.772 kg
Sub-Total		278854.700 kg 30 u.		507398.900 kg	489887.600 kg	407776.800 kg

East and South-East Asia

Brunei Darussalam	No Report	No Report	No Report	1 u.	No Report	No Report
Indonesia	45031 u.	80823 u.	80823 u.	200000.000 kg 132748 u.	47515 u.	78072 u.
Japan	5.134 kg 364 u.	18.188 kg 828 u.	7.247 kg 3301 u.	36.922 kg 2232 u.	23.954 kg 1668 u.	26.422 kg
Korea (Republic of)	No Report	12976 u.	47465 u.	31501 u.	3815 u.	10705 u.
Lao People's Dem. Rep.	9402.000 kg	86424.000 kg [Govt]	104595.000 kg [Govt]	No Report	No Report	No Report
Philippines	4034221 u.	29655644 u.	12161117 u.	No Report	518939.000 kg [ICPO]	5005860 u. [4]
Thailand	75839.031 kg [Govt]	No Report	No Report	19951.301 kg	13401.892 kg	42996.497 kg
Sub-Total	85246.160 kg 4079616 u.	86442.190 kg 29750270 u.	104602.300 kg 12292710 u.	219988.200 kg 166482 u.	532364.900 kg 52998 u.	43022.920 kg 5094637 u.

Source: Annual Report Questionnaire if not otherwise indicated

Region/country or territory	Cannabis plant					
	1994	1995	1996	1997	1998	1999
ASIA						
Near and Middle East /South-West Asia						
Bahrain	No Report	1 u.	0.164 kg	No Report	No Report	No Report
Iraq	No Report	0.166 kg	5.305 kg	34.812 kg	55.905 kg	No Report
Jordan	No Report	No Report	No Report	No Report	1.120 kg	62.525 kg
Kuwait	1.199 kg	6 u. [ICPO]	No Report	No Report	No Report	No Report
Lebanon	No Report	No Report	No Report	No Report	No Report	4445.880 kg
Oman	No Report	0.508 kg	No Report	No Report	No Report	No Report
Qatar	No Report	35.964 kg	220.899 kg	No Report	No Report	No Report
Sub-Total	1.199 kg	36.638 kg 7 u.	226.368 kg	34.812 kg	57.025 kg	4508.405 kg
South Asia						
Bangladesh	62649 u.	No Report	25307 u.	No Report	No Report	11826 u. [F.O.]
India	1073334.000 kg	694617.000 kg	No Report	No Report	No Report	No Report
Nepal	23752 u.	No Report	No Report	No Report	No Report	No Report
Sri Lanka	47735.020 kg	51451.000 kg	65010.000 kg	49900.000 kg	21375.000 kg	372000.000 kg
Sub-Total	1121069.000 kg 86401 u.	746068.000 kg	65010.000 kg 25307 u.	49900.000 kg	21375.000 kg	372000.000 kg 11826 u.
Total region	1206316.000 kg 4166017 u.	1111402.000 kg 29750310 u.	169838.600 kg 12318010 u.	777321.900 kg 166482 u.	1043685.000 kg 52998 u.	827308.100 kg 5106463 u.
EUROPE						
Eastern Europe						
Belarus	No Report	16.000 kg	No Report	No Report	117.000 kg	No Report
Bosnia Herzegovina	No Report	No Report	No Report	No Report	No Report	19342 u. [WIB (5]
Bulgaria	No Report	2828 u.	50000.000 kg	127000.000 kg	16000.000 kg 10943 u.	2742 u.
Croatia	3899 u.	6902 u.	4602 u.	31710 u.	5131 u.	3050 u.
Czech Republic	No Report	No Report	11866.134 kg	No Report	No Report	No Report
Estonia	No Report	No Report	No Report	72 u.	23.184 kg 92 u.	41.973 kg 175 u.
FYR of Macedonia	No Report	107 u.	No Report	No Report	1457 u.	151262 u. [WIB (5]
Hungary	No Report	500.000 kg [ICPO] 650 u.	140 u.	No Report	1033 u.	620.000 kg
Poland	16000 u.	8000.000 kg	200.000 kg	12105.075 kg	1904.362 kg	900.000 kg
Romania	No Report	9 u.	No Report	No Report	215.923 kg	No Report
Slovakia	65.300 kg	No Report	No Report	No Report	2830.680 kg	848.797 kg
Slovenia	8921 u.	No Report	5019 u.	44944 u.	14453 u.	8196 u.
Ukraine	No Report	1547 u. [ICPO]	2159.000 kg	6091.000 kg	5103.364 kg	No Report
Yugoslavia	151.408 kg	No Report	No Report	No Report	No Report	No Report
Sub-Total	216.708 kg 28820 u.	8516.000 kg 12043 u.	64225.130 kg 9761 u.	145196.100 kg 76726 u.	26194.510 kg 33109 u.	2410.770 kg 184767 u.

Source: Annual Report Questionnaire if not otherwise indicated

Region/country or territory	Cannabis plant					
	1994	1995	1996	1997	1998	1999
EUROPE						
Western Europe						
Belgium	22.251 kg 19700 u.	2784 u.	No Report	653.000 kg	6280.000 kg	2911.166 kg
Cyprus	618 u.	847 u.	260 u.	787 u.	276 u.	190 u.
Denmark	No Report	3012.300 kg	2177.600 kg	2692.300 kg	949.969 kg	337.290 kg
Finland	286 u.	2054 u.	2065 u.	82.519 kg 2328 u.	2.334 kg 2900 u.	5.251 kg 2789 u.
France	No Report	21888 u.	38341 u.	38115 u.	34266 u.	23287 u.
Germany	35955 u.	11151 u.	53179 u.	5000.000 kg 67065 u.	81097 u.	168833 u.
Gibraltar	No Report	No Report	1 u.	No Report	13 u.	14 u.
Greece	202846 u.	30499 u.	15192 u.	11010 u.	9967 u.	46198 u.
Iceland	109 u.	221 u.	No Report	No Report	No Report	No Report
Ireland	No Report	No Report	542 u.	753 u.	400 u.	No Report [ICPO]
Italy	708206 u.	411432 u.	491390 u.	379851 u.	190240 u.	
Liechtenstein	No Report	No Report	No Report	No Report	1300.000 kg	3.686 kg
Luxembourg	No Report	No Report	No Report	No Report	222 u.	No Report
Malta	592 u.	24 u.	100 u.	153 u.	5 u.	35 u.
Netherlands	No Report	No Report	No Report	1479821 u.	353208 u.	582588 u.
Norway	3.122 kg	11.609 kg	7.300 kg	23.329 kg	23.041 kg	28.546 kg
Portugal	74 u.	145 u.	1646 u.	7982 u.	17316 u.	1184 u.
Spain	2490.587 kg	1188.080 kg	14001.399 kg	1734.002 kg	3072.938 kg	2319.031 kg
Sweden	20.823 kg	6.917 kg	4.165 kg	2.426 kg 269 u.	6.890 kg	39.820 kg 249 u.
Switzerland	2913 u.	8867 u.	32488 u.	313258 u.	26813 u.	79746 u.
Turkey	No Report	75.816 kg 1989215 u.	No Report	52100620 u.	55655864 u.	19736000 u.
United Kingdom	57846 u.	94202 u.	116218 u.	114988 u.	72040 u.	382 u. [ICPO]
Sub-Total	2536.783 kg 1029145 u.	4294.722 kg 2573329 u.	16190.470 kg 751422 u.	10187.580 kg 54517000 u.	11635.170 kg 56444630 u.	5644.790 kg 20641490 u.
Total region	2753.491 kg 1057965 u.	12810.720 kg 2585372 u.	80415.590 kg 761183 u.	155383.700 kg 54593730 u.	37829.680 kg 56477740 u.	8055.560 kg 20826260 u.
OCEANIA						
Oceania						
Australia	15000 u. [6]	367709 u. [6]	2745.057 kg 187837 u.	4445.335 kg	No Report	No Report
Cook Islands	No Report	No Report	2 u.	No Report	No Report	No Report
Fiji	5.000 kg 1100 u.	2239.000 kg [ICPO]	5388 u.	No Report	No Report	No Report
New Zealand	No Report	291000 u. [Govt]	No Report	266867 u.	164531 u.	173277 u.
Vanuatu	No Report	0.800 kg 2 u.	No Report	No Report	No Report	No Report

Source: Annual Report Questionnaire if not otherwise indicated

Cannabis plant

Region/country or territory	1994	1995	1996	1997	1998	1999
OCEANIA						
Oceania						
Sub-Total	5.000 kg 16100 u.	2239.800 kg 658711 u.	2745.057 kg 193227 u.	4445.335 kg 266867 u.	164531 u.	173277 u.
Total region	5.000 kg 16100 u.	2239.800 kg 658711 u.	2745.057 kg 193227 u.	4445.335 kg 266867 u.	164531 u.	173277 u.
TOTAL	8414605.000 kg 15943720 u.	4492987.000 kg 92564010 u.	2008824.000 kg 246531900 u.	1674292.000 kg 125404900 u.	5015527.000 kg 101624400 u.	857605.000 kg 45048180 u.

1) Including cannabis seeds. 2) Included in cannabis herb. 3) Included in cannabis seeds. 4) Includes seedlings 5) Provisional figures. 6) Fiscal year

Source: Annual Report Questionnaire if not otherwise indicated

Cannabis seed

Region/country or territory	1994	1995	1996	1997	1998	1999
AFRICA						
East Africa						
Ethiopia	7 u.	No Report	No Report	No Report	No Report	No Report
Mauritius	0.080 kg	0.048 kg	167 u.	No Report	No Report	No Report
Uganda	No Report	No Report	10.350 kg	No Report	5.000 kg	No Report
Sub-Total	0.080 kg 7 u.	0.048 kg	10.350 kg 167 u.		5.000 kg	
North Africa						
Algeria	No Report	No Report	No Report	No Report	0.930 kg [ICPO]	No Report
Egypt	No Report	No Report	No Report	33.421 kg	11.504 kg	115.819 kg
Tunisia	0.005 kg	0.095 kg	No Report	No Report	No Report	No Report
Sub-Total	0.005 kg	0.095 kg		33.421 kg	12.434 kg	115.819 kg
Southern Africa						
Lesotho	143 u.	No Report	No Report	No Report	No Report	35.280 kg [ICPO]
Malawi	No Report	0.700 kg	No Report	No Report	No Report	No Report
Namibia	646.336 kg	625.858 kg	278.295 kg	No Report	No Report	No Report
Swaziland	No Report	No Report	No Report	No Report	8.096 kg	No Report
Zambia	No Report	191.941 kg [ICPO]	0.044 kg [ICPO]	No Report	38.597 kg [Govt]	126.280 kg
Zimbabwe	No Report	No Report	No Report	No Report	0.200 kg	No Report
Sub-Total	646.336 kg 143 u.	818.499 kg	278.339 kg		46.893 kg	161.560 kg
West and Central Africa						
Congo	No Report	(1	No Report	No Report	No Report	No Report
Saint Helena	No Report	No Report	No Report	No Report	100 u.	80 u.
Sub-Total					100 u.	80 u.
Total region	646.421 kg 150 u.	818.642 kg	288.689 kg 167 u.	33.421 kg	64.327 kg 100 u.	277.379 kg 80 u.
AMERICAS						
Caribbean						
Anguilla	No Report	No Report	No Report	No Report	8 u.	No Report
Antigua and Barbuda	0.083 kg	No Report	No Report	No Report	No Report	No Report
Bermuda	No Report	No Report	0.010 kg	No Report	No Report	No Report
Cuba	No Report	No Report	2836 u.	No Report	No Report	No Report
Dominica	0.236 kg [ICPO]	No Report	4.248 kg	No Report	No Report	No Report
Dominican Republic	210 u.	134 u.	200 u.	72 u.	1327 u.	3642 u.
Grenada	0.724 kg	No Report	No Report	No Report	0.004 kg	No Report
Jamaica	No Report	No Report	No Report	No Report	No Report	452.630 kg [ICPO]
Trinidad Tobago	52500 u.	No Report	No Report	No Report	No Report	No Report
Sub-Total	1.043 kg 52710 u.	134 u.	4.258 kg 3036 u.	72 u.	0.004 kg 1335 u.	452.630 kg 3642 u.

Source: Annual Report Questionnaire if not otherwise indicated

Region/country or territory	Cannabis seed					
	1994	**1995**	**1996**	**1997**	**1998**	**1999**
AMERICAS						
Central America						
Belize	0.007 kg	No Report	No Report	No Report	No Report	No Report
Guatemala	No Report	No Report	427.607 kg	1.840 kg [Govt]	5.100 kg	78.473 kg
Honduras	No Report	73.480 kg	No Report	3.400 kg	No Report	No Report
Nicaragua	No Report	No Report	5.181 kg	2.063 kg	No Report	No Report
Sub-Total	0.007 kg	73.480 kg	432.788 kg	7.303 kg	5.100 kg	78.473 kg
North America						
Mexico	4638.536 kg	7421.864 kg	5098.837 kg	3968.381 kg	4948.744 kg	5847.545 kg
United States	No Report	No Report	229291.750 kg	No Report	No Report	412271.587 kg 451 u.
Sub-Total	4638.536 kg	7421.863 kg	234390.600 kg	3968.381 kg	4948.744 kg	418119.100 kg 451 u.
South America						
Argentina	1.209 kg	6045 u. [ICPO]	10.970 kg [Govt]	39.440 kg	42.790 kg 1950 u.	0.091 kg
Brazil	95.153 kg [ICPO]	56.833 kg	84.622 kg	68.314 kg	5.179 kg	55.804 kg
Chile	No Report	No Report	0.601 kg	No Report	0.377 kg	No Report
Colombia	65.000 kg	177.500 kg	49.000 kg	120.000 kg [Govt]	127.789 kg	25.214 kg
Guyana	No Report	No Report	6.772 kg	No Report	No Report	No Report
Paraguay	243.125 kg [ICPO]	646.355 kg	207.550 kg	167.550 kg	503.110 kg	2130.025 kg
Peru	No Report	36.178 kg	1.924 kg	9.377 kg	0.241 kg	19.041 kg
Suriname	No Report	7.000 kg	6.000 kg	No Report	No Report	No Report
Venezuela		No Report	No Report	No Report	No Report	No Report
Sub-Total	404.487 kg	923.866 kg 6045 u.	367.439 kg	404.681 kg	679.486 kg 1950 u.	2230.175 kg
Total region	5044.073 kg 52710 u.	8419.209 kg 6179 u.	235195.100 kg 3036 u.	4380.365 kg 72 u.	5633.333 kg 3285 u.	420880.400 kg 4093 u.
ASIA						
Central Asia and Transcaucasian countries						
Kazakhstan	119078.000 kg [(2]	No Report	No Report	No Report	No Report	No Report
Sub-Total	119078.000 kg					
East and South-East Asia						
Brunei Darussalam	No Report	No Report	0.011 kg	No Report	No Report	No Report
China (Hong Kong SAR)	No Report	No Report	No Report	8.200 kg	No Report	No Report
Indonesia	0.188 kg	0.386 kg	0.386 kg	1.218 kg	0.329 kg	1.875 kg
Korea (Republic of)	No Report	No Report	13.866 kg	58.789 kg	No Report	46.067 kg
Philippines	513.684 kg	230.814 kg	267.800 kg	No Report	85007.000 kg [ICPO] 223459 u.	163.000 kg
Thailand	15.260 kg [Govt]	4.464 kg [ICPO]	3.011 kg [ICPO]	12.127 kg	1.225 kg	No Report

Source: Annual Report Questionnaire if not otherwise indicated

Region/country or territory	Cannabis seed					
	1994	1995	1996	1997	1998	1999
ASIA						
East and South-East Asia						
Sub-Total	529.132 kg	235.664 kg	285.074 kg	80.334 kg	85008.560 kg 223459 u.	210.942 kg
Near and Middle East /South-West Asia						
Bahrain	No Report	No Report	No Report	No Report	No Report	0.361 kg [ICPO]
Iraq	No Report	0.001 kg	No Report	No Report	No Report	No Report
Jordan	0.443 kg	0.002 kg	26.315 kg	0.770 kg	1.412 kg	61.461 kg
Lebanon	32.000 kg	No Report	No Report	20.000 kg	No Report	270.000 kg
Qatar	No Report	31 u.	No Report	No Report	No Report	No Report
United Arab Emirates	No Report	0.300 kg	4.876 kg	No Report	No Report	No Report
Sub-Total	32.443 kg	0.303 kg 31 u.	31.191 kg	20.770 kg	1.412 kg	331.822 kg
South Asia						
Maldives	No Report	No Report	No Report	No Report	(3	No Report
Sub-Total						
Total region	119639.600 kg	235.967 kg 31 u.	316.265 kg	101.104 kg	85009.970 kg 223459 u.	542.764 kg
EUROPE						
Eastern Europe						
Bulgaria	No Report	No Report	5.986 kg	1.250 kg	6.556 kg	6.768 kg [ICPO]
Croatia	No Report	88820 u.	13.064 kg	38037 u.	0.053 kg 24133 u.	0.868 kg 17054 u.
FYR of Macedonia	No Report	No Report	No Report	No Report	0.135 kg 508 u.	0.103 kg [ICPO]
Poland	400.000 kg	200.000 kg	150.000 kg	300.000 kg	No Report	4.016 kg
Russian Federation	No Report	No Report	No Report	0.021 kg	No Report	No Report
Sub-Total	400.000 kg	200.000 kg 88820 u.	169.050 kg	301.271 kg 38037 u.	6.744 kg 24641 u.	11.755 kg 17054 u.
Western Europe						
Andorra	No Report	No Report	No Report	No Report	0.576 kg [ICPO]	4.900 kg
Belgium	No Report	0.470 kg	No Report	75 u.	48.190 kg	16.250 kg
Finland	No Report	9 u.	0.924 kg 1108 u.	0.364 kg 369 u.	0.345 kg 1304 u.	0.100 kg 1150 u.
Greece	No Report	0.034 kg	No Report	No Report	No Report	No Report
Iceland	No Report	0.491 kg	No Report	No Report	No Report	No Report
Italy	No Report	No Report	45227 u.	220.116 kg 47646 u.	No Report	No Report
Malta	0.756 kg 2120 u.	129 u.	4.005 kg	0.049 kg	72 u.	5 u.
Portugal	No Report	6 u.	0.464 kg	53 u.	1.563 kg	38.377 kg 45 u.
Spain	No Report	No Report	No Report	1.376 kg	No Report	No Report

Source: Annual Report Questionnaire if not otherwise indicated

Cannabis seed

Region/country or territory	1994	1995	1996	1997	1998	1999
EUROPE						
Western Europe						
Turkey	No Report	9462.074 kg	No Report	No Report	No Report	No Report
Sub-Total	0.756 kg	9463.069 kg	5.393 kg	221.905 kg	50.674 kg	59.627 kg
	2120 u.	144 u.	46335 u.	48143 u.	1376 u.	1200 u.
Total region	400.756 kg	9663.069 kg	174.443 kg	523.176 kg	57.418 kg	71.382 kg
	2120 u.	88964 u.	46335 u.	86180 u.	26017 u.	18254 u.
OCEANIA						
Oceania						
Australia	1.774 kg [4]	237.264 kg [4]	304.094 kg [5]	No Report	No Report	No Report
		1558 u.	39567 u.			
New Zealand	980.666 kg [ICPO]	1545.385 kg [ICPO]	No Report	No Report	244031 u.	253609 u.
Sub-Total	982.440 kg	1782.649 kg	304.094 kg		244031 u.	253609 u.
		1558 u.	39567 u.			
Total region	982.440 kg	1782.649 kg	304.094 kg		244031 u.	253609 u.
		1558 u.	39567 u.			
TOTAL	126713.300 kg	20919.540 kg	236278.600 kg	5038.065 kg	90765.060 kg	421771.900 kg
	54980 u.	96732 u.	89105 u.	86252 u.	496892 u.	276036 u.

1) Included in cannabis plants. 2) Including cannabis plants. 3) Small quantity. 4) Fiscal year 5) Including cannabis resin.

Source: Annual Report Questionnaire if not otherwise indicated

TRAFFICKING IN SYNTHETIC DRUGS

Amphetamine-type stimulants

Trafficking in amphetamine-type stimulants (ATS), excluding ecstasy, continues to be largely intra-regional, often geographically close to the consumer market. The capabilities of enforcement agencies to effectively reduce the amounts in circulation are thus limited and most ATS seizures continue to be small. Nonetheless, trafficking in ATS showed strong growth rates throughout the 1990s. In 1999, seizures almost tripled compared to a year earlier and were ten times larger than in 1990. Most of the increase was due to rising levels of trafficking activities in the East and South-East Asia region. By contrast, trafficking in Europe actually showed signs of stabilization/decline in the late 1990s, opposite to the trend observed a few years earlier. Seizures in both Europe and North America - though higher in absolute terms than at the start of the decade - fell as a proportion of global seizures as a consequence of more ATS trafficking in East and South-East Asia.

In 1999 trafficking in amphetamines was characterized by :

• a massive increase in methamphetamine seizures in Asia, notably in South-East Asia, due to strongly rising seizures reported by Interpol for China - ATS seizures rose from 1.6 tonnes in 1998 to 16 tonnes in 1999 -, and strong increases in most other countries of the region, including Thailand, Japan, the Philippines, and Myanmar, as well as Indonesia, Malaysia, the Lao PDR, the Republic of Korea and Brunei Darussalam. Seizures of ATS, excluding ecstasy, almost quintupled in Asia in 1999 and the

share of that region in global seizures rose from 43% in 1998 to 75% in 1999.

• a decline of amphetamines' seizures in Europe by a fifth, falling back to the lowest level since 1996, reflecting first signs of a stabilization or decline in consumption levels of amphetamine after the strong growth of previous years. The share of Europe in global ATS seizures fell to 12% in 1999.

• an increase in seizures in the Americas (now 11% of global seizures), largely due to greater enforcement activities in Mexico and thus higher levels of methamphetamine seizures; and

• increases in ATS seizures in Africa and Oceania (1% of global seizures, each).

There are still significant concentrations of trafficking within regions (1999):

• More than 99% of Asian seizures took place in East and South-East Asia; the People's Republic of China alone accounted for 63% of seizures in that region, or almost half (48%) of global seizures. China together with Thailand, Japan, the Philippines and Myanmar, accounted for 98% of seizures in the East and South-East Asia region, or 74% of global seizures. China has also been identified by neighbouring countries as the main source of ATS supply in East Asia, while Myanmar and Thailand are the main sources of ATS for countries in South-East Asia. In China, the largest amounts were seized in the province of Guangdong, which encircles Hong Kong (SAR), and of Yunnan, located next to Myanmar. In most other countries/ territories of the region, the largest seizures usually

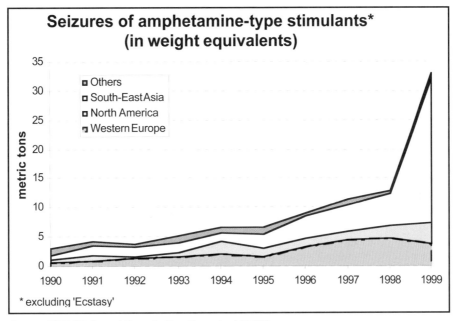

Seizures of amphetamine-type stimulants*
(in weight equivalents)

* excluding 'Ecstasy'

Source: UNDCP, Annual Reports Questionnaire / DELTA

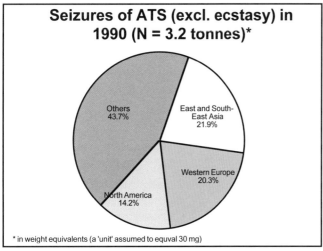

Seizures of ATS (excl. ecstasy) in 1990 (N = 3.2 tonnes)*

Others 43.7%
East and South-East Asia 21.9%
Western Europe 20.3%
North America 14.2%

* in weight equivalents (a 'unit' assumed to equval 30 mg)

Source: UNDCP, Annual Reports Questionnaire / DELTA

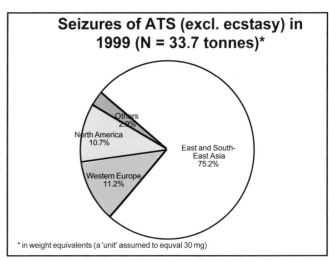

Seizures of ATS (excl. ecstasy) in 1999 (N = 33.7 tonnes)*

Others 2.9%
North America 10.7%
Western Europe 11.2%
East and South-East Asia 75.2%

* in weight equivalents (a 'unit' assumed to equval 30 mg)

Source: UNDCP, Annual Reports Questionnaire / DELTA

took place in the capital cities and/or other metro-politan areas (Bangkok, Manila, Tokyo, Osaka, Hong Kong, Seoul, Jakarta etc.), although large scale seizures were also reported along trafficking routes (e.g. various locations in the north of Thailand or in the south of Japan). Smaller concentrations of ATS trafficking, notably in fenetylline (locally known as Captagon) are also found in the countries of the near and middle east (Saudi Arabia, Syria and Jordan).

• 94% of all European ATS seizures took place in western Europe. The UK and the Netherlands accounted for more than half of all West European seizures, followed by Germany, Belgium, Sweden, France and Spain. Those countries together are responsible for more than 90% of all West European seizures. Seizures are also reported

from eastern Europe, notably from Bulgaria, Poland, the Russian Federation, the Czech Republic, Estonia and Hungary, which account together for 98% of all ATS seizures in East Europe. The Netherlands are seen by most European countries as the main source, even though Belgium and countries of East Europe, notably Poland and the Czech Republic, are also considered to be important source countries. Although the bulk of ATS seizures in Europe are also of European origin, a few seizure cases involved methamphetamine originating in the Philippines and in Thailand.

• 99% of all seizures in the Americas were reported by countries in North America. The USA was responsible for almost three quarters of all North American ATS seizures. Methamphetamine traf-

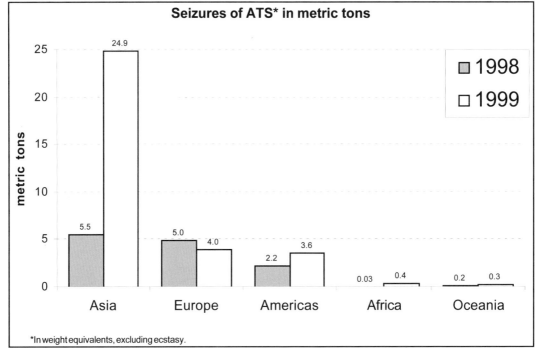

Seizures of ATS* in metric tons

1998 / 1999
Asia: 5.5 / 24.9
Europe: 5.0 / 4.0
Americas: 2.2 / 3.6
Africa: 0.03 / 0.4
Oceania: 0.2 / 0.3

*In weight equivalents, excluding ecstasy.

Source: UNDCP, Annual Reports Questionnaire / DELTA

Methamphetamine trafficking patterns in East and South-East Asia			
Country reporting	Main origin(s)	Main destination(s)	Sources
Japan	China, Hong Kong SAR	domestic	UNDCP/Interpol/WCO
Hong Kong SAR	China (100%)	Japan	ARQ
Rep. of Korea	China (70%), Philippines (20%)	domestic	ARQ
Philippines	China, other neighbouring countries, domestic	Japan, Australia	INCSR
Thailand	Myanmar, Lao PDR	Europe, Singapore	ARQ
Singapore	Philippines	-	ARQ

Sources: UNDCP, Annual Reports Questionnaire Data; UNDCP/Interpol/WCO, Individual seizure cases database; US Dept. of State, International Narcotics Control Strategy Report 2000.

ficking in the USA is still mainly concentrated in the west and southwest, although it is spreading to other parts of the country as well; methamphetamine is mainly produced domestically or imported into the USA from neighbouring Mexico;

• Seizures in Oceania were largely concentrated in Australia (99% of all seizures in the region). 38% of

the ATS (excl. ecstasy) detected by Australian customs in 1999 originated in South-East Asian countries, such as Thailand, the Philippines and Indonesia. There were indications that imports into Australia have declined as domestic production has been increasing. Trafficking in amphetamines within Australia is mainly concentrated in the east of the country, in New South Wales, Queensland

Trafficking patterns of amphetamine in Europe, 1999			
Country reporting	Main origin(s)	Main destination(s)	Sources
UK	Netherlands (90%), Belgium (10%)	domestic	ARQ
Spain	domestic, Netherlands	domestic	UNDCP/Interpol/WCO
Germany	Netherlands (96%), Poland (1.8%), Czech Rep. (1.2%) (as well as domestic)	domestic, Switzerland, Scandinavian countries	ARQ
France	Belgium, Netherlands	other European countries	ARQ
Belgium	domestic, Netherlands, UK	Spain, France, USA	ARQ, UNDCP/Interpol/WCO
Switzerland	Netherlands	domestic	UNDCP/Interpol/WCO
Denmark	Netherlands, Poland, Czech Rep., Belgium	Norway, Sweden	ARQ
Sweden	Poland & Czech Rep. (60%); Netherlands & Belgium (40%);	domestic	ARQ
Norway	Netherlands, other European countries	domestic	ARQ
Finland	Netherlands (49%), Estonia (41%), Russian Fed. (10%)	domestic	UNDCP/Interpol/WCO
Iceland	Netherlands (98%), Poland (2%)	domestic	ARQ
Estonia	Poland	Sweden, Finland	UNDCP/Interpol/WCO
Hungary	Netherlands	domestic	UNDCP/Interpol/WCO
Croatia	Netherlands	domestic	UNDCP/Interpol/WCO

Sources: UNDCP, Annual Reports Questionnaire Data; UNDCP/Interpol/WCO, Individual seizure cases database.

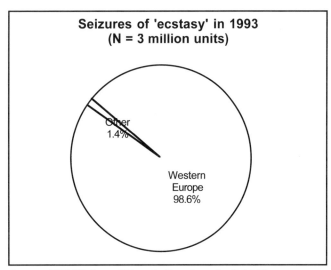

Source: UNDCP, Annual Reports Questionnaire / DELTA

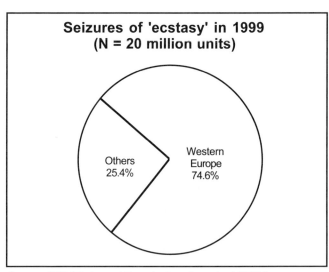

Source: UNDCP, Annual Reports Questionnaire / DELTA

and Victoria.

• Seizures in Africa were largely concentrated in western Africa (94% of all seizures in 1999; Nigeria alone accounted for three quarters of all African seizures of ATS in 1999), while, in the early 1990s, the concentration was mainly in northern Africa, notably in Egypt. Trafficking of ATS in northern Africa, although now at lower levels, is still concentrated in Egypt.

Ecstasy .

Trafficking in ecstasy (MDMA, MDA, MDME) was still mainly concentrated in western Europe, although there have been strong increases in recent years in several other parts of the world as well. In contrast to most other drugs, western Europe is the main source for ecstasy.

As countries are not required - according to the current drug list provided in the Annual Reports Questionnaire - to report specifically on ecstasy seizures, available seizure data have to be treated with caution and only allow for the identification of broad trends. For the time being, most 'ecstasy' seizures are reported by member states under the category of 'other hallucinogens' (i.e. 'hallucinogens excluding LSD'), although a number of countries have started to report specifically on ecstasy seizures in order to avoid confusion. The situation is complicated as a few countries apparently report ecstasy seizures under the category of 'stimulants', because ecstasy (MDMA), for its chemical similarities, is considered to be part of the group of 'amphetamine-type stimulants'.

For the purposes of the following analysis, the two categories - 'ecstasy' and 'other hallucinogens, including ecstasy' - will be combined as this appears to be - for the moment - the best reflection of ecstasy seizures. (In

most of the countries reporting, ecstasy apparently accounts for the bulk of the 'other hallucinogen' category.) Based on seizures reported in units (tablets) only, global seizures rose annually by 18% over the 1990-99 period. In 1999 alone, seizures of tablets doubled. If seizures in weight terms are included - mostly reflecting large scale seizures following the dismantling of clandestine laboratories - and a transformation ratio of 1 unit equalling 100 mg is applied, the growth rate in seizures amounted to 28% per year over the period 1990-99. This, together with 'amphetamines,' was the strongest growth rate of any type of substance worldwide in the 1990s.

While western Europe reported 99% of all ecstasy seizures (in unit terms) in 1992/93, its share fell to 75% by 1999, reflecting the increasing spread of trafficking in ecstasy to other parts of the world. Most countries, however, still identify western Europe (particularly the Netherlands and Belgium) as the main source(s) for their ecstasy imports.

In 1999, the largest seizures of ecstasy tablets worldwide were reported, like in previous years, from the UK. The second largest seizure of ecstasy tablets took place - for the first time in recent years - in the USA. The next largest seizures were reported by the Netherlands, followed by France, Germany, Belgium, Spain, Italy and the Republic of Ireland. Overall, western Europe accounted for 99% of all ecstasy seizures made in Europe. The largest seizures outside Europe and the USA were reported by Canada, the countries of South-East Asia (notably Thailand and, at lower levels, Singapore, Malaysia, Indonesia and Hong Kong, SAR), Australia, Israel, Brazil and the Republic of South Africa. In total, 50 countries and territories reported seizures of ecstasy to UNDCP in 1999, up from 35 in 1998 and 13 in 1990.

Ecstasy trafficking patterns, 1999			
Country reporting	Main origin(s)	Main destination(s)	Source(s)
Western Europe			
United Kingdom	Netherlands (90%), Belgium (9%), Germany (1%)	domestic	ARQ
Netherlands	domestic (77%)	domestic; other Europe; South-East Asia (Thailand, Malaysia, Indonesia, Hong Kong), USA	UNDCP/Interpol/WCO (number of significant seizure cases)
Spain	Netherlands, Belgium	domestic	ARQ
Germany	Netherlands (94.6%), Switzerland (4%), Belgium (1.3%)	domestic, USA; Austria, Italy, Poland, Switzerland, Romania, Slovenia	ARQ
France	UK (79%), Belgium (16%)	USA; Spain, UK, Ireland	ARQ
Belgium	domestic; Netherlands, UK	USA; Spain, France; Israel, South Africa, Japan, China	ARQ; UNDCP/Interpol/WCO
Italy	domestic; Netherlands, Belgium, Germany, France	domestic; USA	UNDCP/Interpol/WCO
Denmark	Netherlands, Belgium	Norway, Sweden, Iceland	ARQ
Norway	Netherlands; UK	domestic	ARQ
Iceland	Netherlands	domestic	ARQ
Ireland	Netherlands	domestic	ARQ
Eastern Europe			
Hungary	Netherlands	domestic	UNDCP/Interpol/WCO
Croatia	Netherlands	domestic, Yugoslavia	UNDCP/Interpol/WCO
Lithuania	n/a	Russian Federation	ARQ
Americas			
USA	Netherlands (60%);Belgium (10%), Germany, France, Spain	domestic	UNDCP/Interpol/WCO (number of significant seizure cases)
Canada	domestic; Netherlands, Belgium, Germany, Spain, France	domestic; USA	UNDCP/Interpol/WCO
Mexico	n/a	domestic	UNDCP/Interpol/WCO
Colombia	n/a	domestic; Mexico, USA	UNDCP/Interpol/WCO
Asia and the Pacific			
Israel	Netherlands, Belgium	domestic	UNDCP/Interpol/WCO
Thailand	domestic; Netherlands	domestic	UNDCP/Interpol/WCO
Hong Kong, SAR	Netherlands, Belarus	domestic	ARQ
Malaysia	Netherlands	domestic	UNDCP/Interpol/WCO
Australia	Netherlands, UK, Indonesia, Belgium, Malaysia, Germany	domestic	UNDCP/Interpol/WCO
New Zealand	Netherlands, Germany	domestic	UNDCP/Interpol/WCO
Africa			
South Africa	Netherlands, domestic	domestic	UNDCP/Interpol/WCO
Zimbabwe	South Africa	domestic	UNDCP/Interpol/WCO

UNDCP, Annual Reports Questionnaire Data; UNDCP/Interpol/WCO, Individual seizure cases database.

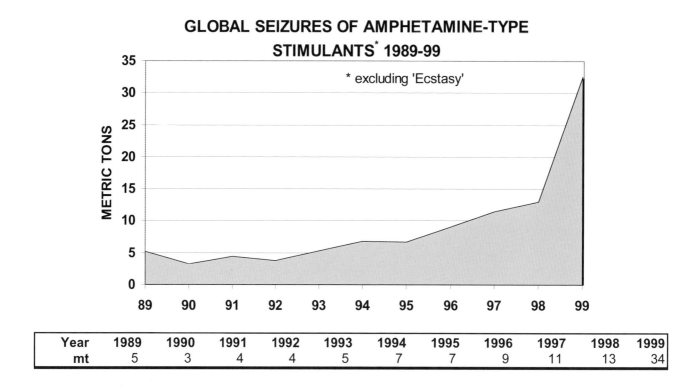

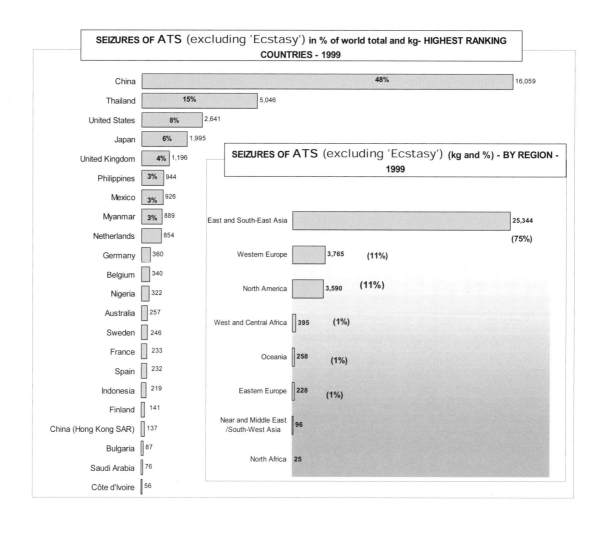

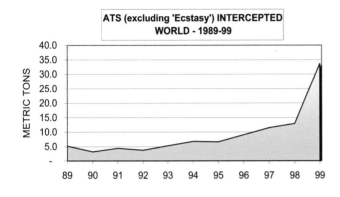

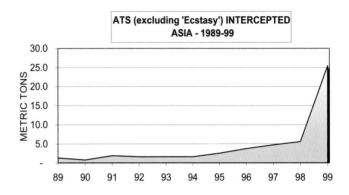

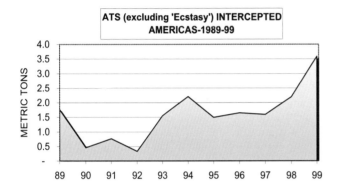

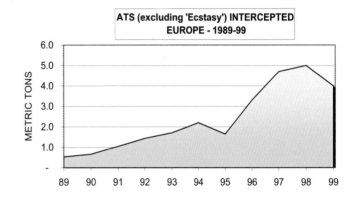

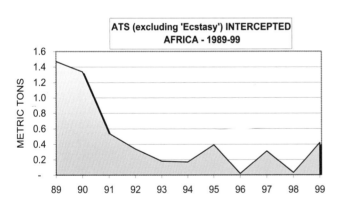

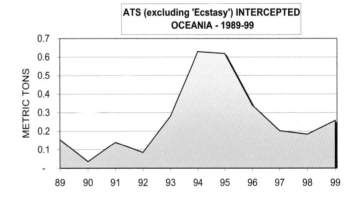

Trafficking of amphetamine-type stimulants 1998-1999: extent and trends (countries reporting seizures of more than 0.001 tons (1kg))

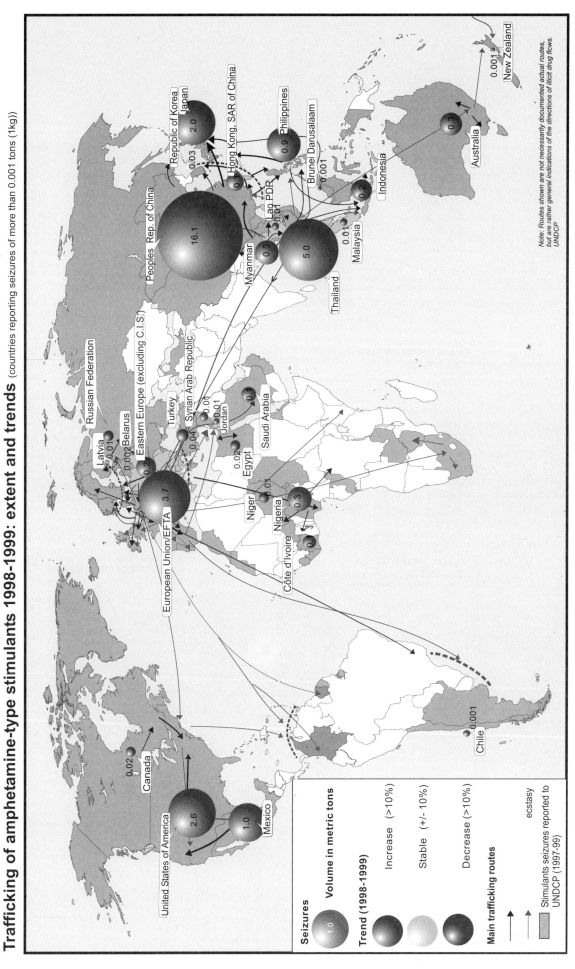

Note: Routes shown are not necessarily documented actual routes, but are rather general indications of the directions of illicit drug flows. UNDCP

New Zealand 0.001

Australia 0.3

Republic of Korea
Japan 2.0
0.03
Hong Kong, SAR of China 0.1
Philippines 0.9
Brunei Darusalaam 0.001
Lao PDR 0.01
Indonesia 0.2
Peoples Rep. of China 16.1
Myanmar 0.3
Thailand 5.0
Malaysia 0.01

Russian Federation
Eastern Europe (excluding C.I.S.)
Turkey
Syrian Arab Republic 0.01
Jordan 0.01
Saudi Arabia 0.1
Belarus 0.002
Latvia 0.01
0.04
European Union/EFTA 3.7
0.2
Egypt 0.02
Niger 0.01
Nigeria 0.3
Côte d'Ivoire 0

Canada 0.02
United States of America 2.6
Mexico 1.0

Chile 0.001

Seizures

Volume in metric tons

1.0

Trend (1998-1999)

Increase (>10%)

Stable (+/- 10%)

Decrease (>10%)

Main trafficking routes

ecstasy

Stimulants seizures reported to UNDCP (1997-99)

Note: The boundaries and names shown and the designations used on this map do not imply official endorsement or acceptance by the United Nations.

Amphetamine-type Stimulants (excluding 'Ecstasy')

Region/country or territory	1994	1995	1996	1997	1998	1999
AFRICA						
East Africa						
United Republic of Tanzania	0.632 kg	No Report	No Report	No Report	No Report	No Report
	65 u.					
Sub-Total	0.632 kg					
	65 u.					
North Africa						
Algeria	36516 u. [ICPO]	No Report	43211 u. [ICPO]	No Report	No Report	No Report
Egypt	64.902 lt.	4088525 u.	415237 u.	94881 u.	15.348 lt.	5.222 kg
						19.023 lt.
Morocco	No Report	No Report	No Report	No Report	49561 u.	73917 u.
Tunisia	No Report	No Report	3 u. [ICPO]	No Report	No Report	No Report
Sub-Total	64.902 lt.	4088525 u.	458451 u.	94881 u.	15.348 lt.	5.222 kg
	36516 u.				49561 u.	19.023 lt.
						73917 u.
Southern Africa						
South Africa	0.030 kg	14 u. [ICPO]	3266 u.	0.280 kg	527 u.	369 u. [ICPO]
Zambia	No Report	282.289 kg [ICPO]	0.091 kg [ICPO]	0.050 kg [ICPO]	No Report	0.018 kg
Zimbabwe	No Report	No Report	No Report	No Report	15.729 kg	No Report
Sub-Total	0.030 kg	282.289 kg	0.091 kg	0.330 kg	15.729 kg	0.018 kg
		14 u.	3266 u.		527 u.	369 u.
West and Central Africa						
Burkina Faso	346903 u. [ICPO]	No Report	No Report	40750 u. [ICPO]	No Report	No Report
Chad	61750 u.	No Report	No Report	No Report	No Report	1620 u. [ICPO]
Congo	Govt (1	No Report	No Report	No Report	No Report	No Report
Côte d'Ivoire	13125 u.	8463 u.	1809 u.	No Report	6385 u.	56.131 kg
Gabon	No Report	25.000 kg [ICPO]	No Report	No Report	No Report	No Report
Gambia	No Report	No Report	No Report	No Report	No Report	328 u.
Mali	32 u. [ICPO]	1207 u. [ICPO]	No Report	No Report	No Report	No Report
Mauritania	1161 u. [ICPO]	No Report	No Report	No Report	No Report	No Report
Niger	661924 u. [ICPO]	No Report	220368 u. [ICPO]	186574 u. [ICPO]	No Report	556537 u. [ICPO]
Nigeria	94.300 kg	45.000 kg [ICPO]	10.652 kg [ICPO]	309.525 kg	No Report	322.071 kg
Senegal	No Report	No Report	17 u. [ICPO]	No Report	No Report	No Report
Sub-Total	94.300 kg	70.000 kg	10.652 kg	309.525 kg	6385 u.	378.202 kg
	1084895 u.	9670 u.	222194 u.	227324 u.		558485 u.
Total region	94.962 kg	352.289 kg	10.743 kg	309.855 kg	15.729 kg	383.442 kg
	64.902 lt.	4098209 u.	683911 u.	322205 u.	15.348 lt.	19.023 lt.
	1121476 u.				56473 u.	632771 u.
AMERICAS						
Caribbean						
Bahamas	No Report	No Report	No Report	0.200 kg [ICPO]	No Report	No Report

Source: Annual Report Questionnaire if not otherwise indicated

Amphetamine-type Stimulants (excluding 'Ecstasy')

Region/country or territory	1994	1995	1996	1997	1998	1999
AMERICAS						
Caribbean						
Cayman Islands	No Report	No Report	0.258 kg	No Report	0.040 kg 120 u.	0.001 kg [ICPO]
Sub-Total			0.258 kg	0.200 kg	0.040 kg 120 u.	0.001 kg
North America						
Canada	0.926 kg	No Report	0.561 kg 1572 u.	2.260 kg 0.225 lt.	0.590 kg 54.500 lt. 11207 u.	20.218 kg 2.306 lt. 4970 u.
Mexico	290.238 kg	499.788 kg	180.723 kg	38.891 kg	98.391 kg	926.011 kg 880 u.
United States	191843104 u.	997.900 kg	1469.164 kg 25890 u.	1428.798 kg 84.942 lt. 3747486 u.	1824.363 kg 215.776 lt. 411768 u.	2641.000 kg 20217 u.
Sub-Total	291.164 kg 191843100 u.	1497.688 kg	1650.448 kg 27462 u.	1469.949 kg 85.167 lt. 3747486 u.	1923.344 kg 270.276 lt. 422975 u.	3587.229 kg 2.306 lt. 26067 u.
South America						
Argentina	1215 u.	13744 u.	480 u. [Govt]	504 u.	600 u.	4103 u.
Brazil	No Report	No Report	0.028 kg	No Report	No Report	No Report
Chile	120493 u.	27044 u.	17463 u.	55686 u.	0.011 kg 6973 u.	104523 u. [CICAD]
Uruguay	No Report	No Report	37 u.	No Report	No Report	No Report
Sub-Total	121708 u.	40788 u.	0.028 kg 17980 u.	56190 u.	0.011 kg 7573 u.	108626 u.
Total region	291.164 kg 191964800 u.	1497.688 kg 40788 u.	1650.734 kg 45442 u.	1470.149 kg 85.167 lt. 3803676 u.	1923.395 kg 270.276 lt. 430668 u.	3587.230 kg 2.306 lt. 134693 u.
ASIA						
Central Asia and Transcaucasian countries						
Armenia	No Report	No Report	No Report	0.040 lt. [ICPO]	No Report	No Report
Georgia	No Report	No Report	0.051 kg [ICPO] 4.373 lt. 224461 u.	No Report	No Report	No Report
Kyrgyzstan	No Report	No Report	No Report	0.020 kg	No Report	No Report
Uzbekistan	No Report	No Report	0.358 kg [ICPO]	0.430 kg [ICPO]	No Report	0.031 kg
Sub-Total			0.409 kg 4.373 lt. 224461 u.	0.450 kg 0.040 lt.		0.031 kg
East and South-East Asia						
Brunei Darussalam	No Report	No Report	0.095 kg 6479 u.	0.123 kg	0.237 kg	1.197 kg
Cambodia	No Report	5.000 kg [Govt]	No Report	13928 u. [ICPO]	No Report	No Report
China	123.000 kg [ICPO]	1303.000 kg	1599.000 kg	1334.000 kg	1608.000 kg	16059.000 kg [ICPO]

Source: Annual Report Questionnaire if not otherwise indicated

Amphetamine-type Stimulants (excluding 'Ecstasy')

Region/country or territory	1994	1995	1996	1997	1998	1999
ASIA						
East and South-East Asia						
China (Hong Kong SAR)	123.081 kg	15.400 kg [Govt]	46.800 kg	73.600 kg	232.700 kg [Govt]	136.369 kg
			14295 u.	3461 u.		29238 u.
Indonesia	25 u.	No Report	0.334 kg	5.621 kg	7.761 kg [HNLP]	218.625 kg
			303 u.			29511 u.
Japan	314.676 kg	89.194 kg	652.192 kg	173.526 kg	549.702 kg	1994.459 kg
	10092 u.	135 u.		2.203 lt.	0.788 lt.	0.589 lt.
				1415 u.	1 u.	4589 u.
Korea (Republic of)	4.504 kg [Govt]	12.978 kg [ICPO]	33.250 kg	24.872 kg	28.311 kg	29.233 kg
Lao People's Dem. Rep.	No Report	No Report	9.698 kg [Govt]	774714 u. [Govt]	No Report	861801 u. [HNLP]
Macau	No Report	0.127 kg [ICPO]	0.252 kg [ICPO]	No Report	0.073 kg [ICPO]	No Report
					187 u.	
Malaysia	71841 u. [ICPO]	No Report	No Report	2.000 kg	No Report	5.411 kg
						329265 u.
Mongolia	No Report	No Report	No Report	No Report	No Report	0.100 kg [ICPO]
Myanmar	No Report	No Report	5906555 u.	5028600 u.	16026688 u.	22.058 kg
						28887514 u.
Philippines	114.581 kg	207.593 kg [ICPO]	797.530 kg	694.480 kg [ICPO]	77.810 kg [ICPO]	943.700 kg
				2.000 lt.		
			2 u.			
Singapore	0.023 kg	0.012 kg	252 u.	0.090 kg	1.711 kg	1.300 kg
				8141 u.	4470 u.	1380 u.
Thailand	812.000 kg [Govt]	561.000 kg [Govt]	442.000 kg [Govt]	2135.889 kg	2827.890 kg	5046.368 kg
Viet Nam	No Report	234.000 kg [ICPO]	No Report	No Report	No Report	6025 u. [ICPO]
Sub-Total	1491.865 kg	2428.304 kg	3581.151 kg	4444.201 kg	5334.195 kg	24457.820 kg
	81958 u.	135 u.	5927886 u.	4.203 lt.	0.788 lt.	0.589 lt.
				5830259 u.	16031350 u.	30149320 u.
Near and Middle East /South-West Asia						
Bahrain	No Report	No Report	No Report	No Report	28 u. [ICPO]	No Report
Israel	13799 u.	7583 u.	50784 u.	30807 u.	No Report	190 u. [ICPO]
Jordan	65773 u.	No Report	2586467 u.	0.290 kg [ICPO]	262071 u.	518813 u.
				2794059 u.		
Kuwait	38231 u.	No Report	3.414 kg [ICPO]	No Report	No Report	No Report
Lebanon	446324 u.	30700 u.	No Report	No Report	No Report	No Report
Qatar	5 u.	4 u.	27 u.	1026 u. [ICPO]	220 u. [ICPO]	14 u. [ICPO]
Saudi Arabia	8807633 u.	6571645 u.	4016752 u. [ICPO]	10852279 u. [ICPO]	3553231 u.	7549665 u. [ICPO]
Syrian Arab Republic	18265 u. [ICPO]	65000 u. [ICPO]	1484690 u.	2463977 u.	No Report	1470831 u.
United Arab Emirates	No Report	No Report	8563 u.	No Report	No Report	No Report
Yemen	1557 u. [Govt]	No Report	No Report	3704 u. [ICPO]	972 u. [ICPO]	No Report
Sub-Total	9391587 u.	6674932 u.	3.414 kg	0.290 kg	3816522 u.	9539513 u.
			8147283 u.	16145850 u.		

Source: Annual Report Questionnaire if not otherwise indicated

Amphetamine-type Stimulants (excluding 'Ecstasy')

Region/country or territory	1994	1995	1996	1997	1998	1999
ASIA						
South Asia						
Maldives	No Report	No Report	No Report	No Report	No Report	0.001 kg
Sub-Total						0.001 kg
Total region	1491.865 kg 9473545 u.	2428.304 kg 6675067 u.	3584.974 kg 4.373 lt. 14299630 u.	4444.941 kg 4.243 lt. 21976110 u.	5334.195 kg 0.788 lt. 19847870 u.	24457.850 kg 0.589 lt. 39688840 u.
EUROPE						
Eastern Europe						
Albania	No Report	No Report	No Report	No Report	No Report	0.009 kg [ICPO]
Belarus	No Report	0.405 kg	No Report	No Report	0.282 kg	1.644 kg
Bulgaria	No Report	No Report	No Report	134.293 kg	150 u.	87.192 kg 22928 u.
Croatia	4138 u.	1739 u.	2075 u.	1.255 kg 1596 u.	0.765 kg 9106 u.	1.110 kg 15429 u.
Czech Republic	3.788 kg	0.165 kg	21.763 kg	0.617 kg 56 u.	76.500 kg [WIB (2]	21.400 kg 673 u.
Estonia	No Report	No Report	0.024 kg [ICPO]	0.725 kg 0.078 lt.	1.955 kg 971 u.	11.507 kg 2707 u.
FYR of Macedonia	No Report	No Report	42 u. [ICPO]	No Report	No Report	No Report
Hungary	27.417 kg [ICPO] 332 u.	3797 u. [ICPO]	2.465 kg 5818 u.	12.326 kg [Govt]	7.605 kg	9.257 kg
Latvia	No Report	1.000 kg 500 u.	1.338 kg	0.370 kg	1.395 kg 1.700 lt. 2671 u.	1.257 kg 55 u.
Lithuania	0.510 lt.	0.344 lt.	0.054 kg 1.035 lt.	0.205 kg 1.348 lt. 5641 u.	0.013 kg 0.994 lt. 142 u.	0.077 kg 0.486 lt. 2297 u.
Poland	35.500 kg	18.870 kg	15.253 kg	27.150 kg	51.503 kg	51.453 kg
Republic of Moldova	0.003 kg [ICPO]	0.009 kg [ICPO]	No Report	20.607 kg 1034 u.	No Report	0.105 lt. [ICPO]
Romania	No Report	14 u.	11420 u.	3289 u. [ICPO]	No Report	10546 u.
Russian Federation	1 652 kg [ICPO]	4.700 kg	21.800 kg	No Report	34.000 kg [F.O.]	40.500 kg [F.O.]
Slovakia	No Report	0.001 kg [ICPO]	No Report	0.094 kg	9.717 kg 35 u.	0.131 kg 22 u.
Slovenia	1196 u.	No Report	18748 u.	1.410 kg	0.339 kg 267 u.	0.625 kg [ICPO] 818 u.
Ukraine	No Report	No Report	7.100 kg	39.500 kg	2.482 kg	No Report
Sub-Total	68.360 kg 0.510 lt. 5666 u.	25.150 kg 0.344 lt. 6050 u.	69.797 kg 1.035 lt. 38103 u.	238.552 kg 1.426 lt. 11616 u.	186.556 kg 2.694 lt. 13342 u.	226.162 kg 0.591 lt. 55475 u.
Western Europe						
Andorra	0.013 kg [ICPO] 29 u.	4 u. [ICPO]	No Report	No Report	143 u. [ICPO]	43 u.

Source: Annual Report Questionnaire if not otherwise indicated

Amphetamine-type Stimulants (excluding 'Ecstasy')

Region/country or territory	1994	1995	1996	1997	1998	1999
EUROPE						
Western Europe						
Austria	0.218 kg 796 u.	1562 u.	3767 u.	7895 u.	9763 u.	5165 u.
Belgium	27.849 kg 0.003 lt. 2259 u.	77.029 kg 504 u.	24.000 kg 184413 u.	77.000 kg 511 u.	445.000 kg 271080 u.	325.070 kg 489566 u.
Cyprus	0.002 kg 1 u.	0.047 kg 120 u.	0.004 kg 18 u.	0.050 kg [ICPO]	No Report	0.012 kg
Denmark	12.600 kg [ICPO]	40.000 kg	26.700 kg	119.400 kg	25.236 kg	31.600 kg
Finland	9.127 kg	20.123 kg 3752 u.	22.408 kg 1011 u.	22.189 kg 1101 u.	24.784 kg 1003 u.	140.464 kg 17665 u.
France	79.657 kg [ICPO]	103.664 kg 273779 u.	127.965 kg 349210 u.	194.047 kg 198941 u.	165.122 kg 1142226 u.	232.941 kg
Germany	119.662 kg	137.852 kg	159.767 kg	233.633 kg	309.602 kg	360.000 kg
Gibraltar	No Report	No Report	No Report	0.030 kg	No Report	1.091 kg
Greece	0.013 kg 11 u.	0.109 kg 1725 u.	0.013 kg 2104 u.	0.034 kg 958 u.	0.003 kg 5 u.	1.380 kg 257 u.
Iceland	0.783 kg 22 u.	5.146 kg	No Report	No Report	No Report	5.078 kg
Ireland	0.534 kg [ICPO] 186 u.	1.500 kg [ICPO]	19244 u.	102.585 kg 22191 u.	43.162 kg 46538 u.	13.300 kg [ICPO] 12015 u.
Italy	3.358 kg 9993 u.	1.099 kg 9071 u.	154503 u.	0.384 kg 10950 u.	2.454 kg 2309 u.	5.131 kg [ICPO] 16115 u.
Liechtenstein	No Report	0.018 kg	122 u.	No Report	No Report	No Report
Luxembourg	No Report	91 u. [ICPO]	No Report	0.010 kg [ICPO]	No Report	0.016 kg [ICPO]
Malta		No Report	686 u.	0.060 kg 100 u.	No Report	No Report
Monaco	No Report	0.020 kg 15 u.	1 u.	No Report	No Report	No Report
Netherlands	316.639 kg [ICPO] 132062 u.	46.000 kg [ICPO] 850 u.	No Report	No Report	1450.000 kg 242425 u.	853.000 kg 45847 u.
Norway	12.696 kg	52.765 kg	30.286 kg	93.241 kg	207.999 kg	52.110 kg 6056 u.
Portugal	No Report	695 u.	4093 u.	0.019 kg 549 u.	1131 u. [(3]	0.087 kg 31393 u.
San Marino	1 u.	No Report	No Report	No Report	No Report	No Report
Spain	31.736 kg	35.038 kg	53.412 kg	119.584 kg	176.985 kg	49.538 kg 182.000 lt.
Sweden	210.215 kg 1164 u.	277.377 kg	163.780 kg	187.374 kg 16057 u.	134.714 kg [(2]	246.310 kg 1099 u.
Switzerland	0.540 kg	2.147 kg	4.521 kg	7.981 kg	No Report	10.700 kg
Turkey	No Report	No Report	No Report	1020130 u.	No Report	4244493 u.
United Kingdom	1305.100 kg	819.000 kg	2624.700 kg	3295.700 kg	1807.847 kg	1194.938 kg [ICPO] 25021 u.

Source: Annual Report Questionnaire if not otherwise indicated

Amphetamine-type Stimulants (excluding 'Ecstasy')

Region/country or territory	1994	1995	1996	1997	1998	1999
EUROPE						
Western Europe						
Sub-Total	2130.742 kg 0.003 lt. 146524 u.	1618.934 kg 292168 u.	3237.556 kg 719172 u.	4453.321 kg 1279383 u.	4792.908 kg 1716623 u.	3522.766 kg 182.000 lt. 4894735 u.
Total region	2199.102 kg 0.513 lt. 152190 u.	1644.084 kg 0.344 lt. 298218 u.	3307.353 kg 1.035 lt. 757275 u.	4691.873 kg 1.426 lt. 1290999 u.	4979.464 kg 2.694 lt. 1729965 u.	3748.928 kg 182.591 lt. 4950210 u.
OCEANIA						
Oceania						
Australia	628.600 kg [4	618.480 kg [4 0.068 lt. 546 u.	339.958 kg 0.101 lt. 13742 u.	202.814 kg	182.220 kg Govt [5	256.978 kg Govt [5
New Zealand	0.867 kg ICPO 343 u.	0.248 kg Govt	No Report	No Report	1.340 kg	1.104 kg 1400 u.
Sub-Total	629.467 kg 343 u.	618.728 kg 0.068 lt. 546 u.	339.958 kg 0.101 lt. 13742 u.	202.814 kg	183.560 kg	258.082 kg 1400 u.
Total region	629.467 kg 343 u.	618.728 kg 0.068 lt. 546 u.	339.958 kg 0.101 lt. 13742 u.	202.814 kg	183.560 kg	258.082 kg 1400 u.
TOTAL	4706.560 kg 65.415 lt. 202712400 u.	6541.093 kg 0.412 lt. 11112830 u.	8893.763 kg 5.509 lt. 15800000 u.	11119.630 kg 90.836 lt. 27392990 u.	12436.340 kg 289.106 lt. 22064970 u.	32435.530 kg 204.509 lt. 45407910 u.

1) Included in methaqualone. 2) Amfetamine 3) Small quantity. 4) Fiscal year 5) Provisional figures.

Source: Annual Report Questionnaire if not otherwise indicated

Depressants (excluding Methaqualone)

Region/country or territory	1994	1995	1996	1997	1998	1999
AFRICA						
East Africa						
Kenya	No Report	No Report	No Report	No Report	9060 u.	No Report
Mauritius	1582 u.	4064 u.	1886 u.	1886 u.	11694 u.	952 u.
Sub-Total	1582 u.	4064 u.	1886 u.	1886 u.	20754 u.	952 u.
North Africa						
Algeria	No Report	No Report	No Report	No Report	No Report	110786 u.
Egypt	No Report	10.277 kg 178815 u.	No Report	No Report	No Report	No Report
Morocco	15918 u. [Govt]	523317 u. [Govt]	28988 u. [Govt]	36236 u. [Govt]	No Report	No Report
Sudan	No Report	No Report	14345 u. [ICPO]	No Report	No Report	No Report
Tunisia	3405 u.	13664 u.	4330 u. [ICPO]	No Report	4439 u.	No Report
Sub-Total	19323 u.	10.277 kg 715796 u.	47663 u.	36236 u.	4439 u.	110786 u.
Southern Africa						
Botswana	No Report	No Report	No Report	No Report	No Report	0.073 kg [ICPO] 500 u.
Mozambique	No Report	No Report	No Report	No Report	5080 u. [ICPO]	No Report
Zambia	No Report	0.477 kg [ICPO] 20715 u.	0.825 kg [ICPO]	No Report	0.908 kg [Govt] 1049 u.	4140 u.
Zimbabwe	No Report	No Report	No Report	No Report	43.640 kg	No Report
Sub-Total		0.477 kg 20715 u.	0.825 kg		44.548 kg 6129 u.	0.073 kg 4640 u.
West and Central Africa						
Benin	No Report	No Report	No Report	24 u. [Govt]	No Report	No Report
Cameroon	14 u. [ICPO]	255 u. [ICPO]	222 u. [ICPO]	No Report	No Report	No Report
Chad	448510 u.	No Report	No Report	No Report	No Report	5360 u. [ICPO]
Côte d'Ivoire	1202 u.	22696 u.	8290 u.	71.500 kg 44699 u.	23.600 kg 9367 u.	66.690 kg
Gabon	No Report	No Report	100 u. [ICPO]	No Report	No Report	No Report
Gambia	No Report	1171 u. [ICPO]	18650 u. [ICPO]	No Report	4500 u. [ICPO]	No Report
Ghana	No Report	0.140 kg 16000 u.	No Report	No Report	No Report	No Report
Mali	19598 u. [ICPO]	3.500 kg [ICPO] 6138 u.	No Report	No Report	No Report	No Report
Niger	No Report	No Report	591703 u. [ICPO]	No Report	679484 u. [ICPO]	367823 u. [ICPO]
Nigeria	No Report	91.000 kg [ICPO]	1183.252 kg [ICPO]	1426.487 kg	No Report	No Report
Senegal	No Report	No Report	No Report	No Report	4063 u. [ICPO]	4737 u. [ICPO]
Togo	No Report	No Report	9.275 kg	No Report	No Report	No Report
Sub-Total	469324 u.	94.640 kg 46260 u.	1192.527 kg 618965 u.	1497.987 kg 44723 u.	23.600 kg 697414 u.	66.690 kg 377920 u.
Total region	490229 u.	105.394 kg 786835 u.	1193.352 kg 668514 u.	1497.987 kg 82845 u.	68.148 kg 728736 u.	66.763 kg 494298 u.

Source: Annual Report Questionnaire if not otherwise indicated

Depressants (excluding Methaqualone)

Region/country or territory	1994	1995	1996	1997	1998	1999
AMERICAS						
Caribbean						
Bahamas	1.360 kg 136000 u.	No Report	No Report	No Report	No Report	No Report
Cayman Islands	No Report	No Report	No Report	No Report	No Report	0.001 kg
Dominican Republic	No Report	No Report	No Report	No Report	No Report	8 u. [ICPO]
Sub-Total	1.360 kg 136000 u.					0.001 kg 8 u.
Central America						
El Salvador	No Report	No Report	No Report	No Report	40000 u. [ICPO]	No Report
Guatemala	No Report	No Report	No Report	No Report	52.000 kg	No Report
Honduras	No Report	106 u.	No Report	1 u.	No Report	No Report
Sub-Total		106 u.		1 u.	52.000 kg 40000 u.	
North America						
Canada	2577 u.	0.474 kg 42386 u.	0.265 kg 25183 u.	0.880 kg 0.120 lt. 122359 u.	0.934 kg 0.686 lt. 12033 u.	0.726 kg 2.439 lt. 8355 u.
Mexico	No Report	No Report	1108863 u.	117104 u.	1484000 u.	182604 u.
United States	25427770 u.	0.071 kg 300331 u.	0.329 kg 442712 u.	0.026 kg 0.867 lt. 709685 u.	No Report	2.646 kg 403724 u.
Sub-Total	25430350 u.	0.545 kg 342717 u.	0.594 kg 1576758 u.	0.906 kg 0.987 lt. 949148 u.	0.934 kg 0.686 lt. 1496033 u.	3.372 kg 2.439 lt. 594683 u.
South America						
Argentina	No Report	No Report	No Report	5759 u.	13125 u.	8055 u.
Chile	No Report	No Report	48392 u.	No Report	0.002 kg 2545 u.	19813 u. [CICAD]
Uruguay	No Report	No Report	2 u.	No Report	No Report	No Report
Sub-Total			48394 u.	5759 u.	0.002 kg 15670 u.	27868 u.
Total region	1.360 kg 25566350 u.	0.545 kg 342823 u.	0.594 kg 1625152 u.	0.906 kg 0.987 lt. 954908 u.	52.936 kg 0.686 lt. 1551703 u.	3.373 kg 2.439 lt. 622559 u.
ASIA						
Central Asia and Transcaucasian countries						
Armenia	No Report	No Report	No Report	No Report	No Report	1209 u. [ICPO]
Georgia	No Report	No Report	0.215 lt. [ICPO] 4956 u.	No Report	180 u. [ICPO]	0.018 kg [ICPO] 1060 u.
Kazakhstan	No Report	No Report	No Report	No Report	No Report	56.000 kg
Kyrgyzstan	No Report	2400 u.	No Report	No Report	No Report	No Report
Uzbekistan	No Report	88 u.	40 u.	970 u.	No Report	No Report
Sub-Total		2488 u.	0.215 lt. 4996 u.	970 u.	180 u.	56.018 kg 2269 u.

Source: Annual Report Questionnaire if not otherwise indicated

Depressants (excluding Methaqualone)

Region/country or territory	1994	1995	1996	1997	1998	1999
ASIA						
East and South-East Asia						
Brunei Darussalam	17801 u.	18186 u.	No Report	3227 u.	No Report	53 u.
Cambodia	No Report [ICPO]	No Report	No Report	No Report	No Report	No Report
China	144829 u. [ICPO]	231419 u.	No Report	No Report	No Report	No Report
China (Hong Kong SAR)	No Report	318142 u. [Govt]	No Report	512832 u.	162850 u. [Govt]	12.208 kg [1] 1134461 u.
Indonesia	43379 u.	48294 u.	0.103 kg 48294 u.	No Report	17793 u.	372494 u. [ICPO]
Japan	154070 u.	0.473 kg 79468 u.	109778 u.	56895 u.	0.024 kg 0.010 lt. 141455 u.	0.003 lt. 97310 u.
Korea (Republic of)	No Report	No Report	130000 u.	681233 u.	1452896 u.	1030567 u.
Macau	16885 u.	23287 u. [ICPO]	5942 u. [ICPO]	No Report	4937 u. [ICPO]	No Report
Philippines	12 u.	1131 u.	No Report	No Report	No Report	No Report
Singapore	12151 u.	48117 u.	273 u.	582 u.	34911 u.	13069 u.
Thailand	No Report	No Report	No Report	No Report	No Report	4.630 kg [ICPO]
Viet Nam	No Report	No Report	No Report	No Report	No Report	74274 u. [ICPO]
Sub-Total	389127 u.	0.473 kg 768044 u.	0.103 kg 294287 u.	1254769 u.	0.024 kg 0.010 lt. 1814842 u.	16.838 kg 0.003 lt. 2722228 u.
Near and Middle East /South-West Asia						
Israel	2136 u.	No Report	No Report	No Report	No Report	936 u. [ICPO]
Jordan	No Report	24.117 kg	No Report	2794 u.	No Report	No Report
Kuwait	No Report	No Report	No Report	No Report	8943 u.	No Report
Lebanon	No Report	No Report	14510 u.	490 u.	No Report	359 u.
Oman	0.751 kg	No Report	No Report	No Report	No Report	No Report
Qatar	No Report	No Report	12 u.	No Report	753 u. [ICPO]	2164 u. [ICPO]
Saudi Arabia	319387 u.	30946 u.	23594 u. [ICPO]	No Report	No Report	No Report
Syrian Arab Republic	No Report	16 u. [ICPO]	17921 u.	No Report	No Report	15117 u. [ICPO]
Yemen	No Report	No Report	No Report	No Report	169 u. [ICPO]	No Report
Sub-Total	0.751 kg 321523 u.	24.117 kg 30962 u.	56037 u.	3284 u.	9865 u.	18576 u.
South Asia						
Nepal	3800 u.	No Report	No Report	No Report	6811 u.	No Report
Sub-Total	3800 u.				6811 u.	
Total region	0.751 kg 714450 u.	24.590 kg 801494 u.	0.103 kg 0.215 lt. 355320 u.	1259023 u.	0.024 kg 0.010 lt. 1831698 u.	72.856 kg 0.003 lt. 2743073 u.
EUROPE						
Eastern Europe						
Belarus	No Report	No Report	No Report	No Report	No Report	0.002 kg

Source: Annual Report Questionnaire if not otherwise indicated

Depressants (excluding Methaqualone)

Region/country or territory	1994	1995	1996	1997	1998	1999
EUROPE						
Eastern Europe						
Bulgaria	No Report	No Report	No Report	0.627 kg	93460 u.	1.500 kg
Croatia	No Report	No Report	No Report	4915 u.	4358 u.	8335 u.
Czech Republic	No Report	No Report	No Report	No Report	No Report	50.000 kg
Estonia	No Report	No Report	0.016 lt. ICPO 120 u.	9.139 kg 908 u.	No Report	0.103 kg 138 u.
Hungary	597 u. ICPO	No Report	No Report	No Report	No Report	No Report
Latvia	No Report	0.100 kg 100 u.	0.975 kg 1731 u.	20830 u.	11244 u.	0.171 kg 13562 u.
Lithuania	No Report	No Report	No Report	No Report	1237 u.	580 u.
Republic of Moldova	No Report	No Report	No Report	No Report	1800 u.	No Report
Russian Federation	32.787 kg ICPO	16.800 kg	91.000 kg	975 u.	No Report	39.500 kg ICPO
Slovakia	No Report	No Report	No Report	10642 u.	1356 u.	1104 u.
Slovenia	No Report	No Report	1138 u.	No Report	5745 u.	621 u.
Ukraine	No Report	No Report	36.868 kg	No Report	No Report	0.001 kg ICPO 8427 u.
Sub-Total	32.787 kg 597 u.	16.900 kg 100 u.	128.843 kg 0.016 lt. 2989 u.	9.766 kg 38270 u.	119200 u.	91.277 kg 32767 u.
Western Europe						
Andorra	No Report	201 u. ICPO	No Report	No Report	No Report	No Report
Belgium	0.007 kg 1400 u.	1284 u.	No Report	No Report	No Report	No Report
Cyprus	No Report	123 u.	No Report	No Report	No Report	No Report
Denmark	No Report	8053 u. ICPO	No Report	No Report	No Report	No Report
Finland	28972 u.	16841 u.	74997 u.	48395 u.	35664 u.	45448 u.
Germany	780 u.	0.100 kg 2345 u.	4195 u.	6035 u.	7071 u.	No Report
Gibraltar	No Report	No Report	569 u.	1058 u.	No Report	64 u. ICPO
Greece	3.954 kg 7644 u.	3.935 kg 9359 u.	6.098 kg 41520 u.	10.400 kg 26403 u.	2.306 kg 18470 u.	80.210 kg 217004 u.
Ireland	No Report	No Report	No Report	0.248 kg 4935 u.	No Report	13793 u. ICPO
Italy	0.055 kg 15684 u.	0.230 kg 4081 u.	2599 u.	14437 u.	0.037 kg 1506 u.	0.232 kg ICPO 3316 u.
Luxembourg	No Report	No Report	No Report	No Report	145 u.	No Report
Malta	1318 u.	395 u.	14 u.	212 u.	353 u.	8 u.
Norway	38589 u.	34079 u.	53908 u.	130000 u.	0.071 kg 101295 u.	0.012 kg 180500 u.
Portugal	No Report	736 u.	1544 u.	1945 u.	2577 u.	2122 u.
Spain	72187 u.	127128 u.	63543 u.	59352 u.	99126 u.	343974 u.
Sweden	No Report	No Report	No Report	No Report	0.302 kg 293508 u.	255000 u.

Source: Annual Report Questionnaire if not otherwise indicated

Depressants (excluding Methaqualone)

Region/country or territory	1994	1995	1996	1997	1998	1999
EUROPE						
Western Europe						
Switzerland	No Report	No Report	No Report	No Report	1204104 u.	554641 u.
Turkey	No Report	No Report	No Report	No Report	3559 u.	No Report
United Kingdom	4.200 kg	6.600 kg	7.700 kg	6.200 kg	No Report	12000 u.[ICPO]
Sub-Total	8.216 kg	10.865 kg	13.798 kg	16.848 kg	2.716 kg	80.454 kg
	166574 u.	204625 u.	242889 u.	292772 u.	1767378 u.	1627870 u.
Total region	41.003 kg	27.765 kg	142.641 kg	26.614 kg	2.716 kg	171.731 kg
	167171 u.	204725 u.	0.016 lt.	331042 u.	1886578 u.	1660637 u.
			245878 u.			
OCEANIA						
Oceania						
Australia	No Report	258 u.[2]	1.823 kg	0.380 kg	No Report	No Report
			336 u.			
New Zealand	709 u.[ICPO]	402 u.[ICPO]	No Report	No Report	445 u.	126 u.
Sub-Total	709 u.	660 u.	1.823 kg	0.380 kg	445 u.	126 u.
			336 u.			
Total region	709 u.	660 u.	1.823 kg	0.380 kg	445 u.	126 u.
			336 u.			
TOTAL	43.114 kg	158.294 kg	1338.513 kg	1525.887 kg	123.824 kg	314.723 kg
	26938900 u.	2136537 u.	0.231 lt.	0.987 lt.	0.696 lt.	2.442 lt.
			2895200 u.	2627818 u.	5999160 u.	5520693 u.

1) Includes mainly benzodiazapines 2) Fiscal year

Source: Annual Report Questionnaire if not otherwise indicated

Hallucinogens (excl. LSD but incl. 'Ecstasy')

Region/country or territory	1994	1995	1996	1997	1998	1999
AFRICA						
East Africa						
Mauritius	No Report	2 u. [ICPO]	No Report	No Report	No Report	No Report
Sub-Total		2 u.				
North Africa						
Egypt	No Report	No Report	19.453 lt.	46.565 lt.	No Report	No Report
Morocco	No Report	28267 u. [ICPO]	No Report	No Report	No Report	No Report
Sub-Total		28267 u.	19.453 lt.	46.565 lt.		
Southern Africa						
Namibia	No Report	No Report	No Report	No Report	No Report	74 u.
South Africa	1262 u.	2135 u.	No Report	118784 u.	111733 u.	30132 u. [ICPO]
Zimbabwe	No Report	No Report	No Report	No Report	No Report	3 u.
Sub-Total	1262 u.	2135 u.		118784 u.	111733 u.	30209 u.
West and Central Africa						
Ghana	9.092 lt.	No Report	No Report	No Report	No Report	No Report
Sub-Total	9.092 lt.					
Total region	9.092 lt. 1262 u.	30404 u.	19.453 lt.	46.565 lt. 118784 u.	111733 u.	30209 u.
AMERICAS						
Caribbean						
Aruba	No Report	No Report	No Report	No Report	No Report	0.004 kg [ICPO] 873 u.
Cayman Islands	No Report	No Report	No Report	No Report	No Report	0.030 kg
Dominican Republic	No Report	No Report	No Report	No Report	No Report	29 u.
Sub-Total						0.034 kg 902 u.
North America						
Canada	68.102 kg	159.829 kg	50.261 kg 719 u.	47.703 kg 9288 u.	64.019 kg 0.022 lt. 25451 u.	561.837 kg 0.503 lt. 3427 u.
Mexico	No Report	No Report	No Report	611.038 kg	93.000 kg	No Report
United States	1504251 u.	43.275 kg 236 u.	83.409 kg 53598 u.	44.588 kg 59.968 lt. 151934 u.	No Report	160.515 kg 4745097 u.
Sub-Total	68.102 kg 1504251 u.	203.104 kg 236 u.	133.670 kg 54317 u.	703.329 kg 59.968 lt. 161222 u.	157.019 kg 0.022 lt. 25451 u.	722.352 kg 0.503 lt. 4748524 u.
South America						
Argentina	260 u.	[ICPO]	No Report		No Report	No Report
Brazil	No Report	No Report	No Report	No Report	No Report	59612 u. [ICPO]
Chile	No Report	No Report	No Report	No Report	2.977 kg	No Report
Colombia	No Report	No Report	No Report	No Report	No Report	1022 u.

Source: Annual Report Questionnaire if not otherwise indicated

Hallucinogens (excl. LSD but incl. 'Ecstasy')

Region/country or territory	1994	1995	1996	1997	1998	1999
AMERICAS						
South America						
Suriname	No Report	No Report	No Report	No Report	6000 u.	No Report
Uruguay	No Report	18 u.	20 u.	No Report	No Report	84 u.
Sub-Total	260 u.	18 u.	20 u.		2.977 kg 6000 u.	60718 u.
Total region	68.102 kg 1504511 u.	203.104 kg 254 u.	133.670 kg 54337 u.	703.329 kg 59.968 lt. 161222 u.	159.996 kg 0.022 lt. 31451 u.	722.386 kg 0.503 lt. 4810144 u.
ASIA						
Central Asia and Transcaucasian countries						
Kazakhstan	No Report	No Report	No Report	No Report	No Report	1099.000 kg
Sub-Total						1099.000 kg
East and South-East Asia						
Brunei Darussalam	No Report	No Report	No Report	No Report	No Report	32 u.
China (Hong Kong SAR)	No Report	20 u. [Govt]	No Report	49613 u.	265 u. [Govt]	21202 u. [ICPO]
Indonesia	7412 u.	0.334 kg 303 u.	0.444 kg 300052 u.	5.197 kg 89413 u.	119655 u.	32361 u.
Japan	2.150 kg 55 u.	0.013 kg	298 u.	56 u.	16 u. [(1]	5273 u.
Macau	No Report	No Report	1452 u. [ICPO]	No Report	64 u. [ICPO]	No Report
Malaysia	No Report	No Report	No Report	1397979 u.	1733335 u.	55975 u.
Singapore	No Report	No Report	No Report	No Report	2175 u.	5.170 kg 17232 u.
Thailand	No Report	15705 u. [HNLP]	9687 u. [HNLP]	13.005 kg 80047 u.	10395 u. [Govt]	269.620 kg [ICPO] [(2]
Sub-Total	2.150 kg 7467 u.	0.347 kg 16028 u.	0.444 kg 311489 u.	18.202 kg 1617108 u.	1865905 u.	274.790 kg 132075 u.
Near and Middle East /South-West Asia						
Israel	483 u.	No Report	No Report	No Report	5.000 kg 118501 u.	130.687 kg [ICPO] 30335 u.
Jordan	342 u.	No Report	No Report	10178 u.	No Report	5000 u. [ICPO]
Saudi Arabia	41516 u.	No Report	No Report	No Report	No Report	No Report
Sub-Total	42341 u.			10178 u.	5.000 kg 118501 u.	130.687 kg 35335 u.
Total region	2.150 kg 49808 u.	0.347 kg 16028 u.	0.444 kg 311489 u.	18.202 kg 1627286 u.	5.000 kg 1984406 u.	1504.477 kg 167410 u.
EUROPE						
Eastern Europe						
Belarus	No Report	No Report	0.305 kg	No Report	No Report	No Report
Bosnia Herzegovina	No Report	No Report	No Report	No Report	1041 u. [ICPO]	No Report
Croatia	No Report	No Report	No Report	0.004 kg	No Report	0.018 kg [ICPO] 15421 u.

Source: Annual Report Questionnaire if not otherwise indicated

Hallucinogens (excl. LSD but incl. 'Ecstasy')

Region/country or territory	1994	1995	1996	1997	1998	1999
EUROPE						
Eastern Europe						
Czech Republic	No Report	No Report	No Report	0.001 kg 4 u.	No Report	No Report
Estonia	No Report	No Report	2058 u. [ICPO]	No Report	No Report	0.000 lt. 1773 u.
FYR of Macedonia	No Report	No Report	No Report	No Report	787 u.	5532 u. [ICPO]
Hungary	No Report	No Report	No Report	No Report	11857 u.	510 u.
Latvia	No Report	0.260 kg 2080 u.	No Report	0.007 kg 23 u.	No Report	0.749 kg [ICPO] 9625 u.
Lithuania	No Report	No Report	56 u.	0.002 kg 1641 u.	831 u.	1122 u. [ICPO]
Poland	No Report	No Report	No Report	No Report	1736 u.	6319 u.
Romania	No Report	No Report	No Report	No Report	1093 u.	No Report
Russian Federation	631.333 kg [ICPO]	1.000 kg	0.800 kg	No Report	No Report	0.153 kg
Slovakia	No Report	No Report	No Report	No Report	No Report	9 u.
Slovenia	No Report	7354 u. [ICPO]	No Report	7440 u.	No Report	1749 u. [ICPO]
Ukraine	No Report	No Report	No Report	No Report	No Report	1.349 kg [ICPO] 18888 u.
Sub-Total	631.333 kg	1.260 kg 9434 u.	1.105 kg 2114 u.	0.014 kg 9108 u.	17345 u.	2.269 kg 0.000 lt. 60948 u.
Western Europe						
Andorra	3 u. [ICPO]	201 u. [ICPO]	No Report	No Report	88 u. [ICPO]	0.002 kg 43 u.
Austria	3.004 kg	31338 u.	25118 u.	23522 u.	114677 u.	31129 u.
Belgium	11.378 kg 55637 u.	12.767 kg 320441 u.	No Report	132.000 kg 125718 u.	33.044 kg	279.620 kg 467506 u.
Cyprus	No Report	No Report	No Report	3 u.	20 u.	0.001 kg 62 u.
Denmark	No Report	2115 u.	15262 u.	0.102 kg 5802 u.	27038 u. [(1]	26117 u.
Finland	No Report	No Report	No Report	0.195 kg 3147 u.	0.130 kg 2396 u.	16578 u. [ICPO]
France	1.076 kg [ICPO] 254804 u.	5.518 kg	1.522 kg	1.607 kg	4.795 kg	14.000 kg 1860402 u.
Germany	1.518 kg 254014 u.	380858 u.	692397 u.	694281 u.	419329 u.	1470507 u.
Gibraltar	No Report	No Report	300 u.	No Report	No Report	1.000 kg 2 u.
Greece	No Report	1554 u.	No Report	0.010 kg 136 u.	85 u.	3095 u.
Iceland	0.813 kg	1820 u.	No Report	No Report	No Report	7478 u.
Ireland	45305 u. [ICPO]	3.700 kg [ICPO] 123699 u.	No Report	9 u.	1.087 kg 616439 u.	74.609 kg 266462 u.

Source: Annual Report Questionnaire if not otherwise indicated

Hallucinogens (excl. LSD but incl. 'Ecstasy')

Region/country or territory	1994	1995	1996	1997	1998	1999
EUROPE						
Western Europe						
Italy	0.195 kg 91183 u.	0.140 kg 160185 u.	22958 u.	0.034 kg 161044 u.	1.580 kg 15 u.	0.673 kg[ICPO] 272397 u.
Liechtenstein	No Report	18 u.[ICPO]	No Report	565 u.	0.500 kg	No Report
Luxembourg	172 u.	784 u.	545 u.	367 u.	No Report	0.167 kg 357 u.
Malta	28 u.	519 u.	No Report	247 u.	153 u.	459 u.
Monaco	No Report	15 u.[ICPO]	No Report	No Report	No Report	3 u.[ICPO]
Netherlands	101.049 kg[INCB] 127037 u.	391.000 kg[ICPO] 40418 u.	No Report	1054918 u.	35.000 kg 1163514 u.	3663608 u.
Norway	810 u.	10103 u.	12852 u.	13182 u.	1.081 kg 15647 u.	0.025 kg 24644 u.
Portugal	614 u.	77 u.[ICPO]	No Report	No Report	10 u.	0.089 kg 31319 u.
San Marino	10 u.	No Report	No Report	No Report	No Report	No Report
Spain	306501 u.	739511 u.	340444 u.	184950 u.	194527 u.	357649 u.
Sweden	0.028 kg 26 u.	0.070 kg	0.122 kg	0.135 kg 1540 u.	0.579 kg	0.504 kg
Switzerland	28071 u.	46467 u.	81917 u.	86676 u.	73914 u.	67353 u.
Turkey	No Report	No Report	No Report	No Report	477250 u.	No Report
United Kingdom	1563800 u.	554800 u.	5798000 u.	1925500 u.	2095879 u.[3]	6323500 u.[NCIS]
Sub-Total	119.061 kg 2728015 u.	413.195 kg 2414923 u.	1.644 kg 6989793 u.	134.083 kg 4281607 u.	77.796 kg 5200981 u.	370.690 kg 14890670 u.
Total region	750.394 kg 2728015 u.	414.455 kg 2424357 u.	2.749 kg 6991907 u.	134.097 kg 4290715 u.	77.796 kg 5218326 u.	372.959 kg 0.000 lt. 14951620 u.
OCEANIA						
Oceania						
Australia	No Report	6.448 kg[4] 476 u.	2.110 kg 56128 u.	1.394 kg	7.380 kg[Govt (5]	16.497 kg[Govt (5]
New Zealand	3.878 kg[ICPO]	3.401 kg[ICPO] 269 u.	No Report	No Report	2665 u.	No Report
Sub-Total	3.878 kg	9.849 kg 745 u.	2.110 kg 56128 u.	1.394 kg	7.380 kg 2665 u.	16.497 kg
Total region	3.878 kg	9.849 kg 745 u.	2.110 kg 56128 u.	1.394 kg	7.380 kg 2665 u.	16.497 kg
TOTAL	824.524 kg 9.092 lt. 4283596 u.	627.755 kg 2471788 u.	138.973 kg 19.453 lt. 7413861 u.	857.022 kg 106.533 lt. 6198007 u.	250.172 kg 0.022 lt. 7348581 u.	2616.319 kg 0.503 lt. 19959380 u.

1) Small quantity. 2) Ketamine 3) Including other opiates. 4) Fiscal year 5) Provisional figures.

Source: Annual Report Questionnaire if not otherwise indicated

Region/country or territory	LSD					
	1994	1995	1996	1997	1998	1999
AFRICA						
North Africa						
Egypt	No Report	406 u.	669 u.	15 u.	514 u.	No Report
Sub-Total		406 u.	669 u.	15 u.	514 u.	
Southern Africa						
South Africa	16701 u.	3107 u.	11804 u.	2730 u.	6426 u.	1549 u.[ICPO]
Zambia	No Report	No Report	No Report	0.080 kg [ICPO]	No Report	No Report
Zimbabwe	No Report	2 u. [ICPO]	No Report	No Report	No Report	30 u.
Sub-Total	16701 u.	3109 u.	11804 u.	0.080 kg 2730 u.	6426 u.	1579 u.
Total region	16701 u.	3515 u.	12473 u.	0.080 kg 2745 u.	6940 u.	1579 u.
AMERICAS						
Caribbean						
Bahamas	3 u.	No Report	No Report	No Report	No Report	No Report
Bermuda	No Report	No Report	No Report	18 u.	No Report	No Report
Sub-Total	3 u.			18 u.		
North America						
Canada	0.227 kg 37049 u.	73523 u.	0.259 kg 17613 u.	22519 u.	0.295 kg 8955 u.	0.098 kg 9852 u.
United States	165232 u.	0.009 kg	0.099 kg 74396 u.	1.488 kg 0.452 lt. 79073 u.	No Report	0.330 kg 165504 u.
Sub-Total	0.227 kg 202281 u.	0.009 kg 73523 u.	0.358 kg 92009 u.	1.488 kg 0.452 lt. 101592 u.	0.295 kg 8955 u.	0.428 kg 175356 u.
South America						
Argentina	14621 u.	49105 u.	1291 u. [Govt]	563 u.	1435 u.	1085 u.
Brazil	47 u. [ICPO]	0.004 kg	No Report	3 u.	No Report	16 u. [Govt]
Chile	3624 u.	34 u. [ICPO]	1205 u.	1764 u.	153 u.	11 u. [CICAD]
Uruguay	No Report	28 u.	13 u. [Govt]	72 u.	1 u.	4 u.
Sub-Total	18292 u.	0.004 kg 49167 u.	2509 u.	2402 u.	1589 u.	1116 u.
Total region	0.227 kg 220576 u.	0.013 kg 122690 u.	0.358 kg 94518 u.	1.488 kg 0.452 lt. 104012 u.	0.295 kg 10544 u.	0.428 kg 176472 u.
ASIA						
Central Asia and Transcaucasian countries						
Uzbekistan	No Report	No Report	No Report	No Report	40 u.	No Report
Sub-Total					40 u.	

Source: Annual Report Questionnaire if not otherwise indicated

LSD

Region/country or territory	1994	1995	1996	1997	1998	1999
ASIA						
East and South-East Asia						
China (Hong Kong SAR)	68 u.	No Report	46 u.	52 u.	No Report	21 u.
Indonesia	No Report	3328 u.	3328 u.	No Report	103368 u.	53160 u.
Japan	3630 u.	2261423 u.	3668201 u.	3471 u.	4802 u.	62618 u.
Thailand	No Report	No Report	No Report	0.031 kg	No Report	No Report
Sub-Total	3698 u.	2264751 u.	3671575 u.	0.031 kg 3523 u.	108170 u.	115799 u.
Near and Middle East /South-West Asia						
Israel	0.360 kg 9150 u.	5796 u.	16660 u.	0.040 lt. 7342 u.	10337 u.	7346 u.[ICPO]
Kuwait	No Report	No Report	No Report	13245 u.	No Report	No Report
Saudi Arabia	No Report	No Report	3882730 u.[ICPO]	No Report	No Report	No Report
Sub-Total	0.360 kg 9150 u.	5796 u.	3899390 u.	0.040 lt. 20587 u.	10337 u.	7346 u.
South Asia						
India	256 u.	113 u.	1285 u.[Govt]	No Report	45 u.	20 u.
Nepal	No Report	18 u.	No Report	No Report	9 u.	No Report
Sub-Total	256 u.	131 u.	1285 u.		54 u.	20 u.
Total region	0.360 kg 13104 u.	2270678 u.	7572250 u.	0.031 kg 0.040 lt. 24110 u.	118601 u.	123165 u.
EUROPE						
Eastern Europe						
Croatia	223 u.	387 u.	172 u.	114 u.	86 u.	247 u.
Czech Republic	530 u.	500 u.	No Report	No Report	No Report	19 u.
Estonia	No Report	No Report	4 u.[ICPO]	No Report	No Report	6 u.
Hungary	665 u.[ICPO]	266 u.[ICPO]	1079 u.	1450 u.[Govt]	3351 u.	1928 u.
Latvia	No Report	No Report	16 u.	205 u.	38 u.	27 u.
Lithuania	No Report	No Report	No Report	2 u.	342 u.	164 u.
Poland	No Report	No Report	No Report	542 u.	14902 u.	14099 u.
Romania	No Report	13 u.	No Report	No Report	No Report	1 u.
Slovakia	No Report	No Report	No Report	2 u.	63 u.	72 u.
Slovenia	124 u.	No Report	947 u.	156 u.	53 u.	512 u.
Ukraine	No Report	No Report	No Report	14 u.	500 u.	36 u.[ICPO]
Yugoslavia	26 u.	No Report	No Report	No Report	No Report	No Report
Sub-Total	1568 u.	1166 u.	2218 u.	2485 u.	19335 u.	17111 u.
Western Europe						
Andorra	13 u.[ICPO]	148 u.[ICPO]	No Report	No Report	28 u.[ICPO]	No Report
Austria	1543 u.	2602 u.	4166 u.	5243 u.	2494 u.	2811 u.
Belgium	5237 u.	5458 u.	13704 u.	621 u.	2050 u.	1047 u.
Cyprus	No Report	No Report	1 u.	No Report	No Report	2 u.

Source: Annual Report Questionnaire if not otherwise indicated

LSD

Region/country or territory	1994	1995	1996	1997	1998	1999
EUROPE						
Western Europe						
Denmark	1335 u. [ICPO]	1282 u.	262 u.	381 u.	108 u.	83 u.
Finland	2541 u.	500 u.	41 u.	323 u.	301 u.	50 u.
France	74004 u. [Govt]	70217 u.	74780 u.	5983 u.	18680 u.	9991 u.
Germany	29627 u.	71069 u.	67082 u.	78430 u.	32250 u.	22965 u.
Gibraltar	No Report	No Report	3 u.	[1]	0.001 kg	No Report
Greece	323 u.	426 u.	1106 u.	166 u.	44 u.	212 u. [ICPO]
Iceland	369 u.	11 u.	No Report	No Report	No Report	339 u.
Ireland	No Report	819 u. [ICPO]	5901 u.	1851 u.	792 u.	648 u.
Italy	28684 u.	35499 u.	14191 u.	8140 u.	0.003 kg 9752 u.	5509 u. [ICPO]
Luxembourg	No Report	100 u. [ICPO]	122 u.	4 u.	0.303 kg	1 u.
Malta	1 u.	9 u.	45 u.	19 u.	123 u.	54 u.
Monaco	3 u.	No Report	No Report	No Report	10 u.	No Report
Netherlands	16030 u. [INCB]	305 u. [ICPO]	No Report	137218 u.	35954 u.	2423 u.
Norway	4758 u.	1321 u.	551 u.	6888 u.	2833 u.	483 u.
Portugal	No Report	11 u.	705 u.	84 u.	261 u.	1845 u.
San Marino	9 u.	No Report	No Report	No Report	No Report	No Report
Spain	7213 u.	15437 u.	13373 u.	25368 u.	9068 u.	3353 u.
Sweden	384 u.	373 u.	2459 u.	1541 u.	0.002 kg 2704 u.	1508 u.
Switzerland	1352 u.	5098 u.	9010 u.	9424 u.	2995 u.	3130 u.
Turkey	No Report	No Report	No Report	No Report	No Report	61 u.
United Kingdom	213500 u.	381800 u.	216400 u.	164100 u.	40070 u.	67400 u. [NCIS]
Sub-Total	386926 u.	592485 u.	423902 u.	445784 u.	0.309 kg 160517 u.	123915 u.
Total region	388494 u.	593651 u.	426120 u.	448269 u.	0.309 kg 179852 u.	141026 u.
OCEANIA						
Oceania						
Australia	22663 u. [2]	0.038 kg [2] 1364 u.	0.647 kg 6180 u.		No Report	No Report
New Zealand	7069 u. [ICPO]	18426 u. [Govt 3]	No Report	No Report	37554 u.	17437 u.
Sub-Total	29632 u.	0.038 kg 19790 u.	0.647 kg 6180 u.		37554 u.	17437 u.
Total region	29632 u.	0.038 kg 19790 u.	0.647 kg 6180 u.		37554 u.	17437 u.
TOTAL	0.587 kg 668507 u.	0.051 kg 3010324 u.	1.005 kg 8111541 u.	1.599 kg 0.492 lt. 579136 u.	0.604 kg 353491 u.	0.428 kg 459679 u.

1) Including depressants. 2) Fiscal year 3) Including cannabis herb.

Source: Annual Report Questionnaire if not otherwise indicated

Region/country or territory	1994	1995	1996	1997	1998	1999
Methaqualone						

AFRICA

East Africa

Region/country or territory	1994	1995	1996	1997	1998	1999
Kenya	22856 u.	537000 u.	(1	5000 u.	No Report	No Report
Uganda	No Report	No Report	78.354 kg	No Report	No Report	No Report
United Republic of Tanzania	778002 u.	14 u.	No Report	57 u.	4 u.	7 u.
Sub-Total	800858 u.	537014 u.	78.354 kg	5057 u.	4 u.	7 u.

North Africa

Region/country or territory	1994	1995	1996	1997	1998	1999
Egypt	143952 u.	No Report	No Report	No Report	No Report	No Report
Sub-Total	143952 u.					

Southern Africa

Region/country or territory	1994	1995	1996	1997	1998	1999
Angola	No Report	No Report	No Report	No Report	1.050 kg [ICPO]	No Report
Botswana	263498 u. [ICPO]	970 u. [ICPO]	No Report	No Report	No Report	No Report
Lesotho	143 u.	No Report	No Report	No Report	No Report	No Report
Malawi	610 u. [ICPO]	1986 u.	1000 u.	185.652 kg 200307 u.	1007 u. [Govt]	1800 u.
Namibia	2030 u.	3719 u.	4846 u.	No Report	6318 u.	2611 u.
South Africa	2668221 u.	30.008 kg 886846 u.	34.200 kg 432807 u.	50.561 kg 1629531 u.	160.000 kg 1307109 u.	2498806 u. [ICPO]
Swaziland	2093765 u. [ICPO]	26830 u. [ICPO]	7408 u. [ICPO]	15245 u. [ICPO]	12015 u.	1621 u.
Zambia	No Report	19550.488 kg [ICPO]	2.784 kg [ICPO]	0.004 kg [ICPO] 611 u.	0.125 kg [Govt]	2368 u.
Zimbabwe	1066 u. [Govt]	459 u. [ICPO]	No Report	No Report	4.300 kg 4431 u.	1701 u.
Sub-Total	5029333 u.	19580.500 kg 920810 u.	36.984 kg 446061 u.	236.217 kg 1845694 u.	165.475 kg 1330880 u.	2508907 u.

West and Central Africa

Region/country or territory	1994	1995	1996	1997	1998	1999
Congo	250000 u. [Govt (2]	No Report	No Report	No Report	No Report	No Report
Sub-Total	250000 u.					
Total region	6224143 u.	19580.500 kg 1457824 u.	115.338 kg 446061 u.	236.217 kg 1850751 u.	165.475 kg 1330884 u.	2508914 u.

AMERICAS

North America

Region/country or territory	1994	1995	1996	1997	1998	1999
Canada	0.183 kg [ICPO]	4 u.	0.002 kg 78 u.		0.007 kg	56.000 kg 123 u.
United States	273755 u.	12972 u.	80585 u.	1330 u.	No Report	32030 u.
Sub-Total	0.183 kg 273755 u.	12976 u.	0.002 kg 80663 u.	1330 u.	0.007 kg	56.000 kg 32153 u.

South America

Region/country or territory	1994	1995	1996	1997	1998	1999
Chile	10133 u.	No Report	No Report	No Report	1390 u.	No Report
Uruguay	19 u. [Govt]	No Report	No Report	No Report	No Report	No Report
Sub-Total	10152 u.				1390 u.	

Source: Annual Report Questionnaire if not otherwise indicated

Region/country or territory	1994	1995	1996	1997	1998	1999
Methaqualone						

AMERICAS

	1994	1995	1996	1997	1998	1999
Total region	0.183 kg 283907 u.	12976 u.	0.002 kg 80663 u.	1330 u.	0.007 kg 1390 u.	56.000 kg 32153 u.

ASIA

East and South-East Asia

	1994	1995	1996	1997	1998	1999
China (Hong Kong SAR)	No Report	No Report	25 u.	4 u.	No Report	187 u. ICPO
Indonesia	No Report	48294 u. ICPO	53290 u.	No Report	No Report	2018 u.
Myanmar	No Report	1002 u.	No Report	No Report	No Report	No Report
Philippines	7000.000 kg	No Report	No Report	No Report	No Report	No Report
Singapore	No Report	No Report		No Report	No Report	No Report
Sub-Total	7000.000 kg	49296 u.	53315 u.	4 u.		2205 u.

Near and Middle East /South-West Asia

	1994	1995	1996	1997	1998	1999
Israel	4177 u.	No Report	No Report	No Report	No Report	No Report
United Arab Emirates	238.000 kg	No Report	No Report	6000.815 kg	No Report	No Report
Sub-Total	238.000 kg 4177 u.			6000.815 kg		

South Asia

	1994	1995	1996	1997	1998	1999
India	45319.000 kg	20485.000 kg	2212.000 kg Govt	1740.000 kg	2257.000 kg	474.000 kg
Sub-Total	45319.000 kg	20485.000 kg	2212.000 kg	1740.000 kg	2257.000 kg	474.000 kg
Total region	52557.000 kg 4177 u.	20485.000 kg 49296 u.	2212.000 kg 53315 u.	7740.815 kg 4 u.	2257.000 kg	474.000 kg 2205 u.

EUROPE

Eastern Europe

	1994	1995	1996	1997	1998	1999
Romania	No Report	No Report	No Report	No Report	1924 u.	8487 u. ICPO
Sub-Total					1924 u.	8487 u.

Western Europe

	1994	1995	1996	1997	1998	1999
Belgium	20 u.	No Report	No Report	No Report	11.000 kg 52 u.	No Report
Cyprus	No Report	123 u. ICPO	No Report	No Report	No Report	No Report
Greece	No Report	No Report	No Report	41 u.	No Report	No Report
Switzerland	No Report	No Report	No Report	No Report	4620 u.	No Report
United Kingdom	5.000 kg					No Report
Sub-Total	5.000 kg 20 u.	123 u.		41 u.	11.000 kg 4672 u.	
Total region	5.000 kg 20 u.	123 u.		41 u.	11.000 kg 6596 u.	8487 u.

OCEANIA

Oceania

	1994	1995	1996	1997	1998	1999
Australia	No Report	(3	No Report	No Report	No Report	No Report
Sub-Total						

Source: Annual Report Questionnaire if not otherwise indicated

Region/country or territory	Methaqualone					
	1994	1995	1996	1997	1998	1999

OCEANIA

Total region

TOTAL	52562.180 kg	40065.500 kg	2327.340 kg	7977.032 kg	2433.482 kg	530.000 kg
	6512247 u.	1520219 u.	580039 u.	1852126 u.	1338870 u.	2551759 u.

1) Small quantity. 2) Including stimulants. 3) Including cannabis resin, liquid cannabis.

Source: Annual Report Questionnaire if not otherwise indicated

Synthetic narcotics

Region/country or territory	1994	1995	1996	1997	1998	1999
AFRICA						
North Africa						
Tunisia	No Report	13656 u. [ICPO]	No Report	No Report	No Report	No Report
Sub-Total		13656 u.				
Southern Africa						
Zambia	No Report	No Report	No Report	0.881 kg [ICPO] 383 u.	2.300 kg [Govt]	No Report
Sub-Total				0.881 kg 383 u.	2.300 kg	
West and Central Africa						
Côte d'Ivoire	No Report	216434 u.	No Report	No Report	No Report	No Report
Gambia	No Report	No Report	No Report	1750 u. [ICPO]	No Report	No Report
Ghana	98 u.	No Report	No Report	No Report	No Report	No Report
Mali	No Report	No Report	No Report	1.100 kg [ICPO] 3336 u.	No Report	No Report
Niger	No Report	No Report	No Report	752718 u. [ICPO]	No Report	No Report
Nigeria	No Report	56 u. [ICPO]	No Report	760.753 kg [ICPO]	No Report	No Report
Senegal	No Report	1264 u. [ICPO]	No Report	No Report	No Report	No Report
Sub-Total	98 u.	217754 u.		761.853 kg 757804 u.		
Total region	98 u.	231410 u.		762.734 kg 758187 u.	2.300 kg	
AMERICAS						
North America						
Canada	0.615 kg	0.173 kg 0.031 lt.	0.400 kg 1.963 lt. 827 u.	154.121 kg 0.286 lt. 2645 u.	0.281 kg 1764.550 lt. 4231 u.	1.025 kg 2.654 lt. 2461 u.
United States	80876 u.	0.027 kg 1652 u.	767.100 kg 6646 u.	No Report	No Report	2.883 kg 39037 u.
Sub-Total	0.615 kg 80876 u.	0.200 kg 0.031 lt. 1652 u.	767.500 kg 1.963 lt. 7473 u.	154.121 kg 0.286 lt. 2645 u.	0.281 kg 1764.550 lt. 4231 u.	3.908 kg 2.654 lt. 41498 u.
South America						
Argentina	No Report	0.359 kg [ICPO] 8406 u.	No Report	No Report	No Report	No Report
Sub-Total		0.359 kg 8406 u.				
Total region	0.615 kg 80876 u.	0.559 kg 0.031 lt. 10058 u.	767.500 kg 1.963 lt. 7473 u.	154.121 kg 0.286 lt. 2645 u.	0.281 kg 1764.550 lt. 4231 u.	3.908 kg 2.654 lt. 41498 u.

Source: Annual Report Questionnaire if not otherwise indicated

Synthetic narcotics

Region/country or territory	1994	1995	1996	1997	1998	1999
ASIA						
Central Asia and Transcaucasian countries						
Armenia	No Report	No Report	1.023 kg 1550 u.	No Report	No Report	No Report
Georgia	No Report	No Report	0.001 kg ICPO	No Report	No Report	No Report
Kazakhstan	No Report	No Report	No Report	No Report	11.576 kg	3.408 kg
Kyrgyzstan	No Report	0.322 kg	13.988 kg	0.020 kg	No Report	0.692 kg
Uzbekistan	No Report	No Report	No Report	287 u.	No Report	No Report
Sub-Total		0.322 kg	15.012 kg 1550 u.	0.020 kg 287 u.	11.576 kg	4.100 kg
East and South-East Asia						
Brunei Darussalam	No Report	145 u. ICPO	No Report	No Report	No Report	No Report
China	1103 u. ICPO	240212 u.	79373 u.	No Report	No Report	No Report
China (Hong Kong SAR)	0.124 kg	212.000 kg ICPO	No Report	No Report	No Report	1000 u.
Indonesia	0.740 kg 67 u.	No Report	138 u.	863 u.	No Report	550 u.
Japan	436 u.	3.011 kg 7411 u.	0.031 kg 15098 u.	0.013 kg 8240 u.	0.097 kg 11483 u.	0.048 kg 17968 u.
Korea (Republic of)	No Report	No Report	200 u.	No Report	No Report	0.046 kg
Macau	No Report	No Report	No Report	8968 u. ICPO	No Report	No Report
Malaysia	No Report	59541 u. ICPO	No Report	No Report	No Report	No Report
Philippines	No Report	No Report	No Report	93 u. ICPO	No Report	No Report
Singapore	280 u.	233 u.	69631 u.	7670 u.	No Report	No Report
Thailand	No Report	No Report	No Report	No Report	593.652 kg	No Report
Sub-Total	0.864 kg 1886 u.	215.011 kg 307542 u.	0.031 kg 164440 u.	0.013 kg 25834 u.	593.749 kg 11483 u.	0.094 kg 19518 u.
Near and Middle East /South-West Asia						
Kuwait	No Report	129832 u. ICPO	No Report	No Report	No Report	No Report
Qatar	No Report	No Report	No Report	2503 u. ICPO	No Report	No Report
Yemen	No Report	No Report	No Report	60 u. ICPO	No Report	No Report
Sub-Total		129832 u.		2563 u.		
South Asia						
Bangladesh	4810 u.	No Report	16075 u.	No Report	No Report	No Report
Maldives	No Report	No Report	No Report	No Report	No Report	140 u.
Nepal	No Report	No Report	No Report	6439 u. ICPO	No Report	No Report
Sub-Total	4810 u.		16075 u.	6439 u.		140 u.
Total region	0.864 kg 6696 u.	215.333 kg 437374 u.	15.043 kg 182065 u.	0.033 kg 35123 u.	605.325 kg 11483 u.	4.194 kg 19658 u.
EUROPE						
Eastern Europe						
Belarus	5.529 kg	No Report	No Report	No Report	0.080 kg	0.025 kg
Bulgaria	1.060 kg	0.343 kg	No Report	No Report	No Report	No Report

Source: Annual Report Questionnaire if not otherwise indicated

Region/country or territory	Synthetic narcotics					
	1994	**1995**	**1996**	**1997**	**1998**	**1999**
EUROPE						
Eastern Europe						
Croatia	2129 u.	3685 u.	4438 u.	3554 u.	6252 u.	635 u.
Estonia	No Report	No Report	No Report	No Report	0.012 kg 44 u.	0.011 kg 43 u.
Hungary	No Report	6.400 kg ^{ICPO}	No Report	No Report	No Report	No Report
Latvia	No Report	No Report	0.015 kg	No Report	No Report	No Report
Lithuania	15000 u.	No Report	0.022 kg 0.015 lt. 92 u.	0.001 lt. [(1]	No Report	No Report
Romania	No Report	No Report	No Report	No Report	1003 u.	No Report
Russian Federation	3427.500 kg ^{Govt}	852.002 kg ^{Govt}	No Report	287 u.	10230 u.	No Report
Slovakia	No Report	No Report	No Report	No Report	No Report	1309 u.
Slovenia	886 u.	No Report	186 u.	81 u.	No Report	No Report
Ukraine	No Report	No Report	9.782 kg	No Report	No Report	No Report
Sub-Total	3434.089 kg 18015 u.	858.745 kg 3685 u.	9.819 kg 0.015 lt. 4716 u.	0.001 lt. 4174 u.	0.092 kg 17529 u.	0.036 kg 1987 u.
Western Europe						
Andorra	No Report	31 u. ^{ICPO}	No Report	No Report	No Report	No Report
Austria	No Report	0.106 kg ^{ICPO}	No Report	No Report	No Report	No Report
Belgium	0.001 kg 0.003 lt. 500 u.	549 u. ^{ICPO}	No Report	1100 u.	No Report	9.300 kg
Denmark	No Report	2273 u. ^{ICPO}	No Report	No Report	No Report	No Report
France	No Report	1164 u.	630 u.	854 u.	5085 u.	521 u.
Germany	0.074 kg 4599 u.	0.555 kg 1932 u.	4443 u.	0.180 kg 0.994 lt. 3482 u.	No Report	No Report
Greece	No Report	0.009 kg 19 u.	No Report	No Report	20 u.	No Report
Ireland	987 u. ^{ICPO}	No Report	No Report	34.000 lt. 408 u.	0.009 kg 1960 u.	No Report
Italy	1.557 kg 2231 u.	3.117 kg 156 u.	1.902 kg	0.077 kg 5080 u.	3.045 kg 134359 u.	No Report
Luxembourg	No Report	5 u. ^{ICPO}	No Report	No Report	No Report	No Report
Malta	0.800 lt. 2 u.	0.121 lt.	94 u.	0.005 kg	0.030 lt. 23 u.	No Report
Netherlands	No Report	1.000 kg ^{ICPO} 2946 u.	No Report	No Report	No Report	No Report
Norway	6507 u.	5877 u.	14431 u.	16076 u.	0.104 kg 17949 u.	0.004 kg 9170 u.
Portugal	No Report	0.200 kg ^{ICPO}	No Report	0.001 kg 7 u.	2 u.	0.021 kg 27 u.
Switzerland	2183 u.	2857 u.	No Report	5.231 kg	33.190 kg	No Report
Turkey	270828 u.	135629 u.	259097 u.	No Report	257493 u.	55067 u.

Source: Annual Report Questionnaire if not otherwise indicated

Region/country or territory	1994	1995	1996	1997	1998	1999
EUROPE						
Western Europe						
United Kingdom	53.500 kg	54.700 kg	87.500 kg	117.200 kg	70.584 kg	No Report
Sub-Total	55.132 kg	59.687 kg	89.402 kg	122.694 kg	106.932 kg	9.325 kg
	0.803 lt.	0.121 lt.	278695 u.	34.994 lt.	0.030 lt.	64785 u.
	287837 u.	153438 u.		27007 u.	416891 u.	
Total region	3489.221 kg	918.432 kg	99.221 kg	122.694 kg	107.024 kg	9.361 kg
	0.803 lt.	0.121 lt.	0.015 lt.	34.995 lt.	0.030 lt.	66772 u.
	305852 u.	157123 u.	283411 u.	31181 u.	434420 u.	
OCEANIA						
Oceania						
Australia	No Report	2.173 kg [2]	2.563 kg	2.259 kg	No Report	No Report
		0.140 lt.	0.250 lt.			
		2 u.	3 u.			
New Zealand	205 u. [ICPO]	2148 u. [ICPO]	No Report	No Report	No Report	No Report
Sub-Total	205 u.	2.173 kg	2.563 kg	2.259 kg		
		0.140 lt.	0.250 lt.			
		2150 u.	3 u.			
Total region	205 u.	2.173 kg	2.563 kg	2.259 kg		
		0.140 lt.	0.250 lt.			
		2150 u.	3 u.			
TOTAL	3490.700 kg	1136.497 kg	884.327 kg	1041.841 kg	714.930 kg	17.463 kg
	0.803 lt.	0.292 lt.	2.228 lt.	35.281 lt.	1764.580 lt.	2.654 lt.
	393727 u.	838115 u.	472952 u.	827136 u.	450134 u.	127928 u.

Synthetic narcotics

1) Including depressants. 2) Fiscal year

Source: Annual Report Questionnaire if not otherwise indicated

Psychotropic substances

Region/country or territory	1994	1995	1996	1997	1998	1999
AFRICA						
West and Central Africa						
Mauritania	No Report	No Report	No Report	147 u. GSR	135 u. GSR	No Report
Sub-Total				147 u.	135 u.	
Total region				147 u.	135 u.	
AMERICAS						
North America						
Mexico	46685 u.	569789 u.	No Report	No Report	1484078 u.	1490152 u.
Sub-Total	46685 u.	569789 u.			1484078 u.	1490152 u.
Total region	46685 u.	569789 u.			1484078 u.	1490152 u.
ASIA						
Central Asia and Transcaucasian countries						
Uzbekistan	No Report	No Report	No Report	No Report	No Report	0.639 kg
Sub-Total						0.639 kg
Near and Middle East /South-West Asia						
United Arab Emirates	No Report	No Report	No Report	No Report	No Report	14460 u.
Sub-Total						14460 u.
Total region						0.639 kg 14460 u.
EUROPE						
Eastern Europe						
Russian Federation	No Report	No Report	No Report	No Report	673.400 kg F.O.	905.500 kg F.O.
Sub-Total					673.400 kg	905.500 kg
Total region					673.400 kg	905.500 kg
TOTAL	46685 u.	569789 u.		147 u.	673.400 kg 1484213 u.	906.139 kg 1504612 u.

Source: Annual Report Questionnaire if not otherwise indicated

HEROIN WHOLESALE AND RETAIL PRICES PER GRAM IN WESTERN EUROPE (*), 1987-1999

(*) Weighted average (by population) of: Austria, Belgium, Denmark, Finland, France, Germany, Greece, Iceland, Ireland, Italy, Luxembourg, Netherlands, Norway, Portugal, Spain, Sweden, Switzerland, United Kingdom

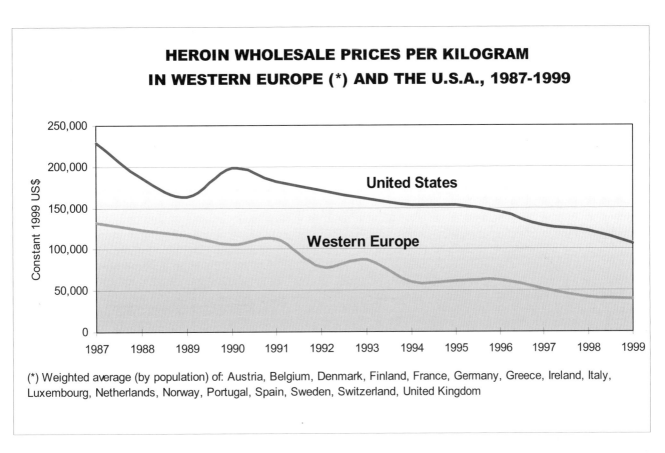

HEROIN WHOLESALE PRICES PER KILOGRAM IN WESTERN EUROPE (*) AND THE U.S.A., 1987-1999

(*) Weighted average (by population) of: Austria, Belgium, Denmark, Finland, France, Germany, Greece, Ireland, Italy, Luxembourg, Netherlands, Norway, Portugal, Spain, Sweden, Switzerland, United Kingdom

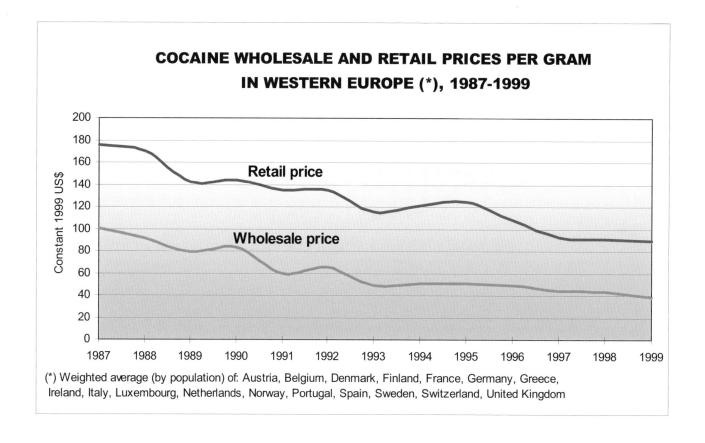

COCAINE WHOLESALE AND RETAIL PRICES PER GRAM IN WESTERN EUROPE (*), 1987-1999

(*) Weighted average (by population) of: Austria, Belgium, Denmark, Finland, France, Germany, Greece, Ireland, Italy, Luxembourg, Netherlands, Norway, Portugal, Spain, Sweden, Switzerland, United Kingdom

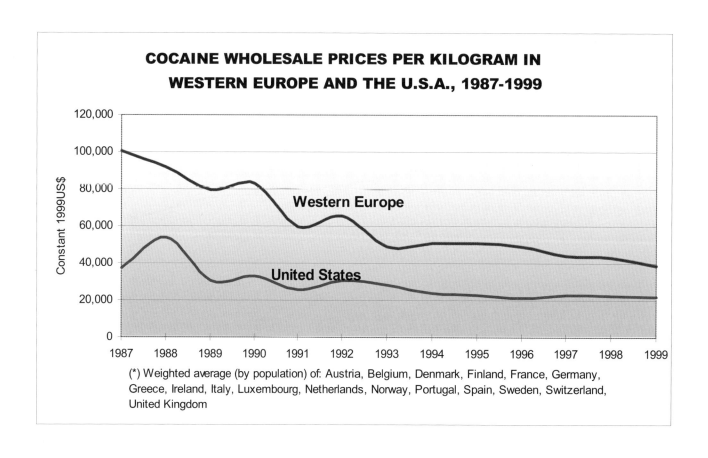

COCAINE WHOLESALE PRICES PER KILOGRAM IN WESTERN EUROPE AND THE U.S.A., 1987-1999

(*) Weighted average (by population) of: Austria, Belgium, Denmark, Finland, France, Germany, Greece, Ireland, Italy, Luxembourg, Netherlands, Norway, Portugal, Spain, Sweden, Switzerland, United Kingdom

WHOLESALE AND STREET PRICES

Retail and wholesale prices and purity levels:
breakdown by drug, region and country or territory
(prices expressed in US$ or converted equivalent, and purity levels in percentage)

Opium

Region / country or territory	RETAIL PRICE (per gram)				WHOLESALE PRICE (per kilogram)			
	Range	Average	Purity	Year	Range	Average	Purity	Year
Africa								
East Africa								
Uganda	17.0 - 30.0	23.5	-	1996				
Southern Africa								
Zambia	10.7	10.7	-	1999				
Americas								
Central America								
Guatemala					1,888.7	1,888.7	-	1996
North America								
Canada	14.0 - 99.3	38.9	-	1999	14,569.5 - 23,178.8	18,543.0	-	1999
South America								
Colombia					400.0	400.0	-	1999
Asia								
Central Asia and Transcaucasia								
Armenia	10.0	10.0	-	2000	1,000.0	1,000.0	-	1999
Azerbaijan					1,500.0 - 2,000.0	1,750.0	-	1999
Kyrgyzstan	0.8	0.8	-	1999	500.0 - 800.0	650.0	-	1999
Tajikistan	0.6 - 0.8	0.7	90.0	1999	80.0 - 300.0	190.0		2000
Turkmenistan					1,000.0 - 2,000.0	1,500.0	-	2000
Uzbekistan	1.0 - 2.5	1.8	-	1999	600.0 - 1,500.0	1,050.0	-	1999
East and South-East Asia								
Malaysia					513.3	513.3	-	1998
Myanmar					241.3	241.3	-	1999
Singapore	4.9 - 5.6	5.3	-	1997				
Viet Nam					300.0 - 1,500.0	900.0	-	1996
Near and Middle East /South-West Asia								
Afghanistan					27.0 - 72.0	49.5	-	1999
Bahrain	2.3	2.3	-	1996				
Iran (Islamic Republic of)	2.4 - 2.9	2.7	-	2000	2,400.0	2,400.0	-	2000
Jordan	70.0	70.0	-	1996				
Pakistan	0.1 - 0.2	0.1	80.0 - 100.0	1999	78.5 - 119.2	98.9	80.0 - 100.0	1999
South Asia								
India	0.3 - 0.4	0.3		1999	98.6 - 369.6	234.1	-	1998
Europe								
Eastern Europe								
Russian Federation	40.0	40.0	-	1999	2,700.0	2,700.0	-	1999
Western Europe								
Cyprus	43.0	43.0	-	1996	12,903.0	12,903.0	-	1996
Greece	7.3	7.3	70.0 - 80.0	1997	5,474.0	5,474.0	80.0 - 90.0	1997
Sweden	22.0	22.0		2000	5,490.0 - 10,990.0	8,240.0	-	2000
Turkey	17.5 - 19.7	18.6		1999	546.7 - 1,093.5	820.1	-	1999
United Kingdom	18.0	18.0		2000				

Heroin

Region / country or territory	RETAIL PRICE (per gram)				WHOLESALE PRICE (per kilogram)			
	Range	Average	Purity	Year	Range	Average	Purity	Year
Africa								
East Africa								
Kenya	10.0 - 13.0	11.5	-	1999	13,000.0	13,000.0	-	1999
Mauritius	402.4	402.4	10.0 - 35.0	1999	201,191.1	201,191.1	10.0 - 35.0	1999
Uganda	7.0 - 10.0	8.5	-	2000	10,000.0 - 14,000.0	12,000.0	80.0	2000
United Republic of Tanzania	25.0	25.0	-	1999	18,800.0	18,800.0	-	1999
North Africa								
Algeria					189,193.9	189,193.9	-	1999
Egypt	71.4 - 85.7	78.6	-	2000	34,290.0 - 42,860.0	38,575.0	-	2000
Southern Africa								
Namibia					65,500.0	65,500.0	-	2000
South Africa	19.6 - 49.1	32.7	-	1999				
Swaziland	75.0	75.0	-	1998	50,000.0	50,000.0	-	1998
West and Central Africa								
Benin	20.2	20.2	-	1998	18,500.0	18,500.0	-	1998
Côte d'Ivoire					28,850.0	28,850.0	-	1996
Ghana	23.5 - 31.4	27.4	60.0 - 90.0	1999	36,000.0	36,000.0	90.0	1997
Americas								
Central America								
Costa Rica					100,000.0	100,000.0	95.0	1999
Guatemala	24.4	24.4	10.0	1996	55,386.3	55,386.3	100.0	1999
Panama					25,000.0	25,000.0	90.0	1998
North America								
Canada	107.3 - 268.3	187.8	-	1999	63.715.6 - 100,603.6	82,159.6	-	1999
United States	50.0 - 900.0	475.0	40.0	1999	14,000.0 - 200,000.0	107,000.00	80.0	1999
South America								
Colombia	25.0	25.0	-	1999	15,000.0 - 20,000.0	17,500.0	-	1999
Ecuador					5,000.0	5,000.0	96.0	1999
Venezuela	25.0	25.0	-	1999	19,989.6	19,989.6	-	1999
Caribbean								
Bermuda	220.0	220.0	-	1997				
Dominican Republic	25.0 - 40.0	32.5	-	1999	25,000.0 - 40,000.0	32,500.0	85.0 - 90.0	1999
Saint Lucia	30.0	30.0	-	2000	25,000.0	25,000.0	-	2000
Asia								
Central Asia and Transcaucasia								
Armenia	120.0	120.0	-	2000				
Azerbaijan	50.0 - 100.0	75.0	-	1999	50,000.0 - 60,000.0	55,000.0	-	1999
Kyrgyzstan	8.0 - 10.0	9.0	-	1999	6,000.0 - 8,000.0	7,000.0	-	1999
Tajikistan	1.7 - 2.0	1.85	90.0	1999	800.0 - 2,800.0	1,270.0		2000
Turkmenistan					12,500.0 - 25,000.0	18,750.0	-	2000
Uzbekistan	10.0 - 20.0	15.0	-	1999	2,000.0 - 10,000.0	5,666.7	-	2000
East and South-East Asia								
Brunei Darussalam	249.1	249.1	-	1998	239,521.0	239,521.0	-	1998
China (Hong Kong SAR)	49.8	49.8	46.4	1999	18,419.2 - 21,377.7	19,898.5	100.0	1999
Indonesia	45.5	45.5	-	1999	42,223.7	42,223.7	-	1999
Malaysia	81.3 - 609.8	355.7	32.5	1997	1,340.0	1,340.0	-	1998
Myanmar					3,619.9	3,619.9	-	1999
Philippines	90.1 - 128.7	109.4	90.0	1999				
Republic of Korea	593.0 - 762.4	677.7	90.0	1999	372,744.6	372,744.6	90.0	1999
Singapore	29.9 - 59.9	44.9	4.0	1998	2,904.3 - 3,300.3	3,102.3	-	1998
Thailand	24.3 - 72.9	48.6	70.0 - 90.0	1998	7,292.2 - 9,722.9	8,507.5	70.0 - 90.0	1998
Near and Middle East/ South- West Asia								
Afghanistan	2.8	2.8	-	1996	2,727.00	2,727.00	-	1996
Iran (Islamic Republic of)					2,400.0	2,400.0	-	2000
Israel	24.8 - 74.0	49.4	-	1998	20,000.0 - 45,000.0	32,500.0	-	1998

Heroin

Region / country or territory	RETAIL PRICE (per gram)				WHOLESALE PRICE (per kilogram)			
	Range	Average	Purity	Year	Range	Average	Purity	Year
Jordan	42.4 - 56.5	49.4	-	2000	19,770.0	19,770.0	-	2000
Kuwait					98,684.2	98,684.2	-	1998
Lebanon	20.0	20.0	40.0	1997	18,000.0 - 22,000.0	20,000.0	60.0 - 80.0	2000
Pakistan	1.8 - 4.0	2.9	50.0 - 80.0	1999	596.1 - 3,676.0	2,136.1	50.0 - 80.0	1999
Qatar	137.0 - 164.1	150.6	-	1996	54,945.0 - 82,420.0	68,682.5	-	1996
Saudi Arabia					266,666.0	266,666.0	25.0	1998
Syrian Arab Republic	43.5	43.5	-	1999	32,608.70	32,608.70	-	1999
South Asia								
India	2.8 - 7.6	5.2	-	1999	1,232.1 - 4,928.5	3,080.3	20.0 - 60.0	1998
Maldives	213.3	213.3	-	1999	85,324.2	85,324.2	-	1999
Nepal	14.3 - 26.9	20.6	-	1996	15,000.0 - 25,000.0	20,000.0	-	1998
Sri Lanka	21.5 - 28.6	25.1	-	1999	11,452.1 - 14,315.2	12,883.6	-	1999
Europe								
Eastern Europe								
Bulgaria	9.8 - 12.0	10.9	10.0	1999	43,739.7	43,739.7	40.0 - 60.0	1999
Croatia	48.0	48.0	10.0 - 15.0	2000	16,200.0 - 18,010.0	17,105.0	50.0 - 80.0	2000
Czech Republic	29.4	29.4	45.0	1999	11,746.4 - 23,492.8	17,619.6	-	1999
Hungary	25.49 - 29.74	27.6	10.0 - 50.0	1999	10,934.9	10,934.9	40.0 - 80.0	1999
Latvia	103.1	103.1	-	1999	34,364.3	34,364.3	-	1999
Lithuania	35.0 - 50.0	42.5	40.0 - 85.0	2000	20,000.0 - 35,000.0	27,500.0	40.0 - 85.0	2000
Poland					52,645.4 - 65,806	59,226.1	-	1999
Romania	22.0 - 35.0	28.5	70.0 - 90.0	1998	18,000.0 - 25,000.0	21,500.0	70.0 - 90.0	1998
Russian Federation	20.0 - 45.0	27.0	-	1999	30,000.0	30,000.0	-	1999
Slovakia	19.5 - 29.2	24.3	5.0 - 12.0	1999	8,201.2 - 16,402.4	12,301.8	20.0 - 90.0	1999
Slovenia	55.6 - 74.1	64.9	25.0 - 30.0	2000	23,140.0 - 27,770.0	25,455.0	30.0 - 50.0	2000
The form.Yug.Rep of Macedonia	28.3 - 39.6	33.9	-	1998	10,175.2 - 12,436.2	11,305.8		1998
Western Europe								
Andorra	128.5	128.5	-	1999				
Austria	72.6 - 112.9	92.7	-	1998	40,322.6 - 64,516.1	52,419.4	60.0 - 70.0	1998
Belgium	39.8	39.8	-	1999	15,905.8 - 21,207.8	18,556.8	-	1999
Cyprus	155.0 - 290.7	222.9	-	1998	38,759.7 - 48,449.6	43,604.7	-	1998
Denmark	89.0 - 237.4	163.2	25.0 - 30.0	1998	10,387.3 - 74,195.0	42,291.1	80.0	1998
Finland	148.9 - 372.3	204.7	-	1999				
France	32.6 - 40.8	36.7	40.0	1999	11,411.8 - 40,756.4	26,084.1	6.0 - 91.0	1999
Germany	19.4 - 58.2	47.8	-	2000	12,920.0 - 27,610.0	20,265.0	-	2000
Gibraltar					117,000.0	117,000.0	20.0	1997
Greece	60.6 - 67.3	64.0	10.0 - 40.0	1998	14,599.0 - 36,494.0	25,547.5	15.0 - 40.0	1998
Iceland	372.0	372.0	-	1998				
Ireland	203.8	203.8	25.0 - 35.0	1999	43,478.3	43,478.3	60.0 - 70.0	1999
Italy	91.9 - 106.2	99.0	-	1998	35,598.1 - 39,043.1	37,320.6	-	1998
Liechtenstein	34.7 - 62.4	48.5	-	1997	27,760.0	27,760.0	-	1997
Luxembourg	108.0 - 170.5	138.5	-	1998	47,717.5 - 53,019.5	50,368.5	-	1999
Malta	70.9	70.9	20.0	2000	47,240.0	47,240.0	60.0	2000
Monaco	86.5	86.5	65.0	1997	87,100.0	87,100.0	65.0	1997
Netherlands	24.3 - 60.7	42.5	-	1999	12,376.2 - 17,708.3	15,757.4	-	1998
Norway	102.3 - 230.2	166.2	10.0 - 70.0	1999	35,805.6 - 63,938.6	49,938.6	10.0 - 70.0	1999
Portugal	33.5	33.5	-	1999	27,777.8 - 47,058.8	36,056.6	-	1997
Spain	76.2	76.2	33.0	1999	45,633.9	45,633.9	-	1999
Sweden	131.9 - 164.8	148.6	30.0	2000	38,460.0 - 87,900.0	63,180.0	50.0 - 60.0	2000
Switzerland	167.1	167.1	20.0	1999	13,369.0 - 53,475.9	33,422.5	-	1999
Turkey					8,750.0 - 9,840.0	9.295.0	-	1999
United Kingdom	123.3	123.3	41.0	1998	25,890.0 - 32,362.5	29126.2	41.0	1999
Oceania								
Australia	63.9 - 319.7	191.8	-	1999	84,030.0 - 127,880.0	105,955.0	-	1999
New Zealand	422.6 - 633.9	528.3	-	1999				

Cocaine

Region / country or territory	RETAIL PRICE (per gram)				WHOLESALE PRICE (per kilogram)			
	Range	Average	Purity	Year	Range	Average	Purity	Year
Africa								
East Africa								
Kenya	60.0	60.0	-	2000	50,000.0	50,000.0	-	2000
Uganda	100.0	100.0	-	2000	200,000.0	200,000.0	90.0	2000
North Africa								
Egypt	200.0 - 228.6	214.3	-	2000	114,300.0 - 142,870.0	128,585.0	-	2000
Southern Africa								
Namibia	65.5	65.5	-	2000	65,500.0	65,500.0	-	2000
South Africa	29.4 - 65.4	40.9	-	1999	26,800.0 - 33,500.0	30,150.0	-	1997
Swaziland					7,600.0	7,600.0	-	1999
Zambia	26.8	26.8	90.0	1999				
Zimbabwe	26.6 - 53.3	40.0		1999				
West and Central Africa								
Côte d'Ivoire					96,150.0	96,150.0	-	1996
Ghana					31,368.5 - 47,052.8	39,210.7	80.0	1999
Nigeria	11.9	11.9	-	1997				
Americas								
Central America								
Costa Rica	8.1 - 9.2	8.6	75.0 - 90.0	1999	6,344.8 - 8,107.3	7,226.0	75.0 - 90.0	1999
El Salvador	6.9	6.9	-	1999	5,733.9 - 6,307.3	6,020.6	75.0 - 80.0	1999
Guatemala	14.3	14.3	80.0	1998	13,846.6	13,846.6	80.0	1999
Honduras					4,690.0	4,690.0	-	1997
Panama	2.0 - 200.0	68.0	10.0 - 90.0	1998	2,500.0	2,500.0	93.0	1998
North America								
Canada	41.1 - 137.0	89.1	75.0	1998	23,474.2 - 40,241.4	31,857.8		1998
United States	17.6 - 275.0	67.1	63.0	1999	8,000.0 - 52,000.0	22,348.0	55.0	1999
South America								
Argentina	1.4 - 3.9	2.6	-	1998	900.0 - 3,510.0	2,080.0	-	1998
Bolivia	0.6	0.6	60.0	1997	1,000.0	1,000.0	100.0	1999
Brazil	4.9	4.9	-	1997	2,500.0	2,500.0	-	1996
Chile	2.4	2.4	-	1997	6,000.0	6,000.0	95.0	1998
Colombia	2.5	2.5	-	1999	1,800.0 - 2,000.0	1,900.0		1999
Ecuador	1.0	1.0	70.0	1999	2,000.0	2,000.0	96.0	1999
Guyana	6.0 - 10.0	8.0	-	1996	4,500.0 - 6,210.0	5,360.0	-	1996
Paraguay	6.5	6.5	-	1999	3,500.0	3,500.0		1999
Peru	0.7 - 1.4	1.1	-	1997				
Suriname	4.0	4.0	-	1998	3,000.0	3,000.0	99.0	1998
Uruguay	12.0	12.0	-	2000	5,200.0	5,200.0	85.0 - 90.0	2000
Venezuela	4.2 - 5.8	5.00	-	1999	3,331.6 - 4,997.4	4,164.5	-	1999
Caribbean								
Bahamas	14.0 - 19.0	16.5	-	1998	8,000.0 - 13,000.0	10,500.0	-	1998
Bermuda	105.8	105.8	-	1999	70,550.0 - 141,100.0	105,830.0	70.0 - 90.0	1997
Cayman Islands	40.0	40.0	60.0	1999	10,000.0 - 12,000.0	11,000.0	80.0	1999
Cuba	100.0	100.0	-	1996	5,000.0 - 10,000.0	7,500.0	70.0 - 90.0	1996
Dominican Republic	8.0 - 9.0	8.5	-	1999	8,000.0 - 9,000.0	8,500.00	85.0 - 90.0	1999
Saint Lucia	10.0	10.0	-	2000	8,000.0	8,000.0	-	2000
Trinidad Tobago					3,500.0 - 5,500.0	4,500.0	-	1998
Turks and Caicos Islands	100.0	100.0	-	1997	150,000.0	150,000.0	-	1999

Cocaine

Region / country or territory	RETAIL PRICE (per gram)				WHOLESALE PRICE (per kilogram)			
	Range	Average	Purity	Year	Range	Average	Purity	Year
Asia								
Central Asia and Transcaucasia								
Azerbaijan	125.00	125.00	-	1999				
East and South-East Asia								
China (Hong Kong SAR)	156.0 - 194.7	175.3	-	1999	38,084.2 - 45,184.6	41,634.4	-	1999
Indonesia	70.0	70.0	-	1998				
Philippines	90.1 - 128.7	109.4	-	1999				
Republic of Korea	593.0 - 847.1	720.1	85.0	1999	338,858.7	338,858.7	85.0	1999
Near and Middle East /South-West Asia								
Israel	119.3 - 159.2	139.3	-	1996	37,000.0 - 52,000.0	44,500.0	-	1998
Jordan	141.2	141.2	-	1998	70,620.0	70,620.0	-	1998
Lebanon	25.0 - 40.0	32.5	30.0	2000	100,000.0	100,000.0	90.0	2000
Saudi Arabia					9,070.0	9,070.0	19.0	1998
Europe								
Eastern Europe								
Bulgaria	53.0 - 64.7	58.9	-	1997	82,350.0	82,350.0	-	1997
Croatia	72.0 - 96.0	84.0	70.0 - 80.0	2000	32,410.0 - 36,010.0	34,210.0	80.0 - 90.0	2000
Czech Republic	73.4 - 88.1	80.8	-	1999	58,732.0 - 73,415.0	66,073.5		1999
Estonia	100.0	100.0	50.0	1999				
Hungary	63.7 - 68.0	65.8	60.0 - 80.0	1999	33,986.4 - 38,234.7	36,110.6	60.0 - 80.0	1999
Lithuania	100.0	100.0	47.0 - 89.0	1999	70,000.0 - 75,000.0	72,500.0	47.0 - 89.0	1999
Poland					65,806.8 - 78,968.1	72,387.5	-	1999
Romania	50.0 - 70.0	60.0	-	1999	33,000.0 - 38,000.0	35,500.0	-	1999
Russian Federation	150.0	150.0	-	1999	75,000.0	75,000.0	-	1999
Slovakia	43.8 - 60.8	52.3	20.0 - 90.0	1999	60,000.0	60,000.0	90.0	1999
Slovenia	40.0 - 100.0	70.0	-	1999	35,000.0 - 50,000.0	42,500.0	-	1999
Ukraine	150.0	150.0	90.0	1999				
Western Europe								
Andorra	64.3 - 77.1	70.7	-	1999				
Austria	69.9 - 116.6	93.3	20.0 - 40.0	1999	31,087.3 - 46,630.9	38,859.1	70.0 - 80.0	1999
Belgium	39.8 - 79.5	59.6	-	1999	15,905.8 - 31,811.7	23,858.8	-	1999
Cyprus	158.1 - 197.6	177.9	-	1998	50,000.0 - 60,000.0	55,000.0	-	1999
Denmark	100.4 - 229.5	165.0	59.0	1999	43,000.0 - 114,800.0	78,900.0	-	1997
Finland	146.8 - 211.9	178.7	-	1998				
France	60.0 - 84.7	72.4	-	2000	27,714.4	27,714.4	60.0 - 93.0	1999
Germany	33.6 - 80.5	57.1	-	2000	23,020 - 44,490.0	37,755.0	-	2000
Gibraltar					117,000.0	117,000.0	90.0	1997
Greece	65.8 - 98.6	82.2	65.0 - 85.0	1999	32,879.9 - 65,759.8	49,319.9	65.0 - 85.0	1999
Iceland	148.8	148.8	-	1998				
Ireland	108.7	108.7	60.0 - 70.0	1999	29,891.3	29,891.3	60.0 - 70.0	1999
Italy	98.6 - 121.1	109.7	-	1998	44,000.0 - 50,500.0	47,250.0	-	1999
Liechtenstein	67.6 - 101.4	84.5	40.0 - 50.0	1998	33,780.0 - 47,300.0	40,540.0	70.0 - 80.0	1998
Luxembourg	79.5 - 159.1	119.3	15.0 - 35.0	1999	42,415.6 - 53,019.5	47,717.5	85.0 - 90.0	1999
Malta	82.7	82.7	40.0	2000	70,870.0	70,870.0	60.0	2000
Monaco	203.0	203.0	-	1997				
Netherlands	48.5 - 72.8	60.7	-	1999	25,000.0 - 30,000.0	27,500.0	-	1999
Norway	102.3 - 153.5	127.9	70.0 - 90.0	1999	38,363.2 - 76,726.3	57,544.8	70.0 - 90.0	1999
Portugal	43.2	43.2	-	1999	25,000.0 - 35,000.0	30,000.0	-	1999
Spain	63.0	63.0	54.5	1999	38,898.1	38,898.1	75.0	1999
Sweden	65.9 - 87.9	76.9	-	2000	32,960.0 - 43,950.0	38,455.0	75.0 - 80.0	2000

Cocaine

Region / country or territory	RETAIL PRICE (per gram)				WHOLESALE PRICE (per kilogram)			
	Range	Average	Purity	Year	Range	Average	Purity	Year
Switzerland	55.6 - 173.6	114.6	-	1997	24,310.0 - 55,560.0	39,940.0	-	1997
Turkey					75,000.0 - 85,000.0	80,000.0	-	1999
United Kingdom	101.9	101.9	61.6	1999	32,362.5 - 35,598.7	33,980.6	-	1999
OCEANIA								
Australia	159.9 - 511.5	335.7	-	1999	70,330.0 - 83,120.0	76,725.0	-	1999
New Zealand	158.5 - 211.3	184.9	-	1999				

Herbal cannabis

Region / country or territory	RETAIL PRICE (per gram)				WHOLESALE PRICE (per kilogram)			
	Range	Average	Purity	Year	Range	Average	Purity	Year
Africa								
East Africa								
Kenya	0.1	0.1	-	1996	119.8	119.8	-	1996
Mauritius	8.0 - 12.1	10.1	-	1999	12,071.5	12,071.5		1999
Seychelles	6.0	6.0	-	1998	3,600.0 - 4,510.0	4,055.0	-	2000
Uganda	0.03 - 0.15	0.1	-	2000	100.0 - 150.0	125.0	-	2000
North Africa								
Egypt	5.1	5.1	-	1996	2,990.0 - 3,580.0	3,285.0	-	1996
Morocco					426.0	426.0	-	1997
Southern Africa								
Malawi					400.0	400.0		1999
Namibia	0.5	0.5		1998	545.6	545.6	-	1998
South Africa	0.2 - 0.3	0.3	-	1997	500.0 - 800.0	650.0	-	1997
Swaziland	0.1 - 0.1	0.1	-	1998	50.0	50.0	-	1998
Zambia	0.6	0.6	-	1998				
Zimbabwe	1.3	1.3	-	1999	266.5	266.5	-	1999
West and Central Africa								
Benin					8.4	8.4	-	1998
Congo	0.3	0.3		1999				
Côte d'Ivoire	1.7	1.7	-	1997	190.0	190.0	-	1996
Ghana					39.2 - 62.7	51.0	-	1999
Nigeria					17.8	17.8	-	1997
Americas								
Central America								
Costa Rica	0.1	0.1	-	1999	63.4 - 70.5	67.0	-	1999
Guatemala					135.3	135.3	-	1996
Honduras					39.0	39.0	-	1997
Panama					80.0	80.0	-	1998
North America								
Canada	6.7 - 13.4	10.1	-	1999	4,024.1 - 5,365.5	4,694.8	-	1999
Mexico					49.0 - 96.8	72.9	-	1996
United States	5.5 - 26.5	10.2	-	1999	3,400.0 - 8,600.0	5,500.0	-	1999
Uruguay	1.0	1.0	-	2000	180.0	180.0	-	2000
South America								
Argentina	0.5 - 0.7	0.6	-	1999	500.0	500.0	-	1999
Brazil	0.9	0.9	-	1997				
Chile	1.0	1.0	-	1996	800.0	800.0	-	1998
Ecuador					600.0	600.0	-	1999
Guyana	0.2	0.2	-	1996	50.0 - 80.0	65.0	-	1996
Paraguay	1.6	1.6	-	1999	32.6 - 48.9	40.7	-	1999
Peru	0.1	0.1	-	1999	50.0	50.0	-	1999
Uruguay	0.4	0.4	-	1999	150.0 - 180.0	165.0	-	1999
Caribbean								
Bahamas	1.9 - 2.6	2.3	-	1998	1,322.8 - 1,543.2	1,433.0	-	1998
Bermuda	17.6	17.6	-	1999	11,023.1 - 15,432.4	13,227.7	-	1999
Cayman Islands	2.2	2.2	-	1999	11,023.0	11,023.0	-	1999
Dominican Republic	4.0 - 5.0	4.5	-	1999	400.0 - 500.0	450.0	-	1998
Saint Lucia	0.8	0.8	-	2000	600.0 - 660.0	630.0	-	2000
Trinidad Tobago	0.6	0.6	-	1998	1.0 - 530.0	265.5	-	1998
Turks and Caicos Islands					1,102.0	1,102.0	-	1998

Herbal cannabis

Region / country or territory	RETAIL PRICE (per gram)				WHOLESALE PRICE (per kilogram)			
	Range	Average	Purity	Year	Range	Average	Purity	Year
Asia								
Central Asia and Transcaucasia								
Armenia					1,000.0	1,000.0	-	1996
Azerbaijan	10.0 - 12.0	11.0	-	1999	1,000.0 - 1,200.0	1,100.0	-	1999
Kyrgyzstan	0.1	0.1	-	1999	70.0 - 80.0	75.0	-	1999
Tajikistan					500.0 - 800.0	650.0	-	1999
Turkmenistan					350.0	350.0	-	2000
Uzbekistan					100.0 - 300.0	200.0	-	1998
East and South-East Asia								
Brunei Darussalam					5,297.2	5,297.2	-	1998
China (Hong Kong SAR)	6.5	6.5	-	1999	1.190.5	1.190.5	-	1999
Indonesia	0.4	0.4	-	1999	129.9	129.9	-	1999
Japan	7.0 - 69.9	38.4	-	1999	8,737.7	8,737.7	-	1999
Malaysia	0.5 - 0.6	0.5	-	1997	265.2 - 397.8	331.5	-	1999
Myanmar					30.2	30.2	-	1999
Philippines	0.1	0.1	-	1999	20.6 - 25.7	23.2	-	1999
Republic of Korea	2.5 - 3.4	3.0	-	1999	1,524.9 - 1,694.3	1,609.6	-	1999
Singapore	3.9	3.9	-	1999	941.7	941.7	-	1999
Thailand	1.2 - 2.4	1.8	-	1999	72.9 - 97.2	85.1	-	1999
Near and Middle East /South-West Asia								
Israel	2.5 - 5.0	3.7	-	1998	200.0 - 500.0	350.0	-	1998
Jordan	0.3 - 0.7	0.5	-	1998	565.0	565.0	-	1998
Lebanon					1,200.0	1,200.0	-	2000
Syrian Arab Republic	1.1	1.1	-	1999	652.2	652.2	-	1999
South Asia								
Nepal					7.4 - 14.7	11.0	-	1999
Europe								
Eastern Europe								
Czech Republic	0.7 - 1.1	0.9	-	1996				
Hungary	7.2	7.2	-	1998	3,338.6	3,338.6	-	1998
Republic of Moldova	0.05	0.05	-	1997	100.0	100.0	-	1997
Slovakia	1.9 - 2.4	2.2	-	1999				
Slovenia	9.3 - 13.9	11.6	-	2000	1,850.0 - 4,630.0	3,240.0	-	2000
Russian Federation	1.0	1.0	-	1999	500.0	500.0	-	1999
The former Yug.Rep of Macedonia					452.2 - 565.3	508.8	-	1998
Ukraine					1,000.0 - 2,000.0	1,500.0	-	1997
Western Europe								
Andorra	3.2	3.2	-	1999				
Austria	7.8 - 11.7	9.7	-	1999	2,720.1 - 3,497.3	3,108.7	-	1999
Belgium	6.6	6.6	-	1999	927.8	927.8	-	1999
Cyprus	20.0	20.0	-	1999	3,000.0 - 4,000.0	3,500.0	-	1999
Denmark	8.8 - 9.2	9.0	-	1999				
Finland	6.4 - 9.6	8.0	-	1999				
France	1.6 - 6.5	4.1	-	1999	652.1 - 1,956.3	1,304.2	-	1999
Germany	3.8 - 8.5	4.7	-	2000	1,400.0 - 3,310.0	2,355.0	-	2000
Gibraltar					5,000.0	5,000.0	-	1997
Greece	1.6 - 3.3	2.5	-	1999	328.8 - 657.6	493.2	-	1999
Iceland	22.3	22.3	-	1998	-	-	-	-
Ireland	14.2	14.2	-	1998	2,549.6 - 2,832.9	2,691.2	-	1998
Italy	4.5 - 7.1	5.8	-	1998	1,408.5 - 2,253.5	1,820.5	-	1998
Liechtenstein	8.2	8.2	-	1996	3,679.5	3,679.5	-	1996
Luxembourg	2.5	2.5	-	1998	1,642.9 - 2,190.5	1,916.7	-	1998
Netherlands	3.6 - 6.1	4.9	-	1999	1,005.0 - 1,538.5	1,269.2	-	1997
Norway	7.0 - 14.1	10.6	-	1997	4,944.0 - 6,356.0	5,650.0	-	1997
Portugal	1.5	1.5	-	1999	543.5 - 1,142.9	836.2	-	1998

Herbal cannabis

Region / country or territory	RETAIL PRICE (per gram)				WHOLESALE PRICE (per kilogram)			
	Range	Average	Purity	Year	Range	Average	Purity	Year
Spain	2.7	2.7	-	1999	1,220.0	1,220.0	-	1999
Switzerland	3.3 - 10.0	6.7	-	1999	133.7 - 4,679.1	2,406.4	-	1999
Turkey					200.0	200.0	-	1996
United Kingdom	5.1	5.1	-	1999	3,000 - 5,000	3,750.0	-	1998
Oceania								
Australia	19.2	19.2	-	1999	3,050.0	3,050.0	-	1999

Cannabis Resin

Region / country or territory	RETAIL PRICE (per gram)				WHOLESALE PRICE (per kilogram)			
	Range	Average	Purity	Year	Range	Average	Purity	Year
Africa								
East Africa								
Seychelles					8,110.0 - 9,010.0	8,560.0	-	2000
Uganda					2,250.0	2,250.0	-	1998
North Africa								
Algeria					2,207.3	2,207.3	-	1999
Egypt	2.8 - 3.5	3.2	-	1998	2,352.0 - 3,393.1	2,822.7	-	1999
Tunisia					1,035.4 - 1,207.9	1,121.7	-	1999
Southern Africa								
South Africa	18.4 - 23.0	20.7	-	1996	9,220.0 - 13,820.0	11,520.0	-	1996
Zambia	0.7	0.7	-	1998				
Americas								
North America								
Canada	6.8 - 16.9	11.8	-	1998	4,736.1 - 6,765.9	5,751.0	-	1998
United States					2,205.0 - 7,720.0	4,962.5	-	1996
Asia								
Central Asia and Transcaucasia								
Armenia	5.0	5.0	-	2000	5,000.0	5,000.0	-	1999
Kyrgyzstan	0.4	0.4	-	1999	300.0	300.0	-	1999
Tajikistan					800.0 - 1,000.0	900.0	-	1997
Uzbekistan	0.7 - 1.5	1.1	-	1999	400.0 - 1,000.0	700.0	-	1999
East and South-East Asia								
China (Hong Kong SAR)	9.0	9.0	-	1999	21,882.3	21,882.3	-	1999
Near and Middle East /South-West Asia								
Afghanistan					28.3 - 69.0	51.7	-	1999
Israel	3.8 - 7.5	5.6	-	1996	2,700.0 - 4,800.0	3,750.0	-	1996
Jordan	1.4	1.4	-	2000	710.0	710.0	-	2000
Kuwait					4,934.2	4,934.2	-	1998
Lebanon	5.0	5.0	-	1997	3,000.0	3,000.0	-	1997
Pakistan	0.1	0.1	-	1999	37.7 - 132.1	70.5	-	2000
Qatar	6.9 - 8.2	7.5	-	1996	5,995.0 - 6,870.0	6,432.5	-	1996
Syrian Arab Republic	1.1	1.1	-	1998	663.0	663.0	-	1998
South Asia								
India	0.2 - 0.4	0.3	-	1999	123.2 - 793.3	431.2	-	1998
Nepal	0.1 - 0.2	0.1	-	1999	36.8 - 44.2	40.5	-	1998
Sri Lanka	0.3	0.3	-	1997	244.0	244.0	-	1997
Europe								
Eastern Europe								
Czech Republic	6.4 - 11.8	9.1	-	1999				
Hungary	3.4 - 10.6	7.0	-	1999	1,274.5 - 1,699.3	1,486.9	-	1999
Russian Federation	15.0	15.0	-	1999	3,000.0	3,000.0	-	1999
Slovenia	5.5 - 8.2	6.8	-	1999				

Cannabis Resin

Region / country or territory	RETAIL PRICE (per gram)				WHOLESALE PRICE (per kilogram)			
	Range	Average	Purity	Year	Range	Average	Purity	Year
Western Europe								
Andorra	2.6	2.6	-	1999				
Austria	4.2 -12.6	8.2	-	1998	2,941.2 - 3,968.3	3,563.6	-	1998
Belgium	6.8	6.8	-	1998	1,910.0	1,910.0	-	1998
Cyprus	20.0	20.0	-	1999	5,000.0 - 6,000.0	5,500.0	-	1999
Denmark	5.7 - 8.6	7.2	-	1999	1,721.4 - 2,869.0	2,295.2	-	1999
Finland	9.0 - 14.4	11.7	-	1999	3,956.8 - 5,395.7	4,676.3	-	1999
France	3.3 - 6.5	4.9	-	1999	1,141.2 - 2,934.5	2,037.8	-	1999
Germany	3.3 - 7.6	5.5	-	2000	1,440.0 - 2,790.0	2,115.0	-	2000
Gibraltar	2.0 - 3.0	2.5	-	1998	1,000.0 - 1,500.0	1,250.0	-	1998
Greece	3.3 - 16.4	9.9	-	1999	1,644.0 - 2,630.4	2,137.2	-	1999
Iceland	21.7	21.7	-	1999				
Ireland	13.6	13.6	-	1999	3,396.7	3,396.7	-	1999
Italy	6.4	6.4	-	1996	1,920.0 - 3,210.0	2,565.0	-	1996
Luxembourg	5.3	5.3	-	1999	2,651.0 - 3,976.5	3,313.7	-	1999
Monaco					5,807.0	5,807.0	-	1997
Netherlands	4.9 - 12.1	8.5	-	1999	1,237.6 - 2,475.2	1,671.7	-	1998
Norway	6.4 - 12.8	9.6	-	1999	4,475.7 - 6,393.9	5,434.8	-	1999
Portugal	1.2	1.2	-	1999	1,087.0 - 2.285.7	1,686.4	-	1998
Spain	4.1	4.1	-	1999	1,639.0	1,639.0	-	1999
Sweden	6.6 - 8.8	7.7	-	2000	2,750.0 - 4,400.0	3,575.0	-	2000
Switzerland	4.1 - 10.3	7.2	-	1998	2,005.3 - 4,679.1	3,342.2	-	1999
Turkey					820.1 - 1,093.5	956.8	-	1999
United Kingdom	5.7	5.7	-	1999	2,427.2 - 4,530.7	3,479.0	-	1999
Oceania								
Australia	32.0	32.0	-	1999	6,550.0	6,550.0	-	1999

Cannabis Oil

Region / country or territory	RETAIL PRICE (per gram)				WHOLESALE PRICE (per kilogram)			
	Range	Average	Purity	Year	Range	Average	Purity	Year
Africa								
Southern Africa								
Zambia	1.3	1.3	-	1998	-	-	-	-
Americas								
North America								
Canada	5.1 - 33.1	15.3		1999	2,899.0	2,899.0	-	1997
United States	35.0 - 55.0	45.0	-	1996	3,510.0 - 8,820.0	6,165.0	-	1996
South America								
Chile	24.7	24.7	-	1996	-	-	-	-
Asia								
Near and Middle East /South-West Asia								
Israel	10.0	10.0	-	1998	-	-	-	-
Europe								
Western Europe								
Cyprus					8,000.0 - 10,000.0	9,000.0	-	1999
Iceland	89.3	89.3	-	1998	-	-	-	-
Spain	9.4	9.4	-	1997	3,288.6	3,288.6	-	1997
Switzerland	17.1 - 34.3	25.7	-	1998	-	-	-	-
United Kingdom	24.3	24.3	-	1999	-	-	-	-
Oceania								
Australia	33.3	33.3	-	1998	6,666.7 - 9,333.3	8,000.0	-	1998

L.S.D

Region / country or territory	RETAIL PRICE (per dose)				WHOLESALE PRICE (per thousand dose)			
	Range	Average	Purity	Year	Range	Average	Purity	Year
Africa								
Southern Africa								
South Africa					5,593.0 - 8,949.0	7,271.0	-	1997
Zambia	42.8	42.8	-	1998				
Americas								
North America								
Canada	3.7 - 7.3	5.5	-	1996	3,380.0 - 6,765.9	5,074.4	-	1998
United States	1.0 - 10.0	5.5	-	1996	250.0 - 500.0	375.0	20.0 - 80.0	1996
Asia								
Near and Middle East /South-West Asia								
Israel	15.0 - 21.0	18.0	-	1996				
Europe								
Eastern Europe								
Czech Republic	3.2 - 6.4	4.8	-	1999				
Hungary	6.0	6.0	46.0 - 77.0	1997				
Poland					5,264.5 - 10,529.1	7,896.8	-	1999
Western Europe								
Austria	6.2 - 9.3	7.8	-	1999	4,663.1 - 7,771.8	6,217.5	-	1999
Belgium	4.3 - 14.2	8.9	-	1998	2,159.2 - 2,272.7	2,216.0	-	1998
Denmark	7.7 - 11.7	9.7	-	1998	4,622.5	4,622.5	-	1999
Finland	9.2 - 19.3	14.1	-	1998	9,174.3 - 9,633.9	9,404.1	-	1998
France	8.3 - 17.5	12.8	-	1998				
Germany	3.8 - 9.9	6.9	-	2000	1,420.0 - 4,730.0	3,075.0	-	2000
Greece	6.7 - 10.1	8.4	-	1998	3,366.1 - 5,049.1	4,207.6	-	1998
Iceland	17.9	17.9	-	1998	-	-	-	-
Ireland	14.1 - 14.6	14.3	-	1998	2,812.9 - 2,919.7	2,866.3	-	1998
Italy	11.5 - 17.2	14.4	-	1998	2,870.8 - 4,593.3	3,732.1	-	1998
Luxembourg	12.3	12.3	-	1998	9,943.2	9,943.2	-	1998
Netherlands	5.2	5.2	-	1998				
Portugal	5.7 - 14.3	10.0	-	1998	-	-	-	-
Spain	8.5	8.5	-	1998	8,965.5	8,965.5	-	1998
Sweden	6.1 - 12.1	9.1	-	1999				
Switzerland	4.1 - 41.2	22.6	-	1998	-	-	-	-
United Kingdom	6.2	6.2	-	1999	1,213.6 - 1,618.1	1,415.9	-	1999
Oceania								
Australia	12.4 - 26.7	16.5	-	1998				
New Zealand	13.2 - 23.8	18.5	-	1999	9,508.7 - 13,206.6	11,357.60	-	1999

Ecstasy

Region / country or territory	RETAIL PRICE (per tablet)				WHOLESALE PRICE (per thousand tablets)			
	Range	Average	Purity	Year	Range	Average	Purity	Year
Africa								
<u>North Africa</u>								
Egypt	8.6 - 14.2	11.4	-	2000	1,430	1,430	-	2000
<u>Southern Africa</u>								
South Africa	6.5 - 24.5	15.4	-	1999	5,592.0 - 8,948.0	7,270.0	-	1997
Americas								
<u>North America</u>								
Canada	26.5 - 33.1	29.8	-	1999	9,933.8 - 13,245.0	11,589.4	-	1999
United States	20.0 - 40.0	30.0	-	2000	2,000.0	2,000.0	-	2000
<u>Caribbean</u>								
Cayman Islands	30.0	30.0	-	1999				
Asia								
<u>East and South-East Asia</u>								
China	34.3	34.3	-	1999	12,909.0	12,909.0	-	1999
Indonesia	30.0	30.0	-	1996	10,730.0	10,730.0	-	1996
Thailand	10.6	10.6	-	1999				
<u>Near and Middle East /South-West Asia</u>								
Israel	14.9 - 30.0	22.4	-	1996	-	-	-	-
Europe								
<u>Eastern Europe</u>								
Croatia	6.0 - 9.6	7.8	-	2000				
Czech Republic	8.6 - 12.8	10.7	-	1999				
Hungary	7.2	7.2	20.0	1998	1,907.8	1,907.8	73.0	1998
Lithuania	6.0 - 12.0	9.0	-	2000	2,000.0 - 4,000.0	3,000.0	11.0 - 40.0	2000
<u>Western Europe</u>								
Austria	15.5 - 23.3	19.4	-	1999	4,663.1 - 7,771.8	6,217.5	25.0 - 90.0	1999
Belgium	8.0 - 26.5	15.0	-	1999	1,060.4 - 2,651.0	1,678.9	-	1999
Denmark	17.2 - 21.5	19.4	-	1999	4,303.5	4,303.5	-	1999
Finland	10.8 - 18.0	14.4	-	1999	5,395.7 - 7,194.2	6,295.0	-	1999
France	16.9	16.9	-	1998				
Germany	5.5 - 13.7	9.6	-	1999	2,132.3 - 5,248.8	3,690.5	-	1999
Greece	16.8 - 26.9	21.9	-	1998	6,732.1 - 10,098.2	8,415.2	-	1998
Iceland	50.6	50.6	-	1999				
Ireland	13.6	13.6	-	1999	1,358.7	1,358.7	-	1999
Italy	31.6 - 40.2	35.9	-	1998	8,450.7 - 10,682.5	9,544.0	-	1998
Luxembourg	13.3	13.3	-	1999	6,747.6 - 7,102.3	6,925.0	-	1998
Netherlands	7.8 - 12.4	10.0	-	1998	2,475.5 - 3,465.3	2,848.3	-	1998
Norway	19.2 - 25.6	22.4	20.0 - 50.0	1999	10,230.2 - 12,787.7	11,509.0	20.0 - 50.0	1999
Portugal	11.4 - 27.2	18.8	-	1998	1.358.7 - 2,857.1	2,104.7	-	1998
Spain	14.6	14.6	-	1999	15,689.7	15,689.7	-	1998
Sweden	18.2 - 24.3	21.2	-	1999	8,489.0	8,489.0	-	1999
Switzerland	6.9 - 41.2	24.0	-	1998				
Turkey					16,958.7 - 22,611.6	19,785.2	-	1998
United Kingdom	17.8	17.8	-	1999	3,236.2 - 4,854.4	4,045.3	-	1999
Oceania								
Australia	9.6 - 51.2	30.4	-	1999	9,590.0 - 15,980.0	12,785.0	-	1999
New Zealand	42.3 - 52.8	47.5	-	1999	21,130.5 - 31,695.7	26,413.1	-	1999

Amphetamine

Region / country or territc	RETAIL PRICE (*)					WHOLESALE PRICE (**)				
	Range	Average	Purity	Year	Unit	Range	Average	Purity	Year	Unit
Africa										
<u>Southern Africa</u>										
South Africa	4.9 - 6.5	5.7	-	1999	T					
Europe										
<u>Eastern Europe</u>										
Croatia	12.3 - 15.4	13.8	-	1998	T					
Estonia	12.0	12.0	20.0	1999		3,500.0	3,500.0	90.0	1999	
Hungary	9.5 - 14.3	11.9	20.0	1998		4,769.5	4,769.5	80.0 - 85.0	1998	
Lithuania	15.0 - 30.0	22.5	-	2000		10,000.0	10,000.0	28.0 - 89.0	2000	
Romania	15.0 - 20.0	17.5	-	1998	T					
Slovakia	0.3	0.3	90.0	1998	T					
Slovenia	6.5 - 11.1	8.8	20.0 - 25.0	2000		2,780.0 - 4,630.0	3,705.0	20.0 - 25.0	2000	
<u>Western Europe</u>										
Austria	15.9 - 42.0	28.6	-	1998		7,936.5 - 16,806.7	11,262.8	-	1998	
Belgium	8.0 - 26.5	15.0	-	1999	T	1,060.4 - 2,651.0	1,678.9	-	1999	
Denmark	17.2 - 35.9	26.5	24.0	1999		5,738.1 - 7,172.6	6,455.3	24.0	1999	
Finland	18.0 - 36.0	27.0	-	1999		9.892.1 - 12,589.9	11,241.0	46.0	1999	
France	8.2 - 16.3	12.2	-	1999	D					
Germany	4.3 - 11.9	8.1	-	2000	D	1,780.0 - 3,850.0	2,815.0	-	2000	TD
Greece	4.0 - 5.0	4.5	-	1998	D	2,797.2 - 3,496.5	3,146.9	-	1998	TD
Iceland	65.1	65.1	-	1999						
Ireland	14.1 - 14.6	14.3	-	1998		2,812.9 - 2,919.7	2,866.3	-	1998	TD
Italy	23.0 - 28.7	25.8	-	1998	D	4,593.3 - 5,741.6	5,167.5	-	1998	TD
Luxembourg	13.3 - 26.5	19.9	-	1999						
Netherlands	2.5 - 7.8	5.1	-	1998		2,604.2 - 3,465.3	3,013.3	-	1998	
Norway	32.0 - 51.2	41.6	20.0 - 90.0	1999		12,787.7 - 19,181.6	15,984.7	20.0 - 90.0	1999	
Portugal	5.7 - 14.3	10.0	-	1998						
Spain	4.2 - 27.1	15.7	-	1998		20,172.4	20,172.4	-	1998	
Sweden	9.9 - 22.4	16.15	-	2000		6,590.0 - 10,990.0	8,790.0	-	2000	
United Kingdom	16.2	16.2	-	1999		1,618.1 - 3,236.2	2,427.2	-	1999	
Oceania										
Australia	44.8 - 191.9	118.4	7.0	1999		12,790.0 - 19,180.0	15,985.0	7.0	1999	
New Zealand	105.7 - 132.1	118.9		1999						

(*) in Gram or otherwise as indicated
(**) in Kilogram or otherwise as indicated
D : Doses unit
T : Tablets unit
TD: Thousand of doses

Methamphetamine

Region / country or territor	RETAIL PRICE (per gram)				WHOLESALE PRICE (per kilogram)			
	Range	Average	Purity	Year	Range	Average	Purity	Year
Africa								
Southern Africa								
Malawi	5.0	5.0	-	1997	2,000.0	2,000.0	-	1997
Namibia	10.0	10.0	-	1996	2,000.0	2,000.0	-	1996
South Africa	3.4 - 8.9	6.2	-	1997	1,800.0 - 2,700.0	2,250.0	-	1997
Americas								
North America								
Canada	101.5	101.5	-	1998	20,882.3 - 26,849.1	23,865.7	-	1998
United States	50.0 - 900.0	224.3	40.0	1999	14,000.0 - 200,000.0	107,000.0	80.0	1999
Asia								
East and South-East Asia								
Brunei Darussalam					58,858.2 - 70,629.8	64,744.0	-	1999
China (Hong Kong SAR	56.5	56.5	99.0	1999	6,153.8	6,153.8	99.0	1999
Japan	556.9 - 2,768.1	1,662.5	100.0	1997	11,637.6 - 33,250.2	22,443.9	100.0	1997
Republic of Korea	491.3	491.3	85.0	1999	67,771.7	67,771.7	85.0	1999
Singapore	147.1	147.1	-	1999	29,429.1 - 58,858.2	44,143.6	-	1999
Thailand	2.4 - 3.6	3.0	-	1998				
Europe								
Eastern Europe								
Czech Republic	23.5 - 35.2	29.4	-	1996	-	-	-	-
Western Europe								
Finland	18.0 - 36.0	27.0	-	1999	9,892.1 - 12,589.9	11,241.0	31.0	1999
Germany	7.1 - 26.5	16.8	-	2000	3,200.0 - 7,990.0	5,595.0	-	2000
Netherlands	7.3 - 12.1	9.7	-	1999	-	-	-	-
Spain	24.3 - 25.8	25.1	-	1997	21,812.1 - 24,305.6	23,058.8	-	1997

CONSUMPTION

OVERVIEW

EXTENT

Assessing the extent of drug abuse (the number of drug abusers) is a particularly difficult undertaking because it involves measuring the size of a hidden population. Margins of error are thus considerable, and tend to multiply as the scale of estimation is raised, from local to country, regional and global levels.

Estimates provided by member states to UNDCP are very heterogenous in terms of quality and reliability. Detailed information is available from countries in North America, a number of countries in Europe, some countries in South and Central America, a few countries in the Oceania region and a limited number of countries in Asia and in Africa. For several other countries, available qualitative information on the drug abuse situation only allows for making some 'guess estimates'. In the case of complete data gaps for individual countries, it was assumed that drug abuse was likely to be close to the respective subregional average, unless other available indicators suggested that abuse levels were likely to be above or below such an average. Even in cases where detailed information is available, there is often considerable divergence in definitions used - general population versus specific surveys of groups in terms of age, special settings (such as hospital or prisons), life-time, annual, or monthly prevalence, etc. In order to reduce the error from simply adding up such diverse estimates, an attempt was made to standardize - as a far as possible - the very heterogenous data set. Thus, all available estimates were transformed into one single indicator – annual prevalence among the general population age 15 and above - using transformation ratios derived from

analysis of the situation in neighbouring countries, and if such data were not available, on estimates from the USA, the most studied country worldwide with regard to drug abuse. In order to minimize the potential error from the use of different methodological approaches, all available estimates for the same country were taken into consideration and - unless methodological considerations suggested a clear superiority of one method over another - the mean of the various estimates was calculated and used as UNDCP's country estimate.

All of this - pooling of national results, standardization and extrapolation from subregional results in the case of data gaps - does not guarantee an accurate picture, but it is sufficient to arrive at reasonable orders of magnitude about the likely extent of drug abuse. The estimates show that worldwide the most widely consumed substances are cannabis (144 million people), followed by amphetamine-type stimulants (29 million people), cocaine (14 million people) and opiates (13.5 million people of whom some 9 million are taking heroin). The total number of drug users was estimated at some 180 million people, equivalent to 3% of the global population or 4.2% of the population age 15 and above[a]. As drug users frequently take more than one substance, it should be noted that the total is not identical with the sum of the individual drug categories. A more detailed geographical breakdown of these estimates will be provided in the individual substance specific sub-chapters.

Trends

In general, replies to UNDCP's Annual Report Questionnaire are far more comprehensive in coverage

Extent of drug abuse (annual prevalence) in the late 1990s						
	Illicit drugs of which:	Cannabis	Amphetamine-type stimulants*	Cocaine	Opiates	of which heroin
GLOBAL (million people)	180	144.1	28.7	14	13.5	9.2
in % of global population	3.0%	2.4%	0.5%	0.2%	0.2%	0.15%
in % of global population age 15 and above	4.2%	3.4%	0.7%	0.3%	0.3%	0.22%

*Amphetamines (methamphetamine and amphetamine) and substances of the ecstasy group.
Source: UNDCP, *World Drug Report 2000.*

a) These estimates were recently published in UNDCP, World Drug Report 2000 (Oxford Univ. Press)

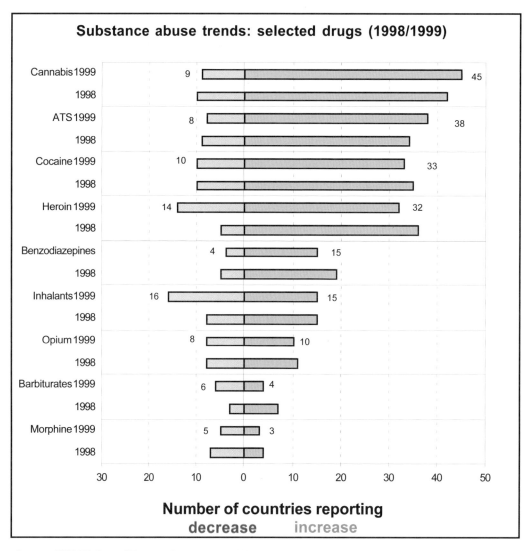

Substance abuse trends: selected drugs (1998/1999)

Number of countries reporting
decrease   increase

Source: UNDCP, Annual Reports Questionnaire / DELTA

with regard to the reporting of trends in substance abuse than on estimates of the numbers of drug users.[b] Nonetheless, one has to be aware that indications of trends in drug abuse are - for many countries - primarily a reflection of the 'perceptions' of the development of the drug problem by the authorities. The perceptions may be influenced by a large number of factors and partial information, including police reports on seizures and on crime, reports from social workers, reports from drug treatment centres, personal impressions from visiting certain areas known for high levels of local drug trafficking and drug abuse, press reports, or a particular political agenda. These factors may have some built-in bias towards reporting an increase rather than a decline in the drug problem though in some cases the opposite may be true as well. Information on trends of drug abuse must therefore be treated with caution as well, and cannot always be taken at face value as a fair reflection of the development of the actual drug abuse situation in a country. Nonetheless, and despite the caveats, trend

data do provide some interesting insights into the growth patterns of individual drug groups and into regional patterns which are worthwhile to highlight.

Trend data, for instance, show that the 'most popular' substances of abuse worldwide in the late 1990s were cannabis and the amphetamine-type stimulants, followed by cocaine and heroin. While the number of countries reporting increasing levels of abuse rose for cannabis and ATS (notably for ecstasy and methamphetamine) between 1998 and 1999, the respective numbers fell for cocaine and heroin as well as for the benzodiazepines, opium, the barbiturates and morphine. In 1999 there were already more countries reporting declines than increases in abuse for morphine, barbiturates, inhalants, LSD and methaqualone while in the case of cannabis, ATS, cocaine, heroin and benzodiazepines the countries reporting increases outnumbered those reporting declines.

b) In 1999, 46 countries provided UNDCP with estimates on the numbers of drug abusers while 137 countries provided UNDCP with information on drug abuse trends.

ABUSE OF OPIATES

EXTENT

Opiate use (including heroin) was estimated at around 0.3% of the population age15 and above in the late 1990s; heroin abuse was estimated to affect 0.2% of the population. More than 60% of the world's users are found in Asia and 20% in Europe. It appears that abuse of opiates in eastern Europe - notably in the C.I.S. states - is already higher than in western Europe. Some of this may be due to differences in methodological approaches at the country level. Similarly, the rather high rates reported from the Oceania region as compared to western Europe may reflect methodological particularities rather than any significant higher levels of abuse. Above average levels of opiate abuse have been reported from countries in Oceania, Europe, Asia as well as North America, while abuse levels in South America and Africa seem to be below average.

Annual prevalence estimates of opiate use in the late 1990s

	Number of people (in million)	in % of population age 15 and above
OCEANIA	0.13	0.58
- Western Europe	1.22	0.34
- Eastern Europe	1.46	0.54
EUROPE	2.68	0.42
ASIA	8.62	0.35
- North America	1.12	0.36
- South America	0.32	0.12
AMERICAS	1.44	0.20
AFRICA	0.63	0.13
GLOBAL	13.5	0.33

Above global average: ▭ below global average: ▭

Source: UNDCP, *World Drug Report 2000.*

Annual prevalence estimates of heroin use in the late 1990s

	Number of people (in million)	in % of population age 15 and above
OCEANIA	0.6	0.27
EUROPE	1.51	0.24
ASIA	5.74	0.24
AMERICAS	1.31	0.22
AFRICA	0.57	0.12
GLOBAL	9.18	0.22

Above global average: ▭ below global average: ▭

Source: UNDCP, *World Drug Report 2000.*

Abuse of opiates (including heroin)

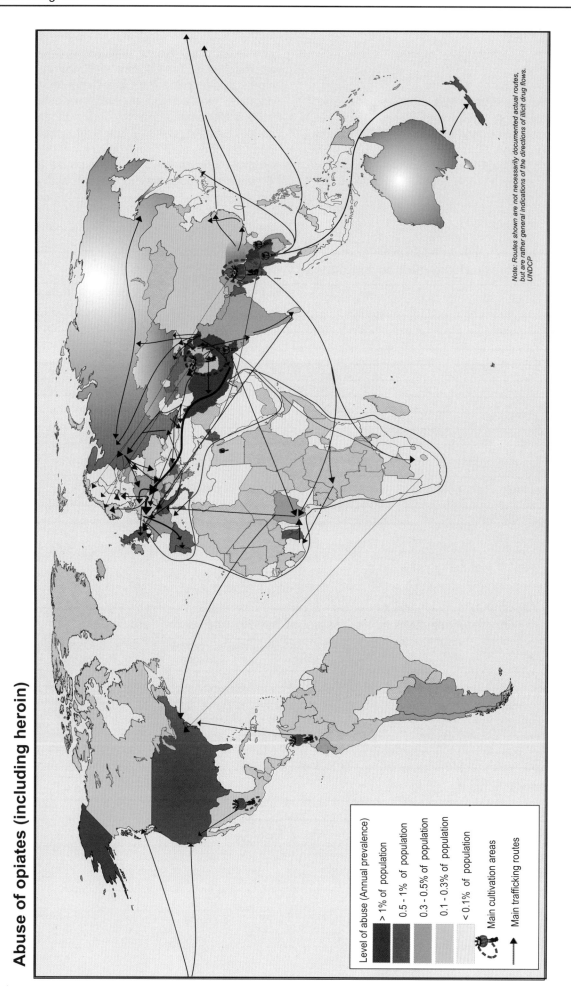

Note: Routes shown are not necessarily documented actual routes, but are rather general indications of the directions of illicit drug flows.
UNDCP

Level of abuse (Annual prevalence)

- > 1% of population
- 0.5 - 1% of population
- 0.3 - 0.5% of population
- 0.1 - 0.3% of population
- < 0.1% of population

Main cultivation areas

Main trafficking routes

Changes in abuse of heroin and other opiates, 1999 (or latest year available)

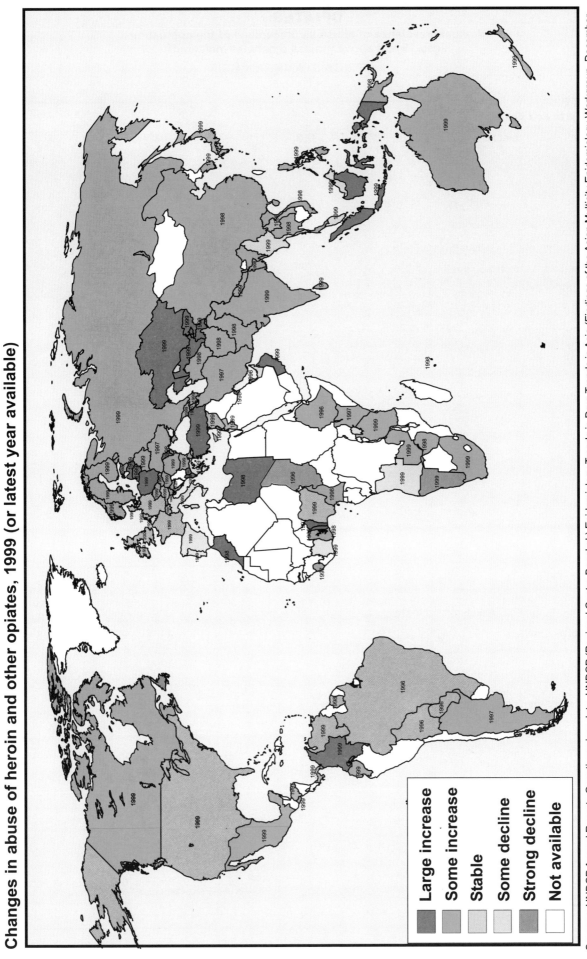

Legend:
- Large increase
- Some increase
- Stable
- Some decline
- Strong decline
- Not available

Sources: UNDCP Annual Reports Questionnaires data, UNDCP (Regional Centre Bangkok) Epidemiology Trends in Drug Trends in Asia (Findings of the Asian Multicity Epidemiology Workgroup, December 1999, National Household Surveys submitted to UNDCP, United States Department of State (Bureau for International Narcotics and Law Enforcement Affairs) International Narcotics Control Strategy Report, 1999;Bundeskriminalamt (BKA) and other Law Enforcement Reports, SACENDU (South African Community Epidemiology Network July - December 1998.

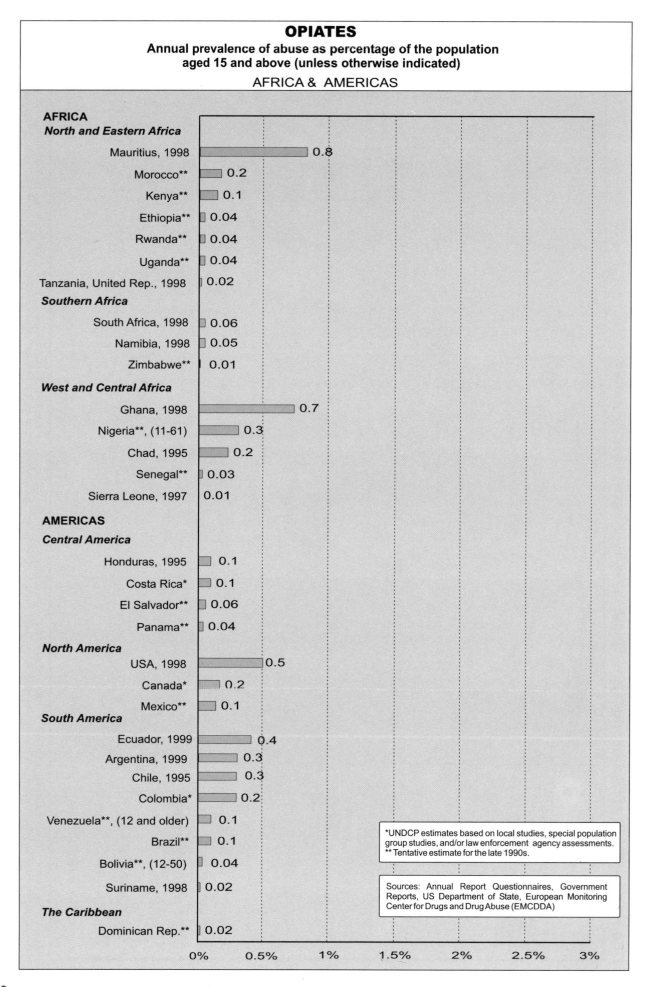

OPIATES

Annual prevalence of abuse as percentage of the population
aged 15 and above (unless otherwise indicated)

AFRICA & AMERICAS

AFRICA
North and Eastern Africa

Mauritius, 1998	0.8
Morocco**	0.2
Kenya**	0.1
Ethiopia**	0.04
Rwanda**	0.04
Uganda**	0.04
Tanzania, United Rep., 1998	0.02

Southern Africa

South Africa, 1998	0.06
Namibia, 1998	0.05
Zimbabwe**	0.01

West and Central Africa

Ghana, 1998	0.7
Nigeria**, (11-61)	0.3
Chad, 1995	0.2
Senegal**	0.03
Sierra Leone, 1997	0.01

AMERICAS
Central America

Honduras, 1995	0.1
Costa Rica*	0.1
El Salvador**	0.06
Panama**	0.04

North America

USA, 1998	0.5
Canada*	0.2
Mexico**	0.1

South America

Ecuador, 1999	0.4
Argentina, 1999	0.3
Chile, 1995	0.3
Colombia*	0.2
Venezuela**, (12 and older)	0.1
Brazil**	0.1
Bolivia**, (12-50)	0.04
Suriname, 1998	0.02

The Caribbean

Dominican Rep.**	0.02

*UNDCP estimates based on local studies, special population group studies, and/or law enforcement agency assessments.
** Tentative estimate for the late 1990s.

Sources: Annual Report Questionnaires, Government Reports, US Department of State, European Monitoring Center for Drugs and Drug Abuse (EMCDDA)

0%   0.5%   1%   1.5%   2%   2.5%   3%

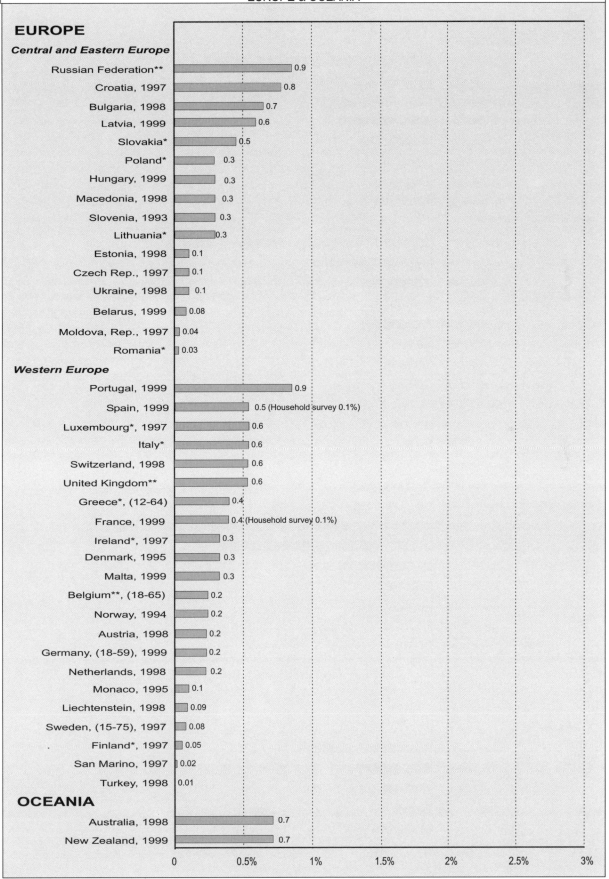

OPIATES

**Annual prevalence of abuse as percentage of the population
aged 15 and above (unless otherwise indicated)**

EUROPE & OCEANIA

EUROPE

Central and Eastern Europe

Russian Federation**	0.9
Croatia, 1997	0.8
Bulgaria, 1998	0.7
Latvia, 1999	0.6
Slovakia*	0.5
Poland*	0.3
Hungary, 1999	0.3
Macedonia, 1998	0.3
Slovenia, 1993	0.3
Lithuania*	0.3
Estonia, 1998	0.1
Czech Rep., 1997	0.1
Ukraine, 1998	0.1
Belarus, 1999	0.08
Moldova, Rep., 1997	0.04
Romania*	0.03

Western Europe

Portugal, 1999	0.9
Spain, 1999	0.5 (Household survey 0.1%)
Luxembourg*, 1997	0.6
Italy*	0.6
Switzerland, 1998	0.6
United Kingdom**	0.6
Greece*, (12-64)	0.4
France, 1999	0.4 (Household survey 0.1%)
Ireland*, 1997	0.3
Denmark, 1995	0.3
Malta, 1999	0.3
Belgium**, (18-65)	0.2
Norway, 1994	0.2
Austria, 1998	0.2
Germany, (18-59), 1999	0.2
Netherlands, 1998	0.2
Monaco, 1995	0.1
Liechtenstein, 1998	0.09
Sweden, (15-75), 1997	0.08
Finland*, 1997	0.05
San Marino, 1997	0.02
Turkey, 1998	0.01

OCEANIA

Australia, 1998	0.7
New Zealand, 1999	0.7

0   0.5%   1%   1.5%   2%   2.5%   3%

OPIATES
Annual prevalence of abuse as percentage of the population aged 15 and above (unless otherwise indicated)

ASIA

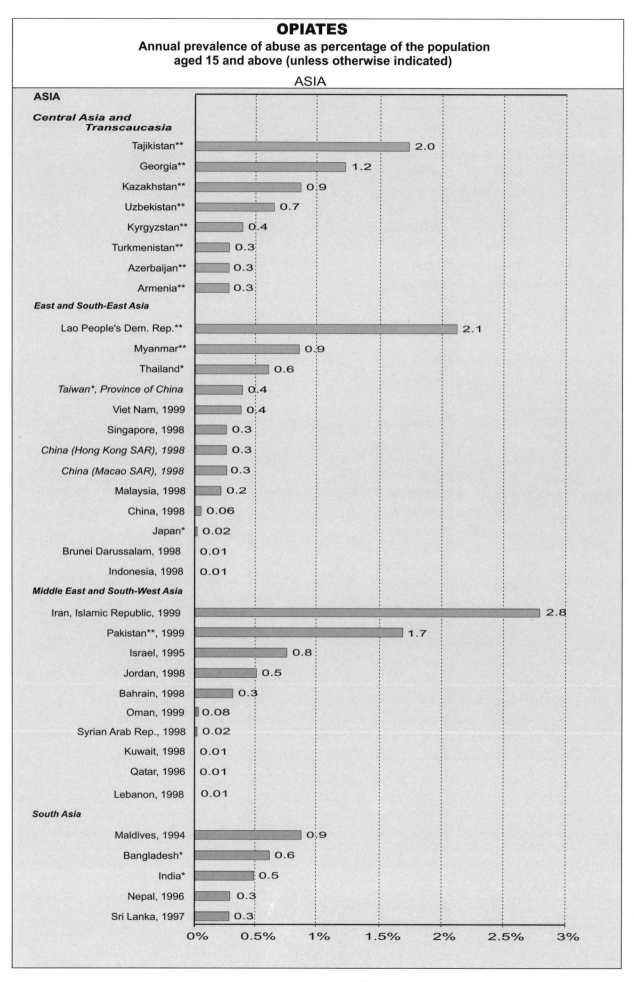

ASIA

Central Asia and Transcaucasia

Tajikistan**	2.0
Georgia**	1.2
Kazakhstan**	0.9
Uzbekistan**	0.7
Kyrgyzstan**	0.4
Turkmenistan**	0.3
Azerbaijan**	0.3
Armenia**	0.3

East and South-East Asia

Lao People's Dem. Rep.**	2.1
Myanmar**	0.9
Thailand*	0.6
Taiwan, Province of China	0.4
Viet Nam, 1999	0.4
Singapore, 1998	0.3
China (Hong Kong SAR), 1998	0.3
China (Macao SAR), 1998	0.3
Malaysia, 1998	0.2
China, 1998	0.06
Japan*	0.02
Brunei Darussalam, 1998	0.01
Indonesia, 1998	0.01

Middle East and South-West Asia

Iran, Islamic Republic, 1999	2.8
Pakistan**, 1999	1.7
Israel, 1995	0.8
Jordan, 1998	0.5
Bahrain, 1998	0.3
Oman, 1999	0.08
Syrian Arab Rep., 1998	0.02
Kuwait, 1998	0.01
Qatar, 1996	0.01
Lebanon, 1998	0.01

South Asia

Maldives, 1994	0.9
Bangladesh*	0.6
India*	0.5
Nepal, 1996	0.3
Sri Lanka, 1997	0.3

0%   0.5%   1%   1.5%   2%   2.5%   3%

TRENDS

Europe

The opiates, particularly heroin, continue to be the main 'problem drug' in Europe, accounting for more than 70 percent of all treatment demand.

Trends show a distinct pattern: while practically all countries of East Europe reported increasing levels of heroin abuse, particularly those along the main heroin trafficking routes, most of the West European countries saw either stable or declining abuse trends.

West European trends are indirectly confirmed by a number of statistical data, including household surveys, treatment, development of HIV/AIDS among drug addicts, first time offenders against the drug laws and drug deaths. Most of these indicators showed a deteri-

oration in the 1980s but suggest a stabilization or decline of abuse levels in the 1990s. Examples for Germany, Spain, Italy and France are given below. The average age of people in treatment has also been rising throughout western Europe in recent years, reflecting a ageing population of heroin addicts.

Reported increases among West European countries were limited to the Nordic countries, which traditionally had very low levels of heroin abuse, as well as in the very south to Turkey and Cyprus, which are also characterized - compared to most other European countries - by low levels of abuse. The situation is less clear for the UK and Ireland. A number of indicators suggested rising levels of abuse in the 1990s, up until 1998. Since then, however, a trend towards stabilization was seen and reported by the authorities (Ireland), and by demand specialists of the REITOX network (UK).

Trends in abuse of heroin in 'Europe' in 1999 (countries sorted according to size of population)			
Stable or declining abuse levels		Rising abuse levels	
Germany, 1999, stable	WE*	Russian Fed., 1999, some increase	CEE*
UK, 1999, stable**	WE*	Turkey, 1999, large increase	WE*
France, 1999, stable	WE*	Ukraine, 1999, some increase	CEE*
Italy, 1999, some decrease	WE*	Poland, 1999, large increase	CEE*
Spain, 1999, some decrease	WE*	Romania, 1999, some increase	CEE*
Netherlands, 1999, stable	WE*	Czech Rep., 1999, some increase	CEE*
Belgium, 1999, some decrease	WE*	Belarus, 1999, large increase	CEE*
Greece, 1999, stable	WE*	Hungary, 1999, some increase	CEE*
Portugal, 1999, some decrease	WE*	Sweden, 1999, some increase	WE*
Austria, 1999, stable/some decrease	WE*	Bulgaria, 1999, some increase	CEE*
Switzerland, 1998, some decrease	WE*	Azerbaijan, 1999, some increase	CEE*
Denmark, 1999, stable	WE*	Finland, 1999, some increase	WE*
Ireland, 1999, stable**	WE*	Georgia, 1999, some increase	CEE*
Luxembourg, 1999, stable	WE*	Norway, 1999, some increase	WE*
Malta, 1999, stable	WE*	Moldova, 1998, large increase	CEE*
Liechtenstein, 1999, some decrease	WE*	Latvia, 1999, large increase	CEE*
		Macedonia, 1998, large increase	CEE*
		Cyprus, 1999, large increase	WE*

* WE = West Europe; CEE = Central and East Europe

** Data for UK based on REITOX report (2000) to EMCDDA; data for Ireland based on explanations provided in the ARQ.

Sources: UNDCP, Annual Reports Questionnaire Data; official reports.

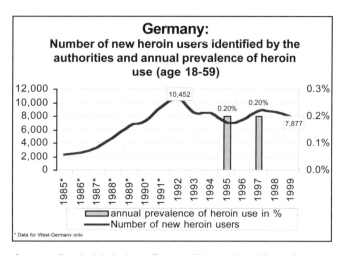

Germany:
Number of new heroin users identified by the authorities and annual prevalence of heroin use (age 18-59)

* Data for West-Germany only.

Sources: Bundeskriminalamt, Rauschgiftkriminalitaet (Erstauffaellige Konsumenten harter Drogen), Wiesbaden 2000, Bundesministerium fuer Gesundheit, *Drogen: Repraesentativerhebung* 1995 and 1997.

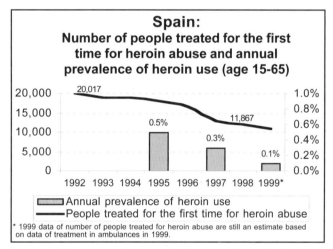

Spain:
Number of people treated for the first time for heroin abuse and annual prevalence of heroin use (age 15-65)

* 1999 data of number of people treated for heroin abuse are still an estimate based on data of treatment in ambulances in 1999.

Sources: Observatorio Espanol sobre Drogas, *Informe No. 3*, and Plan Nacional Sobre Drogas, *Memoria 1999*, UNDCP, Annual Reports Questionnaire, 1999.

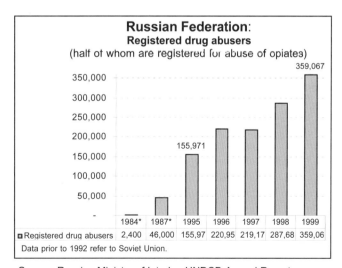

Russian Federation:
Registered drug abusers
(half of whom are registered for abuse of opiates)

	1984*	1987*	1995	1996	1997	1998	1999
Registered drug abusers	2,400	46,000	155,97	220,95	219,17	287,68	359,06

Data prior to 1992 refer to Soviet Union.

Source: Russian Ministry of Interior, UNDCP, Annual Reports Questionnaire Data.

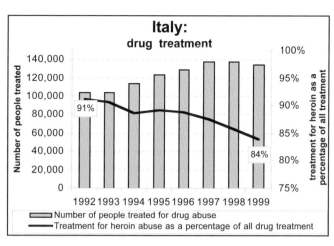

Italy:
drug treatment

Sources: Ministry of the Interior, *Annual Report on the State of the Drugs Problem in Italy for the European Monitoring Centre on Drugs and Drug Addiction*, Rome 1996 and Presidenza del Consiglio del Ministri Dipartmento per gli Affari Sociali, *Tossicodipendenze Annuala al Parlamenta sullo Statu delle Tossicodipendenze in Italy*, 1999, Rome 2000.

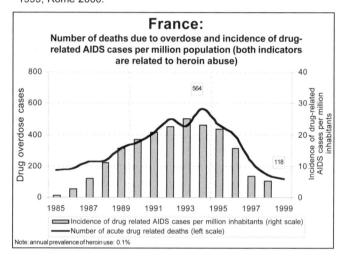

France:
Number of deaths due to overdose and incidence of drug-related AIDS cases per million population (both indicators are related to heroin abuse)

Note: annual prevalence of heroin use: 0.1%

Sources: EMCDDA, *2000 Annual Report on the state of the drugs in the European Union*, Lisbon 2000, UNDCP, Annual Reports Questionnaire Data, CFES, CNAMTS, OFDT, *Baromètre Santé 2000, premiers résultats, Usages de drogues illicites*, Paris 2000.

In contrast to most West European countries, a large number of reports confirm the opposite perception of still rising levels of abuse of heroin and other opiates in most East European countries. There was a shift from simple opiates, such as 'kompot' (a brew made out of poppy straw) to heroin. Strong increases in opiate abuse took place in recent years in a number of drug transit countries, particularly those along the various branches of the Balkan route and the successor states of the former Soviet Union. The number of registered drug addicts in the Russian Federation almost doubled between 1995 and 1999; half of them were registered for abuse of opiates, and the number of heroin users was rising.

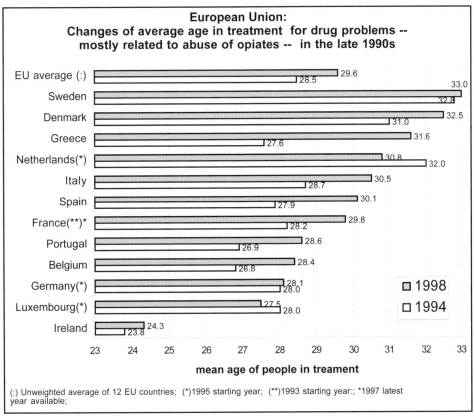

European Union:
Changes of average age in treatment for drug problems --
mostly related to abuse of opiates -- in the late 1990s

Country	1998	1994
EU average (:)	29.6	28.5
Sweden	33.0	32.8
Denmark	32.5	31.0
Greece	31.6	27.6
Netherlands(*)	30.8	32.0
Italy	30.5	28.7
Spain	30.1	27.9
France(**)*	29.8	28.2
Portugal	28.6	26.9
Belgium	28.4	26.8
Germany(*)	28.1	28.0
Luxembourg(*)	27.5	28.0
Ireland	24.3	23.8

mean age of people in treament

(:) Unweighted average of 12 EU countries; (*)1995 starting year; (**)1993 starting year:; *1997 latest year available;

Sources: EMCDDA, Annual Report on the state of the drugs problem in the European Union, Lisbon 2000.

Asia and the Pacific (Oceania)

Abuse levels in most Asian countries increased in 1999. Increases were reported to have been particularly strong in Central Asia, which is increasingly used as a transit zone for opiates produced in Afghanistan though countries in South-West Asia and South Asia also reported increasing abuse. Though injecting heroin is still the exception, there have been reports of it, notably in Pakistan but also in other countries in the region.

The situation is more complex in East and South-East Asia. The main 'growth sector' there was not abuse of opiates but of methamphetamine. Poor opium harvests in South-East Asia, notably Myanmar, apparently played a role as well. Authorities in Myanmar saw a trend towards declining use of opiates, notably for opium but also for heroin. Declines were also reported from Malaysia, Singapore, Brunei Darussalam, Hong-Kong SAR and the eastern provinces of India. The Japanese authorities reported a stabilization of heroin abuse. The picture for Thailand was less clear-cut. The authorities reported some decline in the abuse of opiates in the central provinces as consumption shifted to metham-phetamine. In southern Thailand, however, abuse of opiates continued expanding strongly (1999/2000) and in northern Thailand lower wholesale prices, and thus an overall lower price level for heroin, has been acting as an incentive for rising levels of abuse. Thus, the overall perception of the Thai authorities was that abuse of opiates expanded in the country, though far less than

the use of methamphetamine. The lower prices of opiates were apparently a consequence of some recent shifts in trafficking patterns. While most of the increase in trafficking opiates out of Myanmar in the 1990s was via China, trafficking in 1999/00 partly shifted back to Thailand as China stepped up enforcement efforts in order to stem the rapid rise in domestic abuse. The number of registered drug addicts in China -- mostly related to heroin abuse -- rose almost ten-fold in the 1990s.

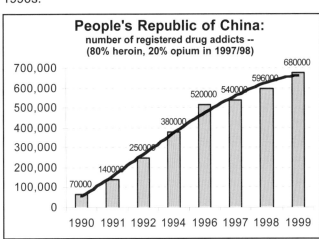

People's Republic of China:
number of registered drug addicts --
(80% heroin, 20% opium in 1997/98)

Source: UNDCP, Annual Reports Questionnaire, U.S. Dept. of State, International Narcotics Control Strategy Report(s), Washington 2001 and previous years.

An increase in the abuse of opiates was also reported by Australia. This was mainly based on results of the 1995 and 1998 household surveys and deaths attrib-

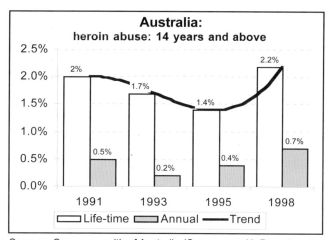

Australia:
heroin abuse: 14 years and above

Sources: Commonwealth of Australia (Commonwealth Department of Health and Family Services), Patterns of Drug Use in Australia 1985-95 - National Drug Strategy; Australian Institute of Health and Welfare, 1998 National Drug Strategy Household Survey.

uted to opiate abuse which showed strong increases in the 1990s. The household surveys suggest that abuse of opiates increased strongly over the 1995-98 period, reversing the trend towards stabilization or decline of the early 1990s. However, there are some indications that the upward trend in heroin use over the 1995-98 period may have been in fact less significant, and that it did not continue in 1999 - in line with lower heroin production in South-East Asia. Several other estimates arrived at substantially lower results for the late 1990s (see Wayne Hall et.al, *How many dependent opioid users are there in Australia?*, NDARC Monograph No. 44, New South Wales, 2000). The numbers of new clients entering methadone maintenance treatment showed in 1999 for the first time in years some decline. Similarly, the weekly numbers of ambulance attendances seem to have declined in late 1999.

Americas

There is generally a low response rate to the question of abuse trends in heroin and other opiates in the Americas, partly reflecting the low importance of opiates as substance of abuse in this region. Five countries, including the two main producers of opium in the region, reported increases in abuse of heroin in 1999: Canada, Colombia, Ecuador, El Salvador and Mexico. However, except for Mexico and Ecuador, the trend data of the other countries were not based on recent epidemiological surveys. Another two countries - Panama and Venezuela - considered abuse levels to have remained stable. For other countries in the region, only reports from previous years are available: they generally saw a stable trend, at relatively low abuse levels.

One exception to this pattern is Argentina, which reported increases in heroin abuse through the 1990s. A national survey in 1999 found life-time prevalence of opiates to affect 0.5% of the population age 12-64 (rising to 0.9% among males) and a monthly prevalence rate of 0.1%, high figures by South American standards. According to national household surveys in Colombia (1996) or in Mexico (1998) life-time prevalence of heroin abuse affected less than 0.1% of the population.

Life-time prevalence of heroin abuse in the USA - based on data of the 1999 household survey - is 1.4% of the population age 12 and above, annual prevalence is 0.2% and monthly prevalence is 0.1% of the population. Heroin abuse levels in the USA are thus not very large by global standards, though they are large by standards in the Americas.

Heroin abuse trends for the USA are, however, rather complex. Though they may appear contradictory at first sight, the various indicators in fact reflect the typical

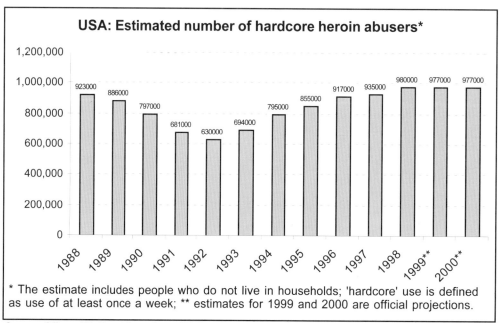

USA: Estimated number of hardcore heroin abusers*

* The estimate includes people who do not live in households; 'hardcore' use is defined as use of at least once a week; ** estimates for 1999 and 2000 are official projections.

Source: Office of National Drug Control Policy, *What American's Users Spend on Illegal Drugs*, 1998-1999

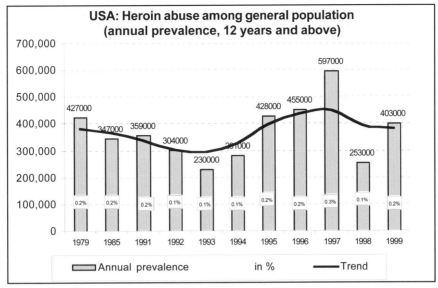

Source: SAMHSA, *US National Household Surveys on Drug Abuse*, 1999 and previous years.

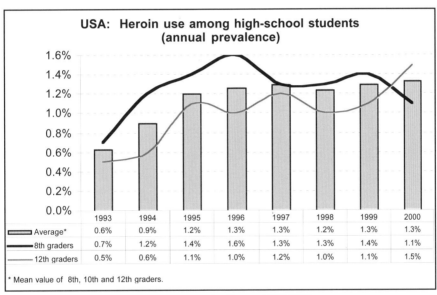

Source: University of Michigan, *Monitoring the Future*, 1975-2000

characteristics of a heroin epidemic in its various phases, basically showing first signs of a stabilization following years of rapid increase in the 1990s. Thus emergency room visits and treatment for heroin abuse continue to go upwards while a number of survey results indicate a stabilization.

Student surveys showed strong increases in the use of heroin in the 1990s up until 1996/97, reflecting the 'heroin chic', among various sections of America's youth at the time. Since then preventions programmes, however, succeeded in bringing down abuse rates among 8th graders and stabilizing those of the 10th graders, as reflected in the latest survey conducted in 2000. Heroin use, however, continues growing among 12th graders,

largely in line with the aging of the 8th grader cohort of the mid 1990s.

General household surveys show that after a decline in the numbers of heroin users in the 1980s, heroin use increased again in the 1990s before levelling off after 1997. While life-time prevalence of heroin use continued rising as the number of people experimenting with heroin was more than those dying from heroin abuse, annual prevalence data showed lower abuse levels for 1999 than for 1997, though they were still higher than1998. This phenomenon, however, may be *inter alia* a reflection of methodological changes in conducting such surveys between 1998 and 1999c. Monthly prevalence rates, a measure of more severe consump-

---

c) In 1999, for the first time, computer assisted interviews were used; they guarantee a higher degree of confidentiality and are thus likely to reduce levels of under-reporting. This should lead to higher results.

tion patterns remained unchanged between 1998 and 1999 and 1999 figures were actually lower than in 1997. Similarly, projections made by the Office of National Drug Control Policy showed the overall number of hard-core heroin users to be stable over the 1998-2000 period, following increases over the 1993-98 period.

Africa

Levels of opiate abuse in Africa - and notably injecting heroin still seem to be low compared to most other regions, mostly due to rather high prices by local purchasing power standards, though the overall abuse trend appears to go upwards. Relatively high levels of abuse have already been reported by some of the island countries, such as Mauritius or Cape Verde, which suffer spill-overs from drug trafficking, and in some of the ports on the mainland.

Abuse trends have been characterized by increases in most East and South African countries along the Indian Ocean, reflecting their growing importance as transshipment points for opiates produced in southwest Asia. By contrast, a number of countries along the Atlantic coast - Angola, Cote d'Ivoire, Namibia and Nigeria - reported abuse trends to have been either stable or declining in 1999, though some other West African countries (including some provinces within Nigeria) still saw abuse of opiates rising. Given trafficking links between some of the countries of West Africa with South-East Asia, lower levels of production in South-East Asia in 1999 may have led to some decline in trafficking and thus to less spill-overs to the local market than in previous years. In some countries, South-East Asian heroin was replaced by shipments originating in South-West Asia.

However, monitoring systems in Africa are sparse and data has to be treated with caution. In several countries, ad-hoc studies have been conducted, usually covering specific sites and population groups. One of the few countries, where a comprehensive national school survey has taken place in recent years - was Tanzania. The survey, undertaken in 1997, found that 0.3% of those 6 to 21 years of age had experimented with opiates, less than the corresponding rates for cannabis (2.2%), sedatives (0.9%) or cocaine (0.5%). In the Republic of South Africa, authorities reported that treatment demand for heroin abuse - though still far less than for cocaine or cannabis - increased in Cape Town, Gauteng (i.e. Johannesburg and Pretoria) and in Port Elizabeth during the first six months of 1999 and then remained stable during the second half of the year. Most of this treatment demand was for first time admissions. The increase was particularly significant among females, reflecting the entrenchment of heroin use among sex workers.

ABUSE OF COCAINE

EXTENT

Cocaine use was estimated to effect 0.3% of the global population. Regional concentrations are more pronounced than for other drugs. More than 70% of all cocaine use takes place in the Americas and some 16% in Europe. Abuse in the Americas, notably in North America, is clearly above average, accounting for half of the total number of cocaine users worldwide. Abuse levels in North America are seven times as large as the global average. By contrast, abuse of cocaine in the Asia region or in eastern Europe, is still at relatively low levels.

Annual prevalence estimates of cocaine use in the late 1990s		
	Number of people (in million)	in % of population age 15 and above
- North America	7.0	2.20
- South America[1]	3.1	1.10
AMERICAS	10.1	1.70
OCEANIA	0.2	0.90
- Western Europe	2.2	0.70
- Eastern Europe	0.1	0.04
EUROPE	2.3	0.40
AFRICA	1.3	0.30
ASIA	0.2	0.01
GLOBAL	14.0	0.30

[1] Data include estimates on cocaine related products (basuco/coca paste)

Above global average*: ▢   close to global average: ▢   below global average**: ▢

* 1 percentage point more than global prevalence rate or 3 times the global prevalence rate.
** 1 percentage point below global prevalence rate or less than 1/3 of global prevalence rate.

Source: UNDCP, *World Drug Report 2000* .

Abuse of cocaine

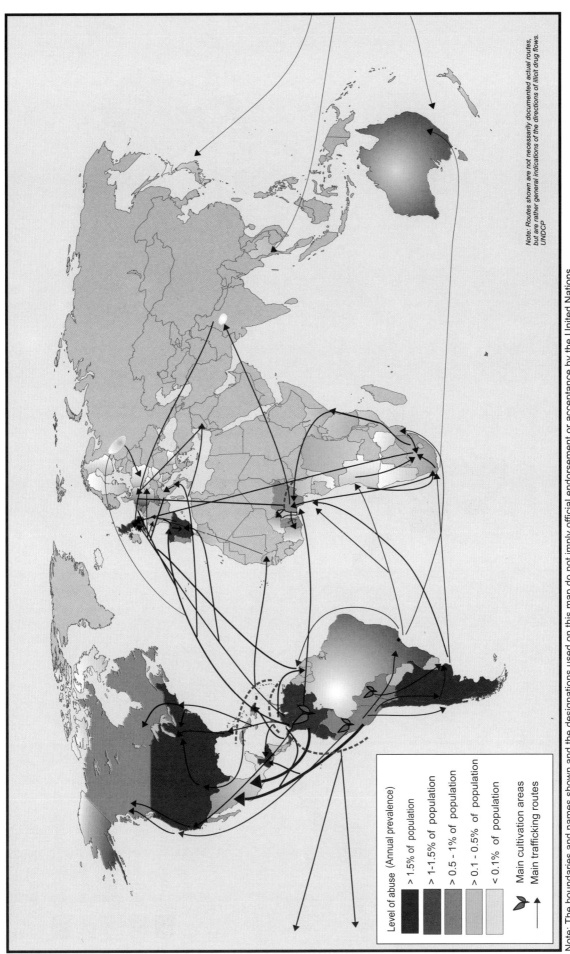

Level of abuse (Annual prevalence)

- \> 1.5% of population
- \> 1-1.5% of population
- \> 0.5 - 1% of population
- \> 0.1 - 0.5% of population
- < 0.1% of population

Main cultivation areas

Main trafficking routes

Note: Routes shown are not necessarily documented actual routes, but are rather general indications of the directions of illicit drug flows. UNDCP

Note: The boundaries and names shown and the designations used on this map do not imply official endorsement or acceptance by the United Nations.

Changes in abuse of cocaine, 1999 (or latest year available)

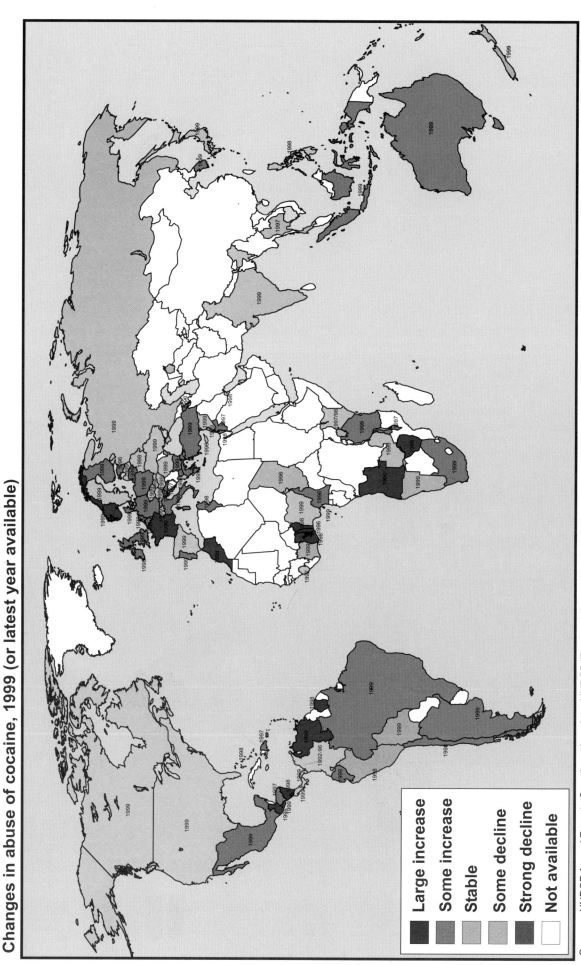

Large increase
Some increase
Stable
Some decline
Strong decline
Not available

Sources: UNDCP Annual Reports Questionnaires data, UNDCP (Regional Centre Bangkok) Epidemiology Workgroup, December 1999, National Household Surveys submitted to UNDCP, United States Department of State (Bureau for International Narcotics and Law Enforcement Affairs) International Narcotics Control Strategy Report, 1999;Bundeskriminalamt (BKA) and other Law Enforcement Reports, SACENDU (South African Community Epidemiology Network July - December 1998,UNDCP and Ministerio de Educacion,Estudio Epidemiologico 1999, CEDRO, Epidemiologia de Drogas en la poblacion urbana Peruana - 1995, INCB, Annual Report for 1999.

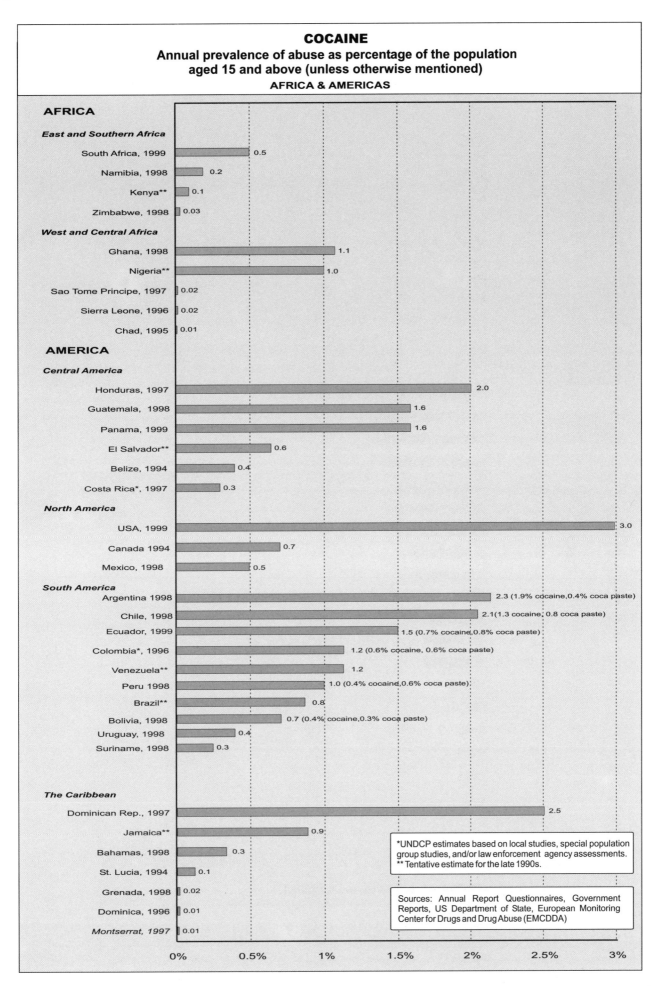

COCAINE
Annual prevalence of abuse as percentage of the population
aged 15 and above (unless otherwise mentioned)
AFRICA & AMERICAS

AFRICA

East and Southern Africa

South Africa, 1999 — 0.5
Namibia, 1998 — 0.2
Kenya** — 0.1
Zimbabwe, 1998 — 0.03

West and Central Africa

Ghana, 1998 — 1.1
Nigeria** — 1.0
Sao Tome Principe, 1997 — 0.02
Sierra Leone, 1996 — 0.02
Chad, 1995 — 0.01

AMERICA

Central America

Honduras, 1997 — 2.0
Guatemala, 1998 — 1.6
Panama, 1999 — 1.6
El Salvador** — 0.6
Belize, 1994 — 0.4
Costa Rica*, 1997 — 0.3

North America

USA, 1999 — 3.0
Canada 1994 — 0.7
Mexico, 1998 — 0.5

South America

Argentina 1998 — 2.3 (1.9% cocaine, 0.4% coca paste)
Chile, 1998 — 2.1 (1.3 cocaine; 0.8 coca paste)
Ecuador, 1999 — 1.5 (0.7% cocaine, 0.8% coca paste)
Colombia*, 1996 — 1.2 (0.6% cocaine, 0.6% coca paste)
Venezuela** — 1.2
Peru 1998 — 1.0 (0.4% cocaine, 0.6% coca paste)
Brazil** — 0.8
Bolivia, 1998 — 0.7 (0.4% cocaine, 0.3% coca paste)
Uruguay, 1998 — 0.4
Suriname, 1998 — 0.3

The Caribbean

Dominican Rep., 1997 — 2.5
Jamaica** — 0.9
Bahamas, 1998 — 0.3
St. Lucia, 1994 — 0.1
Grenada, 1998 — 0.02
Dominica, 1996 — 0.01
Montserrat, 1997 — 0.01

*UNDCP estimates based on local studies, special population group studies, and/or law enforcement agency assessments.
** Tentative estimate for the late 1990s.

Sources: Annual Report Questionnaires, Government Reports, US Department of State, European Monitoring Center for Drugs and Drug Abuse (EMCDDA)

0%   0.5%   1%   1.5%   2%   2.5%   3%

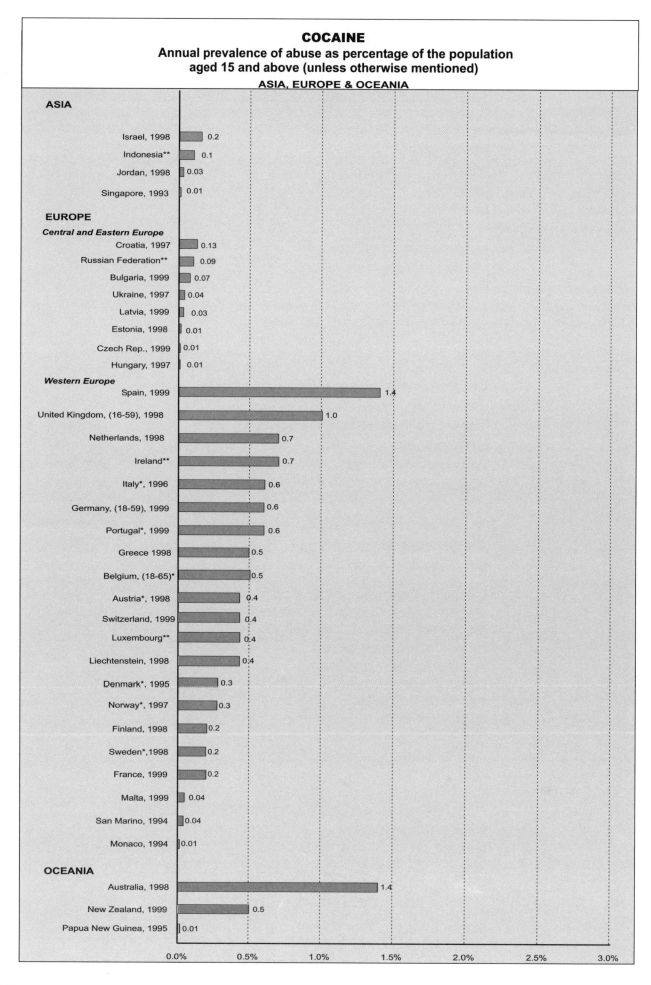

COCAINE
Annual prevalence of abuse as percentage of the population aged 15 and above (unless otherwise mentioned)
ASIA, EUROPE & OCEANIA

ASIA

Israel, 1998	0.2
Indonesia**	0.1
Jordan, 1998	0.03
Singapore, 1993	0.01

EUROPE

Central and Eastern Europe

Croatia, 1997	0.13
Russian Federation**	0.09
Bulgaria, 1999	0.07
Ukraine, 1997	0.04
Latvia, 1999	0.03
Estonia, 1998	0.01
Czech Rep., 1999	0.01
Hungary, 1997	0.01

Western Europe

Spain, 1999	1.4
United Kingdom, (16-59), 1998	1.0
Netherlands, 1998	0.7
Ireland**	0.7
Italy*, 1996	0.6
Germany, (18-59), 1999	0.6
Portugal*, 1999	0.6
Greece 1998	0.5
Belgium, (18-65)*	0.5
Austria*, 1998	0.4
Switzerland, 1999	0.4
Luxembourg**	0.4
Liechtenstein, 1998	0.4
Denmark*, 1995	0.3
Norway*, 1997	0.3
Finland, 1998	0.2
Sweden*,1998	0.2
France, 1999	0.2
Malta, 1999	0.04
San Marino, 1994	0.04
Monaco, 1994	0.01

OCEANIA

Australia, 1998	1.4
New Zealand, 1999	0.5
Papua New Guinea, 1995	0.01

0.0%   0.5%   1.0%   1.5%   2.0%   2.5%   3.0%

TRENDS

Americas

While abuse in several of the cocaine transit countries continued expanding, use of cocaine in the USA -- the world's largest cocaine market — were characterized by a further stabilization. Annual prevalence in 1999 remained unchanged at 1.7% of the population age 12 and above; monthly prevalence remained unchanged at 0.8%. If data from the newly developed computer-assisted interviews methodology (CAI) is used, the monthly prevalence, for 1999, fell to 0.7%. Annual prevalence in 1999 was thus two thirds lower, and monthly prevalence was as much as 70% lower than in 1985.

Most of the decline over the last two decades was related to occasional use of cocaine. Hard- core use of cocaine (i.e. use at least weekly) fell as well, though less significantly. It was 14% lower in 1998 than a decade earlier. Official projections see the downward trend continuing. In 1999 - for the first time in years - the number of cocaine related emergency room visits declined compared to a year earlier and treatment demand for cocaine abuse declined as well in the late 1990s. The numbers of high-school students taking cocaine declined in 2000 -- the first such decline reported in recent years. Nonetheless, hard-core and occasional

use of cocaine taken together still affected 6.6 million people in 1998 or 3% of the US population aged 12 and above, which is the by far largest such number reported worldwide from any country. Even the projected decline to 5.5 million people by the year 2000 or 2.5% of the population aged 12 and above, will not change this assessment though it constitutes a substantial improvement compared to the situation ten or fifteen years ago and is a reflection of the strong US efforts to curb cocaine abuse through a combination of both supply side and demand side measures. Thus, the upward trend in cocaine use among high-school students was stopped in the late 1990s and turned into a decline by the year 2000.

Most other countries in the Americas report less promising trends and cocaine abuse is mostly seen to be on the rise. There are, however, exceptions. The latest surveys undertaken in Peru and in Bolivia - the two main coca leaf producing countries in the Americas up until the mid 1990s - found significantly less people experimenting with cocaine in the late 1990s than were identified in previous surveys, reversing the upward trend of the early 1990s. Though the possibility that methodological issues may have been responsible for some of the decrease, cannot be excluded, the declines are still significant. Declines in production of coca leaf in both Peru and Bolivia, and related awareness of the problems, may have played a role as well as other country

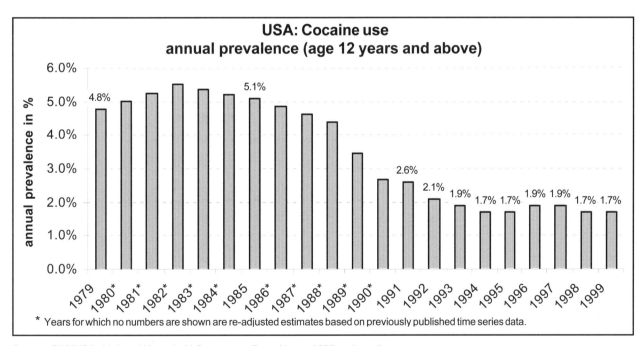

* Years for which no numbers are shown are re-adjusted estimates based on previously published time series data.

Source: SAMHSA, *National Household Surveys on Drug Abuse*, 1999 and previous years.

USA: monthly and life-time cocaine prevalence rates in % of population age 12 and above											
Prevalence	1979	1985	1991	1992	1993	1994	1995	1996	1997	1998	1999[a]	1999[b]
Monthly	2.6	3	1	0.7	0.7	0.7	0.7	0.8	0.7	0.8	0.8	0.7
Life-time	8.6	11.2	11.5	10.9	11.3	10.4	10.3	10.3	10.5	10.6	n/a	11.5

[a]traditional method (PAPI)   [b]new method - computer assisted interviews (CAI)

Source: Substance Abuse and Mental Health Services Administration (SAMHSA), *1999 National Household Survey on Drug Abuse* (and previous years).

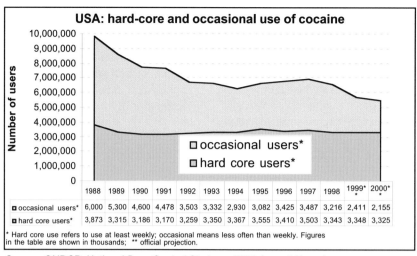

Source: ONDCP, *National Drug Control Strategy, 2001 Annual Report.*

occasional users*	6,000	5,300	4,600	4,478	3,503	3,332	2,930	3,082	3,425	3,487	3,216	2,411	2,155
hard core users*	3,873	3,315	3,186	3,170	3,259	3,350	3,367	3,555	3,410	3,503	3,343	3,348	3,325

* Hard core use refers to use at least weekly; occasional means less often than weekly. Figures in the table are shown in thousands; ** official projection.

Development of cocaine abuse in Bolivia (1992-1999)

Substance	Prevalence:	Year (research institution)			
		1992	1996	1998	1999
Cocaine hydrochloride	Monthly	0.10%	0.50%	0.70%	0.10%
	Annual	0.20%	1.50%	1.30%	0.40%
	Life-time	1.20%	2.40%	2.10%	1.40%
Coca paste / basuco	Monthly	0.20%	0.70%	0.60%	0.10%
	Annual	0.30%	1.70%	1.30%	0..3%
	Life-time	1.20%	2.60%	2.20%	1.00%
Age-group		12-50	12 and above	12 and above	12-64
Sample size		5952	6083	13973	3998
Sample characteristics		cities of more than 30,000 inhabitants	cities of more than 30,000 inhabitants	34 urban and rural areas	national coverage
Research institution		CIEC/PROINCO	CELIN	CELIN	Scientifica

Source: Vice-Ministerio de Prevencion y Rehabilitacion Social / Cientifica, Estudio de Prevalencia del Consumo de Drogas en Bolivia, Encuesta Nacional de Hogares 1999, La Paz, 1999.

Development of cocaine abuse in Peru

Drug	Prevalence	1992	1995	1997	1998 (December)	
Cocaine	Annual	0.5	0.2	n/a	0.5	0.4
	Life-time	1.3	1.9	3.2	1.4	1.3
Coca paste / basuco	Annual	0.8	0.7	n/a	0.6	0.6
	Life-time	2.8	3.1	4.7	3.4	3.1
Age-group		12-50	12-50	12-50	12-64	
Sample characteristics		urban population	urban population	urban population	towns of more than 20,000 inhabitants	
Research institution		CEDRO	CEDRO	CEDRO	NTRADROGAS	

Sources:CEDRO (Centro de Información y Educación para la Prevención del Abuso de Drogas), Epidemiología de Drogas en población Urbana Peruana – 1997 (and previous years); CONTRADROGAS, Encuesta Nacional de Prevencion y Uso de Drogas.

specific factors. In Peru, for instance, the closing of the air corridor to Colombia as of the mid 1990s contributed to an acceleration in the development of a local cocaine processing capacity as well as to temporary excess supply which was dumped on to the local market. Once trafficking links to markets outside the country were re-established, the cocaine began to move to more lucrative markets abroad, as of 1998, and abuse levels began to come down.

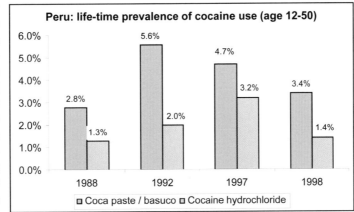

Sources: CEDRO (surveys 1988-97) and CONTRADROGAS (survey 1988), quoted in CEDRO, CONTRADROGAS, PNUFID, UNICRI, *Estudio Global de Mercados de Drogas Illicitas en Lima Metropolitana*, August 2000.

in the cocaine abuse ranking of countries in the Americas[d]. Except for the USA, the largest levels of cocaine hydrochloride use - as measured by life-time prevalence - are now encountered in Chile, Argentina and Brazil (state of Sao Paulo). Peru's and Bolivia's life-time prevalence rates for cocaine are also less than those of Colombia. Peru's life-time prevalence rate for coca paste, however, is still the high-

The apparent declines in abuse levels in the late 1990s also meant that both Peru and Bolivia were falling back

est in the Americas, though the country ranks only third (after Chile and Ecuador), if the analysis is based on annual prevalence data instead. Basing the overall comparisons on annual prevalence data, the most striking

Annual and monthly prevalence of cocaine abuse reported from countries in the Americas (as a percentage of the youth and adult population)

	Annual prevalence		Monthly prevalence	
	Cocaine	Coca Paste	Cocaine	Coca Paste
Argentina, 1999	1.9%	0.4%	1.3%	0.1%
USA, 1999	1.7% (3%)*	-	0.7%	-
Chile, 1998	1.3%	0.8%	0.4%	0.4%
Canada, 1994	0.7%	-	-	-
Ecuador, 1999	0.7%	0.8%	0.4%	0.6%
Mexico, 1998	0.5%	-	0.2%	-
Peru, 1998	0.4%	0.6%	0.1%	0.3%
Bolivia, 1999	0.4%	0.3%	0.1%	0.1%
Uruguay, 1998	0.4%	-	-	-
Costa Rica, 1995	0.2%	-	0.1%	-

* including hard-core cocaine users who do not usually appear in household surveys.

Sources: for Argentina, Bolivia, Chile, Peru and Uruguay: UNDCP, Sistema Subregional de Informacion sobre el Uso Indebido de Drogas; for Canada: Canadian Centre on Substance Abuse; for Costa Rica: El Instituto sobre Alcoholismo y Farmacodependencia; for Edcuador: UNDCP, Annual Reports Questionnaire, for Mexico: Consejo Nacional Sobre Adicciones.

Colombia: life-time prevalence of cocaine use in the late 1990s among youth*

	1996 Household survey*			1999 Youth survey (RUMBOS)*
Age group	12-17	18-24	12-24 (unweighted average)	10-24
Drugs:				
Cocaine hydrochloride	0.5%	1.1%	0.8%	3.6%
Basuco	0.5%	1.3%	0.9%	2.1%
Sample characteristics	150 municipalities in 30 departments			29 capital cities
Sample size	18,770			305,869

* Results are not directly comparable due to differences in methodological approach.
Sources: National Drug Control Office, Use of Psychoactive Drugs in Colombia, 1996, Programa Presidencial RUMBOS, Sondeo Nacional del Consumo de Drogas en Jovenes, 1999.

d) UNDCP supported in 1988/99 national household surveys in Argentina, Bolivia, Chile, Peru and Uruguay (project title "Sistema Subregional de Informacion sobre el Uso Indebido de Drogas") in order to guarantee a greater degree of cross-country comparability.

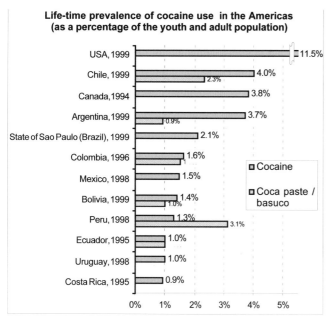

**Life-time prevalence of cocaine use in the Americas
(as a percentage of the youth and adult population)**

USA, 1999	11.5%
Chile, 1999	4.0% / 2.3%
Canada, 1994	3.8%
Argentina, 1999	3.7% / 0.9%
State of Sao Paulo (Brazil), 1999	2.1%
Colombia, 1996	1.6%
Mexico, 1998	1.5%
Bolivia, 1999	1.4% / 1.0%
Peru, 1998	1.3% / 3.1%
Ecuador, 1995	1.0%
Uruguay, 1998	1.0%
Costa Rica, 1995	0.9%

☐ Cocaine
☐ Coca paste / basuco

Sources: for Argentina, Bolivia, Chile, Peru and Uruguay: UNDCP, Sistema Subregional de Informacion sobre el Uso Indebido de Drogas; for Canada: Canadian Centre on Substance Abuse; for Costa Rica: El Instituto sobre Alcoholismo y Farmacodependencia; for Edcuador: UNDCP, Annual Reports Questionnaire, for Mexico: Consejo Nacional Sobre Adicciones; for USA : SAMHSA.

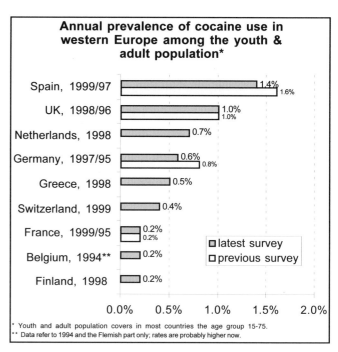

Annual prevalence of cocaine use in western Europe among the youth & adult population*

Spain, 1999/97	1.4% / 1.6%
UK, 1998/96	1.0% / 1.0%
Netherlands, 1998	0.7%
Germany, 1997/95	0.6% / 0.8%
Greece, 1998	0.5%
Switzerland, 1999	0.4%
France, 1999/95	0.2% / 0.2%
Belgium, 1994**	0.2%
Finland, 1998	0.2%

☐ latest survey
☐ previous survey

* Youth and adult population covers in most countries the age group 15-75.
** Data refer to 1994 and the Flemish part only; rates are probably higher now.

Sources: EMCDDA, *2000 Annual Report on the State of the Drug Problem in the European Union*; UNDCP, Annual Reports Questionnaire Data.

results are the very high abuse levels reported from Argentina (1.9%) and Chile (1.3%) which are already at levels similar to those in US household surveys (1.7% in 1999); though they are still below the total estimate of cocaine users in the USA (3% in 1998). The relatively small difference between life-time and annual use of cocaine across South America (between a quarter and half), compared to the USA (less than a fifth) is also an indication of the relatively recent growth of cocaine abuse in South America.

The only country in South America, which did not report an increase in cocaine abuse in 1999 was Colombia. The perception of stable abuse levels was based on national household surveys undertaken in 1992 and 1996. However, it is possible that cocaine abuse started rising again in the second half of the 1990s in the wake of strong domestic growth in coca leaf production, an intensification of trafficking activities and the ongoing civil war. A national youth survey undertaken in 1999 points in this direction, even though the household survey and the youth survey - for methodological reasons - are not directly comparable. By far the highest levels of cocaine use according to the 1999 youth survey - more than twice the national average - were reported from the town of Medellin, known for its vulnerability to cocaine trafficking. All neighbouring countries (except for Peru) have reported increases. A strong increase was reported by the authorities in Venezuela in 1999 while data submitted by the authorities of Ecuador indicate a significant increase over the 1995-99 period.

Europe

In Europe's two main cocaine markets, Spain and the UK, as well as in Sweden, Switzerland and Austria, abuse levels were reported to have stabilized in 1999. However, in most other West European countries, including France, Germany, the Netherlands, Belgium, Denmark, Norway, Portugal, Cyprus and Turkey, authorities reported increases The overall trend in western Europe thus appears to be going upwards. This is reflected in some youth surveys as well as in treatment demand and enforcement data. However, a rising trend in cocaine abuse is not really confirmed by general population survey data which point, rather, to a stabilization of abuse levels in the late 1990s.

Nonetheless, - in contrast to the situation some twenty years ago, data do show that cocaine use is now far more widespread than opiate use of opiates among the general population of western Europe, even though the latter still accounts for the bulk of treatment demand. Cocaine in Europe - similar to the USA in the 1970s prior to the crack-epidemic - is often used recreationally and constitutes less of social problem than in North America. However, there has been a trend towards poly-drug abuse, which not only affects recreational use but also problem drug use. In the European context this means that many heroin addicts consume cocaine, increasingly in the form of crack. Similarly, there have been reports across western Europe of people on methadone maintenance programmes using cocaine to get their 'kick' which, as a consequence of being on methadone, cannot any longer get from heroin.

Cocaine abuse in most east European countries, by contrast, is still far less widespread and less of a problem. A majority of countries in eastern Europe either did not report on cocaine at all, or they perceived abuse levels as stable to declining (Czech Republic, Hungary, Latvia, Romania). Only authorities in Poland, Lithuania and Bulgaria perceived cocaine abuse to be on the rise. The latter case is apparently linked to cocaine having been shipped to Turkey for further distribution - via the Balkan route - to western Europe which led to some spill-overs into the local market.

Africa

Cocaine abuse in Africa continues to be concentrated in southern and western Africa. Reported trends for 1999 show a rather mixed picture. The only country reporting an increase in cocaine use in eastern Africa was Tanzania. While cocaine use has been increasing in the Republic of South Africa and a strong increase was reported by the authorities in Angola - reflecting the ongoing trafficking of cocaine via Brazil to Africa, consumption remained stable in Nigeria and was even decreasing in Cote d'Ivoire which may be a reflection of some shifts in cocaine trafficking routes from western Africa to southern Africa. Though the bulk of cocaine being shipped to Africa is for final destinations in Europe, spill-overs do take place and supply the local market. The only country regularly reporting on cocaine in northern Africa, is Morocco, where abuse levels have been reported to have remained stable in 1999.

Oceania

While authorities of New Zealand found cocaine use to have remained stable, Australia reported an ongoing rise. Increases have indeed been significant in the late1990s. Annual prevalence almost tripled between 1993 and 1998 -- from 0.5% to 1.4% of those aged 14 and above -- which is equivalent to the highest such

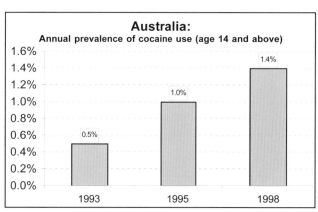

Australia:
Annual prevalence of cocaine use (age 14 and above)

Source: Australian Institute of Health and Welfare, *1988 National Drug Strategy Household Survey*, August 1999 (and previous years).

rates reported from Europe (Spain), and life-time prevalence rates reached 4.3% in 1998, marginally higher than the highest figures reported from countries in South America. Methodological differences, notably a lower tendency to under-report drug abuse in Australia, may be party responsible for the rather high figures, compared to other countries.

Asia

Cocaine abuse in Asian countries, in general, is still a relatively rare phenomenon. Only seven Asian countries reported trends in cocaine consumption in 1999, and most of these showed stable or downward trends.

CANNABIS

EXTENT

Cannabis is the most widely consumed drug worldwide. UNDCP estimates show that 3.4% of the global population (age 15 and above) used cannabis in the late 1990s. Prevalence rates were clearly above average in Oceania, North and South America as well as in Africa

Annual prevalence estimates of cannabis use in the late 1990s		
	Number of people (in million)	in % of population age 15 and above
OCEANIA	4.5	19.3
- North America	22.2	7.2
- South America	14.7	5.3
AMERICAS	36.9	6.3
AFRICA	27.2	5.8
- Western Europe	17.4	5.4
- Eastern Europe	4.7	1.5
EUROPE	22.1	3.5
ASIA	53.5	2.1
GLOBAL	144.1	3.4
Above global average*: ▨ close to global average: ▦ below global average**:▢		
* 1 percentage point more than global prevalence rate or 3 times the global prevalence rate. ** 1 percentage point below global prevalence rate or less than 1/3 of global prevalence rate. Source: UNDCP, *World Drug Report 2000* .		

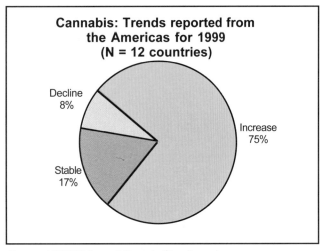

Source: UNDCP, Annual Reports Questionnaire.

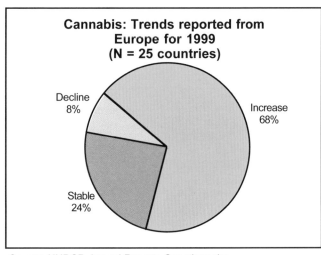

Source: UNDCP, Annual Reports Questionnaire.

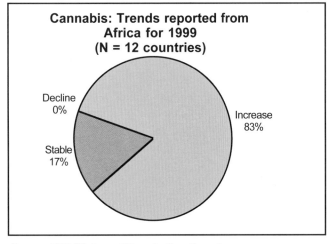

Source: UNDCP, Annual Reports Questionnaire.

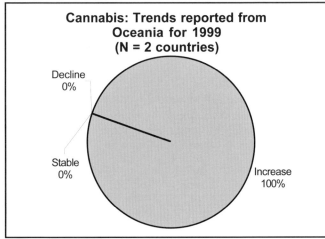

Source: UNDCP, Annual Reports Questionnaire.

and in western Europe. The largest numbers of cannabis users are found in Asia, accounting for more than third of global cannabis consumption, followed by a quarter in the Americas, and a fifth in Africa.

Trends

The general trends of cannabis use, reported by member states to UNDCP for the year 1999, have shown an increase. Increases have been reported by a majority of countries in the Americas (both South and North America), in Europe (both West and East Europe), in Africa (i.e. in southern, western, eastern and northern Africa) and in Oceania. Only in Asia the picture is mixed.

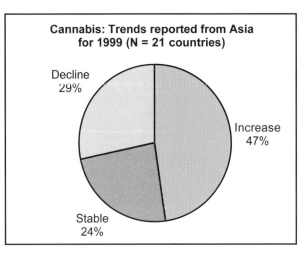

Source: UNDCP, Annual Reports Questionnaire.

Given the large number of countries reporting increases in cannabis use, it would be useful to highlight the countries which deviate from this pattern:
• In Asia, declines have been mainly reported from

countries in South- and South-West Asia as well as from two Central Asian countries bordering the South-West Asia region; in East Asia, authorities of Japan reported as stabilization and so did the authorities of Singapore; in the Near East, Syria reported a stabilization while the authorities of the Lebanon reported a decline;

• In Europe stable trends were reported from the UK and Spain, Europe's two largest cannabis markets as well as from some of the smaller countries; a decline was reported from Greece;

• In Africa stable trends were reported from Nigeria and Tanzania;

• In the Americas stable trends were reported from Mexico while surveys found some decline in Bolivia.

Abuse of Cannabis

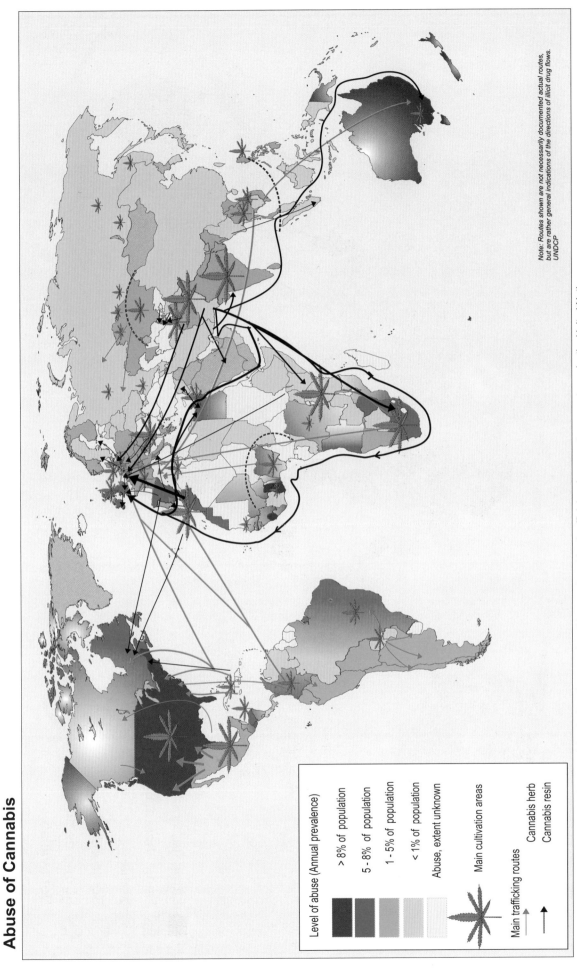

Level of abuse (Annual prevalence)

- > 8% of population
- 5 - 8% of population
- 1 - 5% of population
- < 1% of population
- Abuse, extent unknown

Main cultivation areas

Main trafficking routes

Cannabis herb

Cannabis resin

Note: Routes shown are not necessarily documented actual routes, but are rather general indications of the directions of illicit drug flows.
UNDCP

Note: The boundaries and names shown and the designations used on this map do not imply official endorsement or acceptance by the United Nations.

Changes in abuse of cannabis, 1999 (or latest year available)

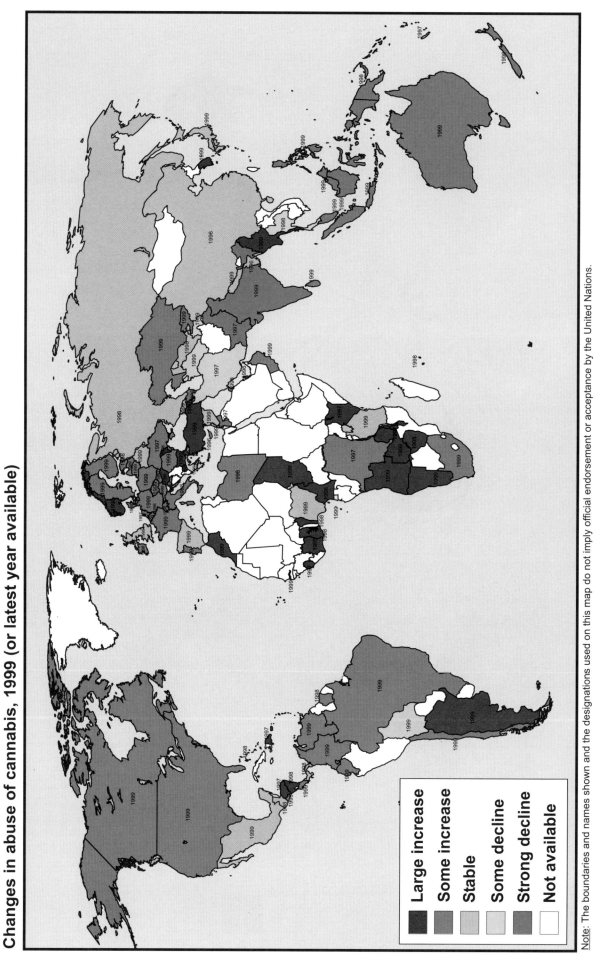

Legend:
- Large increase
- Some increase
- Stable
- Some decline
- Strong decline
- Not available

Note: The boundaries and names shown and the designations used on this map do not imply official endorsement or acceptance by the United Nations.

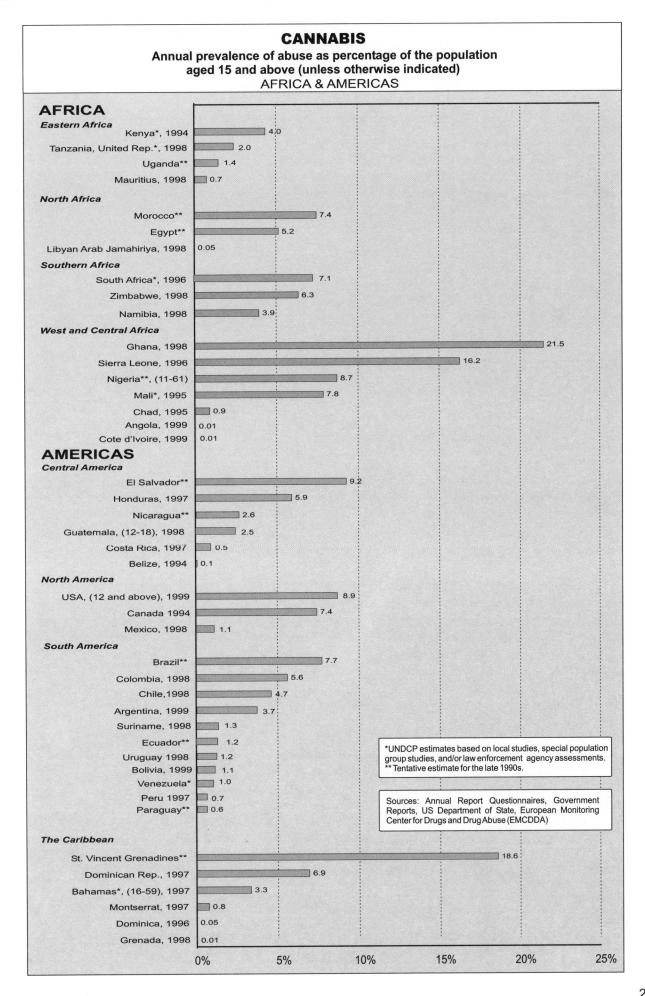

CANNABIS
Annual prevalence of abuse as percentage of the population aged 15 and above (unless otherwise indicated)
AFRICA & AMERICAS

AFRICA

Eastern Africa
- Kenya*, 1994 — 4.0
- Tanzania, United Rep.*, 1998 — 2.0
- Uganda** — 1.4
- Mauritius, 1998 — 0.7

North Africa
- Morocco** — 7.4
- Egypt** — 5.2
- Libyan Arab Jamahiriya, 1998 — 0.05

Southern Africa
- South Africa*, 1996 — 7.1
- Zimbabwe, 1998 — 6.3
- Namibia, 1998 — 3.9

West and Central Africa
- Ghana, 1998 — 21.5
- Sierra Leone, 1996 — 16.2
- Nigeria**, (11-61) — 8.7
- Mali*, 1995 — 7.8
- Chad, 1995 — 0.9
- Angola, 1999 — 0.01
- Cote d'Ivoire, 1999 — 0.01

AMERICAS

Central America
- El Salvador** — 9.2
- Honduras, 1997 — 5.9
- Nicaragua** — 2.6
- Guatemala, (12-18), 1998 — 2.5
- Costa Rica, 1997 — 0.5
- Belize, 1994 — 0.1

North America
- USA, (12 and above), 1999 — 8.9
- Canada 1994 — 7.4
- Mexico, 1998 — 1.1

South America
- Brazil** — 7.7
- Colombia, 1998 — 5.6
- Chile,1998 — 4.7
- Argentina, 1999 — 3.7
- Suriname, 1998 — 1.3
- Ecuador** — 1.2
- Uruguay 1998 — 1.2
- Bolivia, 1999 — 1.1
- Venezuela* — 1.0
- Peru 1997 — 0.7
- Paraguay** — 0.6

The Caribbean
- St. Vincent Grenadines** — 18.6
- Dominican Rep., 1997 — 6.9
- Bahamas*, (16-59), 1997 — 3.3
- Montserrat, 1997 — 0.8
- Dominica, 1996 — 0.05
- Grenada, 1998 — 0.01

*UNDCP estimates based on local studies, special population group studies, and/or law enforcement agency assessments.
** Tentative estimate for the late 1990s.

Sources: Annual Report Questionnaires, Government Reports, US Department of State, European Monitoring Center for Drugs and Drug Abuse (EMCDDA)

0% 5% 10% 15% 20% 25%

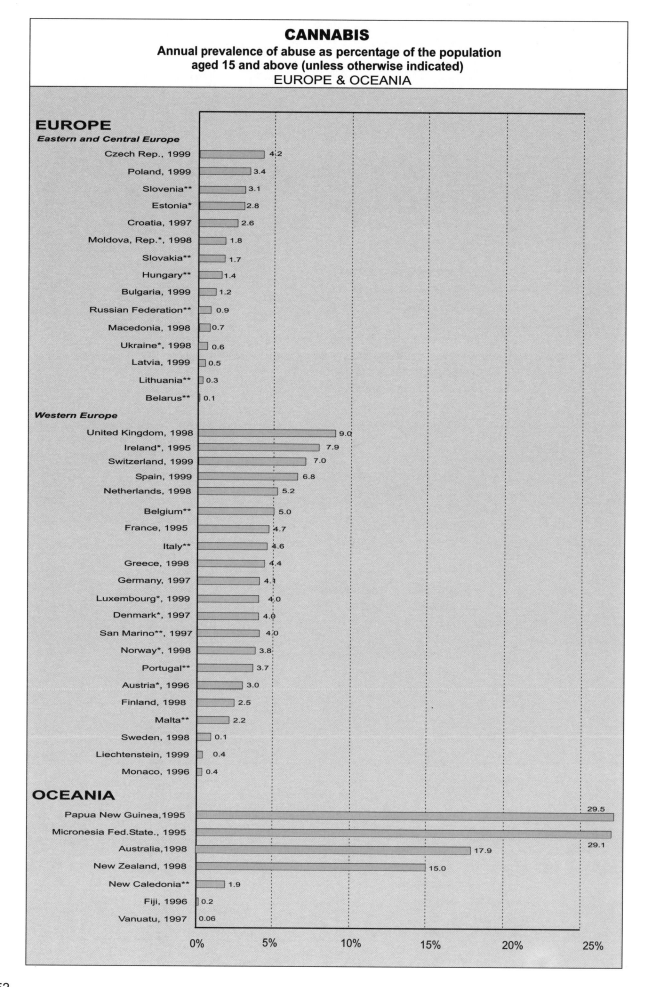

CANNABIS
Annual prevalence of abuse as percentage of the population
aged 15 and above (unless otherwise indicated)
EUROPE & OCEANIA

EUROPE
Eastern and Central Europe

Czech Rep., 1999	4.2
Poland, 1999	3.4
Slovenia**	3.1
Estonia*	2.8
Croatia, 1997	2.6
Moldova, Rep.*, 1998	1.8
Slovakia**	1.7
Hungary**	1.4
Bulgaria, 1999	1.2
Russian Federation**	0.9
Macedonia, 1998	0.7
Ukraine*, 1998	0.6
Latvia, 1999	0.5
Lithuania**	0.3
Belarus**	0.1

Western Europe

United Kingdom, 1998	9.0
Ireland*, 1995	7.9
Switzerland, 1999	7.0
Spain, 1999	6.8
Netherlands, 1998	5.2
Belgium**	5.0
France, 1995	4.7
Italy**	4.6
Greece, 1998	4.4
Germany, 1997	4.1
Luxembourg*, 1999	4.0
Denmark*, 1997	4.0
San Marino**, 1997	4.0
Norway*, 1998	3.8
Portugal**	3.7
Austria*, 1996	3.0
Finland, 1998	2.5
Malta**	2.2
Sweden, 1998	0.1
Liechtenstein, 1999	0.4
Monaco, 1996	0.4

OCEANIA

Papua New Guinea, 1995	29.5
Micronesia Fed.State., 1995	29.1
Australia, 1998	17.9
New Zealand, 1998	15.0
New Caledonia**	1.9
Fiji, 1996	0.2
Vanuatu, 1997	0.06

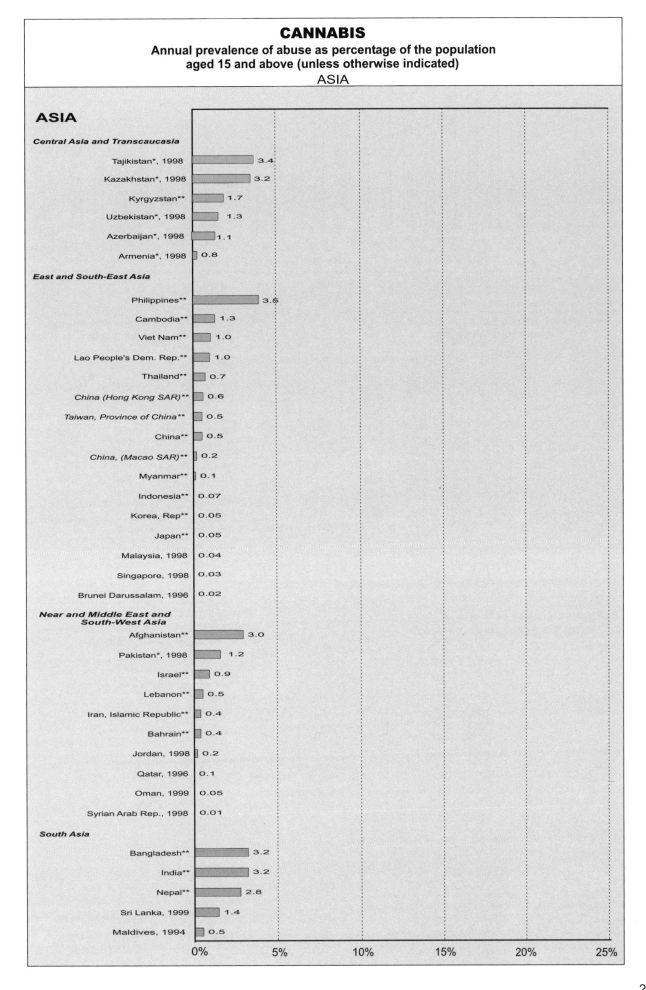

CANNABIS
Annual prevalence of abuse as percentage of the population
aged 15 and above (unless otherwise indicated)
ASIA

ASIA

Central Asia and Transcaucasia

Tajikistan*, 1998	3.4
Kazakhstan*, 1998	3.2
Kyrgyzstan**	1.7
Uzbekistan*, 1998	1.3
Azerbaijan*, 1998	1.1
Armenia*, 1998	0.8

East and South-East Asia

Philippines**	3.5
Cambodia**	1.3
Viet Nam**	1.0
Lao People's Dem. Rep.**	1.0
Thailand**	0.7
China (Hong Kong SAR)**	0.6
Taiwan, Province of China**	0.5
China**	0.5
China, (Macao SAR)**	0.2
Myanmar**	0.1
Indonesia**	0.07
Korea, Rep**	0.05
Japan**	0.05
Malaysia, 1998	0.04
Singapore, 1998	0.03
Brunei Darussalam, 1996	0.02

Near and Middle East and South-West Asia

Afghanistan**	3.0
Pakistan*, 1998	1.2
Israel**	0.9
Lebanon**	0.5
Iran, Islamic Republic**	0.4
Bahrain**	0.4
Jordan, 1998	0.2
Qatar, 1996	0.1
Oman, 1999	0.05
Syrian Arab Rep., 1998	0.01

South Asia

Bangladesh**	3.2
India**	3.2
Nepal**	2.8
Sri Lanka, 1999	1.4
Maldives, 1994	0.5

0%   5%   10%   15%   20%   25%

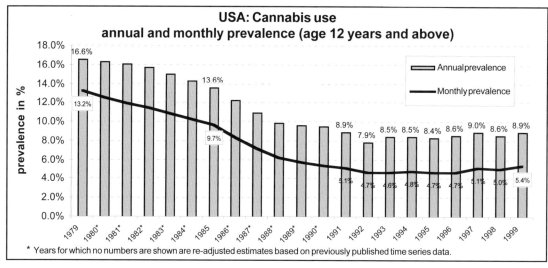

USA: Cannabis use
annual and monthly prevalence (age 12 years and above)

* Years for which no numbers are shown are re-adjusted estimates based on previously published time series data.

Source: Substance Abuse and Mental Health Services Administration, *1999 National Household Survey on Drug Abuse*, and previous years.

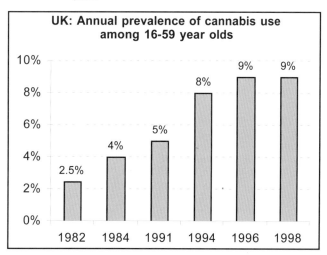

UK: Annual prevalence of cannabis use among 16-59 year olds

Sources: Home Office, *Self-Reported Drug Misuse in England and Wales: finding from the 1992 British Crime Survey*, London 1995, Home Office, *Drug Misuse Declared in 1988: result from the British Crime Survey*, London 1999.

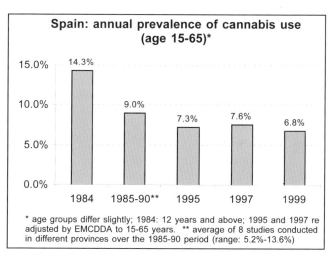

Spain: annual prevalence of cannabis use (age 15-65)*

* age groups differ slightly; 1984: 12 years and above; 1995 and 1997 re adjusted by EMCDDA to 15-65 years. ** average of 8 studies conducted in different provinces over the 1985-90 period (range: 5.2%-13.6%)

Sources: UNDCP, Annual Reports Questionnaire and EMCDDA, *Annual Report on the State of the Drugs Problem in the European Union*, Lisbon 2000,

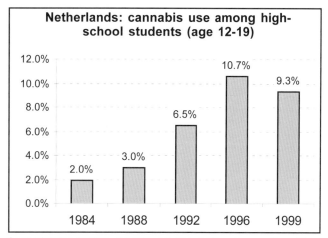

Netherlands: cannabis use among high-school students (age 12-19)

Source: Trimbos Institute, *Key data - smoking, drinking, drug use & gambling among pupils,* Utrecht 1997 and Trimbos Instituut (Zwart WM, Monshouwer K, Smit F), Jeugd en riskant gedrg, Kerngegevens 1999, Roken drinken, drugsgebruik en gokken onder scholieren vanaf tien jaar, Utrecht 2000.

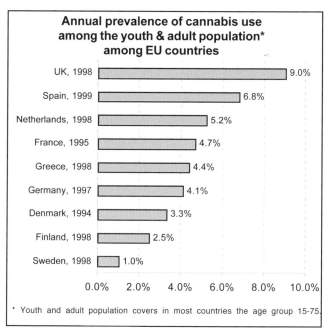

Annual prevalence of cannabis use among the youth & adult population* among EU countries

* Youth and adult population covers in most countries the age group 15-75.

Sources: UNDCP, Annual Reports Questionnaire and EMCDDA, *Annual Report on the State of the Drugs Problem in the European Union*, Lisbon 2000,

Even though in the USA, the world's largest cannabis market, cannabis use increased slightly in 1999 compared to a year earlier (both annual and monthly prevalence rates were going upwards) and compared to the mid 1990s, prevalence rates are still significantly below the levels reported a decade earlier and the market is one that has stabilized in the 1990s. The 1999 US Household Survey also stressed that the reported increase for 1999 was not statistically significant. Given the reported stabilization of cannabis consumption levels in Mexico and no significant increases reported from Canada or the USA, the whole North American cannabis market could be considered to be basically stable. The same, however, cannot be said of Central- and South-America or the Caribbean.

All available evidence also supports the views of the Governments in the Oceania region of rising levels of cannabis use. Similarly, in Africa there is no evidence available, that would question the perception of generally rising levels of cannabis use. A UNDCP study, conducted in several African countries in 1999, came to the same conclusion.

The situation is more complex in Europe. Trends reported by the authorities of most European countries to UNDCP, as mentioned earlier, indicate a rise in consumption. However, there are at the same time indications of a levelling off of consumption in western Europe. An explanation of these conflicting trends for cannabis has been given by the EMCDDA in its latest annual report on the state of the drug problem in the European Union for the year 2000: "*.. continuing rises in countries with previously lower levels and some stabilisation in higher prevalence countries confirm the tendency toward convergence...*" Indeed, in the two main cannabis markets - UK and Spain - consumption has stabilized and the same is also occurring in the

Netherlands, which so far had the third highest levels of cannabis use among the countries of the European Union. The latest high-school survey, conducted in 1999, indeed indicates a stabilization of cannabis use.

AMPHETAMINE-TYPE STIMULANTS

EXTENT

Abuse of amphetamines (i.e. amphetamine or methamphetamine) has been calculated to affect some 0.6% of the global population (age 15 and above). Though rates differ significantly from country to country, the regional averages - except for countries in the Oceania region - are rather close to the global average. About half the users of amphetamines (primarily methamphetamine) are found in Asia (mostly in the countries of East and South-East Asia). The Americas and Europe account for a third of global use of amphetamines. Relatively high levels of consumption have been also reported from countries in South America and in Africa. While consumption of amphetamines in North America, Europe and Asia is largely from clandestine sources, consumption in South America and Africa is still mainly supplied from licit channels where the dividing line between licit and illicit consumption is not always clear. Substances differ as well. While in Europe amphetamine is the ATS of choice, in South-East Asia and North America it is methamphetamine which in general is more potent and causes more health risks than amphetamine. Abuse patterns and risks associated with the abuse of different ATS are thus often not directly comparable with one another.

About 0.1% of the global population (age 15 and above) consume ecstasy. Significantly higher ratios have been reported from countries in Oceania region, western

Annual prevalence estimates of amphetamines' use in the late 1990s		
	Number of people (in million)	in % of population age 15 and above
OCEANIA	0.6	2.9
- Western Europe	3.1	0.8
- Eastern Europe	1.0	0.4
EUROPE	4.1	0.7
ASIA	2.1	0.7
- North America	2.2	0.8
- South America	4.3	0.7
AMERICAS	12.6	0.5
AFRICA	2.5	0.5
GLOBAL	24.2	0.6

Above global average*: [ ]   close to global average: [ ]   below global average**: [ ]

* 1 percentage point more than global prevalence rate or 3 times the global prevalence rate.

Source: UNDCP, *World Drug Report 2000* .

Annual prevalence estimates of ecstasy use in the late 1990s		
	Number of people (in million)	in % of population age 15 and above
OCEANIA	0.40	1.60
- Western Europe	2.30	0.60
- Eastern Europe	0.30	0.10
EUROPE	2.60	0.40
- North America	1.20	0.40
- South America	0.02	0.01
AMERICAS	1.20	0.20
AFRICA	0.10	0.02
ASIA	0.20	0.01
GLOBAL	4.50	0.10

Above global average*: ☐   close to global average: ☐   below global average**: ☐

* 1 percentage point more than global prevalence rate or 3 times the global prevalence rate.
** 1 percentage point below global prevalence rate or less than 1/3 of global prevalence rate.

Source: UNDCP, *World Drug Report 2000* .

Europe and North America. Some 60% of global consumption is concentrated in Europe. West Europe and North America together account for almost 85% of global consumption. Use of ecstasy, however, is increasingly spreading to developing countries as well.

TRENDS

Europe

The number of countries reporting 'large increases' in the abuse of ATS in western Europe halved over the 1995-1999 period, from nine to four. Nonetheless, a clear majority of countries in western Europe (13 out of 19) continue reporting increases in the levels of ATS use. This includes large countries such as Germany or France. Stable or declining levels were reported from Spain, Portugal, Sweden, the UK (with regard to methamphetamine) and two small countries, Andorra and Liechtenstein.

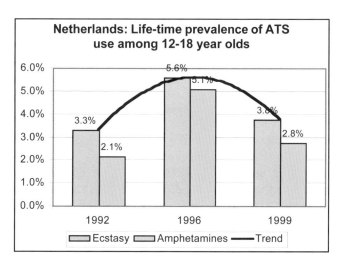

Source: Trimbos Institute, (Netherlands Institute for Mental Health and Addiction), *Jeugd en riskant gedrg,- roken drinken, drugsgebruik en gokken onder scholieren vanaf tien jaar*, Utrecht 2000.

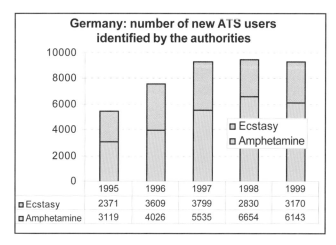

Source: Bundeskriminalamt, *Polizeiliche Kriminalstatistik 1999*, "Erstauffaellige Konsumenten harten Drogen (Falldatei Rauschgift)", Wiesbaden 2000.

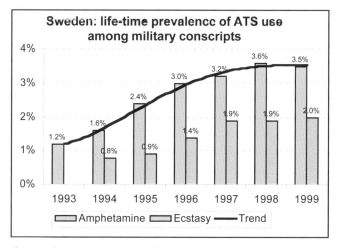

Source: Swedish Council for Information on Alcohol and other Drugs, *Drogutvecklingen i Sverige Rapport 2000*, Stockholm 2000.

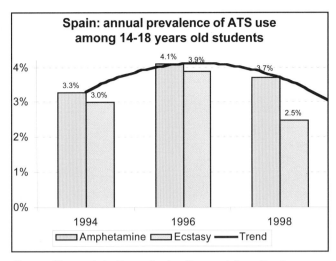

Source: Observatorio Espanol sobre Drogas, *Infome No. 3*, Madrid 2000

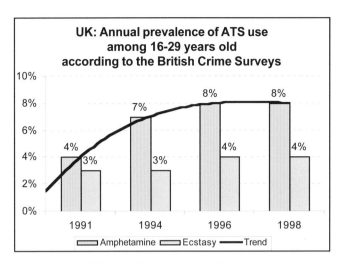

Sources: Home Office, *Self-Reported Drug Misuse in England and Wales: findings from the 1992 British Crime Survey*, London 1995, Home Office, *Drug Misuse Declared in 1998: result from the British Crime Survey*, London 1999.

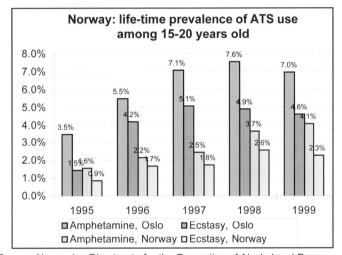

Source: Norwegian Directorate for the Prevention of Alcohol and Drug Problems and National Institute for Alochohol and Drug Research, *Alcohol and Drugs in Norway, Statistikk'99,* Oslo, November 1999.

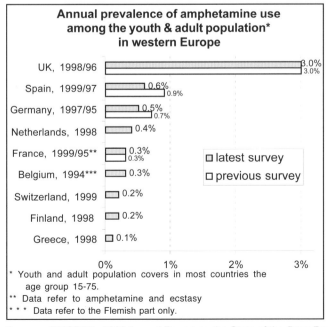

* Youth and adult population covers in most countries the age group 15-75.
** Data refer to amphetamine and ecstasy
* * * Data refer to the Flemish part only.

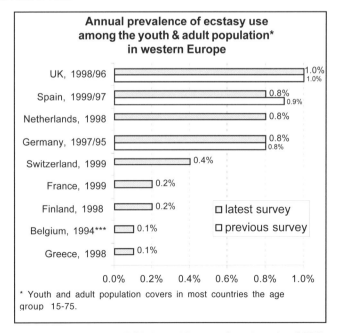

* Youth and adult population covers in most countries the age group 15-75.

Sources: EMCDDA, *2000 Annual Report on the State of the Drug Problem in the European Union*, UNDCP, Annual Reports Questionnaire, OFDT, *Baromètre Santé 2000*.

Changes in life-time prevalence of ATS use among 15-16 year olds (unless otherwise indicated) in the late 1990s in western Europe							
Country	Substance	Age Group	Comparison (years)		Life-time prevalence rates		Change
UK*	Amphetamines	15-16	1995	1997	13.0%	7.3%	-5.7%
	Ecstasy				8.0%	3.0%	-5.0%
Netherlands	Amphetamines	15-16	1996	1999	7.8%	n/a	n/a
	Ecstasy				8.1%	n/a	n/a
	Amphetamines	12-18			5.1%	2.8%	-2.3%
	Ecstasy				5.6%	3.8%	-1.8%
Spain	Amphetamines	15-16	1996	1998	4.1%	4.0%	-0.1%
	Ecstasy				4.6%	2.9%	-1.7%
Denmark	Amphetamines	15-16	1995	1997	1.9%	4.0%	2.1%
	Ecstasy				0.5%	3.1%	2.6%
Belgium (Flemish part of the country)	Amphetamines	15-16	1996	1998	3.2%	3.8%	0.6%
	Ecstasy				5.6%	6.2%	0.6%
Greece	Amphetamines	15-16	1993	1998	4.0%	3.6%	-0.4%
	Ecstasy				n/a	1.8%	n/a
Germany**	Amphetamines***	18-20	1995	1997	6.1%	3.2%	-2.9%
	Ecstasy				5.9%	4.1%	-1.7%
Italy	Amphetamines	15-16	1995	1999	3.0%	2.0%	-1.0%
	Ecstasy				4.0%	4.0%	0.0%
France	Amphetamines	15-16	1993	1997	2.5%****	1.9%	n/a
	Ecstasy				n/a	2.5%	n/a
Sweden	Amphetamines	15-16	1997	1998	0.9%	1.1%	0.2%
	Ecstasy				0.8%	1.0%	0.2%
Unweighted average of 10 EU countries	Amphetamines	15-16	1995	1998	4.4%	3.4%	-1.0%
	Ecstasy				4.4%	3.5%	-0.9%

*   Methodological differences limit comparability of results of 1995 and 1997 UK surveys.

**   Data for West-and East-Germany combined; calculation based on a weight of 80% for West- and 20% for East-Germany, reflecting the population structure.

***   Data for Germany for 1995 refer to stimulants while data for 1997 refer to amphetamines only.

*** *   1993 data for France refer to amphetamine and ecstasy.

Sources: EMCDDA, 2000 Annual Report on the State of the Drugs Problem in the European Union, Lisbon 2000, Trimbos Instituut (Netherlands Institute for Mental Health and Addiction), *Jeugd en riskant gedrag - Roken, drinken, drugsgebruik en gokken onder scholieren vanaf tien jaar*, Utrecht 2000, Ministry of Health, *Population Survey on the Consumption of Psychoactive Substances in the German Adult Population*, 1995 and 1997, Bonn 1997. NIDA, *Monitoring the Future*, 1975-1999.

Nevertheless, there are indications that – in contrast to the trends observed in the early 1990s – the peak in ATS use in western Europe may have passed and that the situation is actually stabilizing following more intensive prevention activities in recent years. Reports on the number of newly identified users by the German authorities as well as school surveys conducted in the Netherlands, Spain, the UK and Italy point in this direction.

In contrast to the countries mentioned before, the table above also shows ATS growing in Belgium and in the Nordic countries. However, there are now also signs of stabilicion in some of the Nordic countries as well. Regular surveys among 18 years-old military conscripts in Sweden, for instance, found in 1999, for the first time over the last decade, a stabilization in the use of

amphetamine. Similarly, surveys in Norway among 15-20 year olds showed in 1999, for the first time in years, a decline in the use of ecstasy while use of amphetamine declined in the capital, Oslo.

Parallel with the stabilization of ATS use among youth in several West European countries, as reflected in school surveys, general population surveys also indicate a stabilization or even a decline in abuse levels in the late 1990s. ATS use in the UK, Europe's largest ATS market, remained stable over the 1996-98 period. The most significant declines for both amphetamine and ecstasy over 1997-99 were reported from Spain, Europe's second largest ATS market It may be also interesting to note that the general population surveys do not indicate a rise in abuse levels in either Germany or in France.

In contrast to signs of a stabilization of ATS consumption levels in western Europe, there is little doubt that ATS use in eastern Europe continues rising. Almost all available studies, notably the ESPAD studies (which are to be published soon), indicate strong increases of ATS use across East Europe in the late 1990s. The authorities share largely the same perceptions as the results of these studies. Six out of eight East European countries reported an increase in 1999 while only one country (Latvia) reported lower levels of ATS abuse in 1999 as compared to a year earlier. Increases were reported by the authorities from Bulgaria, Poland, Hungary, Romania, Lithuania and Belarus.

Americas

Reported trends of ATS use in the Americas for the year 1999 were mixed. A relatively small number of countries (in total nine) reported trends in ATS use, suggesting that ATS were not the main concern of the countries in the Americas. The overall picture is rather diffused. While ecstasy use was generally perceived to be rising, use of amphetamines (i.e. amphetamine or methamphetamine) was reported to have stabilized in about half of the countries. Increases in methamphetamine abuse were reported from Argentina, Colombia, and Venezuela; while consumption of various ATS has had a long tradition in South America (notably those produced

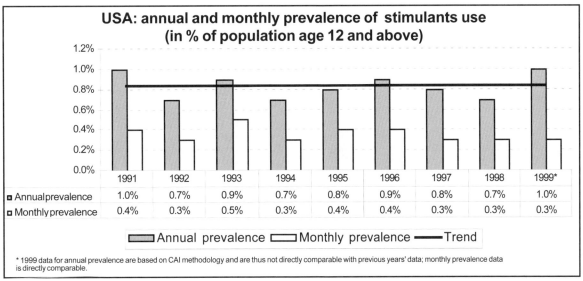

USA: annual and monthly prevalence of stimulants use (in % of population age 12 and above)

	1991	1992	1993	1994	1995	1996	1997	1998	1999*
Annual prevalence	1.0%	0.7%	0.9%	0.7%	0.8%	0.9%	0.8%	0.7%	1.0%
Monthly prevalence	0.4%	0.3%	0.5%	0.3%	0.4%	0.4%	0.3%	0.3%	0.3%

* 1999 data for annual prevalence are based on CAI methodology and are thus not directly comparable with previous years' data; monthly prevalence data is directly comparable.

Source: SAMHSA, *1999 National Household Survey on Drug Abuse* and previous years.

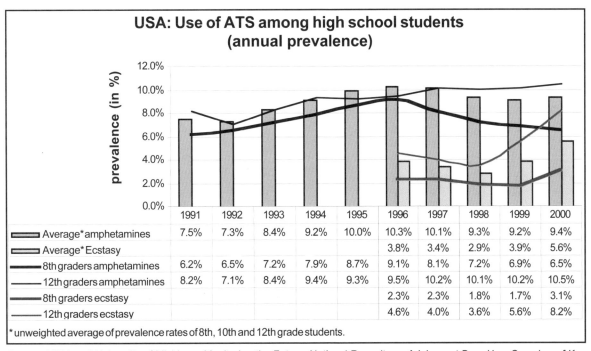

USA: Use of ATS among high school students (annual prevalence)

	1991	1992	1993	1994	1995	1996	1997	1998	1999	2000
Average*amphetamines	7.5%	7.3%	8.4%	9.2%	10.0%	10.3%	10.1%	9.3%	9.2%	9.4%
Average*Ecstasy						3.8%	3.4%	2.9%	3.9%	5.6%
8th graders amphetamines	6.2%	6.5%	7.2%	7.9%	8.7%	9.1%	8.1%	7.2%	6.9%	6.5%
12th graders amphetamines	8.2%	7.1%	8.4%	9.4%	9.3%	9.5%	10.2%	10.1%	10.2%	10.5%
8th graders ecstasy						2.3%	2.3%	1.8%	1.7%	3.1%
12th graders ecstasy						4.6%	4.0%	3.6%	5.6%	8.2%

* unweighted average of prevalence rates of 8th, 10th and 12th grade students.

Source: NIDA and University of Michigan, *Monitoring the Future, National Reusults on Adolescent Drug Use, Overview of Key Findings, 2000*, Washington 2001.

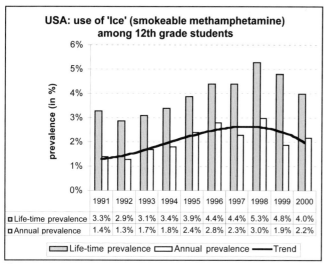

USA: use of 'Ice' (smokeable methamphetamine) among 12th grade students

	1991	1992	1993	1994	1995	1996	1997	1998	1999	2000
Life-time prevalence	3.3%	2.9%	3.1%	3.4%	3.9%	4.4%	4.4%	5.3%	4.8%	4.0%
Annual prevalence	1.4%	1.3%	1.7%	1.8%	2.4%	2.8%	2.3%	3.0%	1.9%	2.2%

Source: NIDA and University of Michigan, *Monitoring the Future*, 2000

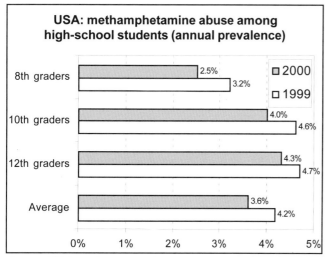

USA: methamphetamine abuse among high-school students (annual prevalence)

Source: NIDA and University of Michigan, *Monitoring the Future*, 2000

and sold as anorectics), methamphetamine was hardly known until a few years ago. By contrast, Mexico and Canada, where methamphetamine has been known for a long time, reported signs of stabilization in consumption levels. An overall decline in the use of ATS was reported by the authorities of El Salvador.

Household surveys in the USA show basically stable levels of stimulants use in recent years. Monthly prevalence of stimulants use -- currently the only directly comparable indicator -- remained unchanged between 1998 and 1999 and is basically at the level of the early 1990s. Annual prevalence data show some fluctuations, but no indications for an upward or a downward trend in the 1990s. Annual prevalence data for 1999 - due to the introduction of a new methodology (computer assisted interviews) are not directly comparable with those of previous years.

Regular studies among high-school students indicate a stabilization in the use of amphetamines, and - since

1996 - even a relatively strong decline among 8th graders. A general decline was reported for methamphetamine abuse in 2000. Ecstasy consumption, by contrast, has been going upwards in 1999 and even more so in 2000, among all age groups of the students.

Asia

In contrast to signs of stabilization in ATS use in western Europe and North America, ATS abuse, notably of methamphetamine, is growing rapidly in Asia. Out of 14 Asian countries reporting to UNDCP, 12 reported an increase. Eleven of them were located in the East and South-East Asia region. The countries & territories reporting strong increases in ATS (mostly methamphetamine) abuse were Hong Kong SAR, Indonesia and Brunei Darussalam; 'some increase' was reported from Thailand, Myanmar, Malaysia, Singapore, the Philippines, the Republic of Korea and Japan. Other reports indicate that the People's Republic of China as well as the Lao PDR, Cambodia and Vietnam are also facing a growing problem of ATS abuse, though starting from relatively low levels. The only Asian country outside the East and South-East Asia subregion, which also reported an increase in 1999, was India. Rising levels of ATS abuse are mostly found in the north-eastern

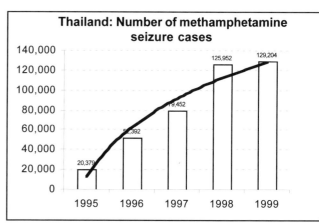

Thailand: Number of methamphetamine seizure cases

Source: Office of the Narcotics Control Board, Statistical Data of the Seized Methamphetamine in Thailand 1995-99.

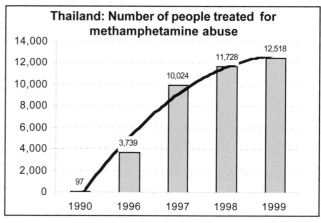

Thailand: Number of people treated for methamphetamine abuse

Source: Office of the Narcotics Control Board, *Thailand Narcotics Annual Report 2000* and previous years.

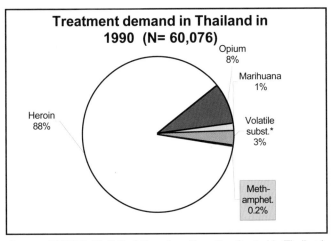

Treatment demand in Thailand in 1990 (N= 60,076)

Source: ONDCB, *Statistical Report on Narcotics Control in Thailand*, 1990-91.

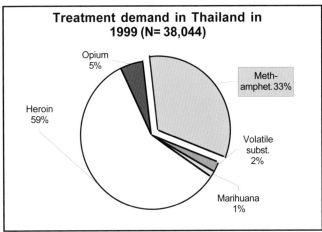

Treatment demand in Thailand in 1999 (N= 38,044)

Source: ONDCB, *Thailand Narcotics Annual Report 2000*.

states which are affected by illegal methamphetamine imports from neighbouring Myanmar.

There are relatively few regular surveys in East and South-East Asia which would allow for identifying abuse trends. In the absence of such studies, perceptions on the development of drug abuse problem are largely based on law enforcement statistics, intelligence reports and, in some countries, on treatment statistics.

Given the massive increases in methamphetamine related trafficking activities throughout the region in recent years, there can be, however, hardly any doubt that abuse has shown an upward trend. The case of Thailand, which keeps systematic records both on enforcement activities and on people in treatment and has conducted a number of surveys, illustrates the point that strong increases in trafficking go hand in hand with rising levels of abuse. Similar correlations can be also expected to hold true for other countries of the region. In Thailand, both the number of methamphetamine seizure cases and the number of people using methamphetamine during the 30 days prior to entering treatment tripled in the second half of the 1990s.

Treatment statistics show that methamphetamine related admissions rose from a negligible 0.2% of overall treatment demand in 1990 to 9% by 1996 and 33% in 1999. In parallel, the shares of opiates - both heroin and opium - declined. Studies indicate that as of the mid 1990s methamphetamine users surpassed the numbers of heroin users (Thailand Development Research Institute Foundation, 1994); it can be assumed that by now methamphetamine use has surpassed the overall number of opiates users in the country. There has been a notable trend of increased ATS use among youth. According to the Office of Narcotics Control Board (ONCB) overall drug use among high-school and college students doubled between 1994 and 1998 (from 72,000 cases in 1994 to 190,000 cases in 1998) and its

appears to have doubled again in 1999 (463,000 cases) with ATS being quoted as one of the main substances responsible for the rise. The 1999 study, conducted on behalf of ONCB, found that 12.4% of students had used drugs at least once in their life (up from 1.4% reported in previous studies)[e]. This approaches levels reported from some European countries and is higher than data reported from several other East and South-Asian countries, though still lower than revealed in surveys from North America or Australia.

The main markets for methamphetamine in Thailand continue to be central Thailand and the capital Bangkok. Methamphetamine use has grown even stronger in Bangkok than in the rest of the country. While the number of people admitted to treatment for methamphetamine abuse rose three-fold in Thailand between 1996-98, the corresponding numbers increased seven-fold in Bangkok and by more than thirty times over the 1994-98 period (from 133 to 4381 according to the Ministry of Public Health). Thus, Bangkok alone now accounts for more than a third of all methamphetamine related treatment demand in Thailand.

Even higher and still growing shares for methamphetamine in treatment were reported by the authorities in the

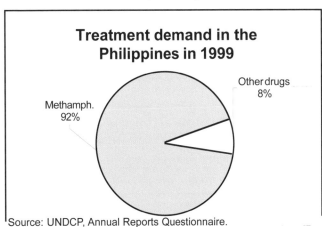

Treatment demand in the Philippines in 1999

Source: UNDCP, Annual Reports Questionnaire.

e) For more details see UNDCP/UNICRI, "Global Study on Illegal Drug Markets: The Case of Bangkok, Thailand", (Draft), February 2000.

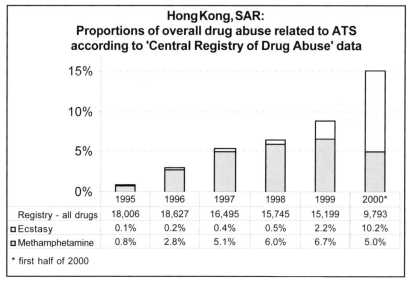

Hong Kong, SAR: Proportions of overall drug abuse related to ATS according to 'Central Registry of Drug Abuse' data

	1995	1996	1997	1998	1999	2000*
Registry - all drugs	18,006	18,627	16,495	15,745	15,199	9,793
▫ Ecstasy	0.1%	0.2%	0.4%	0.5%	2.2%	10.2%
▪ Methamphetamine	0.8%	2.8%	5.1%	6.0%	6.7%	5.0%

* first half of 2000

Source: Central Registry of Drug Abuse, quoted in UNDCP/UNICRI, The Hong Kong Drug Market (Draft), November 2000.

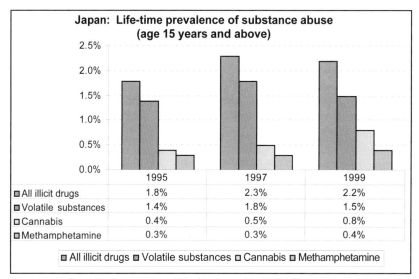

Japan: Life-time prevalence of substance abuse (age 15 years and above)

	1995	1997	1999
▪ All illicit drugs	1.8%	2.3%	2.2%
▪ Volatile substances	1.4%	1.8%	1.5%
▫ Cannabis	0.4%	0.5%	0.8%
▪ Methamphetamine	0.3%	0.3%	0.4%

▪ All illicit drugs ▪ Volatile substances ▫ Cannabis ▪ Methamphetamine

Source: National Institute of Mental Health, quoted in UNDCP/UNICRI, The Illegal Drug Market in Tokyo (Draft), June 2000.

Philippines. 92% of all clients in treatment suffered from methamphetamine related problems in 1999. The number of people officially registered for methamphetamine abuse in the Philippines (4,531 persons) rose in 1999 by 13.3% on a year earlier and was more than three times higher than in 1994. Increasing levels of methamphetamine abuse were notably reported from the work place. A link was also established between methamphetamine

abuse and rising levels of unemployment and rising levels of use in the workplace.

ATS abuse has also grown in Hong-Kong, SAR in the 1990s, notably in the second half of the 1990s. Though most drug abuse identified by the authorities is still linked to abuse of opiates, data contained in Hong-Kong's Central Registry on Drug Abuse show that the

Hong Kong: Drug use among secondary school students (life-time prevalence)

	All drugs*	Cough syrup	Marijuana	Solvents	Amphetamines	Mandrax	Heroin	Cocaine
1992 (age 11-21)	3.50%	1.50%	0.80%	0.50%	0.10%	0.20%	0.30%	0.00%
1996 (age 11-18)	13.50%	7.40%	1.50%	1.00%	0.50%	0.40%	0.20%	0.20%

* including other substances (barbiturates, tranquilizers, hallucinogens, etc.).

Source: Drug Addiction Research Unit (University of Hong Kong) and Narcotics Division (Hong Kong Government) quoted in UNDCP/UNICRI, The Hong Kong Drug Market, November 2000, p. 56.

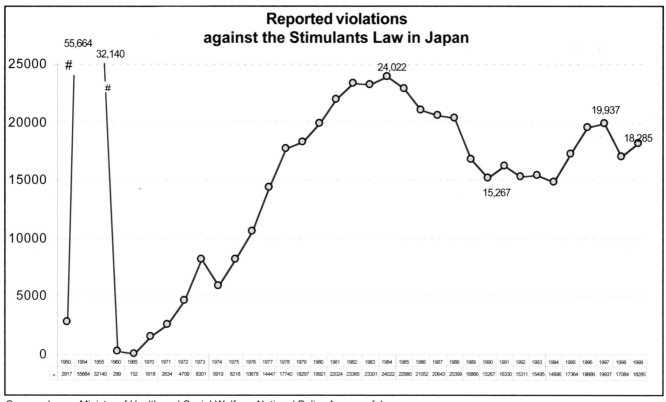

Reported violations against the Stimulants Law in Japan

55,664 #
32,140 #
24,022
19,937
18,285
15,267

1950	1954	1955	1960	1965	1970	1971	1972	1973	1974	1975	1976	1977	1978	1979	1980	1981	1982	1983	1984	1985	1986	1987	1988	1989	1990	1991	1992	1993	1994	1995	1996	1997	1998	1999
2917	55664	32140	299	152	1618	2634	4709	8301	5919	8218	10678	14447	17740	18297	19921	22024	23365	23301	24022	22980	21052	20643	20399	16866	15267	16330	15311	15495	14896	17364	19666	19937	17084	18285

Source: Japan, Ministry of Health and Social Welfare, National Policy Agency of Japan.

overall share of ATS rose from 1% of all people registered in 1995 to 15% over the first six months of 2000. In parallel, the share of opiates fell from 90% in 1995 to 80% (79% heroin) in 2000. While initially the rise was mainly linked to abuse of methamphetamine, data also show that in 2000 Hong Kong was apparently faced with an emerging ecstasy epidemic, mainly affecting youth and young adults The strong emergence of ecstasy in Hong Kong appears to be linked to local Triad groups involved in Hong Kong's club scene, distributing ecstasy which is apparently produced in mainland China[f]. A rise in the popularity of ATS - though then still at low levels - was earlier already identified in school surveys. Between 1992 and 1996 life-time use of amphetamines rose from 0.1% to 0.5% according to surveys conducted in local Chinese secondary schools, while abuse of heroin declined marginally (from 0.3% to 0.2%).

The trend of methamphetamine abuse for Japan is less clear than for other countries in the region where basically all indicators for ATS are showing strong upward trends. However, in contrast to other countries in the region, methamphetamine has already been, for decades, the main problem drug in Japan. About 90% of all reported violations against the drug laws in 1999 and previous years were related to methamphetamine trafficking and abuse while drug treatment in Japan is largely linked to treatment of methamphetamine patients.

The number of reported violations against the Stimulant Law - the main indicator for the development of methamphetamine consumption used by the authorities - increased in 1999 as compared to a year earlier (7%) and was some 20% higher than in the early 1990s. Nonetheless, the reported violations against the Stimulant Law in 1999 were significantly lower than in the early 1950s, lower than in the early 1980s, and remained below the 1996-97 levels. The data may thus be equally well interpreted to signal a stabilization, following an upward trend in the mid 1990s. It may be also noted that in contrast to other countries in the region, there has been a decline in the number of violations against the Stimulant Law among junior high school students in 1999. The outbreak of a major new epidemic of methamphetamine abuse as experienced in the early 1950s and (to a lesser extent) in the early 1980s may have been prevented, despite rapid growth in ATS trafficking and abuse throughout the region. Preliminary data for 2000 of violations against the Stimulant Law seem to confirm the trend towards stabilization. Seizures of methamphetamine, though remaining high, declined in 2000 as compared to 1999.

General population surveys conducted by the National Institute of Mental Health in 1995, 1997 and 1999 also point in the direction of a stabilization. Life-time prevalence of methamphetamine abuse grew over the 1995-99 period only marginally, from 0.3% to 0.4% of the pop-

f) For more details see UNDCP/UNICRI, "Global Study on Illegal Drug Markets: The Hong Kong Market", (Draft), November 2000.

ulation age 15 and above. These data also suggest that methamphetamine abuse in Japan — despite being the most serious drug problem for the country — continues to remain significantly below the levels reported in many other countries[g].

However, preliminary data for 2000 - though still at low levels compared to other countries - show a rather strong increase in seizures of ecstasy, possibly indicating first signs of a an emerging shift among the younger generation from methamphetamine use, which is apparently declining among youth, to ecstasy. In other words, the strong increase in seizures of ecstasy would be in line with trends already observed in Hong Kong, where such a shift among youth took place in 2000.

Oceania

Both Australia and New Zealand reported a further increase in ATS consumption in 1999, confirming the upward trend of ATS use in the region in the second half of the 1990s.

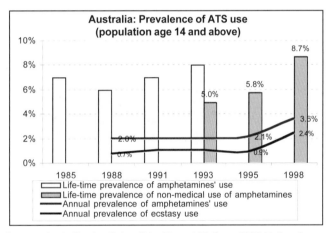

Source: Australian Institute of Health and Welfare, 1988 National Drug Strategy Household Survey, August 1999 (and previous years).

Australia has had a long 'tradition' of amphetamine consumption, reflecting the extensive use of amphetamines in treatment (often for depression) in the 1960 and 1970s . While the medical community over the years became aware of the serious side effects and thus dras-

tically reduced prescriptions, the trade in amphetamines, as of the early 1980s, started shifting into the illegal sector which is now the main source of supply.

Nonetheless, the popularity of amphetamines increased, notably over the 1995-98 period. While overall drug consumption in Australia - measured by annual prevalence - was reported to have grown by some 30% over the 1995-98 period, use of amphetamine increased by some 70%, more than cocaine (some 40%). Amphetamines use thus continues to be more than twice as widespread as cocaine use in Australia. An even stronger growth rate was reported for the use of ecstasy, which almost tripled (from 0.9% to 2.4%).

An annual prevalence rate of 3.6% (1998) for the use of amphetamines in Australia is the highest such rate reported to UNDCP, a higher rate than reported from the UK (3% in 1998), New Zealand (2% in 1998) or the USA (1% in 1999). The same applies to the ecstasy data. Variations in the study designs may account for some of the difference but there is hardly any doubt that ATS use is widespread in Australia and a serious concern.

Africa and the Middle East

No clear overall patterns emerge from trend data provided by African countries for the year 1999. While the authorities of Cameroon, Chad, and Namibia reported an increase, Nigeria, South Africa and Morocco saw consumption levels stable and Cote d'Ivoire reported a decline. Specific trends on ecstasy use were only reported by the authorities of South Africa. Ecstasy use was considered to have remained stable.

While the use of amphetamines is a general problem across Africa, notably in the countries of western Africa where various preparations containing amphetamine-type substances are still widely available in parallel markets, ecstasy use appears to be still largely confined to the Republic of South Africa, and within the country to the white community as revealed in a recent study on the drug markets of Johannesburg[h]. The current stabilization of ecstasy use in South Africa follows a period of rapid growth since the early 1990s. In any case, the

Israel: Annual prevalence of drug use among adults and students in 1998						
	Any drug	Cannabis	Ecstasy	LSD	Opiats (heroin)	Cocaine
Adults (age 18-40)	8.0%	5.6%	0.6%	0.6%	0.4%	0.2%
Students (grades 7-12)	9.8%	5.1%	2.7%	3.0%	2.4%	2.5%
Source: Rahav, Teichmann, Gil and Rosenblum, "The Use of Psychoactive Substances among Residents of the State of Israel: 1998", quoted in UNDCP/UNICRI, The Drug Market in the Greater Tel-Aviv Area (Draft), October 2000, p. 31.						

g) There are, however, other estimates which indicate significantly higher levels of methamphetamine abuse in Japan. The US State Department - referring to estimates made by the Japanese authorities - quotes, for instance, a figure of 600,000 methamphetamine addicts (equivalent to 0.6% of Japan's population age 15 and above) and 2.18 million casual methamphetamine users (2% of the population age 15 and above). For comparison, the methamphetamine prevalence rates for the USA are 0.2% (monthly prevalence), 0.5% (annual prevalence) and 3.5% (life-time use).
(US. Department of State, *International Narcotics Control Strategy Report 2000*, March 2001).

h) For more details see UNDCP/UNICRI, "Global Study on Illegal Drug Markets of Johannesburg" (Draft), May 2000.

problems related to ATS in South Africa are dwarfed by the growing problems related to crack-cocaine abuse.

A marked downward trend in abuse of ATS over the last decade was reported from Egypt. While in the early 1990s 'Maxiton Forte', originally a pharmaceutical preparation of dexamphetamine (and later clandestinely produced methamphetamine) played a significant role in the local drug market, authorities reported a constant decline in subsequent years. This was confirmed in a recent UNDCP sponsored study on illicit drug market of greater Cairo, where abuse of opiates, benzodi-azepines, hashish and codeine containing cough syrups was found to be important while Maxiton Forte was not even mentioned.

Given the low response rate to UNDCP's annual report questionnaire on ATS abuse in the countries of the Near East, it is likely that ATS may play less of a role than in the past when large stocks of fenetylline, locally known as 'captagon' (often of European origin) were dumped on to the local market(s). However, reports of a revival in trafficking activities in 2000 in some countries of the region (notably Jordan and, with regard to transit trade also Syria) could point to a revival . There are also potential threats relating to ecstasy abuse. A recent study of the drug market in Greater Tel-Aviv, showed that ecstasy, usually of European origin, was on the rise in the 1990s - and is now the most common synthetic drug and the second most common substance of abu-

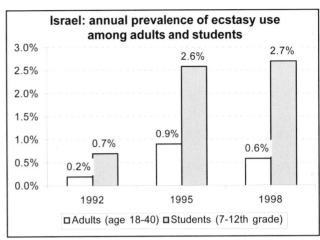

Source: Rahav et at, 1996 and 1999, quoted in UNDCP/UNICRI, The Drug market in the Greater Tel Aviv Area (Draft), Oct. 2000.

se[i]. Like in several of the European countries, the spread of ecstasy use, however, lost momentum in the late 1990s. Nonetheless one cannot exclude the possibility that ecstasy use, once firmly established in a country in the region, will spread to neighbouring countries as well. Reports from Lebanon suggest that this is already the case.

Data presented in this report must be interpreted with caution. All figures provided, particularly those of more recent years, are subject to updating.

---

i) For more details see UNDCP/UNICRI, "Global Study on Illegal Drug Markets:The Drug Market in the Greater Tel- Aviv Area" (Draft),October 2000.

Abuse of Amphetamine-type stimulants

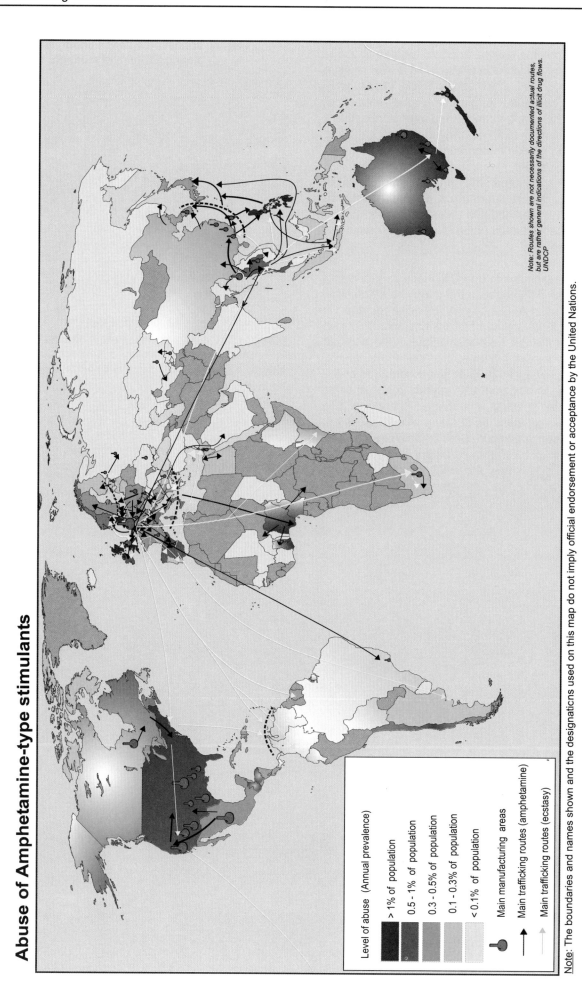

Level of abuse (Annual prevalence)

- \> 1% of population
- 0.5 - 1% of population
- 0.3 - 0.5% of population
- 0.1 - 0.3% of population
- < 0.1% of population

Main manufacturing areas

Main trafficking routes (amphetamine)

Main trafficking routes (ecstasy)

Note: Routes shown are not necessarily documented actual routes, but are rather general indications of the directions of illicit drug flows. UNDCP

Note: The boundaries and names shown and the designations used on this map do not imply official endorsement or acceptance by the United Nations.

Changes in abuse of amphetamine-type stimulants, 1999 (or latest year available)

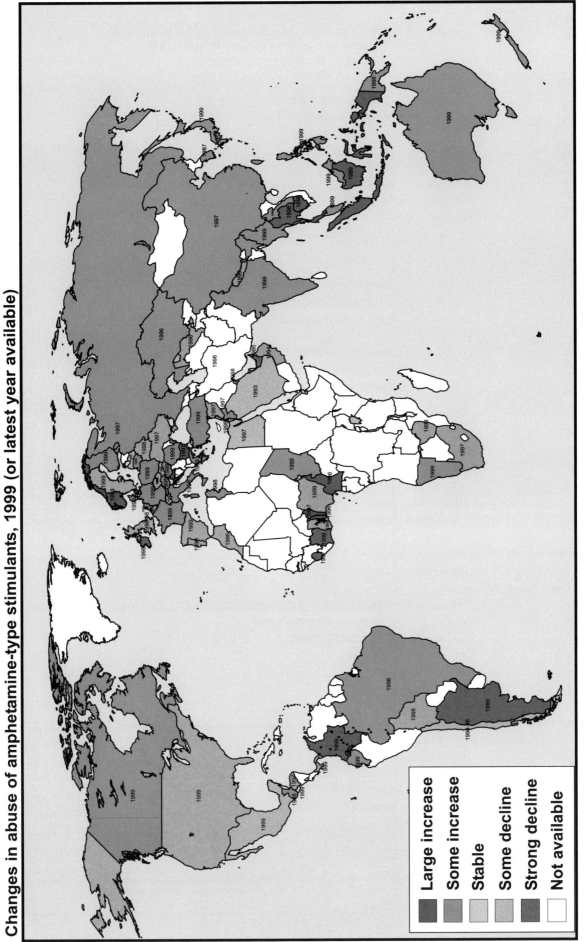

Sources: UNDCP Annual Reports Questionnaires data, UNDCP (Regional Centre Bangkok) Epidemiology Trends in Drug Trends in Asia (Findings of the Asian Multicity Epidemiology Workgroup, December 1999, National Household Surveys submitted to UNDCP, United States Department of State (Bureau for International Narcotics and Law Enforcement Affairs) International Narcotics Control Strategy Report, 1999;Bundeskriminalamt (BKA) and other Law Enforcement Reports.

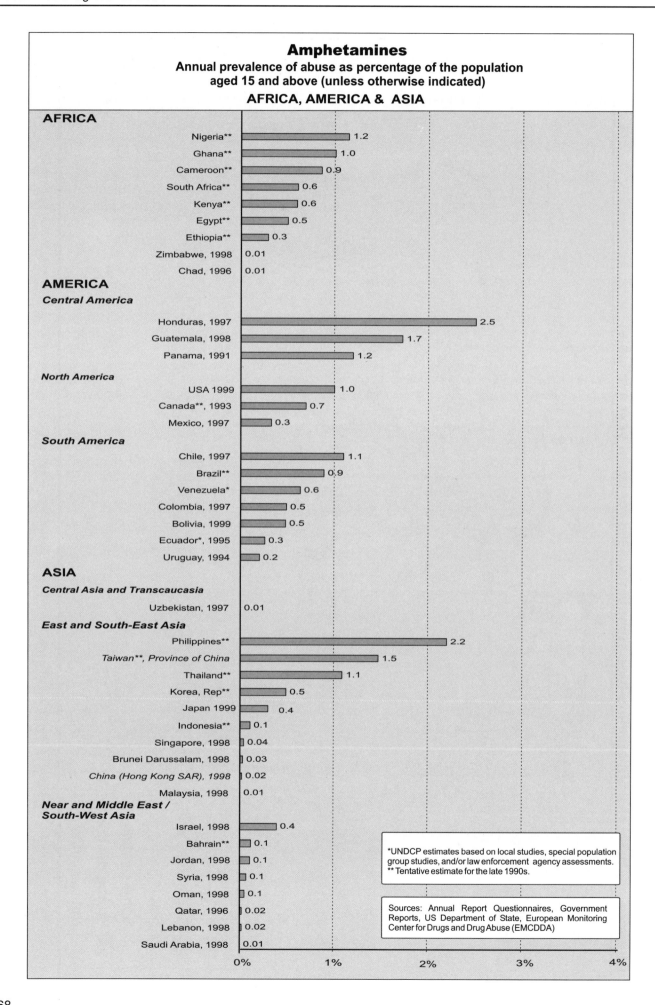

Amphetamines
Annual prevalence of abuse as percentage of the population aged 15 and above (unless otherwise indicated)
AFRICA, AMERICA & ASIA

AFRICA

Nigeria**	1.2
Ghana**	1.0
Cameroon**	0.9
South Africa**	0.6
Kenya**	0.6
Egypt**	0.5
Ethiopia**	0.3
Zimbabwe, 1998	0.01
Chad, 1996	0.01

AMERICA

Central America

Honduras, 1997	2.5
Guatemala, 1998	1.7
Panama, 1991	1.2

North America

USA 1999	1.0
Canada**, 1993	0.7
Mexico, 1997	0.3

South America

Chile, 1997	1.1
Brazil**	0.9
Venezuela*	0.6
Colombia, 1997	0.5
Bolivia, 1999	0.5
Ecuador*, 1995	0.3
Uruguay, 1994	0.2

ASIA

Central Asia and Transcaucasia

Uzbekistan, 1997	0.01

East and South-East Asia

Philippines**	2.2
Taiwan**, Province of China	1.5
Thailand**	1.1
Korea, Rep**	0.5
Japan 1999	0.4
Indonesia**	0.1
Singapore, 1998	0.04
Brunei Darussalam, 1998	0.03
China (Hong Kong SAR), 1998	0.02
Malaysia, 1998	0.01

Near and Middle East / South-West Asia

Israel, 1998	0.4
Bahrain**	0.1
Jordan, 1998	0.1
Syria, 1998	0.1
Oman, 1998	0.1
Qatar, 1996	0.02
Lebanon, 1998	0.02
Saudi Arabia, 1998	0.01

*UNDCP estimates based on local studies, special population group studies, and/or law enforcement agency assessments.
** Tentative estimate for the late 1990s.

Sources: Annual Report Questionnaires, Government Reports, US Department of State, European Monitoring Center for Drugs and Drug Abuse (EMCDDA)

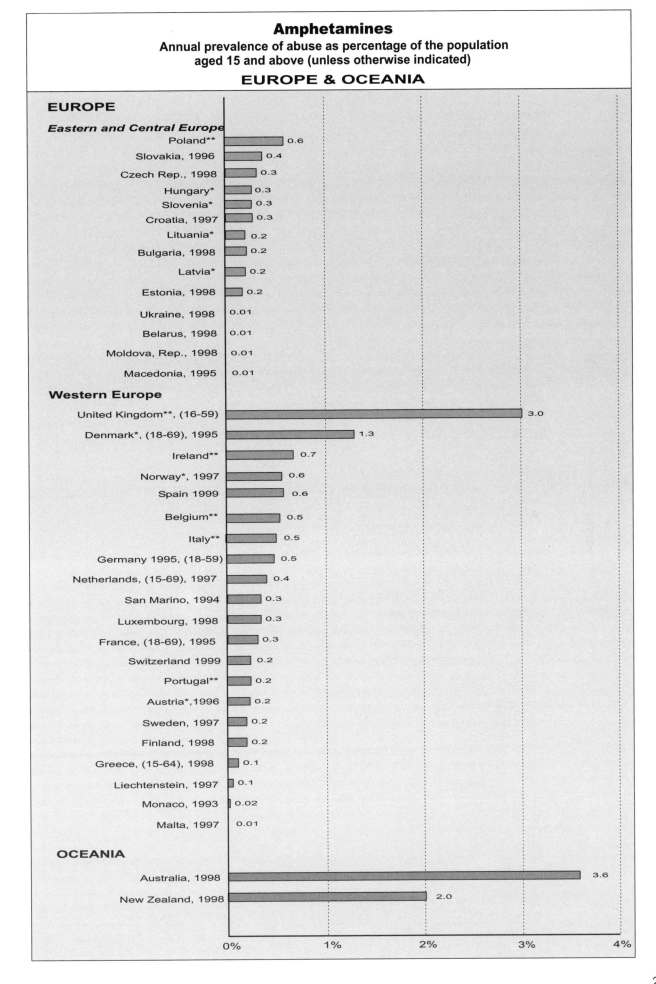

Amphetamines

Annual prevalence of abuse as percentage of the population
aged 15 and above (unless otherwise indicated)

EUROPE & OCEANIA

EUROPE

Eastern and Central Europe

Poland**	0.6
Slovakia, 1996	0.4
Czech Rep., 1998	0.3
Hungary*	0.3
Slovenia*	0.3
Croatia, 1997	0.3
Lituania*	0.2
Bulgaria, 1998	0.2
Latvia*	0.2
Estonia, 1998	0.2
Ukraine, 1998	0.01
Belarus, 1998	0.01
Moldova, Rep., 1998	0.01
Macedonia, 1995	0.01

Western Europe

United Kingdom**, (16-59)	3.0
Denmark*, (18-69), 1995	1.3
Ireland**	0.7
Norway*, 1997	0.6
Spain 1999	0.6
Belgium**	0.5
Italy**	0.5
Germany 1995, (18-59)	0.5
Netherlands, (15-69), 1997	0.4
San Marino, 1994	0.3
Luxembourg, 1998	0.3
France, (18-69), 1995	0.3
Switzerland 1999	0.2
Portugal**	0.2
Austria*,1996	0.2
Sweden, 1997	0.2
Finland, 1998	0.2
Greece, (15-64), 1998	0.1
Liechtenstein, 1997	0.1
Monaco, 1993	0.02
Malta, 1997	0.01

OCEANIA

Australia, 1998	3.6
New Zealand, 1998	2.0

0%   1%   2%   3%   4%

269

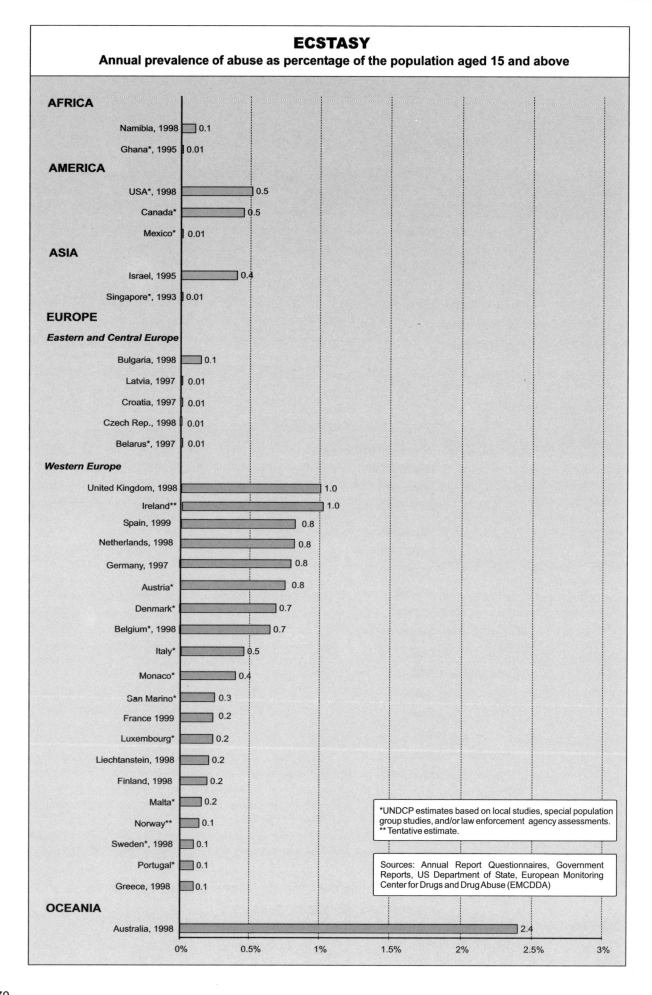

ECSTASY
Annual prevalence of abuse as percentage of the population aged 15 and above

AFRICA

Namibia, 1998	0.1
Ghana*, 1995	0.01

AMERICA

USA*, 1998	0.5
Canada*	0.5
Mexico*	0.01

ASIA

Israel, 1995	0.4
Singapore*, 1993	0.01

EUROPE

Eastern and Central Europe

Bulgaria, 1998	0.1
Latvia, 1997	0.01
Croatia, 1997	0.01
Czech Rep., 1998	0.01
Belarus*, 1997	0.01

Western Europe

United Kingdom, 1998	1.0
Ireland**	1.0
Spain, 1999	0.8
Netherlands, 1998	0.8
Germany, 1997	0.8
Austria*	0.8
Denmark*	0.7
Belgium*, 1998	0.7
Italy*	0.5
Monaco*	0.4
San Marino*	0.3
France 1999	0.2
Luxembourg*	0.2
Liechtanstein, 1998	0.2
Finland, 1998	0.2
Malta*	0.2
Norway**	0.1
Sweden*, 1998	0.1
Portugal*	0.1
Greece, 1998	0.1

OCEANIA

Australia, 1998	2.4

*UNDCP estimates based on local studies, special population group studies, and/or law enforcement agency assessments.
** Tentative estimate.

Sources: Annual Report Questionnaires, Government Reports, US Department of State, European Monitoring Center for Drugs and Drug Abuse (EMCDDA)

PRIMARY DRUGS OF ABUSE AMONG PERSONS TREATED FOR DRUG PROBLEMS IN EUROPEAN COUNTRIES, 1998

Country	Year	Distribution of main drug in percentages				
		Opiates	Cocaine	Amphetamine - type ATS (incl. ecstasy)	Cannabis	Others
BELGIUM (Bru.)	1997	77.1%	7.2%	-	6.6%	9.1%
BELGIUM (Fle.)	1996	39.5%	7.1%	19.9%	22%	11.5%
BELGIUM (Fre.)	1998	69.4%	5.9%	1.5%	14.0%	9.2%
DENMARK	1998	78.0%	1.0%	4%	14.0%	3.0%
FINLAND	1998	27.3%	0.2%	44.3%	22.2%	6.0%
FRANCE	1997	78.6%	3.1%	1.2%	11.0%	6.1%
GERMANY	1998	67.4%	7.4%	3.2%	18.8%	3.2%
GREECE	1998	91.9%	0.7%	0	5.7%	1.7%
IRELAND	1997	78.2%	1.6%	4.9%	11.8%	3.5%
ITALY	1998	85.6%	3.2%	0.9%	7.6%	2.7%
LUXEMBOURG	1998	83.0%	7.0%	3.0%	5.0%	2.0%
NETHERLANDS	1998	65.1%	17.5%	4.1%	10.9%	2.4%
PORTUGAL	1998	92.0%	1.0%	-	-	7.0%
SPAIN	1998	78.3%	11.6%	0.8%	5.5%	3.8%
SWEDEN	1998	26.0%	0.4%	39.7%	14.0%	19.9%
U. KINGDOM (England)	1998	69.2%	5.9%	9.4%	9.7%	5.8%
Average		70.2%	4.8%	9.7%	11.6%	5.5%

Source:EMCDDA, *2000 Annual Report on the State of the Drug Problem in the European Union*

- Belgium (Brussels): cocaine =stimulants including cocaine and amphet. - "Others" include Belgium - Brussels. (hypnotics-sedatives, others)
- France: data refer to specialised centres only.   Belgium - French. (hypnotics-sedatives, solvents, others))
- U. Kingdom (England): data relate to the six months ending 30 September 1998.   France (solvents, hypnotics-sedatives)
   Sweden (multiple abuse)
   Great Britain (hypnotics-sedatives, solvents, others)

PRIMARY DRUGS OF ABUSE AMONG PERSONS TREATED FOR DRUG PROBLEMS IN EUROPEAN CITIES, 1997

City	Year	Distribution of main drug in percentages					Total No.
		Opiates	Cocaine	Amphetamine - type Stimulants (incl. ecstasy)	Cannabis	Hypnotics and Sedatives	
Amsterdam, The Netherlands	1997	38.6%	31.7%	2.6%	21.2%	0.5%	1,018
Athens, Greece	1997	80.7%	0.3%	0.3%	15.5%	1.7%	291
Berlin, Germany**	1997	72.0%	7.0%	1.0%	13.0%		n.a.
Bratislava, Slovakia	1997	94.5%	0.1%	0.9%	1.4%	0.5%	1,002
Brussels, Belgium	1997	70.7%					1,810
Bucharest, Romania	1997	68.6%	0.2%				430
Budapest, Hungary	1997	37.8%	0.7%	10.4%	5.5%	9.8%	3,920
Copenhagen, Denmark	1997	89.6%	0.5%	0.4%	2.3%	0.1%	1,522
Cyprus	1997	32.6%	5.8%	4.7%	52.3%	4.7%	86
Dublin, Ireland	1997	91.1%	0.7%	2.0%	4.6%	1.0%	3,051
Gdansk, Poland	1997	72.3%	0.5%	6.1%	5.1%	3.2%	1,069
Geneva, Switzerland	1997	93.6%	0.6%	1.9%	1.9%	1.3%	342
Helsinki, Finland **	1996	34.8%	0.6%	39.5%	16.5%		
Liège, Belgium	1997	77.3%	4.0%	2.3%	10.7%	5.3%	857
Lisbon, Portugal**	1997	96.9%	1.2%		1.9%	1.5%	
Ljubiljana, Slovenia	1997	96.0%	0.7%		1.9%		270
London, UK **	1997	71.0%	4.0%	9.0%	8.0%	7.0%	
Malta	1997	96.9%	1.6%	0.8%	0.5%	0.1%	741
Madrid, Spain**	1996	93.8%	6.1%				2,511
Orenburg, Russian Federation	1997	70.4%	0.3%	5.2%	8.6%	7.7%	385
Paris, France**	1997	78.6%	3.1%	1.2%	11.0%	5.7%	
Prague, Czech Republic *	1997	41.7%	0.9%	47.2%	5.7%	1.3%	533
Rome, Italy	1997	92.8%	3.8%	0.3%	2.4%	0.4%	5,077
St.Petersburg, Russian Federation	1997	91.7%	0.2%	2.2%	1.0%	1.0%	1,063
Stockholm, Sweden **	1996	39.0%	0.8%	20.0%	7.0%		
Sofia, Bulgaria	1997	94.7%	0.0%				582
Varna, Bulgaria	1997	85.3%	1.3%				75
Vienna, Austria	1997	72.2%					
Warsaw, Poland	1997	66.9%	1.6%	14.1%	11.9%	3.0%	1,068
Zagreb, Croatia	1997	73.4%	1.1%	4.2%	13.7%	5.3%	381
Average		72.7%	2.8%	8.0%	9.6%	3.1%	28,084

This table does not include hallucinogens and "other drugs", therefore the percentages may not add up to 100% for all cities

* First Treatment Demand

Sources: Pompidou Group Project on Treatment Demand, Data 1997; EMCDDA, *1999 Annual Report on the State of the Drug Problem in the European Union*

PRIMARY DRUG OF ABUSE AMONG PERSONS TREATED FOR DRUG PROBLEMS IN ASIAN CITIES, 1998

City	Source	Year	Distribution of main drug in percentages						Total No.
			Opiates	Cocaine	Amphetamine - type Stimulants (incl. ecstasy)	Cannabis	Inhalants	Others (excluding alcohol)	
Alma Ata, Kazakhstan	ARQ	1998	65.1%		1.7%	29.9%			9,458
Bangkok, Thailand (Jan. - June)	AMCEWG	1998	83.4%		14.8%	0.1%		1.7%	5,730
Bahrein	ARQ	1998	100.0%						1,488
Baku, Azerbaijan	ARQ	1998	82.5%			12.4%			97
Brunei Darussalam	ARQ	1996	85.4%						89
Beijing	UNDCPEst.	1998	90.0%						
Colombo, Sri Lanka	AMCEWG	1998	90.6%			0.2%		9.2%	1,250
Dhaka, Bangladesh	AMCEWG	1998	93.3%			5.6%		0.9%	1,862
Djakarta, Indonesia	ARQ	1997	79.6%		3.3%	2.8%			2,977
Dushanbe, Tajikistan	ARQ	1996	92.3%			7.7%			130
Hanoi, Viet Nam (Apr. - Dec.)	AMCEWG	1998	100.0%						2,108
Hongkong, SAR	Govt	1997	99.0%						5,894
Islamabad, Pakistan	AMCEWG	1998	99.7%						775
Kathmandu, Nepal	AMCEWG	1994	87.2%			5.4%			
Kuala Lumpur, Malaysia	AMCEWG	1998	77.2%			21.4%		1.4%	1,914*
Macao, China	ARQ	1998	100.0%						188
Madras, India	AMCEWG	1998	53.5%			24.8%		21.5%	391***
Maldives	ARQ	1998	50.0%			50.0%			120
Manila, Philippines***	AMCEWG	1998	1.0%	0.1%	92.4%	38.6%		63.6%	671*
New Dehli	AMCEWG	1994	81.3%			10.4%			
Qatar	ARQ	1997	25.4%		1.7%	5.1%			59
Seoul, Rep. Korea	ARQ	1998	0.0%		89.3%	7.4%			122
Singapore	AMCEWG	1995	94.0%						
Tashkent, Uzbekistan	ARQ	1998	46.2%			34.2%			917
Teheran, Iran	ARQ	1997	89.8%			5.3%			
Tokyo, Japan	Govt	1996	1.0%		99.0%				
Yangoon, Myanmar	AMCEWG	1996	99.5%						185
Average			73.2%	0.0%	11.6%	8.9%		3.8%	

This table does not include hallucinogens and "other drugs", therefore the percentages may not add up to 100% for all cities

Sources: Asian Multicity Epidemiology work group (AMCEWG); UNDCP ARQ; national reports

* New admissions

** Alcohol, which represents 74% of the total admissions in Madras, is excluded from this figure.

*** Multiple reporting (represents polydrug abuse)

PRIMARY DRUGS OF ABUSE AMONG PERSONS TREATED FOR DRUG PROBLEMS IN THE AMERICAS

Country and year	Source	Cocaine-type (cocaine, basuco & crack-cocaine)	Cocaine	Basuco	Crack	Cannabis	Amphetamines	Inhalants	Tranquilizers	Heroin
Argentina, 1998	SIDUC	77.4%	74.2%	3.2%		6.5%	3.2%		4.9%	
Bahamas, 1998	ARQ	93.0%				7.0%				
Barbados, 1998	SIDUC	72.3%	5.6%		66.7%	27.8%		23.5%		
Bolivia, 1998	SIDUC	54.8%	23.1%	31.8%		14.7%	1.4%	23.5%		
Canada, 1995/96	Profile	63.3%				18.3%	5.3%			45.3%
Brazil, 1999	SIDUC	59.2%	14.4%		44.8%	27.2%		2.0%	2.4%	0.4%
Chile, 1998	SIDUC	89%	21.2%	67.8%		4.1%	4.1%			
Colombia, 1998	SIDUC	56.3%	28.1%	28.2%		13.4%	3.6%	4.8%		
Costa Rica, 1998	SIDUC	90.3%	9.7%	0.2%	80.3%	2.5%		0.5%		
Dominican Rep., 1998	SIDUC	89.5%	19%		70.5%	6.7%	0.7%	0.7%		
Ecuador, 1998	SIDUC	66.1%	13.5%	52.5%		10.2%		4.6%		
El Salvador, 1998	SIDUC	37.1%	30.7%		6.4%	38.7%		11.2%		
Grenada, 1998	ARQ	35.5%				29.0%				
Guatemala, 1997	SIDUC	13.7%	13.7%					11.3%	13.7%	
Honduras, 1998	SIDUC	9.0%	3.1%		5.9%	34.4%		9.0%		
Jamaica, 1998	SIDUC	58%			58%	28.9%				
Mexico, 1998	SIDUC	32.3%	30.9%	0.3%	0.5%	24.3%	0.4%	19.2%		7.2%
Nicaragua, 1998	SIDUC	77.3%	14.5%		62.8%	7.3%		12.7%		
Panama, 1998	SIDUC	49.4%	48.9%	0.5%		5.1%		0.5%		
Peru, 1998	SIDUC	90.8%	20.4%	70.4%		5.6%				
Trinidad & Tobago, 1998	SIDUC	86.9%	16.7%		70.2%	9.5%				
Uruguay, 1998	SIDUC	46.4%	46.4%			12.2%	0.6%	9.2%		
USA, 1997	TEDS	29.1%	7.7%		21%	25.1%	8.8%	0.2%	0.5%	28.5%
Venezuela, 1998	SIDUC	81.4%	22.7%	11.1%	47.6%	11.5%		0.3%		
Average		60.8%	23.2%	26.6%	44.6%	16.1%	3.1%	7.3%	5.4%	3.4%

Note: These drugs represent the most common drugs of impact across countries, therefore the percentages may not add up to 100% for all countries

Sources: SIDUC, Treatment Centres Data 1998, Drug of impact; SIDUC 1997 Report
Treatment episode data set TEDS, USA 1992-1997
Secretaria Nacional Antidrogas, Brazil (Data refer to one treatment centre in Minas Gerais (985 cases))
CCSA, Canadian Profile, 1999

Main problem drugs (as reflected in treatment demand) in the late 1990s

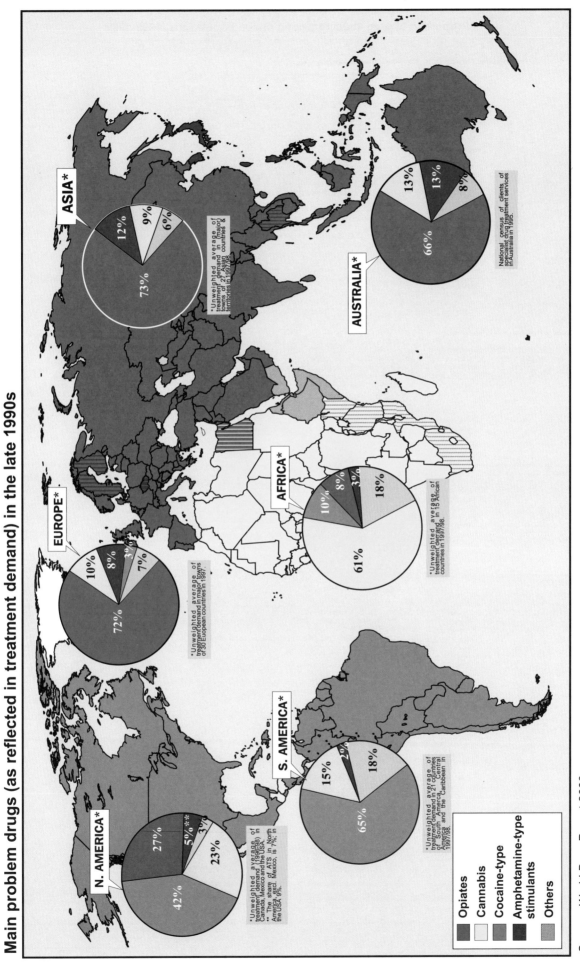

ASIA*

73% 12% 9% 6%

*Unweighted average of treatment demand in major towns of 21 Asian countries & territories in 1997/98.

AUSTRALIA*

66% 13% 13% 8%

National census of clients of specialist drug treatment services in Australia in 1995.

AFRICA*

61% 10% 8% 3% 18%

*Unweighted average of treatment demand in 15 African countries in 1997/98.

EUROPE*

72% 10% 8% 3% 7%

*Unweighted average of treatment demand in major towns of 30 European countries in 1997.

S. AMERICA*

65% 15% 2% 18%

*Unweighted average of treatment demand in 21 countries of South America, Central America and the Caribbean in 1997/98.

N. AMERICA*

42% 27% 5%** 3% 23%

*Unweighted average of treatment demand (1996-98) in Canada, Mexico and the USA. ** The share of ATS in North America, excl. Mexico, is 7%; in the USA 9%.

Legend:
- Opiates
- Cannabis
- Cocaine-type
- Amphetamine-type stimulants
- Others

Source: *World Drug Report 2000*.

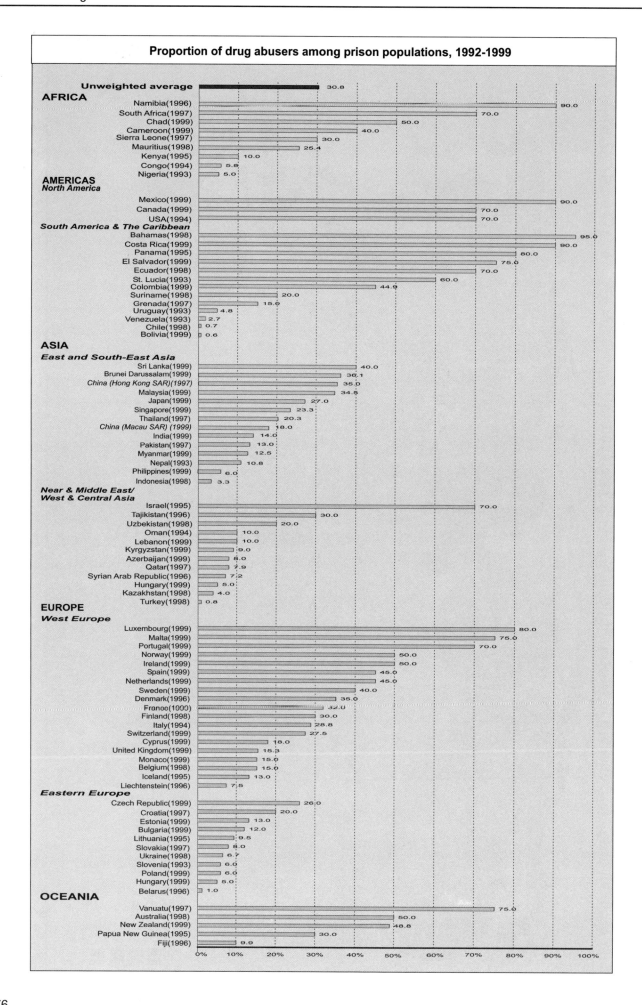

Proportion of drug abusers among prison populations, 1992-1999

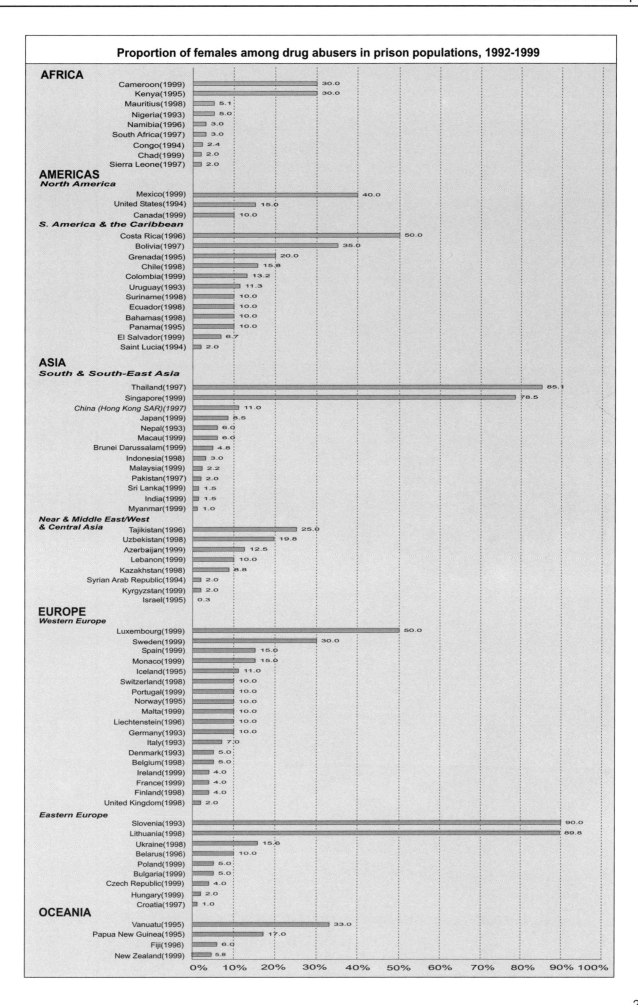

Proportion of females among drug abusers in prison populations, 1992-1999

Countries and territories reporting injecting drug use and HIV infections among IDUs

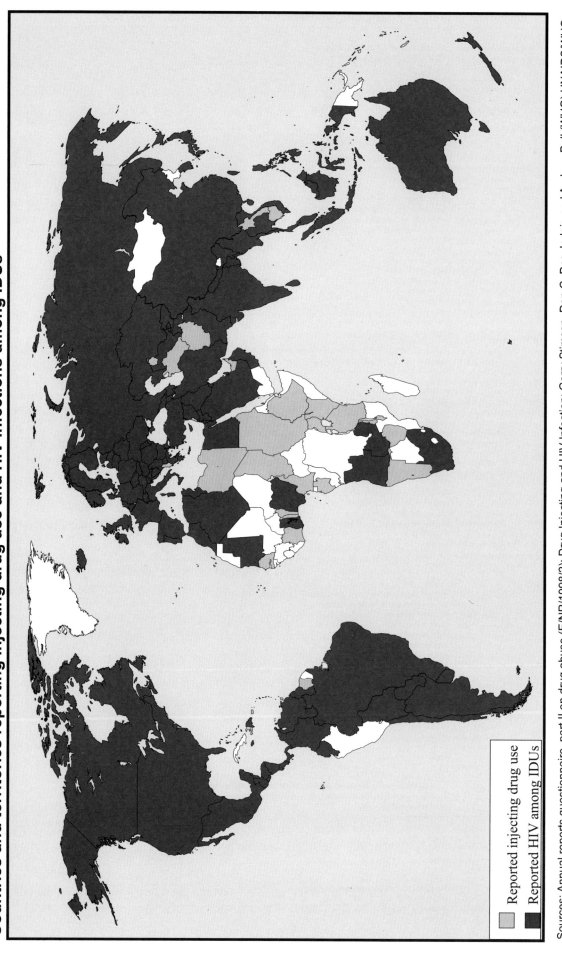

Reported injecting drug use

Reported HIV among IDUs

Sources: Annual reports questionnaire, part II on drug abuse (E/NR/1998/2); Drug Injecting and HIV Infection: Gerry Stimson, Don C. Des Jarlais and Andrew Ball (WHO),UNAIDS/WHO Epi Fact sheet: Prokovski et al, 1999.HIV/AIDS Surveillance in Europe: European Centre for the Epidemiological Monitoring of AIDS. Pompidou Group Project on TreatmentDemand: Final Report on Treated Drug Users in 23 European Cities Data 1997: Trends 1996-97, Parry CDH. HIV among arrestees in Cape Town, Durban and Johannesburg, South Africa (Phase IO). 2000 GRN meeting on HIV prevention in drug-using populations, July 5-7, 2000, Durban, S.Africa, Global AIDS Surveillance. Part II Weekly epidemiological record 2000, 74: 409-414, 75: 386-392, AIDS Epidemic Update December 2000 UNAIDS. Figueroa et al. AIDS 1998, 12 (suppl 2): S89-S98. Dehne K & Kobyshcha Y. The HIV Epidemic in Central and Eastern Europe: Update 2000. Presented at the European HIV Strategy meeting. Copenhagen December 2000. Khwaja et al. AIDS 1997, 11: 843-848. AIDS Cases Country Report Kuwait. HIV/AIDS case country report Nepal.

Note: The boundaries shown on this map do not imply official endorsement or acceptance by the United Nations

SOURCES AND LIMITATIONS OF DATA

SOURCES AND LIMITATIONS OF DATA ON PRODUCTION AND TRAFFICKING

The information on trafficking (and partly on manufacture), as presented in this report, is mainly drawn from annual reports questionnaires (ARQ), relating mostly to 1999 and to previous years, which have been submitted by Governments to UNDCP. Additional sources, such as other governmental reports, the International Criminal Police Organization (Interpol), the World Customs Organization (WCO) and UNDCP's field offices, were used to supplement the information.

Data on cultivation of opium poppy and coca bush and production of opium and coca leaf, which are presented in this report (as UNDCP estimates in the case of opium), are drawn from various sources including Governments, UNDCP field offices and the United States Department of State's Bureau for International Narcotics and Law Enforcement Affairs. The estimates were established by considering all of the various sources available at the time of preparation of this report. These estimates are subject to updating should more reliable data become available.

The main problems with regard to data relate to the irregularity and incompleteness in reporting affecting the quantity, quality and comparability of information received. First, the irregular intervals at which some Governments report may result in absence of data in some years but availability in others. Lack of regular data, for which UNDCP tries to compensate by reference to other sources, could influence trend patterns. Second, submitted questionnaires are not always complete or sufficiently comprehensive. While data on seizures are provided by many Governments in a very detailed manner, information on illicit cultivation and production of drugs, clandestine laboratories and manufacturing activities, as well as on particulars of prices, is often absent. Third, differences in criteria of reporting between countries, or from single countries over a period of time, may distort the trafficking picture and trend analyses. For example, some countries include so-called "kitchen" laboratories in the total number of manufacturing sites detected while others only count fully equipped clandestine laboratories. By the same token, a country which in the past has included "kitchen" laboratories may then change its reporting practice and omit such detections. Also, the extent to which seizure statistics from some countries constitute all reported national cases, regardless of the final destination of the illicit drug, can vary and make it difficult to assess international trafficking.

The utilization of data which are available through the various sources is limited due to two main shortcomings. First, some available information is not fully reliable due to the complexity of the drug phenomenon and problems in assessing the specific nature of an illicit activity. Analyses of illicit drug cultivation/production, for example, rely on estimates and cannot be treated as hard data. Second, data (for example on seizures) reflect different factors, such as changes in reporting modalities or variations in law enforcement practices. However, where such factors do hold constant, changes in seizure statistics can indicate trends in trafficking, and some inferences in the present report are drawn on this very basis.

Despite these limitations, comparisons, on a time-series basis, of different indicators with statistical dependence show high correlations, thus supporting their statistical worth.

SOURCES AND LIMITATIONS OF DATA ON CONSUMPTION

The exact number of drug users worldwide is unknown. There are, however, basic orders of magnitude - which are subject to revision as new and better information is generated. Estimates of illicit consumption for a significantly large number of countries have been received by UNDCP over the years (in the form of annual reports questionnaires (ARQ) submitted by Governments, as well as from additional sources, such as other governmental reports and UNDCP's field offices).

The most widely used indicator at the global level is the "annual prevalence" rate. It relates to the number of people who have consumed an illicit drug at least once over the last twelve months prior to the survey. As "annual prevalence" is the most commonly used indicator to measure prevalence, it has also been adopted by UNDCP as the key indicator for the extent of drug abuse. The use of "annual prevalence" is a compromise between "life-time prevalence" data (drug use at least once in a life-time) and data on current use. Life-time prevalence data are, in general, easier to generate but are not very illustrative. (The fact that a 50-year-old person smoked marijuana at the age of 20 does not provide much insight into the current drug abuse problem). Data on current use (e.g. monthly prevalence) are of more value.

The "annual prevalence" rate number is frequently shown as a percentage of those who are 15 years old and above, or those 12 years old and above, though a number of other age groupings are used as well. However, as most countries do not report prevalence as a percentage of their total population, data presented in this report show the prevalence figures as a percentage of the population above the age of 14. In cases where studies were based on significantly different age groups, the data were adjusted to take into account the fact that drug abuse is usually significantly stronger among younger-age cohorts. In cases where the authorities provided UNDCP only with estimates on the total number of drug abusers, this number has been expressed as a percentage of the population above the age of 14.

The underlying methodological approaches used for collecting data on illicit activities vary from country to country. In some cases, strongly differing results for the same country were obtained. Moreover, in order to arrive at basically comparable results, it was necessary in a number of cases to extrapolate from reported current use or life-time prevalence to annual prevalence rates and/or to adjust results for differences in age groups. These operations can potentially lead to over-estimates or under-estimates. One key problem in currently available prevalence estimates is still the level of accuracy which varies strongly from country to country. While a number of prevalence estimates are based on sound epidemiological surveys, some are obviously the result of guesses. In other cases, the estimates provided simply reflect the aggregate number of drug addicts found in some drug registries which probably cover only a small fraction of the total drug abusing population in a country.

Currently available results presented in this report must therefore be interpreted with a large degree of caution. They can however provide the reader with an idea of the likely magnitudes of drug abuse in the different countries.

The following information was provided to UNDCP by the Government of Colombia on the new national monitoring system it has established. It is reproduced as received:

OFFICIAL FIGURES FOR COCA CULTIVATION IN COLOMBIA 1999 and 2000

In order to obtain accurate, technically specialized, reliable and transparent information on the extent and location of illicit crops and to be able to exercise autonomy in the processing of statistical data, the Colombian Government has, since October 1999, been implementing a national project with the support of the United Nations International Drug Control Programme, entitled Integrated Monitoring System of Illicit Cultivation—the SIMCI Project. The methodology adopted for this System is based on the digital processing of images from satellites such as SPOT, Landsat, IKONOS and ERS and is thus designed to guarantee extensive coverage and high precision in the determination of illicit crops in Colombia.

A further important function of the project is to generate comprehensive technical information such as data identifying licit crops, pastureland, woodland, bodies of water, designated cropland in nature reserve zones and civil infrastructure, on the basis of which it is possible to characterize the environmental status of zones bordering illicit crops.

With the initiation of the SIMCI in Colombia it has been possible to establish a methodology that is unparalleled throughout the world, permitting multitemporal and periodic analysis of the survey results for the purposes of systematic and precise monitoring of the development and behaviour of areas used for illicit crop cultivation in the country. In 1998, Colombia started determining national illicit cultivation figures through the Inter-institutional Illicit Crop Survey[1], conducted by means of aerial surveillance and reconnaissance of areas under cultivation, a methodology which was very helpful at the time but suffered from the extremely extensive area to be measured and the degree of precision necessary for evaluating the changes in cultivation patterns. For the year 1999, for example, a total of 103,500 hectares of coca cultivation (sown) was established using this method.

It should be noted that at each stage of the survey process undertaken by the SIMCI Project, quality control is performed in order to obtain a product with a reliability level of approximately 90 per cent, thereby guaranteeing that, by applying specialized and transparent techniques, highly precise and reliable data can be obtained to be subsequently transferred to the future international illicit crop monitoring network, in response to the recommendations issued by the Commission on Narcotic Drugs at its forty-second session and by the General Assembly, which in its resolution 55/65 of December 2000 called upon States to establish national mechanisms to monitor and verify illicit crops.
The survey process consists of the following stages:

- Identification and acquisition of Landsat and SPOT satellite images covering approximately 14 and 28 million hectares for the 1999 and 2000 figures respectively.

- Development and application of a methodology for interpreting the satellite images in order to ensure correct identification of all coca cultivation sites.

- The images are fully referenced and spatially oriented in order to fill in the coordinates and convert them into maps.

- The images are then inspected visually and improved to allow clearer display and identification of the objects of interest, in this case illicit coca cultivation.

- This improved image is assigned colour combinations giving the sharpest possible contrast and facilitating identification of the different types of vegetation and other aspects of interest for the monitoring system.

- Using the selected colour images, a supervised classification process is then carried out with the support of any available external information such as aerial photographs of illicit cultivation zones and aerial reconnaissance data which, when interpreted by specialists, makes it possible to produce the preliminary coca cultivation map. This map is further improved by a careful process of visual editing and field verifications, whereby the results are matched against the interpretation of the images.

---

[1]This figures for 1998 and 1999 correspond to the First and Second Inter-institutional Illicit Crop Surveys, in which National Anti-Narcotics Police, the National Narcotics Office, the Ministry of the Environment and the National Alternative Development Plan participated.

- The illicit coca crops are then located on the images and measured by applying the results of the methodology developed.

- Each of the coca cultivation sites identified is processed by computer and its position and extent are determined.

- All the sites are then incorporated into a data bank based on the French software ILLISYS, specially designed for this purpose.

Finally, these thematic maps, the statistical information derived from them and other related information are systematically entered into a Geographical Information System, thus providing a valuable management and processing tool with a variety of functions.

By applying this process it was established that the estimated area of coca cultivation (sown) in 1999 and 2000 was 160,119 and 163,289 respectively, giving an increase of 1.98 per cent, on the basis of which it can be stated that a pattern of growth is established for the past two years.